Grave Goods

Objects and Death in Later Prehistoric Britain

Anwen Cooper, Duncan Garrow, Catriona Gibson,
Melanie Giles and Neil Wilkin

OXBOW | books
Oxford & Philadelphia

Published in the United Kingdom in 2022 by
OXBOW BOOKS
The Old Music Hall, 106–108 Cowley Road, Oxford, OX4 1JE

and in the United States by
OXBOW BOOKS
1950 Lawrence Road, Havertown, PA 19083

Hardback edition: ISBN 978-1-78925-747-2
Digital Edition: ISBN 978-1-78925-748-9

A CIP record for this book is available from the British Library

Library of Congress Control Number: 2021947306

Printed in the United Kingdom by Short Run Press

Typeset in India by Lapiz Digital Services, Chennai.

For a complete list of Oxbow titles, please contact:

UNITED KINGDOM
Oxbow Books
Telephone (01865) 241249
Email: oxbow@oxbowbooks.com
www.oxbowbooks.com

UNITED STATES OF AMERICA
Oxbow Books
Telephone (610) 853-9131, Fax (610) 853-9146
Email: queries@casemateacademic.com
www.casemateacademic.com/oxbow

Oxbow Books is part of the Casemate Group

The Grave Goods project database is available online via the Archaeology Data Service: https://doi.
org/10.5284/1052206

Front cover: The Folkton Drums (detail) by Rose Ferraby © 2018, reproduced by kind permission of the artist.

Contents

List of figures

List of tables

Acknowledgements

This book is one output of the AHRC-funded 'Grave goods: objects and death in later prehistoric Britain' project (AH/N001664/1), a collaboration between the Universities of Manchester and Reading and the British Museum. We are sincerely grateful for all the help, advice, support, inspiration and encouragement we have received along the way, and have many, many people to thank. Data and regionally specific advice on our case study regions were provided by Historic Environment Record Officers in Cornwall (Emma Trevarthen), Dorset (Claire Pinder), Gwynedd (Nina Steele), Humber (Victoria Bowns), Kent (Paul Cuming), Orkney (Julie Gibson) and the Outer Hebrides (Kevin Murphy) and by Canmore (Leanne McCafferty). Crispin Flower and Sylvina Tilbury (Exegesis) worked closely with us to enable our enhanced data to be integrated back into HERs. Andy Heath provided characteristically insightful support and ever-present technical know-how in building the project website (and especially in helping to make our grave goods visualisation map). Chris Green designed and built the Grave Goods database and handled our data (and various other complex data demands); he also made available to us his unique expertise in producing a number of 'fuzzy plots' and other graphics that really helped us to present our data in innovative and interesting ways. The *Grave Goods* project database is freely available via the Archaeology Data Service: https://doi.org/10.5284/1052206; various ADS staff kindly assisted us along the way.

Many different people helped us to source and/or very kindly provided us with permission to reproduce images: Hugo Anderson-Whymark (NMS), Kate Bailey and Charlotte Whiting (Society of Antiquaries of Scotland), Martin Bell (Reading), Beverley Ballin-Smith (GUARD), Julia Bastek-Michalska and Rachel McMullan (Headland Archaeology), Megan Berrisford (The Salisbury Museum), Pippa Bradley and Jacqueline McKinley (Wessex Archaeology), Lisa Brown (Wiltshire Museum), Lucy Cooper (Sheffield Museums), John Dent, Julia Farley (British Museum), Ruth Fisher (BAR), Chris Fowler (Newcastle), Julie Gardiner (Oxbow Books and Prehistoric Society), Chris Griffiths (Reading/AC-NMW), Nick Hodgson and Don O'Meara (Society of Antiquaries of Newcastle upon Tyne), Andy M Jones (Cornwall Archaeology Unit), Jaime Kaminski (Sussex Archaeological Society), Rob Law (Museum of Archaeology and Anthropology, Cambridge), Olivia Lelong (University of Bristol), Frances Lynch (Bangor), Andy Margetts (Archaeology South-East), Jamie McIntyre (CUP), Adam Parker (The Yorkshire Museum), Keith Parfitt (Kent Archaeological Society), Clare Randall (Dorset Natural History and Archaeological Society), Andy Richmond (Phoenix Archaeology), Miles Russell (Bournemouth), Lekky Shepherd, Alison Sheridan (NMS) and Ann Woodward (Birmingham).

Michael Rosen inspired us greatly in writing three 'grave goods' poems, focused on three different burials (Folkton, the Knowes of Trotty and Portesham), while artists Rose Ferraby, Chie Kutsuwada and Kelvin Wilson produced a series of fantastic artworks re-imagining those burials. Craig Williams (British Museum) also produced a number of graphical images within the book with his customary subtlety and skill. Speakers and attendees at both of our project conferences (University of Manchester, June 2018 and British Museum, May 2019) helped us to air, refine and test many of our ideas, and inspired us in developing various topics further. John Smythe very generously provided us access to his immensely rich dataset of Bronze Age hoards in Kent, Christie Willis provided us with access to her PhD on Middle to Late Neolithic cremation rites ahead of final submission. Hella Eckardt, J. D. Hill, Charlotte Johnson, Jessica Lutkin, Roger Matthews and Gabor Thomas assisted greatly during the grant application process, helping us to shape the project in its formative stages. Our colleagues more widely in Reading, Manchester and the British Museum also provided help, support, external advice and encouragement along the way. Emily Bateman (Historic England), Harry Fokkens (Leiden), Chris Gosden (Oxford), Jacqueline McKinley (Wessex Archaeology), Chris Scarre (Durham), Alison Sheridan (NMS) and Alex Smith (Headland Archaeology) provided guidance and support along the way as members of our expert Advisory Panel. More widely, Sophia Adams, Richard Bradley, Jo Brück, Julia Farley, Rob Heard, Bob Johnston, Andy M. Jones, Grace Jones, Matt Leivers, Simon Mays, Stuart Needham, Jacky Nowakowski, John Pouncett, Henrietta Quinell, Alison Sheridan, Jake Weekes, Jennifer Wexler, Rachel Wilkinson, Ann Woodward and Debs Young provided various combinations of assistance, guidance, wisdom and inspiration more widely as well.

Julie Gardiner and Jessica Hawxwell (née Scott) (Oxbow Books) have always been on hand to offer advice, support and patience in producing this volume; Sarah Harrison (The Fair Copy) compiled the index. Finally, we'd like to thank John Creighton who very kindly read a complete draft of the book, helping us to improve it greatly in its final stages with several key, characteristically insightful suggestions.

In pulling together the acknowledgements, it has become even more clear to us just how many people assisted in helping us to complete the *Grave Goods* project and in writing this book. We hope they feel we have done the topic justice and that a richer and better understanding of later prehistoric grave goods in Britain has emerged.

Chapter 1

Introduction

1.1. The rationale and scope of the *Grave Goods* project

Britain is internationally renowned for the high quality and exquisite crafting of its later prehistoric grave goods (*c.* 4000 BC–AD 43). Many of prehistoric Britain's most impressive artefacts have come from graves – from the polished beaver incisors at Duggleby Howe, North Yorkshire (Mortimer 1905), to the rich collection of gold plaques and pins, imported bronze daggers, fossil stone macehead and carved bone shaft-decorations at Bush Barrow, Wiltshire (Needham *et al.* 2010), to the coral-encrusted chariot-gear of Wetwang Village, East Yorkshire (Hill 2002). Thousands more arguably less impressive grave goods lie unloved and largely unacknowledged in site reports and archive storerooms. Objects from burials have long been central to how archaeologists have interpreted society at that time. This has happened partly as an interpretive necessity since, for large parts of the Neolithic, Bronze and Iron Ages in Britain settlement evidence can be elusive or difficult to identify archaeologically, ensuring that mortuary evidence is often the best, and sometimes only, information we have to work with. Interred with both inhumations and cremation burials, grave goods provide some of the most durable and well-preserved insights into personal identity and the prehistoric life-course, yet they also speak of the care shown to the dead by the living, and of people's relationships with 'things'. Objects matter. This book's title – *Grave Goods* – is an intentional play on words. These are objects in burials; but they are also goods, material culture, that must be taken seriously. Within it, we outline the results of the first ever long-term, large-scale investigation into grave goods during these periods in Britain, which enables a new level of understanding of mortuary practice and material culture throughout this major period of technological innovation and social transformation.

This book is the primary outcome of an AHRC-funded project (2016–2020) entitled *Grave Goods: objects and death in later prehistory*, a collaboration between researchers at the Universities of Reading (CG/DG) and Manchester (AC/MG) and the British Museum (NW). We set out to study what prehistoric people buried with their dead in Britain, from the beginning of the Neolithic to the end of the Iron Age. In focusing on objects buried with the dead, we are provided with a different lens through which to examine *relationships* between people and materials, complementing those approaches which have looked, for example, at the domain of social production and technology (e.g. Webley *et al.* 2020), ritual performance and adornment (e.g. Woodward and Hunter 2015) or non-funerary deposition (Fontijn 2019). By investigating the 'things' buried with the prehistoric dead, we can critically explore how these moments of funereal practice relate to thresholds of transformation in material technologies and knowledge, as well as the social trajectories or itineraries of objects (which ended up in graves, which did not, and why). We can also explore patterns of object-human association, not only with traditional attributes such as age and sex, but also, through select case studies where the quality of data allows, life histories including the circumstances of dying and death.

The book's analysis is structured at a series of different scales, ranging from macro-scale patterning across Britain, through regional explorations of continuity and change, to site-specific histories of practice and micro-scale analysis of specific graves and the individual objects (and people) within them. At a time when part of our discipline is embracing symmetrical archaeologies of practice or 'flat ontologies' that query or dissolve boundaries *between* past human bodies and objects, we hope that many of our arguments respond creatively and sometimes critically to this paradigm shift, whilst not falling into the trap of what Barrett has called a 'new antiquarianism' (2016, 1685). In the study that follows, we attend to the *mortuary* materialities that emerge from historically specific forms of prehistoric ways of being and lifeways. As we will see, this does at times give us a very different understanding of material relations than those we glimpse through settlement and other non-mortuary depositional contexts.

The nature of our project precluded studying the whole of Britain – it simply would not have been possible to do this in the time available (see discussion in Section 3.1). We have thus focused on six case study regions, identified for a range of reasons: the presence of notable grave good traditions, strong histories of investigation and the accessibility of records and data. Each of the six regions is at least partly coastal in location: Cornwall/Isles of Scilly, Dorset, Kent, East Yorkshire, Orkney/Outer Hebrides and Gwynedd/Anglesey. These situations (north, south, east and west) also allow us, where pertinent, to pick-up on grave goods caught up in debates over migration, mobility and interaction: not just cross-Channel and near-Continent, but inter-island. We have been able to explore the particular 'pulses' when such relationships gained greater visibility in the things buried with the dead and consider these carefully, allowing us a different – or at least additional – perspective on migration during the Early Bronze Age to that recently offered by ancient DNA, for example (e.g. Olalde *et al.* 2018). We are also able to counter the deep-seated focus on 'exotic' materials by studying *all* grave goods, revealing more complex skeins of spatial interactions and social connections, embodied in the things finally given to the dead.

1.2. Grave matters: three preconceptions

This section outlines three preconceptions that we intend to challenge. The first is that prehistorians 'know' the broad pattern of changes in frequencies of prehistoric grave goods. The general perception is that very little is directly associated with individuals in the Neolithic, there is a spike in all sorts of 'personal' grave goods in the Early–Middle Bronze Age, followed by a general lull before the Iron Age, which witnessed the introduction of new and more varied classes of objects in some areas but also significant blank spots where burial is invisible archaeologically. Our project has moved our understanding of this broad-brush sequence from one that is impressionistic to one based on a solid, empirical understanding of the record. Whilst some patterns hold good, our study has shown that the rise and decline of traditions in mortuary materials was experienced in rather different ways in these contrastive areas and it certainly does not map neatly to the overall availability of material culture in a region at any one time. The subtleties matter, not least because our ability to draw upon a large-scale dataset which redresses some of the historical bias in antiquarian activity and focused scholarly research, as it is tempered by information drawn from a wider set of discoveries (including development-led excavations).

The second preconception we have to grapple with is the conceptual 'sorting' that has gone on in archaeological scholarship, which has ruled some things 'in' as grave goods, and others 'out'. In the earliest excavations, this sometimes determined what was kept from the grave and we have had to return to the original accounts to see the wider spectrum of material culture caught up in mortuary practices. Before mid-19th century obsessions with craniology (see Chapter 2) antiquarians were – fortunately for us here – far more likely to retain grave goods than human remains. For example, Thurnam went 'back in' to Wilsford G11 to recover the crania re-interred by its original excavators (Needham *et al.* 2010, 2). This was because objects formed the cultural capital and aesthetic centrepiece of cabinet collections and museum cases, such as Bateman's *Lomberdale House* (Bateman 1855), Mortimer's *Museum of Antiquities and Geological Specimens* (Sheppard 1900) and Pitt Rivers' *Farnham Museum* (Dudley-Buxton 1929). Yet other grave goods were 'divided up' as curios and keepsakes amongst the participants, much to the ire of later archaeologists (Fox 1958, 9). The post-exhumation biography of the Iron Age finds from Arras, East Yorkshire is a good case in point, split into the hands of the three principal excavators: Stillingfleet, Hull and Clarkson, and further subdivided upon their death and dispersal at auction (Stead 1979, 8–11).

Other objects were never retained. Fragile organics, thin sheet bronze, broken glass and decayed and rusted iron seldom survived the labourer's pick unless discovered in a particularly well-preserved burial (as in the Gristhorpe log-coffin; Williamson 1834).

This also applied to poorly fired, broken and undecorated pottery all of which were commonly discarded; some vessels even became the unlikely victims of diggers' ire (see Section 6.1)! Faunal remains, wood and rare examples of vegetation might have been speciated but were rarely kept as they fell outside of the notion of a material 'grave good' (e.g. Bateman 1848, 81; 1861, appendix). Stones of many kinds might again be briefly described but were often thrown away, particularly those acting as capping, covering or plinth stones (see Cooper *et al.* 2019). Fossils and pebbles were often classed as geological specimens – curiosities that were noted but rarely kept (Brück and Jones 2018). Even worked stone had a chequered fate. Bateman kept all the polished axes and leaf-shaped arrowheads from his excavations and the matching upper and lower beehive quern-stones found in neighbouring Iron Age interments at Winster, Derbyshire (1857) were retained long enough to be illustrated in watercolour by Llewellyn Jewitt for his (ultimately unpublished) *Relics of Primeval Life*, *c.* 1850 (Beswick and Wright 1991, fig. 4.3). Yet these more massive and fragmented stones did not survive the loan and final sale of this collection to Sheffield's Weston Park Museum. Someone, at some point, threw them out.

Excavations in the mid-later 20th century did less of this graveside or archival selection, as finds recording became standardised. They were also able to retain more of the fragile fragments, preserved organics and mineralised impressions that reveal 'ghost' grave goods representing our 'missing majority' of perishable materials (Hurcombe 2014). Yet archaeologists continue to do their own 'conceptual sorting' in print: drawing analytical boundaries around items found on or close to the body itself (in inhumations), or those found fused with burned bone and pyre material (in cremation burials). In trying to understand these issues, we analysed a handful of contemporary authors, and how they personally categorise grave goods (see Table 3.02 in Chapter 3). A 'core' group of artefacts are regularly ruled 'in' as grave goods: personal ornaments and dress fittings, weapons or accoutrements of rank and power, which are seen either as personal possessions or part of intimate funerary rites to prepare, dress and adorn the dead (e.g. Whimster 1981; Nowakowski 1991). In a (mostly) unarticulated reading of graveside performance, objects placed at a slight distance tend to be categorised more as 'gifts' or 'tokens of esteem' (Fitzpatrick 2011; Harding 2016). 'Companions' (whether animal or human) are considered particularly problematic (Garwood 2007). Clusters of vessels and faunal remains interpreted as food are sometimes categorised as grave goods but for others these are mere residues of the funeral itself (e.g. Stead 1991). Grave 'furniture' or containers (coffins, cist slabs, coverings etc.) and the small objects that facilitate wrapping or containment (pins and brooches in 'non-normative' positions) often fall into the realm of 'ambiguous' grave goods (Cooper *et al.* 2019). In the *Grave Goods* project database (henceforth shortened to the GGDB) we have included *all* objects associated with burials (see Chapter 3 for a more detailed discussion) to allow us to draw the conceptual boundary of 'grave goods' as widely as possible, even where these no longer exist physically as curated artefacts or substances. The project as a whole, and thus this book specifically, seeks to evaluate and understand more fully the character and role of 'everyday' grave goods, in addition to the spectacular objects that so often capture archaeological attention.

The third and final premise that we seek to challenge is how objects from graves are interpreted. Fundamentally, we have to tackle the concept that they directly represent the identity, status or wealth of the deceased. This is important as the historical rhythms of the rise of individual, furnished burials have been used to evidence the notion of a linear social evolutionary trajectory in prehistoric Britain (see further discussion in Chapter 2). Taking one iconic Early Bronze Age burial – Bush Barrow, from the Normanton Down group on Salisbury Plain, Wiltshire (Needham *et al.* 2010) – we can see how this approach has given us the rise of the chiefdom, exemplified through grave goods as the 'single sepulchres of kings, and great personages' (Stukeley 1740, 43), morphing into Piggott's 'princely' burials of an Armorican elite 'ruling class' (1938, 52). In the later 20th century this discourse may have shifted tone, tempering the social evolutionary model of chiefly warrior elites with a more subtle image of Bush Barrow as a local 'master of ceremonies': 'rising' to 'pre-eminence through the control of particular ceremonies and activities' (Needham *et al.* 2010, 33); one of Van der Noort's 'argonauts', daring voyagers of the North Sea (2006, 269); or even one of Needham's well-connected sacro-political pilgrims (2008). Whichever image best captures the identity of the Bush Barrow individual, we note here how changes in the interpretation of these people have been largely shaped (until the refined application of isotopes and aDNA programmes) *by* their grave goods: where these items came from, what they represented and how they were used to mark, mould or remember a powerful person.

Archaeologists' interpretations of 'rich' Iron Age grave goods are little different. In the early 19th century, the iconic chariot burial from Arras, East Yorkshire was dubbed 'the King', relegating a second wheeled vehicle to that of a 'Charioteer', whilst the richly adorned burial was clearly a 'Queen': 'the chief female of the tribe' (Stillingfleet 1846, 27–28, see Giles *et al.* 2019). Having exhausted the main titles of power, this relegated the 1877 Arras chariot and mirror burial to that of a mere 'Lady' (Greenwell 1877, 454). The notion that these relate to an 'elite' (versus 'commoner' burials) is perpetuated in Parker Pearson's account of the Great Wold Valley (1999a) and Halkon's direct reading of the chariot burials as an iron-controlling elite (2013). By the Late Iron Age, the 'exalted' or 'princely' burials of Welwyn and Lexden type (Evans 1911, 15 cited in Smith 1911, 27) with their feasting equipment and sacrificial accoutrements, were being linked as kin of the 'kings' named in contemporary classical accounts and Late Iron Age coinage (for a more sophisticated reading, see Creighton 2006).

Such images of hierarchies and elites read directly from grave goods have gained near immutable status in accounts of prehistoric Britain because we are repeatedly drawn to suites of shiny and unusual things: caught in the glare of spectacular grave goods. This is not surprising, since it is these very objects that dominate our museum cases as well as our textbooks. Yet it tells us little about how different *kinds* of materials were used to negotiate the loss of all sorts of people from these communities and to confront death itself. Our project thus set out to be conceptually blind to this hierarchy of people and things: it gathered all, to study the specific role of material objects and materials across mortuary rituals. This brings us back to our final point and the double-meaning of our project title mentioned above: these are *grave* goods. Their selection and inclusion began with a death, and our project aims to make a contribution to the 'long view' of how people use things to negotiate human loss, an endeavour which is of both interest and importance not just to the discipline of archaeology but sociology, anthropology and philosophy.

The act of placing an object in a grave makes an important statement not just about the person who has died, but about the mourners themselves; the object crystallises their relationships (Brück 2004). It may be a powerful symbol or metaphor, used to negotiate the event of death, or an apotropaic device for protecting the dead or the living. It may aid passage into an afterlife, providing equipment for the dead, or be a gift to pay a debt or create a new obligation with an ancestor. While extraordinary objects may be selected for their rarity and craft skill, embodying distant or spiritual connections, even relatively mundane artefacts (such as pots or brooches or stones) bring the wider 'living' world into the realm of the dead, evoking kin relations and places to which the deceased belonged. An understanding of how peoples' lives and the lives of objects were intertwined can help us to investigate the dynamic role of materials and technologies that shaped both life and death in the past.

1.3. Research questions and methods: between large-scale datasets and 'object biography'

This volume tackles the following key research questions:

- What do archaeologists mean by 'grave goods'? How have they used (and sometimes abused) this concept, and can we formulate a new, more nuanced and sophisticated understanding of this key category of material culture?
- What kinds of object did people put in graves in later prehistoric Britain? What did 'grave goods' mean to people in the prehistoric past? How were these objects perceived? Why were certain items selected for deposition with the dead? Which were not?

In order to answer these questions, we have carried out a selective historiography of concepts of grave goods, spanning the antiquarian period (broadly, the late 17th–late 19th century) up to the current day. We also tack back-and-forth to these ideas throughout our interpretive chapters. The core of the project, however, was the construction of a database (the GGDB) of all material culture found in formal mortuary contexts during the Neolithic, Bronze Age and Iron Age within our six case study regions. Our methodology is enabled by the use of digitised Historic Environment Records (HERs), which have made a new level of archaeological understanding possible on a nationwide scale. Despite considerable work undertaken over the history of archaeology to log and collate evidence about prehistoric burials, HERs offer the only reliably updated source of information about these sites in Britain. They thus enable patterns to be identified that simply could not be seen before. Equally, development-led archaeology has led to a substantial rise in the number of excavations, uncovering new and unexpected burial types and material culture. Our research methods ensure that these 'grey literature' discoveries were also synthesised in the GGDB. In combining data created as a result of modern development-led excavations with information created by old (often 19th century) excavations, we hope to have unlocked the potential of, and thus reinvigorated, 'old data' and ancient archives as well.

Within much recent theoretically informed work, objects are viewed as being intimately bound up in and contributive to society, and as having the power to affect human action (see Chapter 2 for a more detailed discussion). The primary focus of the *Grave Goods* project was material culture, and its power to 'do' and 'say' things in burial contexts. Prehistory, of course, lacks documents. The mortuary context is an arena in which the body (or parts of it) and objects were laid out in a series of events. On those occasions, people often appear to have gone out of their way to compose a message to be conveyed to other mourners. These might be said to be the fundamental 'documents' of prehistory, which offer us the opportunity to stand in the shoes of the mourners and 'read' the body. Yet in this book, we argue, we need to move beyond this textual analogy to embrace the notion that burial with grave goods was a performance meant to confront mortality. It concerned the dead but it was a live, unfolding piece of funerary theatre in which fundamental ideas about people's role in, and relations with, the world were marked and renegotiated – mourners and mourned. The use of objects in this ontological endeavour literally *mattered*. Grave goods were therefore an important part of what Malafouris has described as a 'mnemo-technology': they created certain possibilities and affordances to people caught up in the rite (2015). Every arrangement of grave goods with the remains of a body, whatever its state or form, was 'social memory in the making' (*ibid.*, 304). Objects were there 'to be talked about' as Rowlands pointed out some time ago (1993, 144). Their obdurate materiality asserted their own stories in the grave but of course, the artful death-worker, kin-member or celebrant-cum-storyteller could invest them with new meanings too. As Rowlands goes on to note, the very act of making something a 'grave good' involved the removal of things from the world of the living – not just spectacular objects of social renown but intimate and familiar, mundane things. It created a powerful 'memory in its absence' (1993, 146). Their passing from view, taking them out of the hands of the living, thus created an absent presence that helped materialise loss.

1.4. Results and outcomes

This book presents an overview of the major results of our research. Very early on in the project, we took a conscious decision *not* to try and write an overarching diachronic narrative of grave goods in Britain, or to compile a series of regional syntheses. The book is not structured regionally or chronologically but thematically: we have conducted a series of studies which investigate grave goods from different perspectives, considering those matters that we felt were the most interesting or most pressing, and the most in need of detailed study. It does not have to be read sequentially but can be dipped into according to reader interests and needs.

We begin with a selective historiography focusing on how grave goods have been conceptualised over time (Chapter 2); this, we feel, is a worthy exercise in itself which also allowed us and our readers to understand the interpretive positions that prehistoric archaeologists have reached, and how our work, as presented here, relates to it. Following this scene setting and conceptual critique, Chapter 3 presents the 'big picture' gleaned from the macro-scale analysis of the GGDB: patterning of grave goods across time and in space, analysed and visualised in a variety of different ways. As discussed above, a key aim of the project was to place impressionistic understandings of regionality and long-term change on a solid empirical footing; this chapter does exactly that. It also looks at how grave goods related to female and male burials, young and old people, cremation and inhumation practices, and other comparable variables. In Chapter 4, we ask the question 'what goes in a grave?'. In order to understand 'grave goods' properly, we argue, it is also vital to consider 'hoard goods', 'settlement goods', and so on, by contrasting mortuary material culture with wider patterns of materiality on settlement sites and in hoards (see also Cooper *et al.* 2020). Our empirical analysis allows us to question long-held assumptions about the relationship between material culture found in graves and on settlements, and to view the complexities of the material record that we, as archaeologists, need to work with in very different way.

Subsequent interpretive chapters adopt a thematic lens through which to explore finer-grained outcomes of the project. Chapter 5 celebrates 'understated' (and usually overlooked) grave goods. In so doing, it complements (and in some ways directly challenges) most previous publications over the past century which have generally focused on the spectacular and the non-everyday. In Chapter 6, we look in detail at the most common grave good of all: the pot, and what we have termed its 'material plasticity' in the arena of burial. This focus on a single object type allows us to bring into especially sharp focus the sometimes-incredible variety of 'things' caught up in mortuary practice, and to explore the effects that grave goods' materiality might have had on both people and practice. Chapter 7 explores object mobility – and indeed immobility – as exemplified in grave goods. Objects whose materials are *known* to have travelled a long way prior to their incorporation in a grave (amber, jet, etc.) have often been drawn into discussions of 'value' and 'wealth' in the prehistoric past.

In considering these concepts – and their constitution in relation to both materials and people in graves – we come to consider the local as well. Local and non-local are mutually constructed concepts and *both* potentially led to 'value' creation in different ways. Our penultimate Chapter 8 turns then to explore elements of time within burial practice. It investigates in detail how the different temporalities of burial sites (especially those of chambered tombs during the Neolithic) affect what we actually see of, and thus how we can possibly begin to understand, grave goods in the present. It also considers the potentially very different temporalities of grave goods caught up in inhumation and cremation practices and, again, the implications these variable tempos had, both for people in the past and in terms of our own interpretations in the present. We also consider how, during the Iron Age, grave goods helped to shape very different temporalities in the context of death and burial. Finally, in Chapter 9, we summarise some of the key outcomes, both empirical and conceptual, of our research.

The key objective of this project has been to create a unique empirical foundation that allows not just us but also future researchers to work with grave goods at a variety of different scales. In so doing, we have aimed to initiate a subtly different conversation about prehistoric death and burial, which opens up new ideas around mortuary material culture: what prehistoric people buried with the dead and what it might have meant. Our final aim then, is to make a small but substantial contribution to the understanding of different kinds of past humanity, and how people have faced and dealt with mortality, in part, through 'things'. It is to the ideas that have governed this discourse so far that the next chapter turns.

Chapter 2

From 'appurtenances of affectionate superstition' to 'vibrant assemblages': an historiography of grave goods

2.1. Introduction

On 3 June 1851, Mrs Sarah Bateman peered into the sandstone cist of a barrow in Monsal Dale in the Peak District of Derbyshire. The sister of William Parker (her husband, antiquarian Thomas Bateman's 'close companion'), her marriage had been an advantageous one given her class, but a necessary one for Thomas, as he cast aside his long-term mistress to fulfil the terms of his grandfather's will and inherit the Middleton estate (Marsden 1974). In the preceding autumn of 1850, it was feared that Thomas himself might die, plagued by gout and severe migraines (*ibid.*). Sarah had yet to provide him with a son and heir but, certainly, her first-born, a daughter, must have been on her mind as she watched the discovery of the 'decayed skeletons of two infants' in the Monsal barrow. Unfortunately, these burials were 'omitted' from the final barrow plan 'to prevent confusion' (Bateman 1861, 79). Just before the trench was backfilled, Thomas 'casually picked up a barbed arrow-head of grey flint, and a piece of hard sandstone that had been used to triturate grain' (*ibid.*). We could read much into these twin symbols of death and life, found close to the infants – the arrow-tip and the quernstone – but whatever Sarah's thoughts, she must have been counting her blessings as she watched her husband enjoy his consuming pastime in the early summer sun. The stones were kept but the bones were not. As she leaned over the grave, Thomas tells us that she had 'the misfortune to drop in, unobserved, a gold ring set with an onyx cameo, representing a classical subject' (Bateman 1861, 79). Thomas was troubled by the notion that its rediscovery someday might 'lead to the conclusion that the Romans [were] buried in these ancient grave-hills' (1861, 79). Was the ring a real Roman relic, already exhumed once from a grave and given to his wife from his own collection, or merely a Victorian reproduction? And did Sarah really lose her ring by accident or was this a small, sentimental offering to accompany the fragile bones thrown back in with the spoil, in lieu of their original grave goods: a kind of exchange with the dead? We will never know. What we can note from

Bateman's account is the importance given to these encounters with prehistoric burials and the care taken to record the things that were interred with them. It is to the origins of this pursuit that this chapter now turns.

Objects buried with the dead in prehistoric Britain have played a central role in archaeological narratives since the discipline's inception. This chapter explores the way in which they drove excavation in the acquisitive era of antiquarians, and shaped impressions of both races and 'states of civilisation' in 19th century discourse. In the 20th century, it examines their mapping to represent culture groups, their deployment to address issues of power and rank, their capacity to reveal underlying structures of society and belief and their mobilisation in narratives of personhood. Most recently, grave good assemblages have been caught up in the rethinking of ontology known as 'new materialism' whilst new analytical techniques have enabled us to follow the itineraries of these objects before (and after) they entered the grave. Yet as this chapter will reveal, they have always led to other kinds of reflections: connecting people with the lives of those long dead, prompting thoughts of mortality and offering a strange kind of solace for the human condition. Whether spectacular or mundane, they have moved archaeologists to consider the social relationships – the 'continuing bonds' to borrow a phrase (Klass 1996) – between the living and the dead. Some of these accounts are emotionally moving, others are more challenging to read, but from the 17th to the 21st century, grave goods have rightly confounded the logic of what Brück and Fontijn dub *Homo economicus* (2013). The giving up of things to the dead demands explanation.

Following a chronological structure, this chapter explores the way in which each different era conceptualised grave goods and categorised artefacts from burials. We will examine what was commented upon, what was kept, what was thrown away and why. We will also explore the constructive role of illustration in these processes, as some objects enchanted the imagination of their finders whilst others were passed over. Throughout, the key influence of ethnographic analogy – learning from the burial rites of other co-present societies and what they gave to their dead – will become clear. We will also see how folklore played its part in understanding some of the more curious, overlooked objects and the ways in which they were treated during prehistoric funerary rites. We take care to contextualise these scholars' opinions in relation to contemporary attitudes towards the dead and their own experience of burial, in order to understand better the approaches they have brought to the topic. It would be possible – and very interesting – to write a whole book on historical approaches to grave goods in Britain, but that is not our intention here. The following historiography is necessarily selective rather than comprehensive, highlighting particular scholars, concepts and definitions that best embody the major paradigm shifts in approaches to grave goods over the centuries.

2.2. Early explorations: *'lasting reliques'*

One of the earliest literary meditations on archaeological grave goods (relating to Anglo-Saxon cremation burials from Norfolk) is Sir Thomas Browne's *Hydriotaphia,* or 'Urn Buriall' (1658, reprinted in 2010 with a preface by W.G. Sebald), seen in literary circles as a reflection on mortality and the vanity of humanity's attempts to overcome it. In Browne's words, 'to subsist in bones … is a fallacy in duration'; such remains are 'Vain ashes … Emblems of mortal vanities'. Yet Browne goes on to list the 'lasting reliques' as he dubs them (2010, 64) in fond detail: from the early medieval cremation burials: 'peeces of small boxes, or combes handsomely wrought, handles of small brasse instruments, brazen nippers, and … some kind of *Opale*' [*sic*] (*ibid.*, 37) and from Roman urned cremation burials: 'Lacrymatories, Lamps, Bottles of Liquor' (*ibid.*, 42).

Browne was writing in the 17th century, at the dawn of antiquarianism among figures such as Leland, Camden, Stukeley, Gough and Aubrey, engaged in the composition of a history of Britain as part of a wider project of nationalism (Sweet 2001; Trigger 2006). By the 18th century, improvement and enclosure, drainage, quarrying and road building were biting deeper into these barrows and turfing up finds from upland moor and downland (Marsden 1974). An Enlightenment education and growing national sentiment encouraged landowners to explore relics from their own estates (such as Colt Hoare in Wiltshire), conduct regional surveys (for example, Hutchins' *History and Antiquities of the County of Dorset* 1774, Leigh's *Natural History of the County of Cheshire, Lancashire and the Peak in Derbyshire etc.* 1700) or conduct their own 'Grand Tours' through Britain, exemplified in Richard Gough's *British Topography* (1780); collating notebooks, itineraries and chorographical accounts that spanned heraldry and antiquities, geology, topography and natural history. In most of these accounts we can still see the primacy of textual evidence: burial mounds and the objects within them were employed as supportive evidence to classical and medieval documents but both were used to counter the bricolage of folklore and myth which enshrined the placenames of sites such as the 'Giant's Grave', 'Waylands Smithy' or 'Danes Graves'. As grave goods came to light associated not just with men but women and children, antiquarians such as Stukeley questioned their link with ancient heroes, battles and the war dead. The aesthetics of these objects came to be valued as the trappings of wealthy figures, naturalising and justifying contemporary social hierarchy. As Stukeley noted:

> Of the Barrows, or sepulchral tumuli about Stonehenge... they are assuredly the single sepulchres of kings and great personages...some note of difference in the persons there interr'd, well known in those ages. (1740, 44)

Yet Browne's account is rather different. These 'reliques' were, he argued, 'appurtenances of affectionate superstition' (2010, 42); 'sacred unto the *Manes*, or passionate expressions of their surviving friends' (*ibid.*, 51), which might have been 'cast into the fire by an affectionate friend' (*ibid.*, 52). He concludes that grave goods were 'things wherein they excelled, delighted, or which were dear to them, either as farewells unto all pleasure, or vain apprehensions that they might use them in the other world' (*ibid.*, 44). We argue here that Browne's prescient sensitivity towards mortality, memory and the negotiation of death through material culture has not been foregrounded strongly enough in subsequent studies of grave goods. For Browne, these were not mere possessions nor markers of status but intimate treasures, good-luck charms, gifts to the dead, tokens of friendship and affection, celebratory 'last hurrahs' or things needed in the afterlife.

This brings us to another key point: it is important not to separate such accounts from the times in which they were written; prevailing mortality patterns, ideologies of death and burial, funerary fashions, as well as personal experiences of mortality all shaped people's encounters with burial objects. Cremation was not just ideologically repugnant to those who believed in a corporeal resurrection but illegal until 1884, yet here were countless individuals reduced to ash and bone, in Neolithic, Bronze Age, Roman and Anglo-Saxon interments. These burials forced antiquarians to rethink their own attitude towards the body and its dissolution. Browne's passion for antiquarianism was also steeped in his professional life as a doctor, living through the heightened mortality rates of the English Civil War and its aftermath. His justification for both his archaeological and poetic endeavours still read as a poignant testimony to the discipline, and its close alliance with medicine:

> Beside, to preserve the living, and make the dead to live, to keep men out of their Urnes, and discourse of human fragments in them, is not impertinent to our profession: whose study is life and death. (Browne 2010, 25)

For Browne, despite his resignation to the ravages of disease and mortality, antiquarian study brought the possibility of a different kind of resurrection. The 2010 reprint of Browne's work includes the academic and novelist W.G. Sebald's engagement with this 1658 essay as a preface, drawn from his part-novel, part-walking tour *The Rings of Saturn* (1998). In Sebald's semi-fictionalised pilgrimage around the Suffolk countryside, he meditates on themes of time, memory and mortality, already torn by the psychological 'fissure that has since riven my life' (cited in the Preface for *Hydriotaphia* 2010, 10). Sebald is spurred by the irony of an idle line in *Urne Buriall* where Browne ponders the 17th century excavation and study of past human lives, lifted from the soil: 'who knows the fate of his bones' Browne asked, 'or how often he is to be buried'? (2010, 23). Sebald finds the quote uncanny since Browne's own skull was exhumed to become a novel kind of funerary object in the collection of archaeologist, ethnographer and evolutionary theorist, John Lubbock. Although Sebald discovers the cranium was finally afforded reburial he finds in Browne's fascination with funerary artefacts a kind of timeless solace:

> things of this kind, unspoiled by the passage of time, are symbols of the indestructibility of the human soul ... he scrutinises that which escaped annihilation for any sign of the mysterious capacity for transmigration he has so often observed in caterpillars and moths. (Sebald in Browne 2010, 19)

In fact, this theme of an ephemeral and fragile object's ability to defy time had already influenced other antiquarians such as Thomas Bateman, whose second great work on the prehistoric burials of the Peak District was published two weeks before his own untimely death. *Ten Years Digging* (1861) opens with a line from *Hydrotaphia* which must have been peculiarly satisfying to this collector and excavator of cinerary or funerary urns:

> in a yard underground... thin walls of clay [have] out-worn all the strong and spacious buildings above it, and quietly rested under the drums and tramplings of three conquests... Time which antiquates antiquities, and hath an art to make dust of all things, hath yet spared these minor monuments. (Browne 2010, 79)

In its first iteration then, 'lasting reliques' came to embody the enduring trace of fleeting humanity. Even as a 17th century doctor, Browne had no real hope of 'reading' the ashes or the bones themselves, and the names of the dead were long lost. Yet, through his essay (and its revisiting by both Bateman and Sebald) we sense a man always close to the reality of disease, the process of ageing and the suddenness of death, enchanted and moved by things that could long outlast the human frame itself.

2.3. Antiquarian excavations: 'All the treasures I could obtain'

As antiquarianism gathered pace over the 18th century, collections of antiquities joined the other domains of curious finds – botanical, geological, folkloric and ethnographic – filling the cabinets of the wealthy (Macgregor and Impey 1997). Alongside privately sponsored monographs, dedicated learned societies (such as the the *Society of Antiquaries of London*, see Pearce 2007) disseminated these finds through influential early publications (notably, *The Gentleman's Magazine* and *The Reliquary*). The overt concerns of antiquarianism with 'property and genealogy' (Sweet 2001, 189) made it an eminently suitable endeavour for the appropriately educated gentleman. The 'taste' exhibited in collecting, the knowledge embodied in arrangement and the finance required to amass these objects (whether through purchase from third parties or the funding of novel excavations) became ways in which status and renown might be assured or inflated (Belk 1994; 1995). In contrast to the ideals of Gough, for example, who valued the evidence base of knowledge that these discoveries provided as an antidote to historical speculation (Sweet 2001, 189–90), grave goods were increasingly sought after by many collectors for their intrinsic 'aesthetic qualities' more than their 'historic value' (Ekengren 2013, 173). Antiquarian collections were also embodiments of social connection (Byrne *et al.* 2011): alongside their monetary value they now conjured cultural capital (Giles 2006). Flurries of letters between renowned scholarly correspondents such as Samuel Pegge and educated clergymen and doctors, began to fuel middle-class aspirations and acquisitiveness. We can see this surge in the early to mid-19th century reflected in our timeline of 'grave goods' organised by date of discovery (Fig. 2.01).

Grave Goods

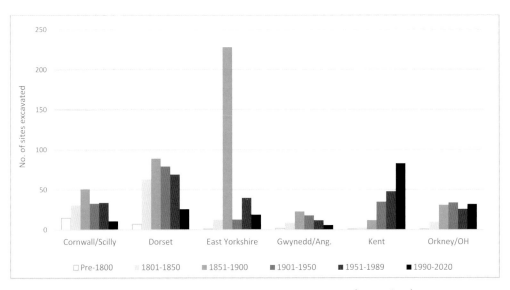

Figure 2.01 Grave good discovery patterns over time (GGDB data).

The seed-merchant John Mortimer (partly responsible for the major spike seen from 1851 to 1900 in East Yorkshire) thus explained how he was driven by the desire that 'there might be brought together in one collection all the treasures I could obtain' (1905, x). This ranged from scouring fellow-collectors' probate sales to purchasing plough-delved finds from the Yorkshire Wolds horselads, on one memorable occasion spotting a particularly fine Beaker masquerading as a flower-pot on a farm-wife's windowsill (see Giles 2006)! This inevitably drove up the prices of such relics during the course of the 19th century (Mortimer 1900, 88), and stimulated the illicit and destructive pillaging of grave goods. In Hudson's *A Shepherd's Life*, Caleb Bawcombe recalls youthful diggings in Wiltshire barrows with farm labourer Dan'l Burdon: an elderly man of 'profound gravity', who was 'always thinking of hidden treasure' in an endless search for (in his own words) 'something he could not find' (1910, 137). In East Yorkshire, the *Driffield Times and General Advertiser* for 1862 noted with distaste the 'unfortunate sepulchral discovery' of human remains left strewn upon the sod of a barrow, disturbed by a labourer 'actuated by desire of profit' (Anon 1862, 4). The disdain shown for blind acquisition is captured in Sir Walter Scott's stock caricature of *The Antiquary*, a 'wild ... eccentric and laughable figure, whose obsession with collecting the detritus of the past has warped his vision and clouded his judgment' (Sweet 2001, 182). It is also echoed in the satirical cartoon entitled *Revenge* depicting a northern barrow labourer, pocketing the 'buryin' (an urn and several arrow-heads) to spite the gentlemen who have failed to share their 'denners' (Fig. 2.02).

As grave goods were either monetised or hoarded for their innate aesthetic value, it is not surprising that only certain objects were deemed worthy of perpetual curation.

REVENGE!

North Country Labourer (who has been engaged to dig). "'THEY THAT EAT ALANE MAY HOWK ALANE!' THESE ARCHI'LOGICAL CHAPS NEVER SO MUCH AS ASKED ME IF AH'D TAK' ANYTHING, AND WHILE THEY'RE HAVIN' THEIR DENNERS AH'VE FOUND THE 'BURYIN''"—*(Pockets Urn and several Flint Arrow-heads)*— "AND THEY MAY WHUSTLE FOR'T!!"

Figure 2.02 Revenge! A satire on the acquisition and ownership of 'grave goods' (originally published in Punch, *21 September 1878 (vol. 75, 129) (© CartoonStock image no. VC122529).*

Bateman's accounts, for instance, record quite faithfully a variety of non-local stones of exquisite colour or interest; a piece of 'spherical iron pyrites, now for the first time noticed as being occasionally found with other relics in the British tumuli' from Elton Moor (1848, 53) and quartzite pebbles (one clutched in the hand of an Anglo-Saxon burial at Alsop-in-the-Dale, 1848, 67) but seldom were these 'mundane' or 'natural' artefacts accessioned (see also Chapter 5). On-site sorting and classification perpetuated certain categories of accepted grave goods: containers, arms/weapons, ornaments, utensils and implements of 'domestic life', as Browne had outlined in *Hydriotaphia*. Illustration played a constitutive part in the ruling in or out of such finds. William Bowman's fine engraving of the Green Lowe, Derbyshire assemblage, for example, includes the ceramic urn, flint dagger and arrowheads as well as bone pin and spatulate osseous objects from this burial but excludes another piece of 'spherical iron ore', even though Bateman argues it was 'an occasional ornament of the Britons' (1848, 59). The ochre pebbles from Liff's Low, Derbyshire which 'even now, on being wetted imparts a bright-red colour to the skin, which is by no means easy to discharge' (1848, 43) were also excluded from Bowman's engraved illustration but they were kept, forming a colourful, glossy centrepiece to the funerary assemblage (Fig. 2.03). We can only imagine the 'ruddy' faces which returned from that particular barrow opening! Llewellyn Jewitt's *Grave Mounds and their Contents* (1870) eschewed any 'historic' or 'ethnological' content in favour of a 'general', 'popular' résumé and illustration of 'varied relics', yet of course he was only able to depict that which was kept from the many excavations covered in his volume.

It is not surprising that fragile shreds of textile, fragments of decayed metal, wood and charcoal, and fused or splintered detritus would not make it out of the spoil, along with the numerous intrusive bones of 'vermin' and 'amphibians' which seem to have made barrow cists their home. We are familiar with the selective collection of skulls (as can be seen 'under the hand' of Bateman in the 1860 oil painting by Thomas Joseph Banks) and the discard of both post-cranial remains and faunal material (unless anthropogenically modified). Yet other discards surprise us. Stone 'lids', plinths or cappings are commonly recorded as part of funerary 'architecture' but seldom made it into the collection (see Cooper *et al.* 2019). Some fossils were kept but these often found their way into the geological sections of antiquarian museums, divorcing them from the assemblage of mortuary objects which had been painstakingly curated for the ancient dead (Brück and Jones 2018). This 'sorting out' (see Bowker and Star 2000) inevitably tacked back-and-forth to their own world of things, not only the new boundaries between the nascent disciplines of 'archaeology' and 'geology' but also the official proscription on grave goods in their own times, patrolled by the Christian church and particularly, non-Conformist ideology. Of course, all humans understand the world through categorisation (Lakoff 1987, 8–9) but we argue here that we need to return to some of these primary antiquarian reports to appreciate the conceptual classification systems of the Georgian, Victorian and Edwardian worlds.

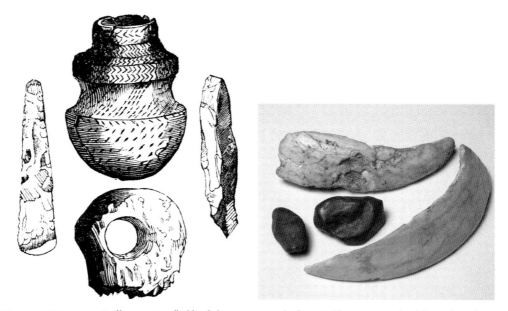

Figure 2.03 Bowman's illustration (left) of the grave goods from Liff's Lowe, Derbyshire, taken from Thomas Bateman's Vestiges *(1848, 43); and photo (right) of worked boar tusks and ochre pebbles from the same funerary context (© Sheffield Museums Trust).*

Despite the avarice evoked above, it would be wrong to dismiss such collections as mere contemporary status symbols or portable forms of wealth. During the mid-19th century, objects from burials began to acquire a special relevance in new models of technological and social change. Jewitt might believe that grave goods had the capacity to 'tell their wondrous tale, in their own language... of ages and races ... long since passed away' but his interest lay in amassing visual foundations from which others could compose their 'theories ... and historical structures' (1870, 1–2) and Bateman's similar aesthetic delight in his collection was clear but so was his wider project: 'to collect and accumulate, with particular industry, every relic brought to light ... in order to elucidate the history and ethnology of the race of people' (cited in Grinsell 1953, 222). By the mid-19th century, as we explore below, grave goods had utility by virtue of the insights they gave into racial or ethnic groups.

2.4. Typologies of things and people: social evolutionary approaches

Colt Hoare (working closely with Cunnington) seems to have been one of the first to create a specific category of 'funerary equipment', mobilising the mortuary associations of objects found with the dead and distinguishing them from other kinds of 'relics' in non-funerary contexts (1812, 6). However, the formal concept of 'grave-goods' was first coined in print within Britain (as far as we know) by Joseph Anderson, during his Rhind Lectures for 1882, entitled *Scotland in Pagan Times: The*

Bronze and Stone Ages. Sometimes hyphenated, sometimes not, Anderson initially uses the term to explain how the presence of 'a thin, knife-like blade of bronze among the grave goods of these interments' (Early Bronze Age burials containing 'bracers' or wristguards) helped place the interments in an intermediate position between the Ages of Stone and Iron (1886, 18). Here we see funerary objects playing their part in the dissemination of the Three Age System developed in Denmark by Thomsen and promoted through the translation of Worsaae's *The Primeval Antiquities of Denmark* into English in 1849. Ekengren argues that Worsaae was 'the first to conceptualise grave goods as a diagnostic feature of the archaeological record' postulating that since the grave was a closed context (unlike a peat bog), 'Here we may therefore, in general, expect to find those objects together which were originally used at the same period' (1849, 76). This 'closed context' concept would be later queried by Olivier who pointed out the 'multi-temporalities' of funerary assemblages which might include ancient 'found' curios, heirlooms as well as 'futural' objects from secondary rites or later insertions (1999), a theme we address directly in Chapter 8. Yet in the mid-19th century, suites of burial objects now took centre-stage in the development of material and form-based typologies, such as those of Montelius, mobilised not just by Wilson but Tylor, Lubbock, Evans and later on, Pitt Rivers.

The notion that the typological system rapidly took hold in British archaeological circles, collections and museum cases has, however, been criticised by Morse (1999). It was an obsession with race, and the role of crania as the defining attribute of different 'peoples', which relegated many grave goods to the role of decorative footnotes in volumes such as *Crania Britannica* (Davis and Thurnam 1865) or 'pretty and attractive' arrangements in museums, as craniologist Thomas Wright derisively put it (1859, 474). Peak District antiquarian Thomas Bateman handed over his impressive collection of crania to form the crux of Davis and Thurnam's case study material, shortly before his untimely death, lured by the hope that this novel 'science' could reveal the racial history of Britain from human remains alone. Craniology ran hand-in-hand with the broader 'ethnological method', promoted by Wright as the 'proper, and the only correct arrangement of a museum of antiquities' (1859, 473). Although ethnographic study had helped elucidate the function and role of many prehistoric grave goods, epitomised in Lubbock's key work *Pre-historic Times, as Illustrated by Ancient Remains, and the Manners and Customs of Modern Savages* (1865), Wright rejected both the typological and comparative ethnographic arrangements favoured by archaeologists such as Pitt Rivers in his Farnham museum: 'Relics of antiquity should be classed according to the peoples and tribes to whom they are known or believed to have belonged, and the localities in which they are found' (1859, 473). In such arrangements, Wright and others believed, burial customs should be neatly mapped against unique artefact classes and human remains, to identify and chart the arrival of different 'races'.

This polygenesist model (which espoused the notion of the distinct physiognomic character and social potential of each race, and thus their unique origin and development) was countered by the monogenesist model (favouring a single racial origin but distinct historical pathways for the emergence of different peoples). For the latter group, modern 'primitives', still wielding the kinds of stone implements found in Neolithic and Early Bronze Age burials in Britain, were merely 'stuck' in time: stilted in their development but capable of change. For the former group, the ethnographic analogy drawn between ancient and modern savage consigned both to a primitive state of social evolution, from which neither group could hope to evolve (see Fabian 1983). Both models relied on the social evolutionary schema developed by Morgan (in *Ancient Society* 1877), which charted the progress of humanity in an inevitable and unilinear trajectory, from 'savagery' to 'civilisation', to which Tylor added a middle stage of 'barbarism' (1871). Whatever model of social change archaeologists opted for (gradual evolution through internal dynamism or change wrought by invasion and supplantation), the overall direction of progress was not in doubt (see Bowler 1994). For Bateman this held out the promise of forming 'a correct opinion as to the real state of the civilisation of the inhabitants of this island' (1848, 5) while Anderson believed they also gave archaeologists a finer grasp on status: 'corresponding to their station or condition in life' (Anderson 1886, 331). Whilst the expert craniologists employed to write specialist appendices fought over the meaning of their measurements (see Giles 2006, 299), this canny elision of race, mortuary practice and material culture change led archaeologists such as Mortimer to conclude from his Iron Age East Yorkshire burials that:

> [the] presence of the chariot with its artistic accomplishments ... seems to point to a somewhat sudden introduction of a higher state of civilisation, as we do not find in any of these barrows, indications of a gradual progression in the arts. (1905, lxxv)

Greenwell was not convinced, however, favouring an admixture of people, resulting from the interbreeding of Neolithic and Bronze Age populations, and the 'natural process of improvement characteristic of man, or through knowledge gained by contact and intercourse' (1877, 212). The notion that funeral rites had the capacity to reveal these attributes should not surprise us given the British Victorian 'way of death': renowned for 'lavish displays of wealth consumption and its close grading of expenditure according to social position', even as higher status groups began to practice a kind of contrary 'good taste' through restraint and modesty, particularly in non-Conformist and atheist circles (Parker Pearson 1999b, 43). By the mid–late 19th century, grave goods had become powerful indices of both states of civilisation and racial identity.

2.5. 'Devoted to the dead': the concept of material affection

While these new paradigms gained archaeology a disciplinary foothold in evolutionary and social science, it is clear that many of these authors were also thinking more creatively about the funerary origin of these finds. Underneath their large-scale models and grandiose pronouncements on racial type or stage of evolutionary progress ran a more subtle narrative: a reflectiveness which builds on Browne's sensibilities. Joseph Anderson for example, evokes particular kinds of gold, jet and bronze objects which were:

> elaborately constructed and carefully ornamented with punctuated patterns which contrast fitly with the ornamented surface of the material. Thus there is taste exhibited in the forms of all these variously fabricated objects, and dexterity and skill implied in their finish and workmanship. Intrinsically they are evidence of the capacity and skill of the men that made them. But, as we find them all in associations which show that they are grave-goods – devoted to the dead, – we see that they are also evidences of the piety and affection which thus expressed themselves in the manner of the time. (1886, 96)

'Taste', 'capacity' and 'skill' might be foregrounded here but Anderson also values these objects as embodiments of belief, even emotion. He finishes his volume with the important point that such objects could have been bequeathed to or kept by the living, yet they were not:

> [through] the costly dedication of articles of use or adornment, freely renounced by the survivors, and set apart from the inheritance of the living, as grave-goods for the dead, we realise the intensity of their devotion to filial memories and family ties, to hereditary tradition and family honour. (1886, 227)

In his final work, Bateman promotes the notion that grave goods relate to:

> the requirements of the future existence ... manifesting itself ... in the splendour with which many of the dead were committed to the grave, not less than in the self-denying affection which suggested the interment of articles valued by the deceased. (1861, iii)

We note here the emerging concept of grave goods as a kind of 'material affection' (Julie Giles, pers. comm.). Thus, Bateman encouraged others to look for 'the glimpses of mental and moral feeling traceable in the make of the accompanying ornament or weapon, and in the motive which prompted its burial with the owner' (1861, ii). As if heading this call, Mortimer noted the difference between old and new ceramic vessels in graves: the former perhaps an actual possession, the later 'specially made for the grave' (1905, lxvii). Greenwell too noted the curious case of 'newly struck flints' alongside old tools in some graves (1877, 36). Concepts of futurity towards an afterlife and what the dead might need, the performance of splendour and largesse, personal possessions indissoluble from the deceased and gift-giving: these are all themes we will take up and consider further throughout this book.

Other archaeologists turned towards their knowledge of ethnography, folklore and local traditions to develop further insights into objects from burials. Mortimer was interested in the peculiar 'gendering' of tools buried with the Samoyads of the Great Tundra (1905, l), a theme also echoed in Greenwell's analogy between

Iron Age grave goods from East Yorkshire and ancient Bavarian laws where property passes down the 'spindle side' of women and the 'spear side' of men (1906, 272). Gendered symbolism begins to emerge in these studies. Meanwhile, Mortimer devoted a whole section to *The Breaking of Weapons and Tools* in his 1905 monograph, using a variety of analogies to explore the motivations behind ritual breakage or damage he saw in his prehistoric grave goods. He described an 'Eskimo' grave where 'a musket and numerous spears … [were] all broken so as to render them useless to the living' (1905, l) while amongst the Samoyads he notes, 'every deposit is somewhat damaged, even the sledge and the harrow … to prevent the unscrupulous from stealing them' (1905, li). A detailed description in Mortimer's footnotes of a Gypsy funeral at Withernsea where personal possessions, including caravan, fiddle and china, were broken and burnt was also used to make sense of ritual destruction. Whilst he sways here towards a prosaic interpretation of deterring post-mortem theft and disturbance of the dead (an ongoing concern in Victorian burial, see Watkins 2013) these themes of dramatic performance and ritual damage would be taken up by Grinsell in the 20th century (see Section 2.7 below; see also Garrow and Gosden 2012; Giles 2016).

Mortimer also touches on care for the dead, citing the frequency of food provision (1905, lxx) such as Greenwell's note regarding a small Food Vessel 'partly pushed into the mouth' of burial no. 40, 'as if it were in the act of taking food' (in Mortimer 1905, lxi). Much excitement was noted on the discovery of pork in Iron Age burials at Danes Graves and Eastburn (East Yorkshire) where newspapers championed evidence for the long-standing Yorkshire tradition of being 'buried with ham' (Anon, *Yorkshire Evening Post,* 24 April 1937). This notion of special, tasty funerary foods rang true for these archaeologists, who were organising and attending such wakes, which still sometimes included a symbolic food-offering to the dead, as in Cheshire:

> When mourners came to the wake, besides other refreshments they were given a piece of cake to eat wrapped up with a sprig of rosemary. The rosemary was either put into the coffin before it was closed or thrown into the grave at the burial'. (cited in Prag 2016, 490)

We should not be surprised by the tone of these insights from antiquarians and early archaeologists. Mortimer had lost both a daughter at the age of eight and his own brother, Robert (his fieldwork partner) by the time he dug at the Iron Age cemetery of Danes Graves with Greenwell (Harrison 2011). Like Browne, he and his peers inhabited worlds of high mortality, where the laying out, washing and preparation of the dead was still largely carried out at home. By being immersed in the memorials and mementos of the long-dead, the brevity of life was given context and meaning. As many of these grave goods moved out of their collector's hands and into formal museums in the 20th century, these more reflective insights ran as an important and subtle counter-narratives of material affection and care for the dead, in contrast to the paradigm that was to become culture history.

2.6. Pots as people? Grave goods and culture history

By the mid-20th century, the notion that crania could be used to directly identify the racial identity of prehistoric peoples might have lost dominance but the paradigm of culture history, instead, picked up the notion that distinctive suites of material culture were associated with particular ways of life. This was a liberating concept when deployed in Boasian cultural anthropology, rejecting the notion of unidirectional progress and social evolution: stressing instead the notion that both historical contingency and acquired social behaviour lay behind patterns in cultural lifeways (Rapport and Overing 2000, 95). Yet in archaeology, a method designed to describe spatial and temporal variation in material culture soon gained ethnic overtones:

> We find certain types of remains – pots, implements, ornaments, burial rites, and house forms – constantly recurring together. Such a complex of associated traits we shall call a 'cultural group' or just a 'culture'. We assume that such a complex is the material expression of what today would be called a people. (Childe 1929, v–vi)

Burial rites, and the distinctive suites of grave goods from them, gained a novel prominence in these models, leading to seminal studies on the 'Rinyo-Clacton folk' (associated with Grooved Ware, Piggott 1954), the 'Wessex Culture' (focused on the distinctive round barrows and 'princely' or 'prestige' grave goods, Piggott 1938), the wider 'Bell Beaker' (Abercromby 1904) or 'Beaker folk' (identified through a specific vessel type, e.g. Childe 1937). In the Iron Age, the 'Arras' (Stead 1965) and 'Aylesford-Swarling' cultures (Birchall 1965) were identified through their distinctive burial rites and grave goods: La Tène influenced artwork, weapons, brooches and ceramic assemblages. Principal exponents in later prehistory beyond Childe included Stuart Piggott, Christopher Hawkes, O.G.S. Crawford, Cyril Fox and F.R. Hodson. Grave goods played a key role in the revisiting of antiquarian datasets, to which were added research and (post)war-era rescue assemblages. They were included in new visualisations by Fox (e.g. 1932, *The Personality of Britain* – featuring in some of archaeology's earliest distribution maps) and Hawkes (e.g. 1959, *The ABC of the British Iron Age* – regional diagrams which 'mapped' cultural variation over space and time; see also Giles 2008).

There were many problems with the culture history paradigm, most notably its ethnic and racist deployment in Nazi-era Germany (see Jones 1997; Trigger 2006). The issue we want to focus on here, however, is its implication for grave goods. Culture history models looked for pattern: supressing variation in funerary assemblages in order to identify coherence. They perpetuated the notion of cultural homogeneity, of conservative customs and stability: for this reason the models valorised funerary ceramics as one of the most 'stable' domestic signatures of a people. They bundled and bounded cultures (and thus funerary assemblages) in time and space (see critique in Ingold 1994). For example, as Fowler points out, the particular 'package' of individual inhumation associated with cord-impressed or incised bipartite vessel, barbed and tanged flint arrowheads, wristguards, copper awls and daggers and 'v' perforated ornaments of jet or shale, created the distinctive Beaker funerary assemblage (2013, 69). This strict approach to boundedness led Ian Stead to believe there was a main Arras square barrow culture and an allied but distinct northern Wolds group distinguished by weapons burials (1965): the latter now recognised through Stead's own fieldwork as a late phase in this regional Iron Age inhumation rite (Stead 1991; Giles 2012).

As many writers have pointed out, culture history was weak at explaining variation and transformation over time. At the same time, archaeological narratives also began to lose their grip on the more idiosyncratic motivations of mourners that had previously been captured in many of the accounts discussed above. The 'event' of a funeral became ossified as a mortuary rite. When rapid change in grave goods was seen, it was inevitable that an external 'prompt' was thought necessary: for Piggott, then, the distinctive ceramic vessels, bronze, jet, gold and amber grave goods of Early Bronze Age Wessex were evidence for the arrival of a 'highly individual culture' arising from an 'actual ethnic movement' (1938, 52). This was not all: the apparently superior technological knowledge, craft skill and exotic materials were (for Stuart Piggott at least) evidence of an 'intrusive ruling class' whose 'delight for barbaric finery' led them to conquer and dominate the indigenous 'uninteresting and unenterprising substratum' (1938, 52). Grave goods had not only become proxies for people: they were material indices of civilisation, mapped against the enduring social evolutionary typologies which were to be reinvigorated by the impact of the processual paradigm.

2.7. Funerals and folklore

Meanwhile, a very different account of grave goods was being produced by the prehistorian Leslie Grinsell: an amateur-turned-professional archaeologist, whose field knowledge of British barrows was unrivalled in his generation. Grinsell specialised in the synthesis of excavations and his interpretation was coloured more by folklore and place-name studies than culture history. In *The Ancient Burial Mounds of England* he made a simple, conceptual distinction between aspects of the burial rite which he believed were for the 'deceased' and those that were orientated towards the 'mourners' (1953 2nd edition, building on his 1936 monograph). The approach required close attention to mortuary practice and the placement of objects in the grave: whether on or off the body, close to it (in the primary interment) or apparently added later (as a secondary insertion). It also required him to 'imagine' something of the funerary performance, its temporal sequence and what was present or absent. He paid more attention to the materials from which things were made than their cultural 'type', using folklore to draw attention to overlooked (and often discarded) substances as well as the treatment of grave goods themselves. Ritual breakage for example, was a consistent theme in his work, as in the case of the 1890 Lincolnshire widow, who had to 'dead' her husband's jug and mug to 'release their spirits' and allow them to accompany her husband into the afterlife (Grinsell 1961, 489). In trying to make sense of the meaning behind mortuary rites in later prehistoric barrows, Grinsell was drawing on

Table 2.01 Re-conceptualizing grave goods, their treatment in death and meaning – the work of Leslie Grinsell.

Aspect of the funerary rite and intended audience	Example of material/object type and interpretation
	For the deceased
Food and drink	Faunal remains and pottery ('token offerings' for the journey, 1953, 26, 34) or means of 'feeding the dead' (e.g. Roman lead pipes)
Inclusion of objects	– as container (especially for cremations but also inhumations): cist, vessel, coffin or cloth, or bier (e.g. palanquin, 1953, 42) – as funerary furniture (1953, 31) – as 'insignia of rank' (e.g. maceheads, 1953, 36) – for 'personal use' (e.g. awls (for tattooing 1953, 35?)), tweezers, knife daggers ('for personal rather than warlike purposes' 1953, 35), razors, flint knives – as 'ornaments for his advantage' (1953, 32) or bodily decoration e.g. shells, teeth, stones, red ochre – as entertainment (e.g. gaming pieces) – as protective or amuletic objects (1953, 32) e.g. horns, tusks, white quartz, 'trinkets of amber, shale and other substances which still have protective powers attributed to them in folklore', 'protection from evil' (1953, 35) or 'beneficial objects' (1953, 36) – as equipment for the afterlife (e.g. knife and whetstone) or 'to enable the dead to keep warm, to cook, or possibly to provide light for the purpose of warding off evil spirits' (1953, 36) (e.g. or iron pyrites and flint 'strike–a–lights') – as vessels or vehicles for journeying to the afterlife e.g. 'boat shaped tree trunk coffins' (1953, 34), chariots and ponies (1953, 41), ships (Anglo-Saxon boats), footwear (Roman hobnailed shoes), or as means of securing passage (Charon's fee, 1953, 42–3) – as substances or objects to ensure or promote rebirth or immortality (1953, 32) e.g. 'crouched' (foetal) posture and substances – red ochre, white pebbles, phallic emblems/symbols, fossil 'echini', haematite, amber, 'stoned or pebbles of unusual shapes or colours', and 'sheaves of wheat or barley' (1953, 37) – as 'miniature' versions for children (e.g. accessory vessels, 1953, 39)
Inclusion of animals	As companions ('a favourite animal accompanied its master or mistress' 1953, 33) e.g. 'hunting dog' (1953, 35), cats (1953, 33) or horse (1953, 40) As guides (1953, 35) or to convey the dead to the afterlife (1961) As protectors (e.g. horned cattle, 1953, 35)

(Continued)

his comparative work during the war amongst Egyptian tombs, ethnographic analogy, as well as a lifelong interest in British folk knowledge and surviving tradition. Whilst we cannot summarise all his ideas, in Table 2.01 we foreground a number of them which stand in subtle contrast to preceding paradigms and endure as salient insights, many of which we will return to in the later chapters of the book.

Table 2.01 (Continued)

Aspect of the funerary rite and intended audience	Example of material/object type and interpretation
Inclusion of other humans	As 'relatives, retainers or slaves' (1953, 35)
Ritual breakage and burning	Broken ceramics, damaged flint artefacts and burned objects: 'to enable the spirits of the objects to reach to afterlife' (1953, 36 and 38) Fragments of broken materials sometimes scattered as part of the rites of making the barrow (1953, 37) Broken swords and spearheads (1953, 43) destroyed 'because of their close association with the deceased' (1961, 477) 'Ceremonial killing' and 'symbolic dedication' (1961, 477 and 485)
Heirloom objects	'In the case of whetstones and bronze implements and some of the pottery, it is ... evident that sometimes they were old and much used' (1953, 36) also gold ornaments (1953, 37)
Making for the dead	Freshly knapped flintwork (1953, 36)
Inversion of objects	Inverted urns which thus 'kept in the spirit of the dead' (1953, 39)
	For the living
Food and drink	Funeral feasts (distinct from offerings to the dead)
Purification rites	Fires close to the barrow (for 'primitive hygiene') in contrast to funerary pyres (1953, 34), charcoal spreads indicating 'fumigation' (1953, 40)
Protection against the dead	Binding, weighting down, covering with slabs (1953, 32 and 39) or 'mutilation of the body of deceased, or the burial of a skull only' (1953, 40): 'to prevent return' (1953, 32) or 'protect ... from the unwelcome attentions of a 'revenant' (1953, 39)
Transformation of the living	Rites involving cutting/shaving of hair, possibly to transfer 'life force' that 'resided in the hair' to the dead (1953, 41)
Ritual breakage	To prevent profane use following funerary rituals (1953, 45) To prevent death claiming another life (1953, 45) To prevent post-mortem theft (1961, 477) To prevent contest or jealousy amongst mourners (1961, 477) Disposal of 'polluted' or spiritually contagious objects (1961) Pragmatic dismantling to fit in the grave (1961, 477)

Grinsell's fascination with apotropaic grave goods (listed in Table 2.01 – horns, tusks, amber, jet, quartz, fossils, haematite, ochre, etc.) has never seemed more timely. Recent excavations by MOLA Headland have discovered 'salt plates' of blue-and-white, willow pattern china interred in 18th–19th century AD burials of men, women and children at St James' and Park Street Burial Grounds in Birmingham (Richardson 2016). A piece of antiquarian folklore suggests that this not only related to an idea around corporeal preservation but protection for the dead (for the 'devil took no salt with his meat') as well as being 'an emblem of the immortal spirit' (John Brand

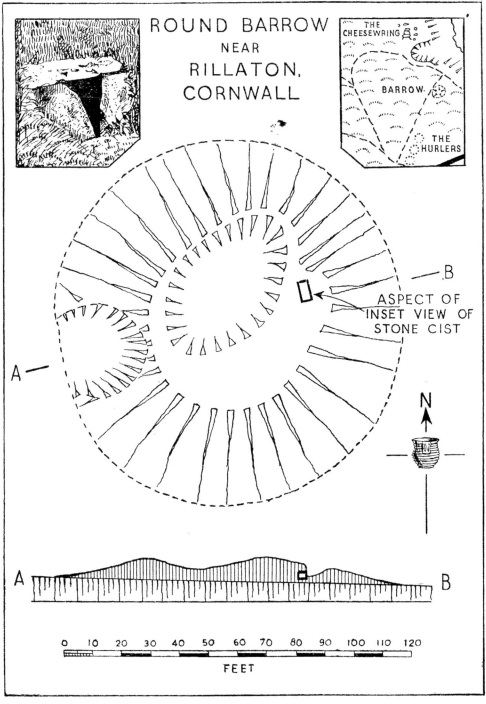

ROUND BARROW
NEAR
RILLATON,
CORNWALL

THE
CHEESEWRING

BARROW.

THE
HURLERS

B

ASPECT OF
INSET VIEW OF
STONE CIST

A

N

A

B

0   10   20   30   40   50   60   70   80   90   100 110 120

FEET

Figure 2.04 'Round Barrow near Rillaton, Cornwall' (Grinsell 1953, fig. 6).

1795 cited in Richardson 2016). These were relatively poor burials, where the living drew a powerful, preservative and tasty substance from the domestic domain into the realm of death, to show their care for the dead, concern for their afterlife and ensure them ongoing protection.

In addition, Grinsell pointed to a number of aspects of mortuary performance which had left no material trace but were likely to have occurred: libations for the dead, funeral orations, dances, wailing and laying in state (1953, 4). He did however observe the frequent inclusion of exotic stones, clay, pebbles and soil, used to compose the burial mound (1953, 52). Whilst not strictly 'grave goods', we can see these instances as part of the wider suite of substances brought together by the living, for the dead. Grinsell's primary fieldwork focused on the monuments and, despite his rich descriptive treatment of grave goods, they seldom feature as illustrations in his work. For example, the Early Bronze Age burial at Rillaton (Fig. 2.04) is represented as a landscape and burial 'infographic' that cleverly captures the grave at a series of nested scales and perspectives. Yet look hard and you will see that the central compass motif – known as the 'rosewind' – is a delicate line drawing of the Rillaton gold cup. Miniature it may be, but it aptly lies at the heart of his study.

In sum, Grinsell's work ran quietly alongside that of his peers, picking up and expanding upon some of the mortuary motivations mentioned by antiquarians but adding nuance in terms of funerary performance, object histories and the meaning of particular substances in the context of death and burial. His egalitarian approach to materials is one we identify with, patiently recording barrows with very few objects of interest. When it came to the East Yorkshire square barrows for instance, this led him to argue (based on the *paucity* of grave goods) that even 'people of small account could be accorded barrow burial' (1953, 4). Despite his unique perspective, not even Grinsell could escape the assumptions of the paradigm which replaced culture history, reconfiguring grave goods not as the signatures of people but as indices of rank and power.

2.8. Rank, status and power

The impact of New Archaeology, the Chicago school of economics, social evolutionary models and middle-range theory on funerary archaeology have been reviewed in some detail by Parker Pearson (1999b, 27–9). He points to the seminal influence of Binford in 1960s–80s mortuary archaeology and his proposal that first, the social 'rank' of the deceased could be correlated with the number of people who had relationships with them and, secondly, that mortuary rites were an exercise in composing a 'social persona': 'a composite of the social identities maintained in life and recognized as appropriate for consideration in death' (Binford 1971, paraphrased in Parker Pearson 1999b, 29). Binford used a cross-cultural ethnographic study to then propose that more complex societies (i.e. sedentary farmers) had more complex mortuary rites and tended to signal sex differences more strongly in their grave goods. To this model, Saxe added the notion that complex societies had more diverse aspects of rank that cut across aspects of identity such as age, sex and achievements in life (1970) which could also be seen in distinctions in grave goods. Carr meanwhile, argued that the *quality* (not *quantity*) of these mortuary assemblages could be correlated with status (1995).

As Brück (2004) and Fowler (2013), among others, have pointed out, the impact on British prehistoric burial archaeology in the mid–later 20th century was to proliferate a kind of circular logic: grave goods became the evidence of status, the grounds upon which 'rank' could be identified (e.g. S. Piggott 1938). Burial monuments, mortuary ideology and grave goods together became one of the main means of charting social evolution from 'simple' (Neolithic) to more 'complex' and 'stratified' (Bronze and Iron Age) societies, before the arrival of state-level mortuary ideology with the Roman invasion (exemplified in Renfrew's 1974 approach, building on Service 1962, see also Earle 1991; 2002). Whilst neo-social evolutionary approaches 'decoupled' themselves from biological models and both lost their emphasis on the inevitability of 'progress' (Fowler 2013, 74), the models tended to stress growing complexity and hierarchy as a feature of later prehistory. In this approach, grave goods were swept up in a tautological model: those who buried their dead without *personalised* 'wealth' were judged, by nature, to be more egalitarian and less advanced forms of society, than those whose dead were explicitly associated with individual panoplies of things: weapons, suites of jewellery, tools, etc. Moreover, mortuary assemblages were read as *direct* reflections of the deceased's wealth and status (e.g. Randsborg 1973; Shennan 1975). Thus Ashbee could write:

> The egregious furnishings in Food Vessel graves are indications of the social status and sex of the deceased... lunulate collars of jet beads or bronze manchettes might betoken office... arrowheads and axe-hammers suggest warrior graves, while awls and plano-convex flint knives could signify the graves of craftsmen concerned with the various aspects of leather-craft. (Ashbee 1978, 146–7)

Importantly, change did not have to arise through actual invasion in these new models: 'peer polity interaction' between elites was seen as replacing the moribund 'ritual authority structures' of the earlier periods (e.g. Thorpe and Richards 1984). Where they had once seen civilised invaders, archaeologists now saw a more entrepreneurial spirit: internal dynamism stimulated by social interaction, characterised in the Beaker period by competitive acquisition *and* consumption, especially in the mortuary sphere where chiefly figures were being shaped (e.g. Shennan 1986; Barrett 1994). Exotic and powerful grave goods naturalised power whilst burials valorised and celebrated such figures (see critique in Fowler 2013, 85 and Brück 2019, 4).

From these accounts emerged a Bronze Age characterised by 'an early warrior-dominated expression of *Heroic* society' (Ashbee 1960, 172, original emphasis) with other burials designated as 'Royal', 'Warrior', 'Female' and 'Poor' graves (Annable and Simpson 1964, 21–8) largely on the basis of their grave goods. Interestingly (as Ucko points out) Childe did not quite agree, noting the Middle Bronze Age 'fall-off' in grave goods, despite an apparent rise in societal wealth (Childe 1944, cited in Ucko 1969). It was left to Ashbee to respond, wondering if 'the greed of the heirs ha[d] overcome their religious scruples?' (1960, 173)! The number, quality, rarity, skill or labour encapsulated in both grave goods and the wider burial rite thus became an index of social stratification – rank – as well as age and sex (Fowler 2013, 70 and table 3.01 for the selective 'features' of identity which processual archaeology took from its ethnographic analogies). Pierpoint's statistical study of select attributes of East Yorkshire Beakers, for example, argued that children and, to a lesser extent, women were buried with fewer and less impressive grave goods than men (1980). Age and sex emerge here as particularly important aspects of the deceased that were being marked in death, not social 'rank', yet as Fowler notes, the 'bias in our imagination is towards vertical or hierarchical differentiation' (2013, 82).

Even the iconic volume celebrating the proliferation of grave goods in the Early Bronze Age, *Symbols of Power at the time of Stonehenge* (Clarke *et al.* 1985; Fig. 2.05) did little to challenge this model. By the 1980s, theoretical approaches in British archaeology were using structural Marxist theory to interrogate ideology and power and examine how status was reproduced (e.g. Frankenstein and Rowlands 1978). Social difference (read through the grave goods) was taken as axiomatic but what had shifted was the focus upon 'prestige' objects (rare, over-size, numerous, extravagant, exotic or exquisitely crafted) which were now understood as the *means* through which new kinds of exclusionary socio-political and/or politico-religious power were symbolised and reproduced (Clarke *et al.* 1985). Only rarely, as Thomas pointed out, do we sense that such authority was 'unstable or imperilled' (2002, 47).

This new paradigm was an important part of the way that material culture itself began to acquire greater agency, as part of what Barrett would later argue were the material conditions of historically specific forms of power (1994). In her study of early medieval graves, Pader also argued the meaning of such objects was not static but could be dynamically renegotiated (1982): what was being projected in death was a social persona, an ideal, which may or may not relate to the biography of the deceased. Yet in later prehistoric studies of grave goods, archaeologists tended to foreground quite a narrow range of burials, often associated with the symbolic regalia of authority (gold plaques, jet maceheads, amber cups) or direct force (weaponry). Such objects were argued to be evidence of close elite control of Continental and Scandinavian exchange routes and their explicit focus on men, metals and power created what Brück and Fontijn have called the 'myth of the warrior chief' (2013). They argue that this revealed an ethnocentric, androcentric and reductive approach to the past, missing much of the 'depth, texture and complexity' of Bronze Age life (Brück 2017a, 37).

Such models endure. A recent account of the cemetery at Varna, for example, led Higham *et al.* to note that 'there can be little doubt about the hierarchical nature of the social relations that resulted in such a massive accumulation of exotic prestige objects' (2007, 641). Meanwhile, the Amesbury Archer is still touted as the 'richest' Early Bronze

Figure 2.05 The front cover of 'Symbols of Power at the Time of Stonehenge' (Clarke et al. *1985).*

Age burial from the landscape around Stonehenge based on a sheer count of grave goods (Wessex Archaeology n.d.). Privileged mobility on the basis of elite connections has become a new vein in these accounts of important figures (Sheridan 2010), whether they were travelling with prized new knowledge of metalworking (Fitzpatrick 2011) or for politico-sacred pilgrimage (Needham 2008). Authority is now sometimes seen as being vested as much in supernatural as worldly social power, reflected in ownership and control of 'magical' materials that were, necessarily, subsequently deposited with that person in the grave (e.g. Sheridan and Shortland 2003; Woodward and Hunter 2015; Brück and Davies 2018). In these narratives, the traditional equation of 'exotic objects = wealth and socio-political power' has simply been translated into one of 'exotic and special objects = supernatural/magical power'. Like Brück, Fowler has done much to pluralise Early Bronze Age burial narratives, showing national and regional variability, unpicking chronology and dissembling the Beaker 'package' (2013, 71–3). Nonetheless, the 'social persona' of the chief still crops up repeatedly as an all-too-familiar trope in others' accounts, especially those focusing on the Early Bronze Age. The subtle symbolism and diversity of grave goods in Gristhorpe man's coffin burial from North Yorkshire, coupled with his complex biography (illness, endemic pain, likely behavioural change and decline) is interpretively reduced in the conclusion to a tale of a well-connected 'paramount chief' (Melton *et al.* 2010, 811). Racton man from Sussex – mature, physically impressive, with a protein-privileged diet – was also buried in a coffin with a rare dagger (Needham *et al.* 2017). His demise by dagger-blade is seen as likely evidence of codified 'combat-contested leadership' (*ibid.*), removing an ageing (silverback?) male from a position of authority. At least in this account, power is treated as momentary, contested and frail.

This approach to evaluating status through mortuary rites can be situated within a contemporary world in which care for the dead was increasingly professionalised, commercialised and codified. For those who could pay, the dead could be removed with speed from their home while embalming alleviated the temporal rhythms normally imposed upon the mourners, and mass-produced coffins, hearses and modes of memorialising shaped acceptable 'social personas' out of the life of the deceased (Davies 2015; Rugg 2017). 'Grave goods' also became more restricted, especially as cremation rose to prominence as a favoured funerary rite (Jupp 2006). It is not surprising then that archaeologists might adopt this pragmatic, rational and scientific approach to analysing wealth and power through funerary material culture: it was shaped not just by the dominant processual paradigm but contemporary mortuary experience.

2.9. 'Where only the heart is competent': the impact of ethnography and mortuary sociology

Yet, as this transformation in contemporary mourning customs took hold in many Western cultures, archaeologists began to draw in a rather different way upon the work of anthropologists. Using ethnographic analogy, Ucko queried many of the underlying assumptions of the 'grave goods=wealth=status' model, arguing that 'richness or poverty of offerings may in no real sense reflect either the actual material contradictions of a society or the actual wealth of any individual' (1969, 266). Ucko argued that what ended up in a grave was usually a tiny fraction of the material culture mobilised in complex and lengthy funerals, of which archaeologists might only see the 'end picture' or tertiary rite. The selection of what went in the grave was thus 'subordinated to social and ritual sanctions' (1969, 266): what was thought to be appropriate according both to custom and belief. Objects might be interred because they related to cults that the dead had been involved in which were not shared by their descendants. Others were simply too potent and dangerous 'to keep' (1969, 267). Ucko also pointed to the classification work that went on in death, where objects might be used to emphasise age as a particular facet of identity not wealth, and kin and lineage rather than status. Others were needed to negotiate certain kinds of demise: from accident, murder, drowning, some infectious diseases, to death in childbirth (1969, 271): what Bloch and Parry would later conceptualise as 'bad deaths' (1982, 16). Artefacts need have no direct association with the deceased: Ucko cites the example of the Nanakanse of Ghana, where objects in the grave represent tokens of *living* souls who have become 'trapped' during the funeral ceremony and are ensured spiritual protection by the intercession of the sexton, who placed material surrogates in the tomb (1969, 256). He also queried the notion that a 'paucity' of grave goods signalled a lack of belief in the afterlife: they might be destroyed before interment as part of the funeral or they might be thought to be 'there' symbolically but not materially, perhaps through being placed close to the dead during their laying out (1969, 266).

The notion that grave goods did not directly reflect the identity of the deceased was taken up by Barrett (1991b), Bradley (1998) and Woodward (2000) among others. The idea that death had the capacity to cause both social and political crises, and that the dead had 'cultural capital' for the living, added further nuance to discourses of power (Barrett 1994). Parker Pearson emphasised that 'funerals are lively, contested events where social roles are manipulated, acquired and discarded' (1999b, 32), noting now-famously that the 'dead do not bury themselves but are treated and disposed of by the living' (1999b, 3). Not even death can 'freeze the picture' as the sociologist Jenkins put it: 'there is always the possibility of a post-mortem revision of identity' (1996, 4). Grave goods could therefore be gifts not possessions, Parker Pearson suggested: repayments of debts or offerings to secure new and favourable relations with a soon-to-be ancestor figure (1999b, 84). Key volumes by Metcalf and Huntingdon explored performance, symbolism and meaning in various 'celebrations' of death (1991 [reprint of 1978]) whilst Bloch and Parry pointed to the theme of regeneration and fertility in funerary rites (1982). 'Symbolic and structural' approaches in archaeology drew on these studies, leading to rather different kinds of data analysis that sought to discern what were thought to be important underlying organising principles related to cosmology, kinship, gender and ideology through statistical patterning in grave goods (e.g. Parker Pearson 1982; 1999a; Shanks and Tilley 1982). Studies of iconography, symbolism and metaphor in mortuary materials gained more prominence (e.g. Thomas 1991), as did the material qualities of the objects themselves. Funerary rites involved incorporations and revelations related to the spiritual as well as the mortal realm, argued Parker Pearson (1999b, 11): some objects may have been meant to dazzle or charm the dead, and the way they were treated in the grave (particularly 'rites of reversal' or object 'killing'; 1999b, 26) may have been meant to confuse otherworldly beings or consign grave goods to the supernatural domain (see also Giles 2016). Grinsell's legacy in burial archaeology is clear here. Some objects, Parker Pearson pointed out, were related not to the deceased but ritual frameworks designed to facilitate acts of separation and processes of transition (1999b). However, as Tarlow (1992) noted early on, the topic of 'emotion' was rarely touched upon. Anthropologists were wary of falling into the trap of ascribing 'psychic universals' to other cultures (Metcalf and Huntingdon 1991, 2) even though they recognized their own work could at times feel both reductive and redundant:

> We believe we know what death is because it is a peculiar event and one that arouses great emotion. It seems both ridiculous and sacrilegious to question the value of this intimate knowledge and to wish to apply reason to a subject where only the heart is competent. (Hertz 2009 [reprint of 1960], 27)

As anthropology entered its own literary turn, sudden moments of clarity began to emerge from personal experience. Rosaldo for example, found it very difficult to understand the relationship between death and Ilongot head-hunting until, as Metcalf and Huntingdon note, 'he himself suffered the loss of his wife in an accident. Then ... distracted by grief, he finally understood the rage that Ilongot expressed in violence' (1991, 4). Bloch and Parry argued that since funerary rituals *structured* socially sanctioned modes of grieving and codes of expression, they could provide a way of exploring emotion (1982): a challenge particularly taken up in historical archaeology by Tarlow (1992; 2012). Wider studies of death, dying and bereavement, and the material culture associated with contemporary burial – what Parker Pearson called 'the ethnoarchaeology of us' (1999b, 40) – also affected studies of prehistoric grave goods. Key thinkers here include Hallam and Hockey who noted how 'material culture mediates our relationship with the dead' (2001, 14). Objects were part of the 'management' of this event (Hockey *et al.* 2010, 1) but, as personal mnemonics, they were especially valent: imbued with a 'visual and emotional affectivity' (Ash 1996, 219), an aesthetics of absence. Things thus assume 'an enhanced agency as fragments which can stand as the individual in their entirety' (Hockey *et al.* 2010, 10). Grave goods therefore allowed the living to do the work of remembering the dead but the tale they told was 'gathered, sifted and recast' (Hallam *et al.* 1999, 5). This was a more subtle understanding of the work of creating a 'social persona' out of death and these sociologists did not gloss over the contest or friction which could arise from competing versions of such lives. Indeed, some of this work could be both 'inflammatory and volatile' (Hockey *et al.* 2010, 207).

An influential paper on contemporary grave goods by Harper (2012) provided particularly rich insights. Its title (*I'm glad she has her glasses on. That really makes the difference*) alluded to the way in which mourners rehumanise the dead by dressing and adorning them. Clothes might be old and familiar or more formal attire, and some were even specially bought, but Harper finds it was the small accoutrements – like glasses – that captured the deceased's personality, which helped connect the living to their relative or friend, during the physical transformations wrought by death. In this contemporary context, grave goods were conceptualised as both 'needful' and 'dear' things that the dead might require. Time was an important factor here. Harper's work in mortuaries and crematoria allowed her to see the period just after death when the deceased still required tending. The boundary between palliative care and post-mortem attention was a very thin one: mourners were not quite done with the dead it seemed, and their last acts were important ways they continued to offer a kind of care whilst such bonds began to loosen. Dressing and wrapping, pinning and coffining were powerful gestures as persons both literally and metaphorically 'fell apart' (Croucher and Richards 2014; see also Cooper *et al.* 2019). We can see grave goods as part of the material expression of this this practical, solidary and emotional labour. One family surrounded the deceased with photographs so that they were 'put all round 'im' (cited in Harper 2012, 51): providing a sense of post-mortem company and affection which might be mimicked in prehistory by objects that embodied such bonds. Yet Harper also noted that, in what van Gennep would call this 'liminal' phase (1960), grave goods came and went: things were put in the coffin during a period of laying out and visiting of the deceased, but they sometimes came out again (medals for example). Some gifts given to the living were now returned to the deceased giver, whilst others were bought and given as new things to the dead (rings and necklaces – potent symbols of bonds – fell into both categories). Through this to-and-fro of grave goods, mourners had the chance to 'catch up' and renew ties (Harper 2010, 107) especially through objects like letters, and their own identity and relationship could be 'remade' through bereavement practices (Walter 1996; see also Gilchrist and Sloane 2005 for an account which expertly highlights the complex temporalities of medieval funerary practices and the grave goods caught up in these).

The 'symbolic efficacy' of objects was seen as vital to the negotiation of these rites of transition (Hockey *et al.* 2010, 6). Materials which conjured the fleeting intangibility of life (flowers, wax, wood, bone, cloth, hair) compared with substances that evoked permanence and constancy (untarnishable gold, granite inscriptions) could both be selectively deployed in the grave, the funeral ceremony and the memorial, to contrastive effect. This 'interplay of longevity and transience' (Hallam and Hockey 2001, 3) is something we have to look hard for in our prehistoric burials, given the bias of preservation we inherit. Objects could also help normalise death, as 'ideas from one domain of life that has a familiar, taken-for-granted status' were used to create 'knowledge about one that is more abstract, mysterious or frightening' (Hockey *et al.* 2010, 5). Death is unknowable: it *has* to be conceptualised through metaphor, proceeding from 'the known to the unknown' (Nisbet 1969, 4). Here, Metcalf and Huntington note the 'paradoxical prevalence of symbolism of rebirth' (1991, 11) as a way of working through the existential threat posed by death. Objects that offered some sense of continued contact with the deceased or eventual reunion were particularly important where death was conceptualised as a loss, departure or journey (Hallam and Hockey 2001, 20). Other aspects of mortuary culture were never aimed at the living nor the deceased but the community they were about to join: the writer and art critic John Berger memorably describes inscriptions on headstones as 'letters of recommendation to the dead, concerning the newly departed' (1984, 44).

Why all this bother? As Hertz put it, 'the living owe all kinds of care to the dead who reside amongst them' (2009, 30), yet the 'uncertainty of the outcomes' (Metcalf and Huntingdon 1991, 6) still haunt us. All death-work risks failure and, as Grinsell (1953) and more recently Watkins (2013) have reiterated, failure of mortuary rites can result in revenancy. As this section has tried to evoke through both ethnographic and sociological examples, grave goods are, and always have been, a kind of care: *part* of 'doing right' by the dead and our relationship with them. Yet where there is doubt, guilt, contest or concern, grave goods can also be used to flatter and appease, or constrain and contain the post-mortem agency of the deceased. In our contemporary landscape, we are used to seeing 'not-grave goods': acts of material deposition that draw attention to places of loss and particular kinds of death ... helmets and 'ghost bikes' left as tangible evocations of road traffic accidents, or mass floral tributes laid in acts of collective mourning. Studies of these artefacts remind us that not all 'mortuary material culture' ended up in a grave or needed to be associated with a corpse (see our development of these ideas in Cooper *et al.* 2020).

The impact of these ideas is still being felt at the interstices of mortuary material culture studies, such as Croucher's interdisciplinary *Continuing Bonds* project (see Croucher *et al.* 2020). Here, the notion that our relationship with the dead is never finished but continues, changing over time, has been used as a starting point for creative conversations between contemporary 'death-workers' (in palliative care) and archaeologists: mutually exploring the meaning of objects caught up in death, dying and memory work. Meanwhile, as we explore below, in prehistory, the paradigm of post-humanism, 'flat ontology' and symmetrical archaeology has once again shifted our perspective on grave goods.

2.10. Relational, vibrant assemblages and kinwork

Since the turn of the millennium, British prehistorians in particular have been increasingly influenced by critical approaches to personhood, which argue that the concept of the individual modern, Western self and post-Enlightenment dualisms between the human and the non-human, does a disservice to the ways in which prehistoric peoples might have conceptualised their identity and being in the world. Brück explicitly takes up this theme in relation to grave goods, arguing that:

identity is not something that people have, an unchanging set of qualities; rather, it is an ongoing act of production – an inherently fluid set of properties under continual construction and revision. As such, Early Bronze Age grave goods do not simply reflect the social identity of the deceased; they communicate the character of the relationships that made that person what he or she was. (2004, 311)

This approach argues for a *relational* model of personhood, in which the boundaries of the body did not neatly 'cohere' with the epidermis (Jones 2002) but extended to 'incorporate other objects, places and people' (Brück 2004, 313). Grave goods were not mere symbols then but 'intrinsic components of selfhood' (*ibid.*). Goodenough's study of the 'social persona' was revisited in its original sense as 'transitive, contextual and relational' (Fowler 2013, 77). Since personhood 'unfolds as a process of growth and maturation' within those relationships (Giles 2012, 34) it is an ongoing project (Jones 2002) and grave goods are part of the practices through which people are constituted at the time of death and in its wake, not a passive reflection of fully formed and finished identity. These ideas found resonance in a wider interest in practices of sociality around death in the work of Whittle (2003) for example. The very obvious fragmentation of the corporeal body following death in Neolithic chambered tombs encouraged archaeologists such as Thomas (1999) and Fowler (2004) to propose that models of partible or permeable identity might be more relevant to this period, based on work drawn from ethnographers such as Strathern (1988), Busby (1997) and LiPuma (1998).

In her study of Early Bronze Age burials, Brück reconceptualised objects that were too 'big' for a child or were composed of composite elements (jet or amber necklaces) as potential gifts that embodied the 'ties that bind': expressing links between the living and the dead (2004, 314 and 316). She argued that this produced a graveside *mappa mundi* in which the position of the person within their world was expressed and contextualised. Tools like awls for leather-working might not be personal possessions or equipment for the afterlife then but evocations of other times, places and tasks that knitted the deceased back into their kin, kine and land (2004, 318). Other tools might be caught up in the work for the funeral: the making of shrouds or coffins, and the 'death-work' of those preparing the corpse. Wrapping was a particularly significant act which Brück argues had metaphoric value of tying up bonds: it also 'assembled' a particular constellation of substances, 'expressing, reaffirming or altering' interpersonal relationships (2004, 319). In contrast, blades could be used to evoke the 'cutting' of such ties (Fowler 2004, 74). There was room here for the kind of politics of death discussed above, where 'descent groups, neighbours and friends were recast in the face of profound personal loss' (Brück 2004, 321). Ritual damage and fragmentation were also reinterpreted as part of how the living coped with the social impact of loss, the wrench and rift of death (2004, 320).

In Jones' study of durable, shiny, colourful and luminous materials from graves (like copper and bronze, gold, jet and amber) he emphasised their animacy and vitality, beginning to grant objects greater agency and potency in terms of their affects (2002).

It was a theme echoed by Ingold who stressed these were not 'fixed' attributes of matter but relational properties arising from their positioning within wider fluxes and flows of materials (2007). Like Brück, Jones moved beyond Hoskins' important concept of 'biographical objects' (1998) to evoke how things were also enmeshed in relations. Whilst objects *could* be used 'to tell the stories of people's lives' (the subtitle of Hoskins book, 1998), Jones argued it was not necessarily the individual being scrutinised, consolidated and celebrated in the grave so much as the density and reach of their relations (2002). This was not limited to social bonds with people: other kinds of grave 'substance' considered by a number of authors were the 'foreign' clays and soils found in barrow-mounds or particular stones and pebbles. They brought together a landscape in microcosm, reflective not just of personal journeys but wider relations with places (Owoc 2002; Brück 2004, 321). Brück also breaks down some of the conceptual boundaries between people and animals, arguing that the inclusion of certain (non-meat bearing) faunal remains might not be simply an expression of clan or moiety (as Parker Pearson had proposed in the Iron Age East Yorkshire burials, 1999a). The metaphoric power of animal remains might be used to evoke particular qualities of the deceased, their skills and behaviour, through analogy with particular species (see also Jones 1998 and Wilkin 2011).

As attentiveness to substance grew, other overlooked materials began to gain greater prominence in such accounts. Assemblages of shells and fossils might be 'metonymic referents' to meaningful locations in someone's life (Brück 2004, 321), a theme we take up in Chapters 5 and 7. For Fowler, the 'five periwinkle shells, fish vertebrae, teeth and bird bones' at Hasting Hill cist burial 1 for instance, 'speak of the sea, the shore, the sky' (2013, 134). They remind him of sacred 'medicine' bundles from North America which comprise 'carefully curated assemblages of powerful, elemental and mnemonic objects, or substances ... that articulated a set of larger personal, community or social relations' (Pauketat and Alt 2018, 77). Pauketat and Alt thus see these gatherings not just as suites of sacred things but material 'territorialisations' of fluid fields of relations (after Deleuze and Guattari 1987): temporarily bounded, crystallising or cohering into a recognised entity with 'palpable agentic and affordant qualities' (2018, 78).

The impact of 'new materialism' begins to be felt in these accounts, a body of thought ultimately derived from key thinkers Latour (1993), Delueze and Guattari (1987), as well as the development of these approaches by sociologists Bennett (2010) and DeLanda (2016). It finds expression in symmetrical archaeology (Harris and Cipolla 2017): an embracing of 'flat ontology' that refuses to privilege the human, recognising that it is only within a field of relations that a component derives its properties and potentialities (Crellin 2017, 113). For Latour, this can be described as a 'sociology of associations' or actor-networks (2005) whilst for Ingold the concept of the 'meshwork' reprioritised lines and flows of relations rather than actants (2011). The key idea for funerary archaeology is that a burial is not just an 'assemblage' in traditional archaeological terms: a gathering of human remains, architecture and artefacts bounded in space-time, but a conceptual 'ad hoc grouping ... of diverse elements, of vibrant materials of all sorts. Assemblages are living, throbbing confederations' (Bennett 2010, 33). The method has strong descriptive rather than explanatory power as Johnston argues (2020, 12), enabling us to capture the temporary constellation of things in motion and follow how they might move between different assemblages over time (Harris 2013). Fowler (2013) and Crellin (2017, 115) both see burial practices as effectively *black boxing* this flow and fluidity of relations, so that we no longer see the 'vibrant, fluxing heterogeneous assemblage' for what it is. Much of the recent work of Harris (2013), Hamilakis and Jones (2017) and Crellin (2020) consists of opening up those black boxes, to reveal the multiple assemblages temporarily crystallised in graves. Returning to objects such as jet bead necklaces, Brück thus captures the 'composite' nature of persons behind such artefacts, and how the 'circulation, dissolution, and reassembly of such collections acted as a means of giving material form to interpersonal relationships that extended across time and space' (2019, 74). Any individual grave good is a 'thing in motion' as Joyce and Gillespie have put it (2015): objects with itineraries (Hahn and Weiss 2013) which pause for a while in a grave to form particular connections with people, other things and places, but which may not 'rest' there (not least because their exhumation by the trowel begins yet another journey: Lucas 2012; Fowler 2013 – see Fig. 2.06 for a representation of the 'lines of becoming' in the Kyloe cist burial).

A slight riposte to this blurring of ontological categories is the notion that human bone itself is a substance with exaggerated 'emotive materiality and affective valence', as Krmpotich *et al.* (2010, 371) put it. Whilst grounding their study in

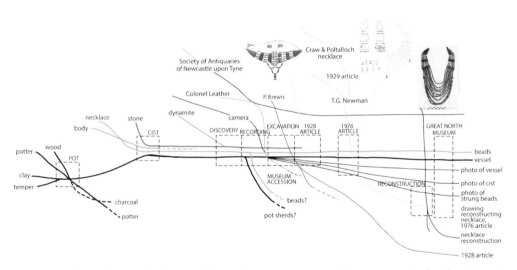

Figure 2.06 'Lines of becoming' involved in the Kyloe cist burial and its grave goods (Fowler 2013, 47, fig. 2.2. Originally drawn by Sheila Severn Newton. Photographs from Brewis (1928) and Newman (1976), reproduced courtesy of the Society of Antiquaries of Newcastle-upon-Tyne).

Ingold's 'injunction to return to materials and their transforming and transferring properties and affordances ... bones as things, bones as substance', Krmpotich *et al.* also press home that they are 'not rendering bones as other-than-humans' (2010, 372). As Barrett argues, 'living and non-living matter are ... conceptually distinct' (2016, 1684). As Fowler notes, bones (whether skeletonised or cremated) as well as flesh (consumed or preserved) could become particularly potent media of kinship (2013, 103). A new appreciation of the fragmentary amounts of bone ending up in cremation burials and their partibility and dispersal (e.g. Brück 2006; Fowler 2013, 163) as well as the discovery of curated bone 'bundles' or selective body parts interred in secondary rites within inhumations (Brück 2019; Booth and Brück 2020) continues to be an important counter to the conceptual model of individuated personhood.

Johnston, for example, uses the key concept of kinship and 'kinwork' in his latest account of grave goods (2020). Like the above authors, he refuses to 'place hard boundaries between the humans, animals and things' that compose assemblages such as hoards and burials, and he lauds the 'decentring' of humans and 'dispersal' of agency that this brings. Yet he notes how prehistorians have been criticised in the past for 'giving things undue priority in social processes' (2020, 13). This ontological 'return to things' has been criticised by Barrett for valourising 'descriptive richness' (Olsen 2012, 27) to create a 'discipline of things' (Witmore 2014, 203) instead of investigating the particular 'forms of life, and the materialities which emerge from it' which Barrett believes is the proper object of historical enquiry (2016, 1684). The key problem in such approaches is the risk of 'exorcised depth and humanness' (Johnston 2020, 13). Kinship, for Johnston, retains 'an attention on humanity' because it is a 'distinct form of relation' that focuses on 'intensity and mutuality' which allows him to 'identify and represent the depth and persistence of certain relations over time' (2020, 13): Lucas's 'iterative assemblages' (2012, 200). The processes through which these are examined include the 'sharing of substances and presences', keeping sight of the fact that kinship is an ongoing process which is 'creative, performative and political' (2020, 17). Thus, the Amesbury Archer emerges not as the 'expression of a powerful individual' since this 'beaker person was assembled by kinsfolk *for* the grave' (Johnston 2020, 36–7, our emphasis). The 'spectacular' grave goods buried with him were only facilitated by 'widely dispersed kin networks' performed and given expression locally (2020, 38). In Johnston's account, as in Brück's (2004, 325), the Amesbury burial is wrested out of the domain of the 'intrinsic' qualities of a uniquely gifted individual: this traveller, his navigational knowledge and any craft skills he possessed, are recontextualised *in* kin ... 'the relatedness that shaped mortuary ceremonies and grave assemblages, and the conduit along which beliefs, technologies, materials, things, people and other animals were exchanged and moved' (Johnston 2020, 38). Importantly, Johnston's concept of kinship is a 'genealogical' not a biological one: an important riposte to the new emphasis on aDNA in burial archaeology, where deep-time affiliations at a population level are being given both high academic priority and public exposure (see Carlin 2020 for a critique). The risk is that its coarse application may yet see grave goods once more reduced to the mere 'signature' of a gene pool. As Johnston argues, the art lies in keeping dialogue open between the natural and social sciences, to generate sophisticated accounts of social life (2020, 15).

2.11. Osteobiographies and object histories

It is not surprising that this relational approach to grave goods has become more 'thinkable' in an era of diverse funerary practice in Britain. The dominant contemporary rite of cremation allows people to be deposited and remembered in multiple places or kept in perpetuity in a vast array of mass-made or bespoke receptacles. 'Green burial' enables the inhumed dead to be regenerated in new woodland growth. Sudden deaths are commemorated in surrogate offerings such as ghost bikes whilst 'love locks' enable the memory of the dead to be literally fixed in place. Ashes can be packed into a firework, incorporated into a charm-bead or compressed to create a 'diamond'. The partibility, portability and fluidity of things and people have never seemed so relevant, even as crematoria staff wrestle with the illicit or banned categories of grave goods still 'smuggled' into coffins (BBC 2018).

Yet many archaeologists and curators working in burial archaeology are not driven by the 'new materialism'. Instead, local society journals, major field monographs and museum displays favour a rather different approach, driven by the aim of constructing 'osteobiographies' (Saul 1972; Sofaer 2006). In its simplest iteration, this involves 'assembling all information available from the skeleton to create a life narrative for a single individual' (Hosek and Robb 2019, 2). Hosek and Robb see this as an important, indeed necessary, corollary to large-scale, big-data biomedical research which looks at the population level (2019, 1) – part of a more humanistic bioarchaeological approach to the dead which restores context to an individual's life. They cite nuanced studies of intersectionality, bodily plasticity, ageing as a social process and bioarchaeologies of care which have enriched studies of burials and, thus, appreciations of the grave goods found with them. Hosek and Robb see its future potential in understanding *how* people perceived and dealt with aspects of 'appearance, health and illness, violence, aging, and death', exploring what may seem abstract social and historical conditions in terms of the 'shape of human lives' they constrained and enabled, to contextualise the contingencies of a particular life-course (2019, 3): or as Robb puts it, 'the biography as a cultural narrative' (2002, 160). Importantly, 'death histories' and 'post-mortem trajectories' also form part of these accounts (Hosek and Robb 2019, 4). Developments in palaepathology, studies of origin, diet and mobility (through isotope analysis), biological relatedness (using aDNA) and facial reconstruction, as well as life-style biomarkers, trauma and violence, and peri/post-mortem treatments of the corpse, enhance the ability of archaeologists to tell rich and detailed stories of past lives.

Parallel to this work, the concept of object *histories* or, as outlined above, object *itineraries* (Joyce and Gillespie 2015) arose to counter what were seen as the deficiencies of the anthropocentric analogy at the heart of the 'object biography' approach (Kopytoff 1986, revisited by Joy 2009; 2010). These authors rejected the single, unidirectional journey of 'birth, life-use and death', pointing to the frequency of repair and recycling in artefacts which sit at odds with the human life-cycle metaphor. Beyond its past life, the notion of an object itinerary could also embrace post-excavation trajectories through archives, museums and media life. These new concepts thus helped to capture the different fields in which objects had circulated and were active, the places in which they 'came to rest' and the means through which they moved on (Joyce and Gillespie 2015). Again, this approach was facilitated by a suite of enhanced scientific techniques that shed light on provenance, use-wear, modification, patina and repair. In prehistoric grave goods studies, this approach has been most successfully deployed at a large-scale in Woodward and Hunter's *Ritual in Early Bronze Age Grave Goods* project (2015).

When these two approaches are kept separate, they patrol the kinds of boundaries rejected by new materialism, but when brought together well, they have the capacity to both expand that approach and tell extraordinary stories of ordinary lives. In reality of course, this kind of mutually enriching (but costly) study of personhood and grave goods tends to be deployed only on the spectacular grave or 'celebrity' figure (Hosek and Robb 2019, 5). In British prehistory, the Amesbury Archer and Boscombe Bowmen (Fitzpatrick 2011), Gristhorpe man (Melton *et al.* 2013) and Racton man (Needham *et al.* 2017) stand out as 'the usual suspects' of Early Bronze Age inhumations with weapons, but the Iron Age mirror and sword burial from Bryher, Isles of Scilly, provides a subtle story of ambiguous personhood told through its 'grave goods' (Johns 2006). The twin study of the Brisley Farm 'warriors' is exemplary in terms of its relational approach to these burials, as well as its consideration of performance – the temporal, spatial and material dimensions of these funerals and how objects came to finally 'rest' in particular places and states (Stevenson 2013). The Whitehorse Hill cairn woman – a well-preserved cremation burial (Jones 2016) – forms an important contrast to these male case studies, which not only opened up the 'missing majority' of organic grave goods (Hurcombe 2014) but the wider landscape and world of connections in which she lived and died. Meanwhile, Giles has also used an entwined osteobiographical and artefact history approach to foreground the lives of many different kinds of women in Iron Age East Yorkshire, from chariot burials to death in childbirth, to elderly, curated corpses (2012; Giles *et al.* 2019). We do not see this approach as antithetical to the objectives of symmetrical archaeology, nor do they necessarily perpetuate the 'myth' of the individual, though care needs to be taken. By moving between our 'big data' and its longitudinal study of patterns over time and in space, we can deploy these approaches in finer-grained case studies, to investigate the relations through which both people and grave goods have coalesced into such 'vibrant' assemblages.

2.12. Discussion

We want to end our selective historiography with a serious consideration of Barrett's warning that if 'antiquarianism is the attention paid to ancient artefacts ... "new materialism" risks becoming little more than 'new antiquarianism' (2016, 1685). Our brief survey acknowledges that some antiquarians were undoubtedly driven by acquisitive avarice: it governed early excavations. Yet others brought a greater sensibility to encounters with things from graves, influenced by their closeness to death. Alongside our account of major paradigms which have shaped interpretations of grave goods, we have thus sought out important counter-narratives: the 'material affection' of the antiquarians, the folk-knowledge of Grinsell and the reflective insights of anthropology and sociology, to enrich our understanding of the things humans have buried with their dead and what we, as archaeologists, have made of them. We have also tried to set those approaches back within the funerary customs of the day, mindful of the fact that we can never quite escape our own attitudes towards mortality and mortuary material culture. In the chapters that follow, tacking back-and-forth between our large-scale dataset in the form of the GGDB and detailed stories of people and things, we hope to avoid fetishising these objects, re-sensitising us to how things can be used to mediate loss. Each and every one of them began with a death: we do not want to lose sight of this.

Yet in drawing our 'long view' of grave goods to a close, we want to discuss a painting in which they do take centre-stage. In his discussion of Thomas Guest's *Bronze Age Grave Group Excavated at Winterslow in 1814* (Fig. 2.07), Smiles has made a convincing argument that Guest's treatment of the burial assemblage as a kind of Dutch 'still life', combined with the exquisite medium of oil painting, give the objects a peculiar vivacity (2008). The gloss of the oil-paint, their 'propped' closeness to the viewer and their 'thereness' enabled them to attain a kind of animacy: 'catching and receiving light', inhabiting their frame, luring in and commanding the viewer (*ibid.*, 146). For Smiles, the grave goods begin to escape 'antiquarian scrutiny, moving beyond 'docility' to begin to lead their own lives' (*ibid.*). Before we can consider these lives – and afterlives – we need to see the 'big picture'.

Figure 2.07 Thomas Guest's Bronze Age grave group excavated at Winterslow in 1814, *oil on canvas, originally in colour (with kind permission © The Salisbury Museum).*

Chapter 3

Grave goods: the big picture

3.1. The foundations of the project

In this chapter, we focus on the *Grave Goods* project's core – the database. In the first section, we look at how and where the boundaries of data gathering were drawn, as well as the methodological strategies involved in data collection. The latter part of the chapter reports on the key macro-level patterns that emerged out of this data: we outline large-scale changes through time and across space and consider what grave goods can tell us about 'people' (at the broad scale) and about wider societal processes relating to the mortuary sphere.

From the outset, the *Grave Goods* project's central aim was to investigate mortuary material culture at a large scale, in the long term. To ensure as comprehensive an understanding of grave goods as possible, and to distinguish our study from all others that had gone before, we sought to collect information about *all* material culture found in formal burials during the Neolithic, Bronze Age and Iron Age in Britain. As a result of our desire to capture the entire mortuary material repertoire over this period – meaning that we would have to look at every excavated site with burials, recording a complex series of information about each grave good encountered – total coverage across the whole of Britain was not feasible (within the confines of this study). Consequently, we selected six case study regions on which to focus, applying total data collection within them to construct the Grave Goods database (GGDB). It is also important to stress at this point that we did *not* gather any data about burials in our case study areas that did not have grave goods. While this would undoubtedly have been interesting information to work with (for example, it would be fascinating to establish who was buried with grave goods and who was not), we simply did not have time to record burials that were not associated with our core research focus.

The very substantial dataset recorded within the GGDB provided a core, empirical foundation from which to consider later prehistoric grave goods in Britain as a whole – as we hope will become clear in the remainder of this chapter and beyond. Our wider study (including this book) fully embraced grave goods and other mortuary practices outside our case study areas as well. The GGDB is freely available online via the Archaeology Data Service: https://doi.org/10.5284/1052206. A significant element of the data collected was also fed back into relevant Historic Environment Record digital datasets, meaning that a substantial proportion of the GGDB now forms part of those resources as well.

Case study areas

The case study areas selected for detailed 'total' data collection were: Cornwall/ Isles of Scilly, Dorset, Kent, Gwynedd/Anglesey, East Yorkshire and Orkney/Outer Hebrides (Fig. 3.01; Table 3.01). These areas were chosen first and foremost to provide wide geographical coverage across Britain. It was also considered important that each had at least a reasonably good burial record for most of the period we were interested in and sufficient numbers of excavated sites representing traditions of antiquarian, research-driven and developer-funded archaeology. Largely by chance, all the regions we selected were coastal. The fact that our case study areas are so widely dispersed has both advantages and disadvantages which become most visible in mapping. It was, for example, simply not meaningful to plot broad spatial trends across Britain – the kinds of map we are used to seeing in studies conducted at this scale (e.g. Woodward and Hunter 2015, figs 12.1–4; Gosden *et al.* 2021) – due to the huge gaps in between our study regions. However, equally, those very same gaps facilitate better regional analysis in some ways, creating hard, spatially significant boundaries between regions across which meaningful comparisons can be made; the gradual clines in distributions that would exist if all counties had been included (and which raise problems as to where a pattern begins and ends) simply are not there. In a similar vein, the spatially dispersed nature of our study areas actively enables us to map long-distance material connections and exchange patterns very effectively across Britain (see for example Chapter 7). It is difficult to know if we would choose a different set of case study areas if we were to start the project again – on balance, probably not. It might have been preferable to include a 'more representative' land-locked county in the English Midlands or southern Scotland, for example, but then we would have missed out on one of those areas we did study, all of which proved interesting in their very different ways. It might also have been 'more representative' to include a region with a less well-known and/or less prolific burial record than those we selected; however, equally, it is always important to establish an effective and engaging narrative about the past and, to do that, you need good numbers of sites, objects and excavations. Ultimately, at the end of our study (and thus with all of the new knowledge it has given us), we feel confident that the case study areas selected worked very well for our purposes, providing a geographically dispersed, regionally variable (in terms of mortuary practice), multi-period, materially rich and representative dataset with which to work.

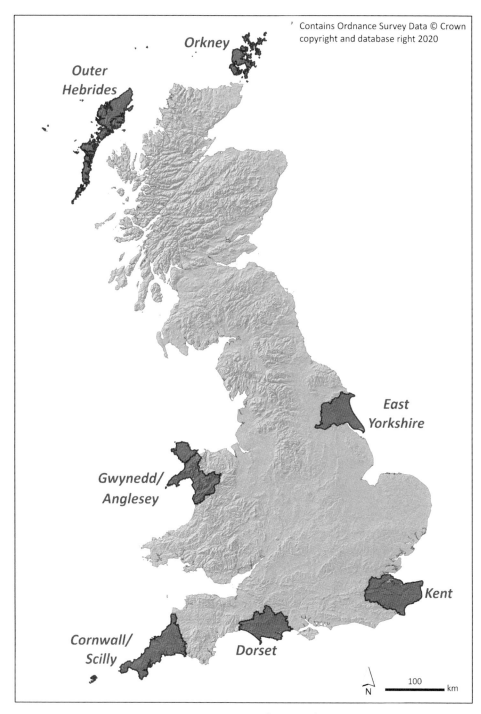

Figure 3.01 Location map of case study areas.

Table 3.01 Basic outline of data within the GGDB, by case study area.

Case study area	Sites (no.)	Burials (no.)	Grave goods (no.)
Cornwall/Isles of Scilly	170	270	551
Dorset	306	1036	1582
Kent	173	375	964
Gwynedd/Anglesey	66	169	299
East Yorkshire	283	1078	2147
Orkney/Outer Hebrides	121	201	501
Grand total	*1119*	*3129*	*6044*

Data acquisition

In line with our ambition to gather information from every known site with grave goods, our starting point for data collection was the relevant Historic Environment Record (HER) for each case study area: Cornwall, Dorset, East Yorkshire (Humber HER), Gwynedd/Anglesey, Kent, Orkney and the Outer Hebrides (Canmore, supplemented by information from individual Scottish island group HERs). In order to find all the sites that could possibly be relevant to our study, we requested HER searches using a wide set of terms that would potentially relate to excavated burial (and thus grave goods) evidence; these included, for example, funerary site types (e.g. 'burial', 'barrow') and also funerary-related terms within descriptive fields (e.g. 'cremation', 'urn', etc.). A full explanation of the data acquisition process can be found on the *Grave Goods* project's ADS webpage. Information acquired from HERs about all *potentially* relevant sites was transferred into an interim database, where details of each site based HER record (e.g. a round barrow) were assessed individually in order to 'clean' these data. All the records associated with sites thought likely to have produced grave goods were then transferred into the main Grave Goods database. Various difficulties were inevitably encountered in acquiring and aligning these data. Some HERs hold more complete/ up to date and/or detailed digital records than others, and so on. The structuring of HER records for funerary sites also differs significantly – in some HERs whole groups of Bronze Age barrows are described in one record, in others, individual graves from cemeteries and even individual finds from barrows are recorded separately (see Cooper and Green 2016 for further discussion of this issue and its interpretative repercussions). Although, wherever possible, we have sought broadly to align funerary site records, this unevenness in our source data caused inevitable lumps in the GGDB data at a site level. It was important to retain some lumpiness in this respect given our intention to return research data to HERs – this would simply not have been possible if we had entirely restructured the information that we were given. It is worth stressing that any such variability in the GGDB at the level of funerary sites did not impact significantly upon our recording of more detailed information at the level of individual graves, deposits of human remains and objects – the main levels at which our analysis operates.

Once all sites viewed as having potential to produce grave goods were identified, relevant published sources relating to those sites were consulted to acquire the necessary detailed information (which is only rarely recorded in HER records). These included the usual range of archaeological site reports, including grey literature, fully published monographs and journal articles. In addition to these site-specific resources, relevant regional and period-specific syntheses (e.g. Grinsell 1959; Henshall 1972; Whimster 1981; Lynch 1970; Giles 2000; Bristow 2001; A.M. Jones 2005; Woodward and Hunter 2015) were also consulted in order to capture more detailed information and potentially to fill in any gaps within HER datasets. Evidence from very recently excavated sites, ongoing excavations and unpublished fieldwork projects was not included systematically. Where it was felt that information from recently excavated/ unpublished sites was important to our analysis (e.g. findings from the Thanet Earth excavations in Kent, Rady and Holman 2019), key project personnel were contacted directly and, in many cases, relevant information was forthcoming. Through our direct discussions with local researchers and fieldwork organisations, we also added important new information to the GGDB about other key unpublished funerary sites that were not recorded in the HER or in previous syntheses.

Defining 'grave goods'

In the original *Grave Goods* project design, our stated intention was to construct a database of all material culture found in formal burials during the Neolithic, Bronze Age and Iron Age. From the outset, we were fully aware of the difficulties sometimes involved in defining 'formal burials' and in establishing an unambiguous relationship between artefacts and body to identify 'grave goods'. During the process of constructing the GGDB, confronted head-on by the complex realities of past practice, these difficulties, perhaps unsurprisingly, became ever more clear. The process of defining 'formal burials' and 'grave goods' is undeniably sometimes a tricky one. What might be viewed as an 'ideal' scenario – a clearly-defined grave containing a single, articulated, complete inhumation, perhaps within a wider cemetery of similar graves, accompanied by a few items (e.g. a pot, a necklace, a joint of meat and a brooch) that had clearly been placed in the grave with or on the body – is in fact a surprisingly rare occurrence throughout later prehistory in Britain.

The key difficulties involved in defining what a grave good is can be characterised as stemming largely from an extension – either spatial or temporal – of the relationship between objects and body. As we explain in more detail below and in subsequent chapters, as a result of these extensions (beyond the hazy edges of 'normal' burials-with-grave-goods), we were compelled to make a series of choices in determining which burials and which objects to include in our study. These decisions were made both on conceptual grounds (e.g. whether the objects were actually close enough to archaeology's core idea as to what a grave good should be) and on the basis of logistical reasoning (i.e. if a certain stance was decided upon in especially complex or unusual scenarios, would it be feasible to construct a meaningful database in a reasonable length of time). In order to provide a more concrete sense of our data collection parameters we provide some examples of the archaeological deposits and associated decision-making processes below. Ultimately, we hope to have come to a series of reasoned and generally acceptable decisions as to which objects and which burials should be included in our study.

The difficulties involved in defining what is a clear and/or *formal burial context* are also significant. As part of the project's wider research scope we have already explored the complexities involved when the relationship between objects and body is extended in an article about object deposits at funerary sites *which were not directly associated with human remains* (Cooper *et al.* 2020). In that work, we looked at the ways in which what can be counted as a grave good, and what should not be, become increasingly hazy as you reach the 'edges' of this category. The inclusion of grave goods in a burial can, of course, be situated within a much wider 'spectrum' of depositional practice (*ibid.*). For example, certain deposits of material culture had been placed on a site, in amongst definite burials-with-grave-goods, that had all the attributes of grave goods themselves but lacked any human remains. These deposits appear very likely to have been related to mortuary activity (broadly defined) but – not being with a body – cannot straightforwardly be classed as grave goods. Similarly, a temporal separation also creates complexity with regards to the identification of grave goods. Objects were, for example, sometimes placed in the ground at a burial site (sometimes even within a grave) but did not seemingly have a direct or immediate temporal relationship with the body – Early Bronze Age axes deposited into a barrow mound or items placed on top of (not within) a stone cist. Again, these items were not included within our dataset because the necessary *direct* relationship between body and objects was absent.

The relationship between obvious 'burials' and associated material culture was sometimes unclear in other ways as well. Neolithic chambered tombs (and related monuments) represent a particularly complex and challenging category to deal with – being, in most cases, such a long way from the 'ideal' body-grave-objects scenario described above. Due to these monuments' often long-term usage and the very common practice of bodies (and bits of bodies) and artefacts being moved around inside them, it is generally very difficult to establish how closely a given 'individual' and the material culture within the tomb were associated – in both a temporal and a conceptual sense (this issue is discussed in much more detail in Section 8.1). For example, it could be argued that certain pottery vessels found in a tomb had originally been placed in relation to specific individuals but had come to be more loosely associated with them following subsequent addition of further burials and movement of material culture. Ultimately, in an attempt *not* to exclude the vast majority of Neolithic burials/material culture from our study on the basis of this very common uncertainty, for this category of evidence we decided to record all objects found in close physical association with human remains in the GGDB. This allowed us some capability to carry out a large-scale assessment of the objects included 'with' burials in Neolithic tombs but, at the same time, clearly does not represent a total study of all material culture from Neolithic tombs and includes object-body relationships that, in reality, are more uncertain in temporal terms than we would ideally have liked (again see Section 8.1). Where such complexities were identified, these records were flagged up in the GGDB and necessarily excluded from certain broad-scale quantifications (e.g. those to do with objects per grave).

Bronze and Iron Age burials within pits (and other contexts) presented us with a comparable scenario. In these cases, sometimes whole bodies were buried in amongst a matrix of what might be termed 'settlement rubbish' (Hill 1995; Sharples 2010, 251–72; Brück 2019, 50–6). Arguably, in such a context, the individual artefacts (including, for example, broken pottery, animal bones, charred plant remains, burnt clay, etc.) were not specifically buried 'with' that person as grave goods in any meaningful sense, although that is not to say that their inclusion in the pit with the body was not meaningful (Brudenell and Cooper 2008, 24–30). Consequently, in contexts such as these, objects were only included when they appeared to have been incorporated specifically as grave goods – e.g. at White Horse Stone, Kent, where the fragments of human bone in Iron Age Pit 8012 were carefully arranged and were closely associated with a flint hammerstone, a slingshot and a jar containing a dark organic substance (Hayden with Stafford 2006, 159, figs 98–9, pl. 30). Again, this represents a subjective, but necessary, distinction on our part. In a similar vein, apparently isolated, disarticulated human bones that were not in a clear mortuary context were not included in our study (not least because they cannot be classified as 'formal burials'). Consequently, a single skull on the bottom of the causewayed enclosure ditch at Hambledon Hill, associated with dumps of pottery, flint, etc., will not have been included; however, the few articulated burials on the same site which did appear to have placed grave goods associated with them (e.g. the child in segment 18 buried with a flint flake and three tubular bone beads; Mercer and Healy 2008, 55) have been. We took a similar approach to disarticulated human remains on Bronze Age and Iron Age sites as well.

Beyond the complexities involved in defining 'formal burials', other challenges arose with the recording of funerary sites excavated during the 19th century – when recording methods were much more variable and/or where finds, almost certainly representing grave goods, were recovered during quarrying or other development work with little, if any, recording. This includes the evidence from many of the 'type sites' in our case study regions, e.g. Rimbury for Middle Bronze Age Dorset, Arras for Middle Iron Age East Yorkshire, Harlyn Bay for Middle/Late Iron Age Cornwall and Aylesford for Late Iron Age Kent. Although for these sites it was not possible to establish clear relationships between objects and bodies, our understanding of grave goods would have been hugely diminished had the objects from them not been included at some level in our analysis. For obvious reasons, these sites were not included in our broad-scale quantifications of the GGDB (presented below) at the grave level (e.g. in considering numbers of graves, relationships between certain types of bodies and objects, etc.). Where possible, however, a minimum number of individuals (MNI) for human burials from these sites, including the main rite identified (cremation or inhumation), was recorded. Where it was likely that all or most of the objects recovered were grave goods (e.g. Late Iron Age cremation cemeteries in Kent), these were logged in one 'grave' record. Where it is uncertain that all of the objects recovered were, strictly speaking, grave goods (e.g. at Middle Bronze Age cremation cemeteries in Dorset, where pots were often interred without human remains), a 'best fit' approach was taken. For this last set of sites, wherever possible, only objects associated directly with human remains were recorded. Where this was not possible (e.g. where significant numbers of objects were recovered clearly from a burial site but no human remains were specifically mentioned at all), only the items known to exist, having been recorded in museum collections, were logged. In both cases, it is likely that our recording of grave goods from these sites *under-represents* the total number of objects deposited.

In circumstances where (1) a sufficiently 'formal' burial context was identified and (2) a sufficiently clear relationship between body/bodies and object/objects could be determined, *every* item of material culture with that burial was included within the GGDB. The issue of whether *all* objects within a grave should necessarily be considered 'grave goods' has been much debated over the years (see also Cooper *et al.* 2020). Examining past discussions of this issue from British prehistory and beyond, it becomes clear that certain objects within graves have not always fitted everyone's interpretive schemes as to what a 'grave good' should be (Table 3.02). Items which occupy this ambivalent territory include dress fastenings (which may simply have been worn by the deceased), containers of cremation burials (e.g. pots), food from associated funerary rituals, weapons embedded within the body, objects that had been burnt along with the body on a cremation pyre, fragments (e.g. pot sherds, waste flint flakes) and even certain categories of human body (e.g. children). Grave goods actually made out of human bone (e.g. Woodward and Hunter 2015, 56) further complicate our categorisations in this regard. Despite – and perhaps also to a certain extent *because of* – these past omissions, we are strongly of the opinion that all objects should be treated, and thus recorded, equally in this regard, in contrast to others who have sometimes sought to eliminate certain items (Table 3.02). To our minds, conceptually, *all* artefacts that were included with a burial were – at a certain level – *chosen* specifically to accompany that burial and so are significant as 'grave goods'. Thus coffins, pots, etc. were all included in the GGDB as 'grave goods'.

Material culture that we did *not* record in the GGDB included items that might be termed 'grave architecture' (e.g. the slabs of stone defining a cist) and, as discussed above, objects on burial sites that were not directly associated with a body themselves (e.g. animal bone or pots deposited within a barrow ditch). We do, of course, recognise, first, that all of these items could well have been significant with regards to mortuary practice more widely (see for example Cooper *et al.* 2020)

Table 3.02 'Ambivalent' grave goods: objects that have been excluded/included within selected other studies.

Object category	Excluded as grave goods	Included as grave goods
Dress fittings	Whimster 1981; Nowakowski 1991	–
Containers of the dead	Wainwright 1967; Kaliff 2005; Caswell 2013	–
Embedded weapons	Sharples 2010	–
Food from funerary rituals	Grajetzki 2014	–
Objects deposited to protect the living	Grajetzki 2014	–
Pyre goods	McKinley 1997	–
Object fragments	–	Chapman 2000
Human remains (e.g. children)	–	Garwood 2007

but they cannot be described as grave goods in a strict sense and so were not included. Secondly, although the distinction that Gilchrist and Sloane (2005) made between 'grave goods' (things interred directly with the body) and what might be termed 'grave architecture' (components of the grave that may have been added at a different time, e.g. grave liners) was methodologically and interpretatively productive in the context of their examination of medieval burials, in a prehistoric context it was not always easy to draw strict lines in this respect: defining the point at which the ephemeral traces of a coffin or bier become a timber grave lining or at which a scatter of stones in the base of a grave become a (temporally removed) grave fixture is necessarily a subjective process. We have addressed many of these issues in a separate paper investigating the various ways in which the dead were 'covered' during burial (Cooper *et al.* 2019).

Database structure

The GGDB, a relational Filemaker Pro database, captured data about a series of different, but related, things: the site, the grave, the object(s) and the associated human remains. To give an example, where a site-based record existed for an Early Bronze Age round barrow, separate, related records were created for each grave within the round barrow, for each body and for each object buried within the grave. Key additional information recorded included details about: bibliographic sources, excavation (where available), scientific dating (where easily accessible) and links/cross-references to relevant information in other key datasets (e.g. Bristow 2001, the National Record of the Historic Environment (NRHE), the British Museum, regional museums, etc.).

A list of the fields recorded at each level of the database can be found on the *Grave Goods* project's ADS webpage (https://doi.org/10.5284/1052206). Key points to highlight are listed below. First, potentially interesting interpretative themes (e.g.

particularly good examples of covering and wrapping, of 'understated' objects, of exotic or well-travelled objects, etc.) were flagged at a grave level; this allowed us to return to these graves more easily when it came to undertaking subsequent, more in-depth, analysis. Highly detailed recording of human remains was not a primary concern. However specific details about human remains were included where they were easily accessible. In order to insure that our coverage of human remains tallied with specialist recommendations we also received specialist input from Jackie McKinley (Wessex Archaeology). Understandably, our efforts in terms of detailed recording within the GGDB were focused at the object level. In addition to logging the broad types of objects deposited in graves (e.g. a brooch of a particular type), we noted their material makeup (e.g. iron, coral), any more specific identifications (e.g. *Knotenfibeln*, La Tène III), the object's state of completeness and condition upon deposition (e.g. fragment, burnt), its orientation (where relevant) and placement relative to the body (e.g. a direct relationship, at the head, in front of the nose), its current museum location and accession number (where available), information about directly relevant publications/images and its date. If an object was clearly associated with one particular body from a grave with multiple interments, this connection was noted specifically.

Unless more detailed information was available (e.g. radiocarbon dates relating to specific objects), the date range attributed to grave goods followed that given to the grave as a whole; this date range was usually attributed typologically on the basis of the grave goods, rather than on the basis of absolute dates. Details about any scientific dates from objects, human remains and graves were logged within the GGDB where these were readily accessible and used preferentially for dating each or all of these things as appropriate. In attributing typologically derived date ranges to artefacts, we sought specialist regional advice where we felt this would potentially provide more specific information. Most objects were attributable typologically to one (and sometimes more than one) sub-period, although occasionally, in the case of certain object types (e.g. Iron Age brooches), more specific dates could be assigned. The date ranges used for each sub-period (and thus assigned to each object falling typologically within that sub-period) are detailed in Table 3.03. Further detailed information about our database input methods relating to dates can be found on the project's ADS webpage.

Where an object deposited in a grave was old/curated upon deposition (e.g. an Early Bronze Age flint arrowhead in a Late Iron Age inhumation burial) the object was given the

Table 3.03. Sub-period date ranges used within the GGDB.

Sub-period	Date range
Early Neolithic	4000–3300 BC
Middle Neolithic	3300–2900 BC
Late Neolithic	2900–2450 BC
Beaker/Chalcolithic	2450–2200 BC
Early Bronze Age	2200–1500 BC
Middle Bronze Age	1500–1150 BC
Late Bronze Age	1150–800 BC
Early Iron Age	800–400 BC
Middle Iron Age	400–100 BC
Late Iron Age	100 BC–AD 42

date of its time of burial (e.g. Late Iron Age) but was flagged up as being 'old' and the likely date of its initial production and use logged in the object description field.

Data analysis

In certain instances, in order to make our primary data more suitable for specific subsequent analyses (e.g. as presented in this chapter), further work was undertaken on top of that originally collected within the GGDB. For example, the 216 individual object *types* in the GGDB were also grouped together into much broader object *categories*, facilitating comparison across the dataset (see Appendix). It is also important to note that not all information recorded within the GGDB will necessarily have been created according to modern standards (e.g. ageing and sexing data relating to human remains; the identification of certain materials such as 'shale'; etc.). In more detailed analyses relating to these specific variables, we have used our discretion as to whether such information is appropriate to use (or not), and clearly stated how we elected to deal with it.

In order to represent the chronological changes evident in many aspects of our data, working closely with archaeological data specialist Chris Green, we produced a series of 'fuzzy' models/plots which feature throughout the book (e.g. Fig. 3.02). In these plots, time is represented along the X axis, usually in 100-year slices from *c.* 4000 BC to AD 43. The Y axis generally depicts the summed probability that all objects (or other things) of the type being analysed were deposited within that 100-year block of time. In some cases, artefacts could, of course, be dated accurately to within a century. In most cases, however, the knowable date range of an artefact was much wider; these objects were therefore assigned to more than one 100-year block on the basis of the likelihood (or 'summed probability') that they fell within it. Thus, for example, a Collared Urn dated no more closely than to the 'Early Bronze Age' or *c.* 2000–1500 BC (the main period of currency of Collared Urns) would be split across five blocks, with that one object contributing a total count of 0.2 (i.e. 20%) to each of the five centuries. The process of 'calibrating' our data into 100-year time-slices in this way makes it possible to compare objects (or other variables) directly with different date resolutions, and to move beyond simple sub-period blocks (such as 'Middle Neolithic' or 'Late Iron Age') which can be difficult to compare equitably because they lasted different lengths of time. A more detailed explanation of the 'fuzzy modelling' process can be found in Green (2011).

It is also worth noting that, throughout the book, we have often had to amalgamate sub-periods and sub-phases in our analysis – thus, for example, we have sometimes treated the Beaker/Early Bronze Age 'period' or entire 'Iron Age' as single entities. While this lumping certainly can and does mask complexities and nuances within the data, it is absolutely necessary from an analytical point of view, especially given the longevity of our overall study period. As will become clear, in many other instances, we have shifted our scale of analysis inwards, looking, for example, at differences between sub-phases of the Early Bronze Age in order to capture those nuances effectively as well. We hope that a good balance of 'big picture' and detailed stories has been achieved overall.

A note of caution about the Neolithic

As discussed above, the complex dynamics in evidence within many Neolithic burial monuments often made it difficult to enter data about grave goods for that period in the same way as was possible for other periods. In many cases it was impossible to tell without further detailed primary research, for example, how many bodies had been buried, how many individual (but subsequently fragmented) artefacts were in evidence, whether an artefact had been introduced with a specific person, and so on. As we discuss in substantial detail within Section 8.1, mortuary practice in many Neolithic contexts simply did not lend itself well to the format of the GGDB that was necessary to capture the information required for the majority of our study period. Consequently, for many Neolithic sites, data had to be entered into the GGDB in a different way. Often, the number of 'burials' (with grave goods) could not be meaningfully established; consequently, for those sites, a separate record was not created for each recorded burial within a grave context (e.g. the chamber of a tomb). Equally, 'grave goods' were defined, in these circumstances, as objects that had been found *in direct association* with human remains (a subjective decision in many cases); other objects which were in the wider mortuary realm but not directly associated with human remains were not recorded. As a consequence of these 'Neolithic complexities' (as we have termed them in the database in order that these burials can be excluded from quantitative analysis where necessary), it is important to recognise that the Neolithic might in some ways be said to be under-represented in our dataset. In some cases this does, of course, reflect the actualities of the past – for example, in comparison to the Early Bronze Age, relatively few clear and obvious grave goods are found then; equally, not as many people were clearly and obviously buried with artefacts at that time. The period *c.* 4000–2450 BC therefore often appears relatively 'low' in comparison to other periods in our broad-scale analyses, and especially within the fuzzy models, for these reasons.

3.2. Grave goods in later prehistoric Britain: broad-scale patterning

Change through time

Figure 3.02, our first 'fuzzy' plot, depicts the *total number of objects* placed in graves through time in 100-year time slices, plotted alongside the *total number of graves* (with grave goods). The Neolithic sees generally low numbers. A gradual increase in grave goods is visible from the start of the Beaker period *c.* 2450 BC, rising to a notable peak during the core of the Early Bronze Age *c.* 1900–1800 BC. Relatively high numbers are maintained to an extent through the Middle Bronze Age before plummeting in the Late Bronze Age/Early Iron Age *c.* 1000–500 BC. We then see a steady rise in grave good numbers again throughout the Middle and Late Iron Age, with the highest peak of deposition overall occurring in the years immediately before the Roman conquest.

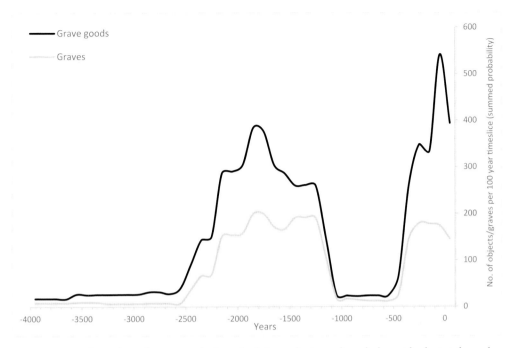

Figure 3.02 Total number of grave goods deposited through time, plotted alongside the total number of graves with grave goods in our case study areas (summed probability per 100 year time slice).

In order to give a broad impression of the types of grave good encountered and the periods when they feature, in Figure 3.03 we have plotted the Top 50 most common grave goods through time, all of which had a minimum of five individual items listed within the GGDB (see Appendix for a full list of object types recorded). Within this chart the density of the shading is normalised relative to the prevalence of each object type so that all artefact types are equally visible; this means that, for those artefacts present in highest numbers overall (pots), a greater summed probability per century value was required for darker shading.

Figure 3.03 indicates clearly that the number of grave goods deposited overall varies considerably throughout our study period, as we might expect. The Early Bronze Age stands our particularly clearly in the centre of the image, having seen the deposition of a substantial *range* of object types in large *numbers*. Objects such as arrowheads, maceheads and querns are the most visible for the Neolithic, while pots and lids continued to be deposited in substantial numbers into the Middle Bronze Age. As you would expect, quite a few specific object types (including brooches, coins, swords, etc.) only feature towards the right-hand side of the image in the Iron Age. Many other patterns are discernible on close inspection and Figure 3.03 certainly rewards detailed scrutiny.

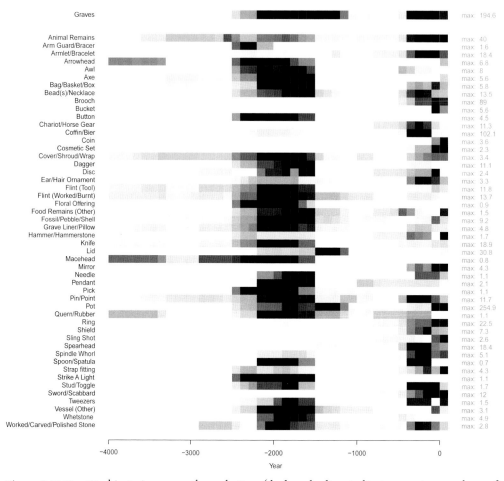

Figure 3.03 Top 50 objects in graves through time (darker shading indicates greater numbers of objects; maximum value for each object type per 100 year time slice (summed probability) is shown on the right-hand side).

Object types

It is possible to refine this very broad-brush, yet at the same time also quite detailed, picture of grave goods through time further to bring out specific aspects of the record. Figure 3.04 depicts the prevalence of the seven most common grave good *object categories* through time, enabling us to assess the contribution of different kinds of artefact to the overall total (again, see Appendix for details of object categories). In Figure 3.04, during the Neolithic, tools (mainly flint) are most common initially, with animal bone taking over later on and peaking noticeably right at the end of the Neolithic. From that point onwards, and throughout the whole of the Bronze Age, pots dominate the picture to a considerable extent, with

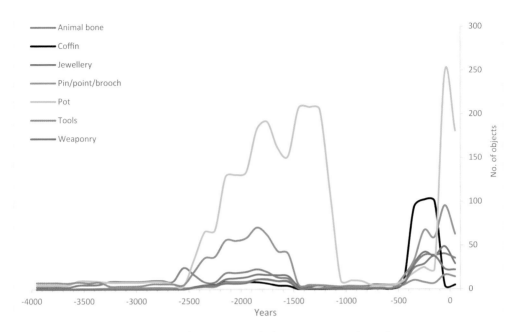

Figure 3.04 Top 7 (most common) object categories through time.

tools remaining as the second highest category. Interestingly, pots were actually deposited in greater numbers (per century) during the Middle Bronze Age *c.* 1500–1200 BC, a period when very few other types of object feature at all. The high peak in total numbers of grave goods overall observed during the Early Bronze Age (in Fig. 3.02) was a result of different artefacts combined – most notably tools (mainly flint), animal bone and jewellery. The Iron Age sees significant deposition of a wide variety of object types, with coffins, brooches, other jewellery, animal bone and weaponry all initially outnumbering pots. With the re-introduction of cremation on a large scale during the Late Iron Age, pots come to dominate the picture once again. It is interesting to note the discrepancy highlighted within this graph between the kinds of object which have featured most prominently in previous accounts of later prehistoric burial (e.g. daggers, necklaces, swords, chariots, etc.) and the 'real' picture (that is dominated by pots and coffins).

Figure 3.05 represents a similar dataset in a different format, this time depicting the relative proportions of each of the Top 10 grave good categories overall, within each sub-period. The domination of pots throughout the Bronze Age is, again, clear, most impressively so in the Middle Bronze Age where they comprise 96% of all grave goods. The fairly even representation of a wide variety of items in the Late Bronze Age/Early Iron Age (despite the small sample size), and especially the Middle Iron Age, is also notable. The very common occurrence of coffins in the Middle Iron Age also stands out strongly in comparison to other sub-periods.

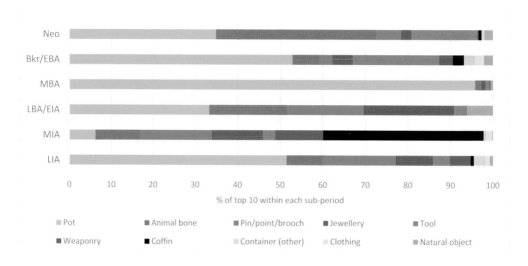

Figure 3.05 Top 10 most common object categories, by sub-period; n = 298 (Neo), 2243 (Bkr/EBA), 718 (MBA), 33 (LBA/EIA), 770 (MIA), 826 (LIA).

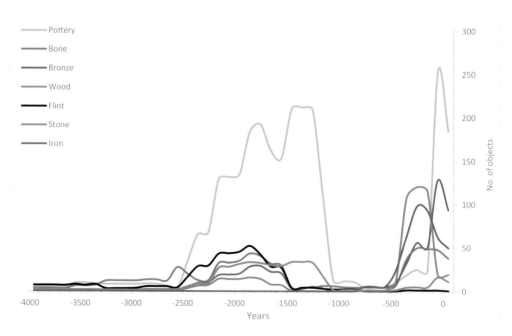

Figure 3.06 Top 7 materials through time.

Materials

Figure 3.06 shows the different *materials* that were employed as grave goods through time. To a considerable extent, it maps closely onto the artefact categories shown in Figure 3.04 (e.g. the peak in wood reflects the peak in coffins). However, certain other novel elements do stand out, such as the Middle Bronze Age prevalence of 'stone' (mainly 'lids' on top of urns – see also Section 7.6), or the noticeable rise in bronze objects, far outnumbering iron, in the Late Iron Age (largely a result of the change in material used for making brooches). It is worth noting that, as with a lot of our broad patterns, this graph masks certain nuances (such as multi-material objects). We discuss the effects of the introduction of 'new' materials in specific periods within later chapters as well.

Regionality

The patterns we have looked at so far at the 'national' level (as represented by our sample of six case study areas) are clearly an amalgamation of potentially more variable, regionally specific trends. Figure 3.07 plots sites recorded in the GGDB against a background 'heat map' of *all* known burial sites (i.e. also including those which have not been excavated and/or have not produced grave goods) recorded within the relevant Historic Environment Record. In the absence of a detailed record of all prehistoric burials in Britain, this image gives us a sense of the spatial relationship between burials with grave goods and burial sites generally. The 'density' of burial sites has been 'normalised' for each case study area in order to make them directly comparable; it should also be noted that the number of 'sites' recorded will have been affected by the specific excavation history of each region, the topographic character of the area (and thus survival of upstanding archaeology) and the variable quality of HER data available. In most regions, grave goods have tended to come from areas of high-density burial overall. In Gwynedd and especially Cornwall, however, denser hotspots in the heatmap are not matched by denser clusters of grave good-producing 'sites' – in both cases this is probably because mostly upland and upstanding burial sites (e.g. barrows, cairns) have been recorded, but have not necessarily been excavated.

Clear and significant chronological patterning in terms of the prevalence of grave goods by region is visible within the GGDB dataset (Fig. 3.08). While several of the peaks shown in Figure 3.08 were certainly expected from the outset, since some regional trends in the burial evidence are well-known (e.g. Neolithic Orkney or Middle Iron Age East Yorkshire), it is nonetheless rewarding to have demonstrated these empirically and to be able to visualise them graphically on the basis of that dataset. Equally, the data presented in Figure 3.08 also challenge some of our preconceptions. We might not have expected East Yorkshire to be quite so far ahead of Dorset, for example, in terms of grave good numbers throughout the Beaker/ Early Bronze Age period. Similarly, the dominance of Dorset during the Middle Bronze Age stands out as perhaps more extreme than we might have imagined, as does the peak in Late Iron Age Kent.

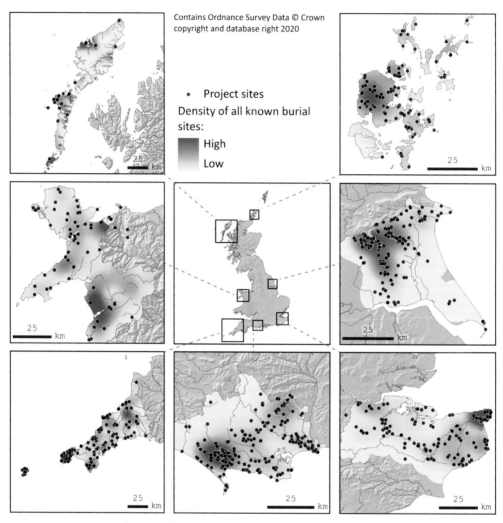

Figure 3.07 Locations of sites with grave goods plotted against background 'heat map' of all known burial sites recorded within the relevant HER.

The kinds of material deposited varied considerably by region as well. Figure 3.09 depicts the materials employed as grave goods during the Beaker/Early Bronze Age period, when most materials were in use. While, broadly, similar materials were used in similar quantities across most regions, some clear regional elements stand out – such as flint in East Yorkshire, pottery in Gwynedd/Anglesey and especially stone in Orkney/Outer Hebrides.

People

It is also possible to use the GGDB dataset to investigate how grave goods related to different 'kinds' of people. Clearly, in this regard, we are limited to the aspects

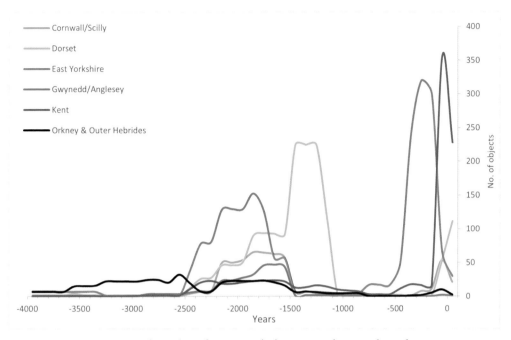

Figure 3.08 Total number of grave goods, by case study area, through time.

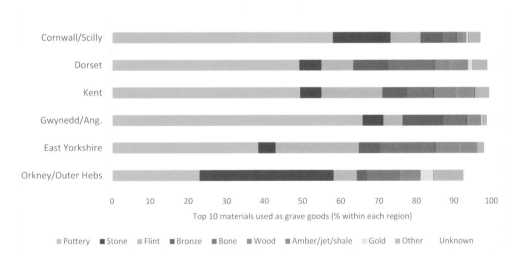

Figure 3.09 Proportions of different materials employed as grave goods, by region, during the Beaker/ Early Bronze Age period; n = 416 (Cornwall), 577 (Dorset), 182 (Kent), 257 (Gwynedd/Anglesey), 992 (East Yorkshire), 148 (Orkney/Outer Hebrides).

of people that are archaeologically visible such as skeletally determined sex and estimated age. Nonetheless, in working with these traits (whilst acknowledging, of course, that many other categories of person may have existed in the past, and that

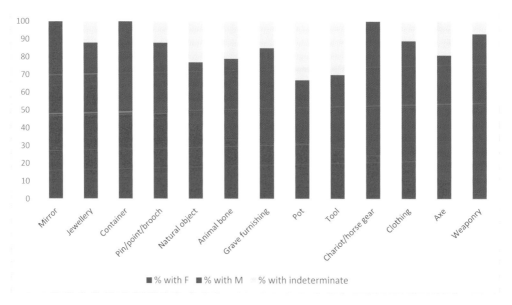

Figure 3.10 Percentage of each object category buried with females/males (n = 1055).

those which are visible to us were not necessarily relevant during later prehistory), a set of interesting patterns does emerge.

Female and male burials
Figure 3.10 clearly demonstrates that certain object types were generally seen as appropriate to accompany both female and male sexed bodies: mirrors and jewellery were preferentially deposited with female burials, axes, weapons and chariot/horse gear were preferentially deposited with males; notably, 'clothing' (a category which included buttons, buckles, studs, etc.) was also deposited mainly with male burials. All percentages in this section are expressed in relation to all grave goods associated with human remains which had been sexed within the GGDB (n = 1055). It should be noted that, especially for older excavations, the 'sex' of individuals may well have been defined according to the grave goods they were buried with. This will inevitably therefore lead to a slightly circular argument in those cases.

Figure 3.11 plots the number of female/male burials (with grave goods) and the number of grave goods associated with females/males, through time. The earliest notable spike comes at the start of the Beaker period with both (a) male burials and (b) grave goods buried with males outnumbering those of/with females. The high peak visible in the total number of grave goods buried with males is especially notable, clearly demonstrating – empirically – the widely held view that, at the start of the Beaker period, men were buried more often and were buried in materially 'richer' graves, than women (e.g. Woodward and Hunter 2015, 518–19; Parker Pearson *et al.* 2019, 200). It is notable that by *c.* 2100 BC, the numbers of female burials and

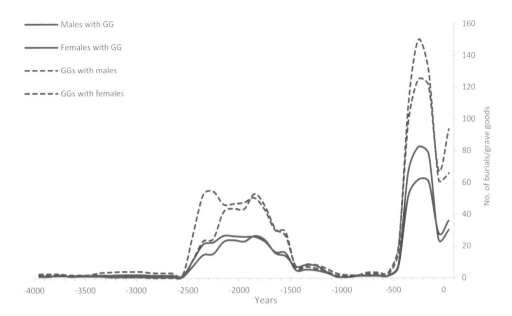

Figure 3.11 Numbers of female/male burials (with grave goods) and numbers of grave goods associated with females/males through time.

female-associated grave goods become directly comparable to those of males, a pattern which continues throughout the rest of the Bronze Age and into the Early Iron Age. The Middle Iron Age presents us with the next clear, sex-based difference; this time, both female burials and female-associated grave goods significantly outnumber those of males, from c. 400-200 BC. In contrast to the Beaker patterning just described, this trend has not previously been widely noted. At this time, in the Middle Iron Age, East Yorkshire contributes the vast majority of burials; clearly, at that time in that region, women were buried more regularly than men. Dent (1982) suggested that this was the result of men dying away from 'home', perhaps as a result of conflict where a body lay unburied or was taken as trophy, but death while travelling or voyaging is also plausible. Perhaps less likely are scenarios of a polygamous society or one with significantly higher numbers of adult women than men (unmarried female relatives, servants or even slaves) 'living in' and being buried as full members of the community, with grave goods (see discussion in Giles 2012, 99). Our final notable peak comes right at the end of the Iron Age – while female and male burials with grave goods are broadly comparable in number, male burials received more grave goods at this time.

Young and old people
It is also possible to assess the relationship between burials of different ages and the grave goods that accompanied them. Grave goods buried with children (defined here as babies, infants and children under 13 years old) comprised 12% of our dataset,

while grave goods buried with older adults (defined here as 35+ years old) comprised 14% of our dataset. All percentages in this section are expressed in relation to all burials with grave goods whose age had been estimated within the GGDB (n=2075). This variability emphasises again the fact that grave goods represent a complex mix of social relationships (perhaps most likely to be extensive in the prime of life), markers of identity (perhaps most vibrant and distinctive in adult life) and objects required for an afterlife (perhaps seldom 'needed' by infants or juveniles and waning again in the fewer needs or roles expected of elders). The proportion of all burials with grave goods that were children varied considerably between periods, ranging from 23% in both the Neolithic and Bronze Age, to just 8% in the Iron Age. Equally, the proportions varied by region as well: 23% of the burials in both Dorset and Orkney/Outer Hebrides were of children, whilst in Cornwall it was just 11%. An even more varied picture is in evidence for older people as well. The representation of older adults within the GGDB ranged from 10% in the Neolithic, to 8% in the Bronze Age, to 28% of all burials in the Iron Age. Notably, numbers also varied greatly by region: 21% of burials in East Yorkshire were of older adults, whilst the total was just 6% in both Cornwall and Dorset. These patterns offer us windows into the differences of emphasis placed on intersectional aspects of identity, particularly the way in which mortuary rites and grave goods were used to deal with the death of older members of society.

Significant variability was also seen in terms of the *types* of object buried with young and old people (Fig. 3.12). Interestingly, 'covers' (e.g. stone lids) and 'grave furnishings' (e.g. scatters of pebbles, wooden liners) were especially common with

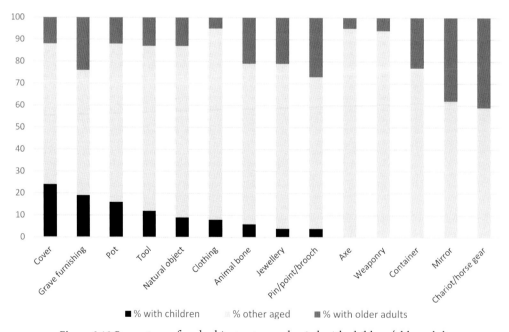

Figure 3.12 Percentage of each object category buried with children/older adults.

children – perhaps indicating a concern with wrapping, covering and caring for the most vulnerable of corpses (see discussion in Cooper *et al.* 2019). Notably, certain object categories were *never* buried with children (within our case study areas): axes, weapons, containers, mirrors and chariot/horse gear. Equally, a number of object categories were preferentially buried with older adults, most notably chariot/horse gear and mirrors (in which cases the percentage of these items far outweighs the average for all grave goods of 14%), but pins/points/brooches, grave furnishings, containers, animal bones and jewellery also stand out strongly as being buried preferentially with older adults. Notably, it is the two martial categories – axes and weaponry – that appear to have been buried preferentially with young and mid-adults.

Cremation and inhumation
Using the GGDB dataset, it is also possible to investigate specific elements of funerary practice beyond material culture alone. For example, we were able to shed light on the varying practices of inhumation and cremation through time more generally, as in this case there is a close correlation between our sample of 3129 burials with grave goods (including both cremation burials and inhumations) and the total buried population. The ebbs and flows of the two rites through time are already well known, but our GGDB dataset provides a solid empirical demonstration of these (Fig. 3.13). It is interesting to note that the overlap between the two burial

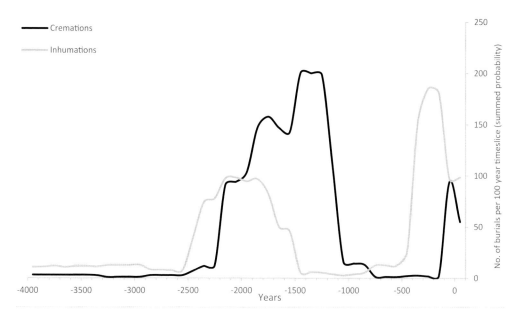

Figure 3.13 Number of inhumations/cremation burials (with grave goods) through time. Note that typologically assigned dates for burials have been included as well as radiocarbon dates. This graph therefore provides a broad impression, not a fully accurate picture, of burial practices through time.

Table 3.04. Occurrence of different object categories with Beaker/EBA inhumation and cremation burials (% of all grave goods with inhumations/cremation burials).

Object category	Inhumations (%) (n=1078)	Cremation burials (%) (n=1333)
Animal bone	8	7
Axe	2	3
Clothing	4	1
Cover	1	0
Grave furnishing	2	0
Jewellery	5	7
Natural object	3	2
Pin/point	3	6
Pot (accompanying)	38	33
Tool	26	22
Weaponry	3	5

n=2495; pots and coffins containing the body excluded.

rites during the Early Bronze Age occurs at around the same time as the highest peak in grave good deposition (see Fig. 3.02).

Working with this burial rite information, it was possible to dig deeper, investigating the kinds of object buried with people who had been subject to each rite. It was only really possible to draw such comparisons meaningfully during those sub-periods when *both* inhumation and cremation were practised, i.e. the Beaker/ Early Bronze Age and Late Iron Age. In order to facilitate a more equitable comparison between the two, we omitted coffins (which are almost exclusively found with inhumations) and pots that were 'containing' or 'covering' the body (which are almost exclusively found with cremation burials) from the following analysis.

Interestingly, across the entire Beaker/Early Bronze Age period, the object categories that were buried with inhumations and with cremation burials were extremely similar. Broad parity is discernible across the board in terms of the kinds of grave goods included with both rites (Table 3.04). It is notable that, even with 'accompanying' (as opposed to 'containing') pots, a roughly equal proportion was included with both cremation and inhumation burials.

There is of course a gradual underlying chronological shift (from inhumation to cremation) to take into account over this Beaker/Early Bronze Age period (see Fig. 3.13). Even despite this, it appears that, overall at this very broad level, from *c*. 2450–1500 BC the same kinds of artefact were placed with those people that were inhumed and those that were cremated. If indeed the 'kind' of person you were in life influenced either the burial rite you were accorded or the objects you were buried with, it seems that these two archaeologically visible expressions of personhood cross-cut each other rather than being parallel or mutually reinforcing.

During the Late Iron Age, the variability of grave goods placed with inhumations and cremation burials was significantly greater, in certain object categories at least (see Table 3.05). Jewellery and weapons stand out most clearly as having been buried more commonly with inhumation burials, perhaps a reflection of the importance of 'dressing' the dead appropriately, either through arming or adorning the corpse, where the full articulated body was on display. In the other direction, interestingly, pots *accompanying* (rather than containing) the body were far more prevalent with cremation burials than they were with inhumations. The key point to highlight here is that, in some ways surprisingly, the mode of burial (cremation or inhumation) was only loosely related to the character of grave goods deposited overall in the Bronze Age. In the Late Iron Age, however, there was a much closer correlation between funerary rites and the kinds of grave goods interred.

Table 3.05 Occurrence of different object categories with Late Iron Age inhumations and cremation burials (% of all grave goods with inhumations/cremation burials).

Object category	Inhumations (%) (n=287)	Cremation burials (%) (n=304)
Animal bone	14	6
Clothing	3	0
Cover	1	0
Jewellery	15	3
Natural object	0	2
Pin/point/brooch	15	22
Pot (accompanying)	25	55
Tool	6	1
Weaponry	14	0

n=888; pots and coffins containing the body excluded

Position of grave goods relative to the body
Using the large-scale data recorded in the GGDB, it was also possible to investigate the position in which objects had been placed in relation to the body (inhumations) or to cremated remains, through time. The key long-term change evident within Figure 3.14

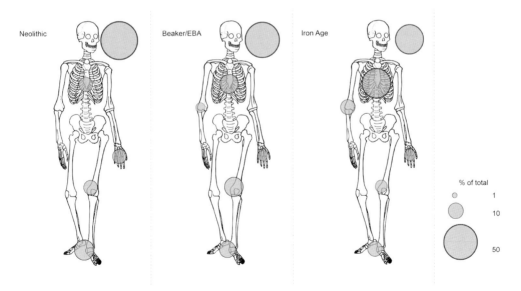

Figure 3.14 Proportions of all grave goods placed in specific positions in relation to the body for the periods when inhumation was most commonly practised. Positions represented: next to the head, on the torso, by the arm(s), by the hand(s), by the leg(s) and by the feet; n = 33 (Neolithic), 711 (Beaker/EBA), 1100 (Iron Age).

Figure 3.15 Proportions of all grave goods placed in specific positions in relation to cremated remains for the periods when cremation was most commonly practised. Positions represented: vessel containing the remains (mostly upright pots), vessel covering the remains (mostly inverted pots), object on top of bones, underneath bones, next to bones and mixed in with bones (all unurned); n = 1099 (Beaker/ EBA), 636 (MBA), 204 (LIA).

is the subtle trend for objects to be deposited increasingly less close to the head and increasingly more towards the torso (although the low Neolithic sample size should be noted). This perhaps reflects an increased tendency for objects to be worn on the body in burial through time, rather than to be placed by mourners adjacent to it. It is also interesting to note that the proportions of objects placed in all areas around the lower part of the body remained relatively constant.

Figure 3.15 shows where grave goods were positioned in relation to cremation burials, for those periods when this rite was most common. A variety of patterns can be discerned. Burials where an urn (or other vessel) contained the cremated bone but had been inverted were relatively common in the Early and Middle Bronze Ages, but extremely rare in the Late Iron Age period. Equally, cremation burials without an urn were much rarer during the Middle Bronze Age, and relatively more common in the other two periods. Un-urned cremation burials were most common during the Late Iron Age, at which time it was also fairly usual for grave goods to be mixed in with the cremated bone upon burial. The Late Iron Age identifiable object types that most often came to be mixed with bone were items likely to have been associated directly with the body – brooches, bangles, rings and cosmetic sets. Interestingly, although in some cases these objects were burnt with the body on the pyre (many of the unidentified masses of copper-alloy found with cremated bone may also represent remnants of these object types), most were seemingly added at a later point to the cremated bone (see also Section 8.2).

Numbers of objects
As discussed in Chapter 2, a considerable proportion of past discussions of grave goods has focused on the signification of wealth and status through material culture, sometimes informed crudely by the numbers of objects buried with a person. It is not our intention to get into such discussions here (see, for example, Fowler 2013 for an effective critique). However, basic counts of grave goods with a burial can be used to gain insight into certain aspects of mortuary practice without venturing into the thornier aspects of 'wealth' and 'status' (see also Chapter 5 for further discussion of

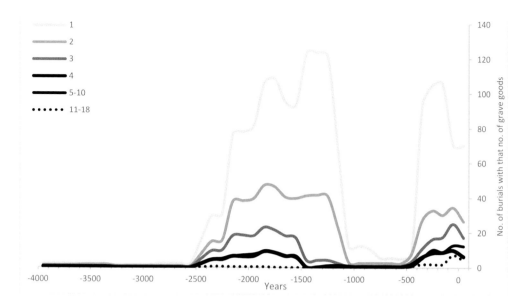

Figure 3.16 Numbers of objects per grave, through time.

this issue). Figure 3.16 shows the number of objects per grave through time. The upper, one-object curve broadly follows the total number of burials overall (see Fig. 3.02). The Neolithic period generally is not well-represented because of the methodological complexities of recording objects 'per grave' in many – if by no means all – cases (see above). At a very general level, Figure 3.16 suggests that the more burials/grave goods there were at a given time, the more likely it is that burials with multiple grave goods were made – a pattern that might have been expected, but nonetheless is good to see demonstrated empirically. Especially high peaks of one-object graves are noticeable in both the Middle Bronze Age and the Middle Iron Age. While the number of three+ object graves tails off at the start of the Middle Bronze Age, interestingly, the level of two-object graves is maintained from *c.* 1500 BC to *c.* 1100 BC (until the substantial Late Bronze Age drop in all burials). As discussed above, the character of grave goods overall changed dramatically in the Middle Bronze Age, with the variety of artefacts dropping markedly and pots coming to dominate the picture (see Fig. 3.05); the data presented in Figure 3.16 suggests that, seemingly, 'a pot plus one other item' remained as a fairly normal rite throughout the Middle Bronze Age, but the placement of more than that in a grave became much rarer. In the Middle Iron Age, we see a common practice of small to medium numbers of grave goods, but the Late Iron Age shows an emerging pattern of some burials with numerous grave goods and rich funerary 'suites' (particularly, here, from inhumations in Dorset and cremation burials in Kent).

Figure 3.17 shows the same data in a different way, with the box and whisker format revealing individual graves with very high numbers of objects more clearly (as 'outlier' circles). In this diagram, the average (median) value is shown as a thick

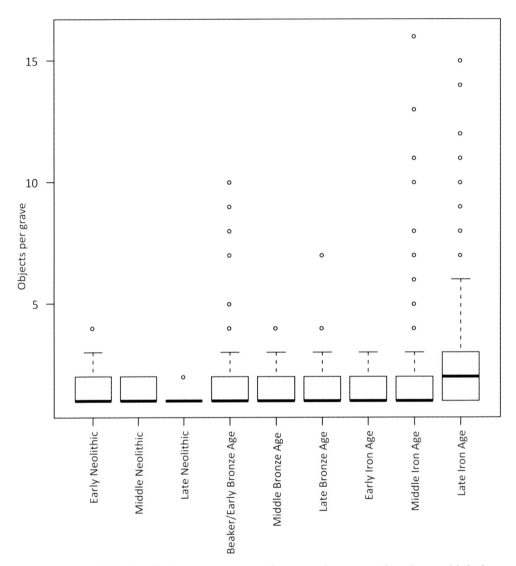

Figure 3.17 Box and whisker plot showing quantities of grave goods per grave, by sub-period (whiskers drawn at 1.5× the interquartile range, outliers plotted as circles).

black line, the middle 50% of values are contained within the boxes (the interquartile range), and the 'whiskers' (vertical dashed lines) run out to 1.5 times the interquartile range, with any values beyond the whiskers defined as outliers (circles). It is notable that, in the Beaker/Early Bronze Age period – which has the most grave goods and greatest variety of object types – no graves in our case study areas contained more than ten objects. The grave with the greatest number of grave goods was the primary burial within Barrow 9, Oakley Down, Dorset (Colt Hoare 1812, 239; Grinsell 1959, 144).

Here, a 'robust' man was buried with four barbed and tanged arrowheads (potentially in a bag), a butt-riveted dagger in a wooden sheath, a Beaker pot, a worn shale button and a shale belt fitting. However, during the Middle–Late Iron Age, it was seemingly much more common for such 'complex' arrangements of multiple grave goods to be deposited. The upper whisker of the Late Iron Age plot shows clearly that, then, it was relatively more common for graves to contain up to six objects. The outlying burials for the Iron Age, all single cremation/inhumation burials (in roughly equal numbers) with more than ten objects, and from four of our case study regions, are, almost without exception, dramatic burials which already feature prominently in archaeological discourse. They include the Whitcombe warrior burial (Dorset), the Bryher mirror burial (Scilly), the Wetwang Village chariot burial (East Yorkshire) and 'bucket burials' from Aylesford, Swarling and Malmains Farm (Kent). Clearly, our analysis does not include the materially richest Beaker/Early Bronze Age burials known from Wiltshire (the 'Amesbury Archer', Bush Barrow, and so on) – equally iconic burials, for this period. What our analysis does highlight, however, is that these Beaker/Early Bronze Age burials with exceptional numbers of grave goods were, arguably, anomalous and restricted to one specific sub-region within Wessex. Most 'rich' Beaker/Early Bronze Age burials are labelled as such because of the exceptional qualities of one or two of the objects they contained rather than necessarily because there were many objects in the grave. During the peak in grave good deposition in the Iron Age (from *c.* 500 BC onwards), a much clearer and more extreme set of materially rich/performative burials emerged in different forms across Britain.

3.3. Discussion

A key aspiration of the *Grave Goods* project from the start was to ensure that we placed ourselves in a position to assess changing burial practices in general, and the nature of grave goods specifically, *on a firm empirical basis* throughout the Neolithic, Bronze Age and Iron Age. As will have become clear, this required a significant amount of primary data collection, 'cleaning', sorting, quantification, analysis and modelling. We hope that the benefits of this large-scale dataset, and the new lines of vision into the past that it has opened up, are clear.

Some of the patterns discussed within this chapter were, of course, well-known prior to our research. These include, for example, the peaks of burial in certain regions (e.g. East Yorkshire during the Iron Age), the well-recognised predominance of male burials often with high numbers of grave goods in the Beaker period, and the shift from inhumation to cremation during the Early Bronze Age. Nonetheless, as we have stressed throughout, it is pleasing to be able to confirm these general impressions, demonstrating them on a firm empirical basis sometimes for the first time. Other patterns that emerged out of the data, however, came as rather more of a surprise or – in some cases – simply could not have been considered previously at all without a dataset on the scale of the GGDB to work with. The huge contribution of Middle Bronze Age pots to total grave goods numbers overall (thanks to Dorset, particularly, in our case study areas) represents an original and unexpectedly significant outcome of this analysis, especially when it is noted that, during this sub-period, pots were deposited in even greater numbers per century than in the well-renowned and materially richer Early Bronze Age. Similarly, the fact that both female burials (with grave goods) and grave goods associated with females would outnumber males during the Middle Iron Age was not expected at all, especially given the arguable dominance of 'charioteer', 'warrior', 'kingly' or 'priestly' burials in the public imagination, museum displays and indeed many archaeological accounts. On top of these surprises, the kinds of patterning that have been revealed uniquely and on an empirical basis by the substantial GGDB dataset include the different materials used for grave goods in different periods, the clear regional variability in grave good deposition, and the kinds of object deposited with cremation burials and inhumations, to name but a few.

It is worth noting at the end of this overview chapter that the huge quantity of data collected within the GGDB means that we have only really been able to scratch the surface of this rich body of information – to plot the most fundamental patterning at a large spatial scale and/or in the long-term. Many more patterns are certain to lie, undiscussed, deeper within that dataset, especially at the regional level. Some of these we are able to explore in later chapters, but others must await further analysis and future research. Equally, it would be possible to add new information to our dataset as well – relating to other case study areas and even perhaps new periods. We very much hope that the free availability of the GGDB for all to use will ensure that this happens.

Chapter 4

What goes in a grave? Situating prehistoric grave goods in relation to the wider materials of life

4.1. Introduction

Excavations carried out following coastal erosion damage on the foreshore at Lopness, Sanday, Orkney in 2000 (Innes 2016) revealed an Early Bronze Age cist burial that might be considered both 'normal' and 'unusual' in a number of ways. The seemingly isolated cist was constructed from large beach flagstones. It contained the incomplete, crouched skeleton of an arthritic 40–50-year-old woman within a matrix of 'midden-like' material (Fig. 4.01). The latter comprised coarse pottery, including large conjoining sherds, flint knapping debris, mammal, fish and bird bones, seaweed and charred weed seeds and barley grains. A potentially later deposit of two neonatal lambs and limpet shells was found at the woman's feet; radiocarbon dating could not establish the contemporaneity (or not) of these with the woman herself (*ibid.*, 13). Similarly, stratigraphic evidence and material analysis could not confirm conclusively whether or not the midden-like deposit was deliberate or incidental. Ultimately, the excavators had to keep open both the interpretative possibility that settlement debris fell into the cist following its collapse sometime after the burial and the option that at least some of this material was inserted intentionally during the burial, as a 'grave good' of sorts.

The Lopness burial assemblage relates to the theme of this chapter in two main ways. First, the occurrence of midden-like material around the skeleton defies traditional archaeological understandings of what *should* be deposited formally in a grave. Most prehistorians are, by now, used to the idea that human remains may have circulated widely among the living during certain periods of prehistory and were ultimately deposited in a range of contexts, including in settlements (e.g. Brück 1995; 2019). Only very rarely, however, does a mixed deposit of settlement debris occur in a potentially closed, and seemingly isolated, Bronze Age grave. Secondly, and most importantly here, the Lopness burial emphasises the extent to which archaeologists assume that the objects buried formally with the dead – and indeed those objects deposited formally elsewhere (e.g. in hoards) – were carefully selected from a much wider material repertoire available. To use Fontijn's terminology developed primarily for hoards (2019, 26–8 and 78–9), we generally expect that there was a 'right way to

Figure 4.01 The Early Bronze Age cist burial at Lopness, Sanday, Orkney (Innes 2016, pl. 4; © GUARD Archaeology Ltd 2016).

act' in depositing material in prehistoric graves which involved choosing objects of an appropriate character and also treating these objects correctly before burying them in the ground. The Lopness burial challenges this expectation in the sense that, if the 'midden-like' material *was* a form of grave good, the selection process is unusual and, in some ways, difficult for us to understand – this deposit comes closer to what we might understand as the 'wider material repertoire' than it does to an easily recognisable 'grave good'.

In this context, but also in relation to grave goods more generally, it seems important to ask what this wider or 'living' material repertoire was, how it relates to the objects that people chose to deposit formally and what this tells us about how prehistoric people tried to make sense of their material and depositional worlds. This chapter aims to tackle this set of questions head-on, focusing in particular on what went into prehistoric graves relative to what was available more widely to, and deposited by, prehistoric people. This topic is of key relevance since it relates closely to one of our central aims – to scrutinise exactly how we define the seemingly well-understood category of 'grave goods'. Our consideration of how grave goods relate to the wider material world is perhaps of particular importance because grave goods have usually been studied in isolation (e.g. S. Piggott 1938; Woodward and Hunter 2015). While traditional grave goods-only studies are certainly valuable in their own right, they have tended to overlook the broader context in which these object deposits took place and through which their meanings were animated. As Barrett *et al.* argued many years ago, in order to develop a richer understanding of the operation of prehistoric societies, it is vital to examine how different aspects of people's lives (in this case settlement, funerary and farming practices) were 'welded together' (1991, 224).

The *Grave Goods* project's work in this vein has followed two main strands. In an initial study of 'spectrums of depositional practice' (Cooper *et al.* 2020) we sought to investigate the sometimes blurred boundaries of traditional depositional categories like hoard, grave/grave good and settlement by highlighting a range of prehistoric object deposits that do not sit easily within these categories and which are therefore often overlooked analytically. This study raised the important point that the key categories via which we approach archaeological evidence can sometimes be unhelpful interpretatively – they can oversimplify (and thus make less interesting) the complexity of prehistoric practices. Additionally, our analysis stressed the vital (but often side-lined) reality that modern archaeological categories do not necessarily correspond neatly with those through which prehistoric people structured their own worlds (see also Barrett 1991a, 203–4). The study presented in this chapter offers an important counterpart to our discussion of spectrums of depositional practice. It attends specifically to the practical consideration that, although traditional archaeological categories – grave good, hoard, settlement find, single find – can sometimes be problematic and/or blur into one another, they are nonetheless essential to archaeological understandings of past practices. If we are to continue to rely on these categories, we argue, it is vital that we develop a stronger sense of how they are constituted materially, how they intersect and relate to one another, and how they potentially link to the 'total' material repertoires available to prehistoric people. Only by doing so can we potentially understand grave goods (as well as hoards, settlement finds, and so on) in a fuller, more dynamic and contextually rich way.

The detailed account of the material relationships between burials and other depositional contexts outlined here offers the first long-term and regionally nuanced consideration of this topic. We will draw together key insights from existing period and/or material-specific studies, add substantial detail to high level summaries (e.g. Brück 2019, 70–1), explore new ways of approaching the materiality of and relationships between depositional contexts, and raise methodological issues of key relevance for future work in this vein.

4.2. Previous approaches to material relationships between archaeological contexts

Active considerations of the material makeup of and relationships between separate archaeological contexts – in particular burial, hoard and settlement assemblages – and of how these deposits relate to what might be termed the 'wider material repertoire', have arisen in distinct waves over the last 150 years or so. At one level, substantial existing work has been undertaken. This topic has, however, been approached only via studies of specific materials and object types – almost exclusively pottery and metalwork – and of relationships between specific pairs of depositional contexts – between settlements and burials, or hoards and burials. Overall, therefore, the important theme of how different prehistoric evidence sets are made up, link up, and, indeed, flow materially is, at the same time, both well-trodden and under-theorised. The summary presented here focuses mainly on discussions within British Bronze Age studies since this is the main setting in which the different archaeological evidence sets has been discussed at length and from which the detailed case studies explored in this chapter are taken. Relevant insights from Neolithic and Iron Age studies in Britain, and from similar considerations on the near Continent, are also highlighted where possible.

One of the earliest published reflections on how prehistoric grave goods related to the wider material repertoire is Thurnam's (1872) thoughtful consideration of the origins of pottery found in Bronze Age burial contexts (see also Greenwell 1865, 99; Stanley and Way 1868, 291; Evans 1881, 274 for other, broadly contemporary discussions about the relationship between objects found in graves and those found in settlements and in metalwork deposits). Thurnam (1872) identified subtle distinctions between three overlapping groups of pottery vessels: (a) 'strictly sepulchral vessels', specifically made for the burial and including 'rude pots' (potentially fired on the funerary pyre) and fine pots/incense cups; (b) 'tableware' (Beakers and Food Vessels), made 'for the living' but 'habitually buried with the dead' (so ultimately passing into the 'sepulchral class'); and (c) 'culinary vessels', used for burials 'in the absence of vessels more suitable or especially fabricated for the purpose' and characterised primarily by their 'exceptional rudeness and the almost entire absence of surface-ornament' (*ibid.*, 338) (Fig. 4.02). In making these distinctions, Thurnam was among the first to appreciate that potentially

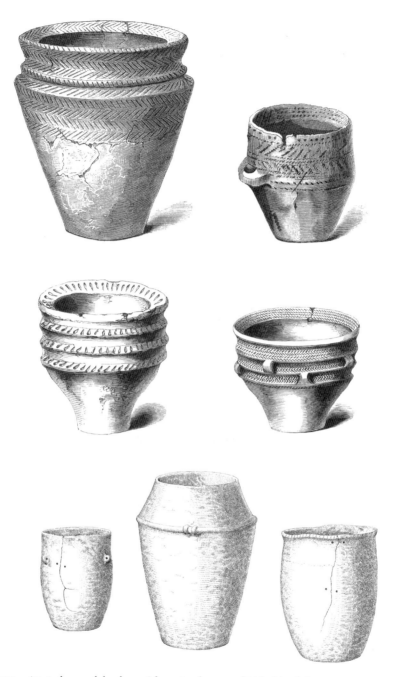

Figure 4.02 Top: 'Strictly sepulchral urns' from Anglesey and Wiltshire (Thurnam 1870, 348, figs 24–5). Middle: 'the tableware of prehistoric Britain' from East Yorkshire – made 'for the living' but 'habitually buried with the dead' (Thurnam 1870, 380, figs 69–70). Bottom: 'culinary vessels' from Dorset and Wiltshire, used in burials only 'in the absence of vessels more suitable or especially fabricated for the purpose' (Thurnam 1870, 338, pl. xxix, figs 6, 8 & 9).

complex processes were involved in selecting objects from one context or 'domain' and depositing them in another, and that this had functional and conceptual implications for the objects concerned. Without having access to substantial settlement assemblages at the time, such antiquarian considerations, while seminal and insightful, were also necessarily somewhat abstract in character.

Relating burial and settlement deposits in later prehistory

Jones' (1998) comparison of depositional practices in Neolithic tombs and settlements on Orkney is a rare example of a direct consideration of material relationships between separate depositional contexts for this period. Uniquely in the setting of our overview, Jones focused on the character of animal bone assemblages (rather than on metalwork or pottery). Both similarities and clear differences were highlighted in the character of animal remains deposited in each context. Bones from ungulates (cattle, sheep, pig, deer) were, overall, similarly represented and treated in both tomb and settlement deposits. Cattle long bones were also used in walling in both tombs and settlements. Jones saw this patterning as evidence that tomb users were referring symbolically to 'the community of the living' (*ibid.*, 312). By contrast, he found that the age ranges and demography of other animal species represented in tombs were markedly different to those found in contemporary settlements, as was the makeup and treatment of specific animal parts – for instance, different bird elements were represented in tombs and in settlements. While the contemporaneity of human and animal bone deposits in some Orkney chambered tombs has since been questioned (see Section 8.1), Jones' study importantly highlighted the possibility that Neolithic funerary and settlement deposits were both broadly related and subtly different. He also emphasised the importance of considering both the basic character of the items deposited (e.g. animal types/parts) and how they were treated both before and during their deposition.

Two substantial studies of Beaker pottery in the 1990s made strong cases (in different ways) for the idea that the vessels deposited in Beaker/Early Bronze Age burials were both connected to, and also distinctly different from, those used and deposited in contemporary settlements. Case noted a higher incidence of small Beakers in funerary contexts in Oxfordshire, Wiltshire and East Yorkshire (1995, 56). This could suggest that the vessels chosen for burial were used for drinking. Where tested, however, their contents at the point of deposition – including mead, flowers, flint objects and cremated human bone – are varied (*ibid.*, 60–3). Beyond the clear selection of smaller vessels for graves, Case noted general commonalities in those Beakers found in graves and in settlements in terms of their decorative features (*ibid.*, 56). Overall, he suggested, Beaker-using communities held common ideas about the right kinds of vessel to deposit with the dead. However, they applied these ideas pragmatically, as appropriate pots were not always readily to hand (*ibid.*, 60). Boast's nuanced study of shifts in the manifestations of Beakers in burials and in settlements over the period 2500–1600 BC indicated, in contrast, that many of the Beakers interred in burials were made specifically for the grave (1995, 76). Beakers from graves were often fashioned from rough fabrics which were then 'made good' by applying a high standard of surface treatment. Using an abstract but productive scheme for distinguishing between 'open' and 'closed' decorative Beaker designs, Boast highlighted close similarities in the decorative designs of pots deposited in graves and in settlements prior to 1800 BC. After this point, however, the Beakers deposited in graves tended to be adorned with more complex, closed motifs than those deposited in settlement contexts (*ibid.,* 76). Towards the end of the Early Bronze Age therefore, a more specialised category of 'funerary Beaker pot' emerged. Interestingly, Boast argued that whatever their immediate makeup and appearance, Beakers deposited in graves were ultimately understood to be special specifically because of their association with daily life – they carried references to food production, communal feasting and so on, to the grave even if they were not taken directly from daily life (*ibid.,* 78). According to Boast's reckoning therefore, the material relationship between burial and settlement deposits was largely abstract/conceptual rather than direct/practical.

Across much of Britain, Early Bronze Age pottery types beyond Beakers are rarely found in contexts beyond burials. It is therefore unsurprising that considerations of material relationships between different Early Bronze Age depositional contexts are scarce (although note Healy's (1995) cautionary comments about depositional practices involving Collard Urns). The Middle Bronze Age pottery sherds from Itford Hill, Sussex (Fig. 4.03), thought to be from the same vessel and found in settlement and cremation cemetery deposits located *c.* 100 m apart (Holden 1972), have offered a powerful image of the proximity of funerary and domestic spheres in the Middle and Late Bronze Age. This image has played a key role in many subsequent discussions about relationships between burials and settlements for this period (e.g. Brück 2001a; 2006; Johnston 2020, 96). Building specifically on the Itford Hill finding, Bradley (1981, 94) saw the rare survival of burial, settlement and farming remains from the Middle and Late Bronze Ages in southern Britain as a unique opportunity to relate the evidence from these different depositional domains. Based on the occurrence of similar Middle Bronze Age pottery vessels in burial and settlement contexts (see also Ellison 1975), on the close spatial location of at least some Middle Bronze Age settlements and cemeteries, and on the arrangement of Middle Bronze Age burial pits in 'family groups', Bradley argued that a particularly strong relationship developed between funerary and domestic spheres at this time (1981, 99). Barrett *et al.* (1991) extended these arguments on the back of a major programme of excavation and re-analysis of earlier excavated material from Bronze Age cemeteries and settlements in Cranborne Chase, Dorset in the late 1970s–1980s. Central to their approach (see also Barrett 1994) to understanding social developments in the mid-2nd millennium BC was the idea that funerary, domestic and farming practices were closely entwined at this time: in order to explain societal change, it was necessary to explore how these separate domains of practice were interconnected (Barrett *et al.* 1991, 224). In this context, the association of 'domestic ceramics' with cremation cemeteries was seen to exemplify close connectivity between the spheres of the living and the dead: 'the widespread use of the full range of domestic containers in mortuary contexts in the Middle Bronze Age represents a significant degree of cross-referencing between these different fields of practice' (Barrett 1991a, 206). Moreover, 'the dead were even accompanied to the grave by the vessels used to store and cook food' (Barrett *et al.* 1991, 225). Although recent analyses have challenged the idea that Middle Bronze Age settlements and burials were closely related spatially (Caswell and Roberts 2018), and have nuanced other parallels drawn between settlement and burial evidence at this time (e.g. Brück 2019, 46), the idea that funerary and settlement practices were closely related materially and metaphorically in the Middle Bronze Age still holds sway.

Given the scarcity of formal burials across much of Britain during the Early and Middle Iron Ages, the rarity of excavated settlements contemporary with Middle and Late Iron Age cemeteries in East Yorkshire (Giles 2012, 72), and the high incidence of other modes of formal deposit (beyond burials and hoards) in this period (e.g. Hill 1995), it is perhaps unsurprising that direct considerations of material relationships between Iron Age burials and settlements are few and far between. With good reason, Iron Age researchers have focused instead on trying to understand how the objects that animated life related to those deposited in a range of formal contexts – occasionally in burials, but also in pits, houses and so on (e.g. Sharples 2010, 300–1; Brudenell 2012, 346).

Giles' (2012, chap. 3) consideration of how Middle and Late Iron Age cemeteries relate to contemporary settlements in East Yorkshire is a rare exception in this respect. Her main focus was on the spatial proximity of these cemeteries and settlements and on the common use of architectural devices to express and to

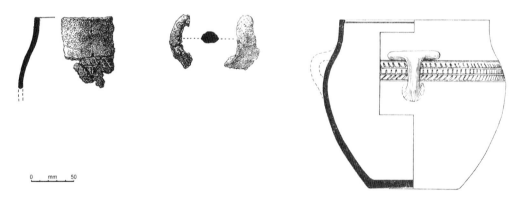

Figure 4.03 Sherds thought to be from the same vessel deposited in the settlement (left/centre; Burstow et al. 1958, fig. 24, sherds A & B) and in the cemetery (right; Holden 1972, fig. 8, pot 7) at Itford Hill, Sussex. Note that sherd B is recorded as missing from the Barbican House Museum, Lewes. In this case, therefore, direct comparison with the vessel found in the cemetery was not possible (images reproduced by kind permission of the Prehistoric Society and the Sussex Archaeological Society).

reproduce understandings of social order in both settings (2012, 59–60). In discussing the ceramics and food remains found in burials, however, Giles noted (following Rigby in Stead 1991, 110) that the pots chosen for deposition in graves were made of a narrow range of fabric types – a noticeably wider range of fabric types is found in contemporary settlement contexts. Additionally, although some of these pots were potentially used for cooking prior to being deposited in graves, others appear to have been made specifically for funerary purposes – many of the vessels from burials are fragile, distorted and/or ill-fired (Rigby in Stead 1991, 105). For the Late Iron Age, and at a site-specific level, Mepham (1997) considered in detail the 'framework' of pottery assemblages from the cremation cemetery at Westhampnett, West Sussex and from contemporary settlements around the local area and successfully identified parallels in the specific pot forms represented at the Westhampnett cemetery and on contemporary settlement sites. Overall, however, she emphasised the highly distinctive character of the cemetery assemblage – larger storage vessels and specialist pots (e.g. for cheese-making) and amphorae/Armorican imports were lacking in burials, an extremely high proportion of cemetery vessels were grog-tempered and highly decorated, and forms which were typically wheel-thrown in settlement contexts were often handmade when found in burials: 'if many of these pots were not specifically made for use and/or burial in the mortuary rituals, then at least they were carefully selected' (Mepham 1997, 133). Once again therefore, for the Iron Age, it appears that material relationships between settlement and burial assemblages are complex and nuanced rather than being straightforwardly either 'close' or 'remote'.

Relating Bronze Age hoard and burial deposits

Evans (1881) was among the first to note the absence from British graves of certain types of Bronze Age metalwork (e.g. swords) that were included as grave goods in other areas of north-west Europe. Almost a century later, Burgess (1976) reviewed the metalwork evidence from Middle and Late Bronze Age burials in Britain and Ireland. He restated what had been clear since Evans' time: that a 'watershed' occurred in the deposition of metalwork as a grave good at the end of the Early Bronze Age, related to major changes in burial and ritual practices, including the emergence of what he called a 'water-dominated cult' (*ibid.*, 82). Burgess was optimistic, however, that more could be said about the relationship between metalwork from burials and hoards if it was tackled empirically and he assembled a list of 47 burials with Middle and Late Bronze Age metalwork. Many of these were, by his own admission, based on 'old and vague sources' (*ibid.*, 88) but they provided a valuable opportunity to consider the relationship between metalwork deposited in hoards and burials during this period. Burgess also made the important point that metalwork deposits in 'wet places' could represent burials with grave goods from which only the objects had survived or been recovered.

Needham (1988) illuminated the relationship(s) between metalwork found in hoards and as single finds and from burials for the Early Bronze Age by undertaking a ground-breaking empirical and typological comparison for the whole of Britain. By bringing together the evidence for the deposition of metalwork in both burials and non-funerary contexts for the first time, Needham was able to identify compelling patterns in the kind and number of objects in burials compared to hoards – and as single finds – through both space and time. To explain these relationships he drew on the notion of prescribed 'sets' or 'repertoires' of metalwork types, which he took to reflect social and symbolic rules that underpinned behaviours (*ibid.*, 245). Needham noted the relatively small size and weight of bronze objects from burials – compared to those from hoards or single finds – and suggested it was the result of 'economic determinism' acting on metal supply and circulation (*ibid.*, 245). Having quantified the rise of metal hoards relative to metalwork from burial contexts, Needham sought to develop a 'general theory' of Early Bronze Age metalwork deposition, suggesting that hoards represented 'community' deposits in contrast to grave goods made of metal, which he linked instead to the 'personal aggrandisement' of important individuals (*ibid*, 245–6). Like Burgess, Needham sought to explain this change in metalwork deposition within the wider context of major – but ultimately difficult to comprehend – changes in symbolic and ritual behaviour across Britain during the later phases of the Early Bronze Age. These changes involved a shift from burials as foci for some metalwork being deposited as high status grave goods to non-funerary 'ceremonies' that involved the deposition of metal objects for the benefit of the community at large (*ibid.*, 246). In seeking to relate metalwork deposits in burials and in other formal contexts, both Burgess and Needham ultimately ended up explaining them – chronologically and conceptually – as distinct realms of practice.

Alongside his important work considering the relationship between Middle and Late Bronze Age settlement and burials (see above), Bradley (e.g. 1981; 2017; 2019; Barrett *et al.* 1991) played a central role in developing wider and theoretically-orientated understandings of the shifting context of metalwork deposition over the Bronze Age as a whole, extending Burgess' and Needham's earlier observations. Bradley took a long-term and landscape-based approach to understanding the relationship between metalwork from burials and from other formal Bronze Age deposits. His work was also instrumental in exploring links between burials and other metalwork deposits beyond the immediate typology of their contents. Bradley asserted directly, for instance, that metalwork deposited in rivers may, at times, have operated as a form of grave good, whether or not human remains were deposited at the same time (1998, 107–8). More recently, Bradley has extended these arguments, highlighting the parallel treatment (e.g. in terms of their arrangement) of metal objects deposited in burials and in hoards at different times in the Bronze Age (2017, 99; see also Needham 1988; Wilkin 2017).

Looking further afield to continental Europe, Fontijn has undertaken a series of detailed empirical studies examining the specific character of metal objects deposited in separate archaeological contexts in the southern Netherlands (2002) and more widely (2020). Key findings from Fontijn's analyses include his demonstration that certain metal objects were selected for deposition in certain ways and in specific contexts – settlements, hoards, burials – over the duration of the Bronze Age in this region. Additionally, Fontijn highlighted the regionally specific character of such practices – sets of objects typically deposited in graves in one region (e.g. weaponry) might be found exclusively in hoards in another (2002, 229–30). On this basis, Fontijn re-emphasised the close relationship between metalwork deposited in Bronze Age hoards and in burials, raising, for instance, the hybrid concept of 'funerary hoards' – object deposits that resemble burial deposits but which lack human remains, and which may have been deposited at a significant moment in the human life cycle other than death (*ibid.*, 230–1). More recently, Fontijn (2019, 147) has noted that in many regions of Europe, material culture from settlements gives the impression of self-sufficient, local communities, while the evidence from hoards highlights foreign or exotic networks. On this basis, he warns against overly simple conceptualisations of Bronze Age society based on only one or two strands of evidence. At a diachronic level and with much of western Europe in mind, Fontijn (2019, 78–9) has also made a case for regarding the patterns or 'rules' of association and disassociation that were established for depositing metalwork in Early Bronze Age graves as vital forerunners to Middle and Late Bronze Age conventions of deposition followed in metalwork hoards.

Material relationships across depositional contexts

Over the last 20 years or so, and via an impressive body of theoretically-orientated analyses that actively take into account a much fuller range of material culture, Brück (e.g. 1999; 2001a; 2004; 2006; 2019), among others (e.g. Jones 2012), has made a further vital contribution to understandings of material relations between different depositional contexts in later prehistory. Although most of Brück's work focuses on Bronze Age evidence, her ideas have been influential much more widely across prehistory and beyond.

Key to Brück's argument has been a fundamental challenge to the idea that human remains and objects were necessarily viewed as ontologically distinct in later prehistory. While human remains are arguably essential to the identification of formal 'graves' (see discussion in Cooper *et al.* 2020), they also occur in a range of other contexts (settlements, field ditches, etc.), particularly from the Middle Bronze Age onwards. Given their occurrence as discrete interments in diverse contexts, removed physically, temporally and conceptually from the immediate context of death, Brück has argued that human remains may sometimes have operated more like objects at the point of deposition (2019, 380). Equally, objects (like pots) and other materials (like charcoal) were sometimes deposited in a manner akin to human remains and may have been seen to operate as burials (*ibid.*, 71). In this light, human remains can be viewed as a vital point of connection between depositional contexts rather than necessarily being a primary means of distinguishing between 'graves' and other types of deposit. Another of Brück's major contributions to the theme of this chapter has been her disruption of the idea that there was a straightforward transition from a 'living' material repertoire to archaeological assemblages deposited variously in the ground. Rather, prehistoric object deposits – particularly graves and hoards – were often revisited; items were removed and recirculated amongst the living as well as potentially being redeposited elsewhere (2019, 29; see also Booth and Brück 2020). On this basis, formal deposits can and should be understood as temporarily removed elements of the living material repertoire rather than as static end points of it. Brück has also spearheaded discussions regarding the parallel treatment (for instance the burning, fragmentation and containment) of objects deposited in different excavated contexts, raising the possibility that the way in which objects were handled prior to and during their deposition was sometimes more important to prehistoric people than the objects' precise character – their type, material, and so on. For instance broken objects (sherds and/or metalwork fragments) are a feature of burials, settlements and hoards at certain times and in particular places over the Bronze Age (*ibid.*, 102).

Summary
The overarching pattern in studies of the material makeup and links between 'different' archaeological contexts in recent years has therefore been towards greater integration and complexity. It has been increasingly recognised that there are multiple material links and overlaps between depositional contexts and that there are many more ways to approach this topic analytically than comparing the types of objects deposited in separate contexts.

Period-specific analyses of the material relationships between burials and settlements are broadly in agreement that burial and settlement deposits were, overall, closely linked both materially and conceptually. Where direct material comparisons are possible, close similarities have been identified in the makeup of pottery (and animal bone) assemblages in both contexts. For all times other than in the Middle Bronze Age, however, it has been argued that the objects deposited in burials represented a selection of the full settlement repertoire, or, alternatively, a simulacrum of a particular aspect of this repertoire – the materiality of 'everyday life' was being cited in specific and varied ways in the funerary arena.

Researchers investigating material relationships between hoards and burials have had to be more creative and conceptual in identifying connections between these domains. Metalwork was deposited in significant numbers in both burials and hoards together only during the Early Bronze Age. Even during this sub-period, there was little direct overlap in the typological makeup of objects from hoards and burials. Given the clear divergence between the material character of hoards and burials, it is particularly interesting that the desire to relate them conceptually has nevertheless persisted in archaeological interpretations (e.g. Roberts 2007; Bradley 2017; Brück 2019; Fontijn 2019; Wilkin 2017). The connection that Fontijn (2019, 78–9) draws between Early Bronze Age burial and Middle and Late Bronze Age hoard/single object deposition hinges on patterns of 'association' and 'disassociation' in particular types of metal valuable that were transposed from one context (burial) to another (hoards) over a considerable time period. Wilkin's (2017) discussion of the evocation of *absent* bodies in the stacking, looping and spatial patterning of ornaments within hoards during the Middle Bronze Age similarly requires a leap of interpretative faith. The fact that it is so difficult to identify material connections between burials and of hoards over much of our study period is, in itself, notable. It has been best described by Fontijn (2002, 274–5; 2019, 153–72) as evidence of a set of strong pan-European ideas concerning how things, especially metal, should be treated, derived in turn from a guiding 'system' of values and beliefs.

Before presenting our own analysis of material relationships between depositional contexts, it is worth highlighting some of the limits of the existing understandings outlined above. At a broad level, previous analyses are extremely patchy in terms of their coverage of the period 4000 BC–AD 43, of different parts of Britain, and of different aspects of the material repertoire. Understandings of material relationships between burials and settlements have been developed almost exclusively through the lens of pottery assemblages – the full array of other objects and materials deposited in both contexts has rarely been brought into consideration. Beyond Jones' (1998) comparison of animal remains from Orkney chambered tombs and broadly contemporary settlements, few, if any, direct investigations have been undertaken of material relationships between Neolithic settlements and burials. Similar appraisals for the Bronze and Iron Ages have been made only in specific regions. Considerations of material relationships between Bronze Age hoards, burials and settlements have been hampered by the lack of recent detailed or contextual studies of metalwork deposition across Britain, in contrast to the situation on the near continent (e.g. Fontijn 2002; 2019). Although the concepts and theories developed to connect hoards to other contemporary contexts are increasingly sophisticated and compelling, the detailed, diachronic, national and regional picture of metalwork deposition across Bronze Age Britain remains rather vaguely understood and articulated. Material relationships between Iron Age hoards and burials have never been scrutinised in detail (see, however, Wilkinson 2019).

Importantly, most detailed comparisons of the material makeup of different depositional contexts were undertaken before the onset of developer-funded archaeology and the Portable Antiquities Scheme in Britain – they are all, as a result, substantially out of date. Bold and pervasive interpretative statements were made about the operation of Bronze Age societies based on studies of material relationships between settlements and burials in the 1980s and 1990s which, in practice, drew on a very narrow evidence base. Recent discussions about the parallel treatment of objects deposited in hoards, burials and settlements are undoubtedly persuasive and interesting. However, these arguments are generally illustrated with piecemeal examples – they have yet to be underpinned by systematic empirical enquiry. Meanwhile, although the closed character of formal deposits has been questioned

(Brück 2019; see also Needham 2000; Sharples 2010), most existing studies still ultimately assume that the objects deposited in burials and in hoards were selected from a 'living material repertoire', the character of which is never specifically brought into question.

Clearly, not all these matters can be addressed in the context of this chapter. Rather we will focus here on developing key aspects of existing studies that we feel benefit from more specific/immediate consideration. Accepting the argument that there was a mutual flow of objects between 'living' and 'depositional' domains in later prehistory, we start by asking if, how and whether it is appropriate to develop an archaeological understanding of the 'living material repertoire' from which formal deposits, such as burials, are meant to have derived. To counterbalance previous studies which have compared only metalwork and pottery deposited in different contexts, and the makeup of depositional domains either at a national level or within one region, we will attempt to trace the broad ebb and flow of *all* objects deposited in hoards, burials and settlements across later prehistory in two case study regions – Dorset and Kent. Having identified the Early Bronze Age as a key period for understanding the emergence of hoarding and burial as distinct spheres of practice in the Middle and Late Bronze Ages, we will explore what the changing value and symbolic significance of metalwork during this period can tell us about the relationship between these depositional contexts. Tackling one key finding from previous studies, we will also re-visit the idea that the material relationship between Middle Bronze Age settlements and burials was straightforwardly close.

4.3. Accessing the 'living material repertoire'?

As discussed above, our interest in investigating the character of the full 'living material repertoire' in later prehistory stems, in part, from the fact that material relationships between graves and other depositional contexts have thus far been investigated directly only via a narrow range of object types – pots and metalwork. It thus feels important to bring a wider range of materials and objects into consideration. Our interest in this topic also stems from our ambivalence about two related assumptions that underpin most previous studies of material relationships between depositional contexts. First, it is broadly assumed that objects deposited formally in burials, hoards and so on, were drawn from a somewhat abstract living material repertoire or, as Sharples puts it, from the array of objects which 'circulated in life' (2010, 301). Secondly, it is often assumed (mostly implicitly) that this living material repertoire relates most closely to the assemblages we encounter archaeologically in *settlement* deposits. It goes without saying that we do not imagine that it is actually possible to recreate 'total' living material repertoires from archaeological assemblages – evaluating the character of these repertoires will always be, to a certain extent, hypothetical. On the other hand, it does seem important that we consider what 'full' or 'living' later prehistoric living material repertoires may have looked like and how we might approach them archaeologically, rather than treating them as a somewhat abstract yet generally accepted 'black box'.

Before considering this topic in more detail, in order to emphasise a couple of our key points, it is worth outlining an example of an excavated assemblage that perhaps comes as close as any to what we might imagine a living material repertoire to be – the spectacular finds from the Late Bronze Age pile-dwelling settlement at Must Farm, Cambridgeshire (Knight *et al.* 2019). The process by which the Must Farm settlement was abandoned (in a catastrophic fire that destroyed the entire settlement less than a year after it was built) and by which its traces were preserved (in a Bronze Age river channel that remained waterlogged until the point of excavation) ensured that a very full range of material culture associated with this archaeological site survived. The material intensity of this assemblage, most notably the organic objects, is dazzling – ranging from spools of yarn, woven fabrics and wooden troughs crusted with dough residues, to a hafted bronze axe, a 'set' of in use and discarded/broken pottery vessels, a potential metalwork hoard 'in the making' and even the chips of wood and lumps of clay left over from constructing the pile-dwellings. The Must Farm assemblage throws into relief the incredible material richness of (at least some) Late Bronze Age life in Britain.

Two other points spring to mind in relation to the Must Farm assemblage. The abundance of the finds reinforces the extent to which 'typical' excavated settlement assemblages represent an extremely partial version of prehistoric material lives. This must cast doubt over the idea that settlement deposits in general offer a reasonable representation of a living material repertoire. Additionally, although it is very tempting to understand the Must Farm assemblage as being a much closer depiction of the 'full' Late Bronze Age material repertoire in eastern England than typical excavated assemblages, it is also vital to remember that even this incredibly rich assemblage is an isolated snapshot – albeit a particularly vivid one – of living material dynamics. The specific makeup of the metal items – in particular axes – was, overall, distinctly different to that typically encountered in contemporary hoards (Appleby *et al.* forthcoming) while the emphasis on 'wild' animals within the faunal assemblage was unique in the context of Late Bronze Age settlement assemblages more broadly in Britain (Rajkovača forthcoming). As Fontijn noted for the Middle and Late Bronze Ages in Europe, settlement assemblages can give an impression of life that is directly contradicted by the material found in other depositional contexts (2019, 147); there is no real reason why the settlement evidence should be viewed as more 'normal' or 'representative'.

Clearly it would be extremely complicated to attempt to build a representation of the living material repertoire over our entire study period – even if only at a regional level, and even today when 'born digital' excavation archives from extensive landscape-scale fieldwork projects are increasingly available. It was possible (and productive) within the context of this study, however, to conduct a simpler exercise in this vein using published material for one particular period and case study area – the Middle Bronze Age in Dorset. A survey was undertaken of the object types recovered from excavated burials, hoards and settlements using information from the GGDB and key published datasets: Pearce (1983) and the corpus of metalwork deposits in south-west Britain (Knight *et al.* 2015); fieldwork reports from excavated settlements at Shearplace Hill (Rahtz and ApSimon 1962), Poundbury (Sparey-Green 1987), Down Farm, Cranborne Chase (Barrett *et al.* 1991), Rowden (Woodward 1991), Middle Farm, Dorchester (Smith *et al.* 1997) and Bestwall Quarry (Ladle and Woodward 2009). One striking outcome of this analysis is the diversity of objects deposited in settlement contexts that are *not* found in burials and hoards (Table 4.01). If settlement and funerary domains were as 'welded together' in the Middle Bronze Age in Dorset as Barrett *et al.* suggest (1991, 224), the version of settlement that was cited in graves was certainly limited. Additionally, although pots deposited in prehistoric burials *may* have been used to refer conceptually to settlement (see above), pots were also deposited in hoards (e.g. South Lodge Camp; Knight *et al.* 2015, no. 200) – an occurrence that similarly needs explaining. Taking the living material repertoire for the Middle Bronze Age in Dorset represented here as a whole, it appears that certain objects/ materials from this matrix were ultimately only deposited in certain contexts – lids in graves, dirks and rapiers in hoards or as single deposits, flint cores in settlements, and so on; meanwhile certain other objects – pots, beads, pins, etc. – transcended depositional domains and, perhaps, offer an archaeological key to understanding how these were related. Although the range of objects deposited in settlements is wider than in hoards and burials, certain objects found in hoards and/or in burials are missing from settlement assemblages.

Although material connections between settlement and hoard deposits in Middle Bronze Age Dorset are slight, it is worth noting that this is not the case across Britain more widely, or over the whole of the Bronze Age. For instance, in contrast to the situation in the Middle and Late Bronze Ages in southern England, many Late Bronze Age hoards in northern England include both metalwork and organic materials – bone, amber, wood and fragments of textile (Matthews 2008). It is also important to highlight that disconnects between the material makeup of different depositional contexts almost certainly arise not only because of what people chose to put in deposits (e.g. gold torcs in hoards but not in settlements) but also what they chose to leave out – whether or not they chose to include the everyday or 'living' parts of composite metal objects such as axe hafts and fabric wrappings. Both Needham (2001, 289) and Matthews (2008, 116) have argued convincingly that the process of actively divorcing objects from their living associations may, in itself, have been socially significant.

In summary, we hope to have made clear that the 'living material repertoire' is not specific to, nor anymore 'real' in, settlements than it is in any other deposited context – all contexts need to be considered together in trying to establish the full materiality of past lives.

Table 4.01 Approaching a later prehistoric 'living material repertoire': object types found in settlements (n=8), burials (n=576) and hoards (n=24) during the Middle Bronze Age in Dorset.

Object type	Burial	Hoard	Settlement
Animal remains	•		•
Axe-head			•
Bead	•	•	•
Bracelet/arm-ring		•	•
Burnisher			•
Burnt flint	•		•
Comb			•
Cover/lid	•		
Daub			•
Finger-ring	•	•	
Flint core			•
Flint flake	•		•
Flint scraper			•
Flint tool (other)			•
Furnace lining			•
Grinding stone			•
Hammer stone			•
Human remains	•		•
Loom/roof weight			•
Metalworking mould			•
Necklace	•		
Palstave		•	•
Pebble	•		•
Pin	•	•	
Plant remains	•		•
Point			•
Pot	•	•	•
Quern	•		•
Rapier		•	
Sharpening stone			•
Slag			•
Spearhead	•	•	
Spindle whorl			•
Torc		•	
Whetstone			•
Worked stone	•		•

4.4. Charting the ebb and flow of objects deposited in burials, hoards and settlements, 4000 BC–AD 43

As well as considering how to approach the makeup and dynamics of later prehistoric 'living material repertoires', it is also interesting to investigate at a broad level shifts in the overall quantities of material entering different depositional contexts over the course of our study period. Many archaeologists will already have a general sense of peaks and dips in the deposition of metal objects in hoards, of grave goods in graves, and so on, over the course of later prehistory. Only very rarely, however, has this topic been directly investigated empirically, or has the amount of material entering different depositional contexts been actively compared. In particular, few, if any, such comparisons have been made at a regional level using the wealth of information now available from developer-funded archaeology and the Portable Antiquities Scheme (PAS). Patterning in the flow of material entering the ground in different contexts and at different times is important because it offers both specific insight into shifting emphases in depositional practices, and a new perspective on the character of the prehistoric lives that gave rise to these deposits.

In order to investigate this theme, we approached the evidence at a regional level within two case study areas – Dorset and Kent – focusing on the objects deposited in hoards, burials and settlements. It is important to highlight at this point that the occurrence of substantial, broadly contemporary evidence across three of these key depositional categories all together is relatively rare in all our case study areas, as it is in many other regions – an outcome that almost certainly relates both to the character of prehistoric activity and to specific regional histories of research and recovery. Taking the evidence from all six of the *Grave Goods* project's case study areas, only during the Middle Bronze Age in Dorset, the Middle and Late Bronze Age in Kent, and the Late Iron Age in Dorset and Kent was it possible to compare meaningfully the amount of material entering the ground across all three depositional contexts (Table 4.02).

The number of objects deposited in burials in Kent and Dorset over the period 4000 BC–AD 43 was extracted from the GGDB. Equivalent information for hoards was collated from detailed regional syntheses for the Bronze Age (O'Connor 1980; Pearce 1983; Perkins 2000; Knight *et al.* 2015; Smythe unpublished data) and Iron Age (Wilkinson 2019). This information was augmented with evidence for recent Bronze and Iron Age finds recorded in the PAS database (https://finds.org.uk/database).

Ideally, we would have liked to chart, in a similar way, the overall volume of objects deposited in settlements over the same period. In practice, however, this was not possible. 'Settlement goods' (and, indeed, objects from other specific depositional contexts – burials, hoards, field ditches and so on) are not generally separated out, at least in terms of their quantification, in specialist finds analyses resulting from fieldwork. In order to gain a very broad-brush understanding of shifting levels of settlement evidence over our period we therefore had to be inventive. According to the best available evidence, different proxies for ebbs and flows in settlement evidence over our study period were generated for each of the two case study areas. In Dorset, where few extensive landscape-scale excavations

Table 4.02 Availability by sub-period of substantial evidence (i.e. more than a handful of excavated sites with securely-dated evidence) for settlement (S), burials with grave goods (B) and metalwork hoards (H) in our six case study areas.

Sub-period	Cornwall/ Scilly			Dorset			E. Yorkshire			Gwynedd/ Anglesey			Kent			Orkney/ Outer Hebs		
	S	B	H	S	B	H	S	B	H	S	B	H	S	B	H	S	B	H
Early Neolithic	–	–		–	Y		–	Y		–	–		–	–		Y	Y	
Middle Neolithic	–	–		–	–		–	–		–	–		–	–		Y	Y	
Late Neolithic	–	–		–	–		–	–		–	–		–	–		Y	Y	
Early Bronze Age	–	Y	–	Y	Y	–	–	Y	–	–	Y	–	–	Y	–	–	Y	–
Middle Bronze Age	Y	–	–	Y	Y	Y	Y	–	–	–	–	–	Y	Y	Y	–	Y	–
Late Bronze Age	Y	–	Y	Y	–	Y	Y	–	Y	–	–	–	Y	Y	Y	–	–	–
Early Iron Age	–	–	–	Y	–	Y	–	–	–	–	–	–	–	–	–	–	–	–
Middle Iron Age	–	–	–	Y	–	Y	–	Y	–	–	–	–	–	Y	–	–	–	–
Late Iron Age	Y	Y	–	Y	Y	Y	–	Y	–	–	–	–	Y	Y	Y	–	–	–

Shading indicates regions/periods when all three evidence types were available

have been published in recent years, we extracted information from the regional HER about the number of settlement 'sites' recorded by sub-period between 4000 BC and AD 43. This included sites recorded specifically as 'settlement' or 'occupation' and also sites where settlement-related features – pits, gullies, post-holes, huts, roundhouses, structures, etc. – had been identified. In Kent, we used material quantifications from the finds specialist reports of major fieldwork publications as a broad proxy for the overall trajectory of material deposited (mostly) in settlements over the period 4000 BC–AD 43. This included evidence from the East Kent Access Route investigations – comprising 21 extensively excavated landscape zones in north-east Kent (Andrews *et al.* 2011) – and from the A2 Pepperhill to Cobham road scheme – comprising 14 excavated areas across a *c.* 4 km swathe of north-west Kent (Allen *et al.* 2012).

The findings are presented in Figures 4.04 and 4.05. These temporal models show a 'best fit' of the overall level of object deposition in burials, hoards and settlements in Dorset and Kent over our study period within 100-year time slices (see Chapter 3 for an explanation of the fuzzy temporal model method). Given the disparity between the overall number and condition of objects deposited in burials and in hoards – for instance 6403 (often fragmentary) objects were deposited in metalwork hoards in Kent over the Bronze Age, compared to the 283 (often complete) objects deposited in formal burials – and the lack of directly comparable evidence in this respect for settlements, the figures for each different context type have been normalised so that they can be viewed together on the same plot.

Three main observations emerge from this exercise. The first is that the patterning of object deposition in hoards and burials in Kent and in Dorset over our study period is very different. In Kent, the gradual fall of object deposits in graves over the course

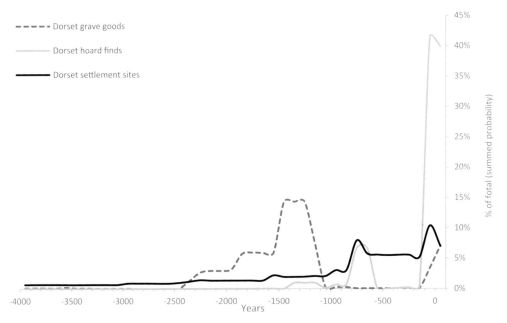

Figure 4.04 Ebb and flow of grave goods, hoard finds and settlement finds in Dorset, 4000 BC–AD 43 (expressed as % of all finds in each category).

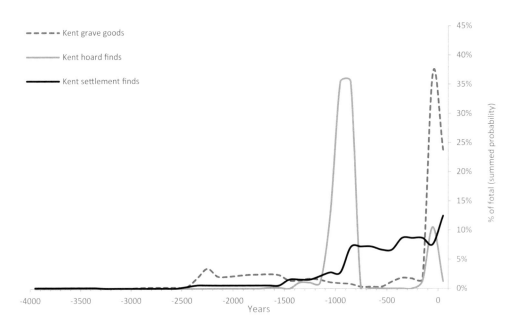

Figure 4.05 Ebb and flow of grave goods, hoard finds and settlement finds in Kent, 4000 BC–AD 43 (expressed as % of all finds in each category).

of the Bronze Age contrasts starkly with the surge in object deposits in hoards in the Late Bronze Age. In Dorset, the Late Bronze Age/Early Iron Age peak in objects deposited in hoards is both later and much slighter than it was in Kent, occurring several centuries after the steep decline in grave good deposition towards the end of the Middle Bronze Age. Indeed, the spike that is visible in the plot centring on the period *c.* 700 BC is made up primarily of a single, exceptional hoard from Langton Matravers, consisting of *c.* 373 complete and 404 fragmentary high-tin axeheads (Roberts *et al.* 2015). Rather than the multiple hoards of fragmentary objects that characterise the Late Bronze Age in Kent *c.* 900–800 BC, this was a massive depositional event that took place during the very final phase of bronze use and the earliest use of iron in Dorset (*c.* 800–600 BC). The main period of object (mostly coin) deposition in hoards in Dorset is in the Late Iron Age. It is possible to interpret these patterns as evidence of regional and chronological differences in attitudes towards the deposition, retention and recycling of metal(work).

In neither study region is there a clear sense that ebbs and flows in grave good deposition relate to those in hoard deposition in any straightforward way. The notion of 'swings' between the respective depositional contexts is harder to support when faced with the kind of data plotted in Figure 4.04 and 4.05, highlighting the (often large) time lapses between depositional peaks and troughs. The second point to make is that, despite our slightly divergent methods for tracing shifts in the volumes of material deposited in settlements in Kent and Dorset over our study period, the overall patterning for both regions is broadly similar, with levels of 'settlement' material visibility increasing significantly at the beginning of the Iron Age, at broadly the same time as peaks in object deposition in hoards in both regions. Thirdly, it is important to remember the variability in numbers lying behind these plots; as discussed above, the numbers of grave goods deposited overall was very low relative to the number of objects deposited in hoards and in settlements over the duration of our study period – a discrepancy that is easy to overlook given the prominence of grave goods in mainstream archaeological analyses, museum displays and elsewhere.

4.5. Relating burials, hoards and settlements: detailed case studies from Dorset and Kent

We will now shift our scale of analysis and examine, more closely, material relationships between burials, hoards and settlements in periods and regions where detailed scrutiny is both possible and productive – focusing on the evidence from Dorset and Kent during the Bronze Age (Table 4.02). Wider examples from across Britain are considered where relevant.

Relating hoards and grave goods: Early Bronze Age metalwork deposition
The relationship between hoards and burials has been shown to be clearer during the Early Bronze Age than during the Middle and Late Bronze Ages (e.g. Needham 1988).

The final centuries of the Early Bronze Age (*c.* 1700–1500 BC) are particularly interesting in these regions. During this period, similar kinds of objects were deposited both in graves and in hoards (Needham *et al.* 2010, table 1), an overlap that was first recognised long ago (S. Piggott 1938, 88–90). The bronze dagger is of particular interest as it occurs in both contexts. There is, however, no geographical overlap between the distribution of daggers in hoards (or as single finds) and in burials (Gerloff 1975, 155), suggesting that a distinction existed in how they were perceived in different regions. From *c.* 1500 BC until at least the end of the Bronze Age, *c.* 800 BC, the character of metalwork deposition in graves and hoards diverged dramatically (see also Figs 4.04 and 4.05). The number of objects, their completeness and character varied between hoards and burials. As we have already highlighted, this picture is regionally specific – with a greater emphasis on complete objects in Dorset and a preference for fragmentation in Kent – but the most striking distinction is between contexts. The large, often fragmented hoards of bronze tools and weapons that are such a distinctive feature of Late Bronze Age Kent find no comparison among the region's grave goods. By focusing on the Early Bronze Age, when the same types of objects were still being placed in both hoards and burials, we can explore the relationship at a significant crossroad in depositional practices.

Exploring the place of daggers in burials and hoards
Dagger burials of the period *c.* 1700–1500 BC are relatively common in Dorset – there are seven examples in the GGDB, in addition to three examples that are likely, but not definitely, from funerary contexts (Gerloff 1975, nos 161, 174, 178). In contrast, there are no daggers from burials in Kent during the same period. The difference reflects their Wessex-focused distribution overall, with just under half of all daggers of this date from all contexts recovered from sites in Wiltshire and Dorset (based on data from Gerloff 1975 and Woodward and Hunter 2015). The other types of object associated with daggers in burials of this period are remarkably consistent across southern England. In Dorset graves, the dagger from Dewlish G7 (Gerloff 1975, no. 169) was associated with a whetstone, a bone crutch-headed pin and a pair of bone tweezers, while the dagger burial from Edmondsham G2 (*ibid.*, no. 182) included a whetstone, a decorated bone pin, and a pair of bone tweezers. In a third example, from Winterbourne Steepleton (Cowleaze Down), the types of objects and materials typically combined within a single dagger assemblage (the dagger itself, a whetstone, and amber and jet/shale beads) were separated across three distinct burial deposits within an enclosure (Woodward 1983). These assemblages give a sense of a unified burial 'tradition' involving a defined 'set' of objects and materials. Drawing on the wider evidence for contemporary dagger burials across southern England, a range of materials (amber, bone, faience, stone/flint, pottery and bronze) were regularly brought together as assemblages. The variety of materials contrasts strongly with hoard deposits during the same period in Dorset, Kent and beyond, in which metal objects were only deposited with other metal objects.

Daggers were associated with other metal objects in grave assemblages too, including pins and additional daggers. There are three examples of two daggers placed together in graves in Dorset: the poorly contextualised finds from a barrow at Winterbourn St Martin 50A (Gerloff 1975, no. 178), and the more securely contextualised finds from Cranborne G4 (Beveridge House) (*ibid.*, no. 144) and Dorchester G4 (Lawrence Barrow, Fordington) (*ibid.*, no. 145). All three burials combined *both* long dagger blades with a rapid taper of the blade below the hilt, which Needham (2015, 9) has called 5C2 ('Bourbriac') type, with another blade: two with distinctive daggers with broad midribs and grooved decoration (Needham's type 5D) and one with a smaller knife-dagger. The combination of these different blade types is interesting, as the rare 5C2 blades (the only three such daggers recorded in Dorset to date) are considered to be direct imports from Brittany, while 5D type daggers and knife-daggers are thought to be locally conceived and produced objects (*ibid.*, 9). It appears to have been important to associate imported, 'foreign' objects with those of a more 'local' character.

Elaborate bronze pins (crutch-headed, bulbous and ring-decorated) were very occasionally deposited in dagger burials of this period and are very rare in contemporary hoards or settlements. Gerloff (1975, 110–12) has established the strong Continental character of these pins, a connection that is likely to be more significant to their inclusion in the grave than their size or any notions of their limited economic 'value' (*pace* Needham 1988, 245). As with imported French daggers, the presence of exotic bronze pins may have been 'balanced' or complemented by locally conceived and produced 5D type daggers. In Dorset there are no examples of bronze pins of this type, but there are numerous bone pins, many with comparable features to their bronze counterparts (e.g. spiral grooving and crutch-heads). This example of skeuomorphism may be explained in economic terms – as a kind of thrifty practice – but it could equally reflect the transformation of an 'exotic' object into a material more suited to the local funerary tradition.

Turning to hoards of the same period that also contained daggers, there are only six examples from the 19 documented hoards from Britain dating to the period 1700–1500 BC. Half of these contained daggers of a type that were also placed in graves (i.e. Needham's 5C and 5D types). This could reflect a chronological shift away from metalwork deposition in burials and towards hoards, with increasing evidence that the dagger burials started earlier than previously thought (see Needham 2015, 10–11). However, the geographical distinction noted above suggests there was a social or cultural dimension to the difference between metalwork from hoard and burial contexts.

Daggers deployed in hoards were clearly associated with a different range of objects and materials compared to daggers from burials. It is, however, still possible that the occasional presence of funerary-appropriate daggers in hoards created a meaningful link between contexts that otherwise remained quite separate. An interesting feature links the treatment of metalwork in both contexts. Woodward and Hunter's (2015, 32–4) study of the completeness of daggers of this type from burials revealed that they show regular damage to their hilt plates, indicative of the intentional removal of their organic handles prior to deposition. This is in keeping with the treatment of spearheads and axes from contemporary hoards, which were apparently stripped down to their metal components prior to deposition. This pre-depositional practice continued and developed in the course of the Middle and Late Bronze Ages, culminating in the 'fragmentary' hoards that are such a feature of Kent's evidence set.

Overall, daggers appear to have been deployed in quite different ways in burials and hoards. The geographical separation between burials with daggers (focused on Wessex) and hoards (found more widely and especially in regions beyond Wessex) is reinforced by the distinctive material makeup of the respective deposits, with burials containing a wealth of *different* materials compared to the metal-only makeup of hoards. Occasionally, similar forms of daggers occur in both hoards and contemporary burials. It was also a common practice in both settings to remove the organic components of composite metal objects before depositing them. It is tempting to make the most of such connections in order to tell a more coherent or joined-up story; however, by our reckoning the differences between contexts were quite marked, even when similar objects functions (and even very particular forms or types) were involved.

The similarities and differences between daggers and spearheads
The vast majority of spearheads from the Early Bronze Age have been found as single finds or else within hoards (Davis 2012). Most hoards that contain spearheads also contain daggers (daggers usually substantially outnumbering the spearheads) and only two geographically outlying hoards contain daggers but no spearheads (Needham 1988, 237, table 3). In preparing this chapter we examined a substantial new 'Arreton Down' tradition hoard from Westenhanger in Kent (PAS number KENT-0330CE; Treasure case 2019 T962). The hoard included a number of spearheads, one of which is so similar to a dagger blade that it was at first erroneously catalogued as such. The curiously similar appearance of some daggers and spearheads, a feature of the Early Bronze Age metalwork repertoire, is unlikely to be accidental and has the potential to further illuminate the relationship between Early Bronze Age burials and hoards.

Only a small number of spearheads (six from the whole of Britain) have been found in funerary contexts (Davis 2012, nos 28, 30, 42, 45, 47, 52). Most of these were found either outwith secure grave deposits (e.g. from barrow mounds) and were therefore potentially deposited without bodies, or else are not typical of the usual size and form of spearheads found in hoards. Only one grave in the whole of Britain – an inhumation burial from Snowshill in Gloucestershire – contains a spearhead that is typical of non-funerary contexts (Kinnes and Longworth 1985, 297: 1). The grave also contained a stone battle-axe, a bronze crutch-headed pin, and a dagger of 5D type (Fig. 4.06). Both spearhead and dagger are remarkably similar in their shape and in key details of their design: especially the grooved decoration, as well as the presence of three rivets set in a triangle formation – a diagnostic attribute of Needham's 5D type daggers (2015, table 3.1.1). The similarity is unlikely to be accidental and the dagger and spearhead were seemingly conceived and made as a matching pair, or at least as part of a set.

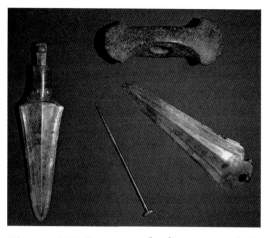

Figure 4.06 Grave goods from Snowshill, Gloucestershire, including an exceptional combination of spearhead and dagger (© The Trustees of the British Museum).

The only spearhead from a burial (of a type that is commonly deposited in hoards) is therefore the only example from the whole corpus that qualifies in almost every respect as a dagger. It is possible that this is why it *could* be deposited within a funerary context. This is a notable observation for two reasons. First, it highlights that there were very particular and detailed conventions or principles governing the selection of objects for deposition in either hoards or burials during the Early Bronze Age. Secondly, the very close relationship between the Snowshill spearhead and dagger highlights broader similarities between Early Bronze Age spearheads and daggers: their blades have similar forms and cross-sections and they could both be decorated with grooved lines and pointillé applied in the post-casting stage. The general similarities may be due to technological development and efficiency: the spearhead was a new weapon introduced during the Early Bronze Age and the dagger probably provided a guide for its form. However, the addition of decoration was clearly well within the control of contemporary metalworkers. Early Bronze Age spearheads were hybrids between local, established, traditions and continental European types, and this novelty may have made them inappropriate for inclusion as grave goods (Gerloff 1975, 130). Spearheads may have possessed 'foreign' connotations and meanings that had to be negotiated and expressed within non-funerary contexts.

The process of differentiation and symbolic negotiation may have been interwoven with the depositional treatment of metalwork: by making conceptual space for a new object type, a physical space needed to be opened for their deposition. The increase in metalwork hoards in southern England from *c.* 1700 BC (Needham 1988, 236–9) was arguably a response to this new set of conditions, instigated by the rapidly expanding availability of Continental European metal supplies, technology and object types. The need to negotiate new meanings for a novel type of object may also account for one of the most interesting features of Early Bronze Age spearheads: the presence of decorated metal collars that appear to be skeuomorphs of the organic features of contemporary dagger handles, complete with multiple false rivets that are inexplicable on objects that were attached by a single rivet through their tangs or by a single peg through their collars (Davis 2012, nos 46b–52, and a new example from Westenhanger, Kent (PAS number KENT-0330CE; Treasure case 2019 T962). This may represent the 'metallisation' of the organic features of daggers, transformed for a new set of practices involving the deposition of new types of metal object.

In summary, at one level, there was a close morphological and conceptual relationship between spearheads and daggers in the later part of the Early Bronze Age – a relationship that is seen within a single depositional context only in the exceptional Snowshill burial from Gloucestershire. At another level, the two object types were viewed as quite distinct from one another, as reflected in the different depositional contexts they almost always ended up within.

Summary
The Early Bronze Age sub-period of *c.* 1700–1500 BC represents an important moment of change in southern England in terms of the increased availability and cultural importance of continental European sources of metal and metalwork, an influence that in general persisted and strengthened during the rest of the Bronze Age, especially after *c.* 1400 BC (Rohl and Needham 1998; Williams and Carlier de Veslud 2019). In a discussion of the wider European picture, Fontijn (2019, 36) noted that the 2nd millennium BC was a period when the contrast between local and foreign objects gained greater cultural significance, as pan-European exchange networks became increasingly important. He also observed that contrasts or tensions between bronze objects with different origins were negotiated differently between regions of Europe (*ibid.*). Sometimes this involved bringing local and foreign objects – and the values and meanings they possessed – together in productive and complementary ways, and sometimes keeping them apart. In the case of burials from the southern Netherlands, Fontijn (2002, 93–5) argued that the foreign origin or appearance of some objects allowed for strict conventions governing grave good selection to be broken. In the case of the Early Bronze Age in Dorset and Kent, we noted rare but significant examples of intersection, where continentally made or inspired pins and daggers were placed in graves but accompanied or 'shadowed' by metalwork with distributions localised to southern England.

Fontijn's observations of local/foreign tensions do not try to predict the particular social, cultural or cosmological meanings that people ascribed to these conventions and contrasts. This remains to be settled on a regional, case-by-case basis. During the period *c.* 1700–1500 BC in southern England, the validity and purpose of grave goods as a means of expressing a range of social and cosmological principles seem to have been brought into question. Careful attempts were made to create a balance between the respective depositional contexts so that the values expressed by grave goods could draw on but not be overshadowed by the novelty or external value of European metalwork. This does not mean that these communities were hostile to those influences or materials; they may simply have been different or incompatible with the values of the funerary context. In contrast, hoarding practices may have provided opportunities to create balance and blending of local and foreign metalwork in the opposite direction so that the novelty and European influences could be emphasised and commended.

The apparent attempt to obtain a symbolic connection and balance between burial and hoard contexts is perhaps best captured by the Early Bronze Age spearhead, a valued, primarily non-funerary object introduced for the first time during this period. Its particular form and decoration were seemingly based on daggers with a strong local and funerary pedigree. The *similarity* between these object types contrasted with their *different* deposition treatment provides a rare glimpse of the overlap between burial and hoard contexts and, perhaps more importantly, evidence of how the contrast or tension between local and foreign metalwork was actively negotiated by Early Bronze Age communities. For much of the Bronze Age (especially the Middle and Late Bronze Ages), the processes of selection and exclusion mean that we can find few tangible connections between burials and hoards. That is both understandable and important. The different contexts appear to have dealt with quite different matters of life and death and we should not suppose they had to be connected by a simple symbolic or cosmological scheme or by pendulum-like swings between sprees of depositional activity. The metalwork of the Early Bronze Age in southern England serves as an important reminder that Bronze Age people lived in a rich and complex material world in which decisions and values were developed not in isolation but with reference to a wider repertoire of materials and depositional practices. It is only by setting metalwork within this more fully contextual *and* conceptual framework that we can identify contrast and tensions and try to interpret the meaning of these patterns.

Relating settlements and burials: revisiting the 'domestic' character of Middle Bronze Age grave goods

As we discussed at the start of the chapter, evidence from the Middle Bronze Age in Wessex has provided a rich source of inspiration for previous theorisations of how grave deposits relate materially to other depositional contexts. The ideas that a particularly close relationship developed between cemeteries and settlements, that this close relationship was essential to broader social changes at this time, and that one important expression of this close relationship is the occurrence of a 'full range' of 'domestic' pottery vessels in both contexts have been widely accepted until very recently (e.g. Barrett *et al.* 1991; Brück 2000, 290). Recent analyses have challenged the notion that Middle Bronze Age settlement and burial practices were closely related spatially (Caswell and Roberts 2018) and have added subtleties to broad parallels that were previously drawn between the spatial organisation of Middle Bronze Age settlements and cemeteries (Brück 2019, 46; see also Johnston 2020, 95–7). However, the idea that a shared ceramic repertoire was a core point of connection between funerary and settlement practices has not been revisited in depth. We attend to this question below in the light of substantial new excavated evidence for this period across southern Britain, and with an open mind as to the significance of this relationship as a basis for building overarching social models. As will become clear, one criticism that can be directed at discussions of relationships between settlements and burials over the last 30 years is that the overall emphasis on *interpretation* over and above direct *empirical analysis* means that the subtleties of settlements and burial assemblages have sometimes been overlooked in important ways.

Material relationships between burials and settlements in the Middle Bronze Age
Given the general acceptance within broad Bronze Age narratives that there was an unusually close relationship – material, conceptual and sometimes spatial – between burial and domestic life in the Middle Bronze Age, it would be easy to assume that the process of examining this relationship is relatively straightforward. This is not actually the case. It is important, therefore, to highlight first some of the challenges involved in approaching this topic.

Within Wessex itself, even early proponents of arguments for the close proximity of domestic and funerary worlds in the Middle Bronze Age acknowledged that it was sometimes difficult to relate precisely the evidence from separate contextual domains. Looking specifically at the 'pairs' of settlements and cemeteries analysed on Cranborne Chase, Dorset (Barrett *et al.* 1991), we can highlight further methodological complexities. The enclosed Middle Bronze Age settlement and cemetery at Firtree Field, Down Farm are perhaps the strongest candidates for being intimately linked based on their close spatial proximity (comparison is also aided by the directly comparable finds collection methods applied to them). However, information about the pottery assemblage from the cremation cemetery at Down Farm was *not* included in the published Cranborne Chase pottery catalogue (Barrett 1991a; pottery from the Angle Ditch settlement located close to Handley Barrow 24 is also missing from this volume). In summarising the evidence from this cemetery at a broad level, somewhat surprisingly and contrary to the overall thrust of Barrett's arguments, Barrett *et al.* concluded that the vessels used in the Down Farm cremation burials were 'restricted to cemetery use' (1991, 224). Additionally, the only grave good from the small inhumation cemetery at Down Farm was a pierced shell necklace found with a child burial, an object which had no parallels within the settlement assemblage (*ibid.*, 214).

Evidence from the South Lodge Middle Bronze Age enclosed settlement and cremation cemetery, located just over 100m apart (and just outside our Dorset case study area), was central to the arguments of Barrett *et al.* (1991) regarding the proximity of funerary and domestic worlds. Although the cemetery was excavated in the late 19th century, and the settlement in both the late 19th and 20th centuries, both were well recorded for the times of excavation and produced substantial quantities of material for analysis. Unfortunately, the 19th century excavators' finds retention method was much more selective than that of their 20th century counterparts. Barrett's attempt to 'shed the tyranny of typology' that characterised Culture Historical approaches to material analysis, and thus to eschew approaches requiring a 'detailed comparanda of traits' (1991a, 207; Barrett's pottery catalogue, frustratingly to our minds, includes information on fabric types but not on form, decorative traits, vessel sizes or production processes) arguably cut off important avenues for approaching the same social processes that he sought to interpret. If we also consider the uncertainties raised about the precise contemporaneity of the cemetery and the settlement at South Lodge (Barrett *et al.* 1991, 183), it is arguably very difficult to compare directly the pottery assemblages from these domains. To introduce a further complexity, arguably the strongest material link between the settlement and the cemetery at South Lodge is the occurrence of similar Middle Bronze Age copper-alloy spearheads (a complete example and a smaller fragment, respectively) in the ditches surrounding the barrow and the settlement enclosure (O'Connor 1991, 234) – objects that were potentially deposited after the main periods of 'funerary' and 'settlement' activity at these sites.

Looking more widely at evidence from other regions of southern Britain where detailed studies have been undertaken of Middle Bronze Age material culture (mainly pottery) from different archaeological contexts, it is clear that difficulties identified above in comparing the character of pottery recovered from cemeteries and settlements are not confined to Wessex. In Essex, for example, the vast majority of cemeteries associated with Middle Bronze Age Ardleigh pottery are located in the north and east of the county while most of the major Middle Bronze Age settlement evidence is in central and southern Essex (Brown 1995, 128). Although more recent large-scale excavations have identified a handful of Middle Bronze Age settlement sites in northern and eastern Essex, the overall patterning has remained the same (Nigel Brown, pers. comm.). Although Brown felt that 'there is no reason to suppose that [Middle Bronze Age] Deverel Rimbury pots from this region were separated into domestic and funerary vessels' (1995, 128), given the geographical separation of Middle Bronze Age settlements and cemeteries in Essex and the imprecise chronological hold on these sites, it is also very difficult to argue that any clear association was being made between funerary and domestic spheres. In Kent, meanwhile, McNee (2012) felt unable to undertake a detailed comparison of the Middle Bronze Age pottery from burials and settlements due to the relative rarity of urned Middle Bronze Age cremation burials in this region. McNee's comprehensive catalogue of Middle Bronze Age pottery from Kent included 13 sites that produced vessels from burial contexts compared to 27 that produced settlement assemblages (2012, appx 1). Moreover, urned Middle Bronze Age cremation burials in this area tend to be singular, or to occur in small groups, often within settlement contexts. Here, the dislocation between the Middle Bronze Age pottery from burials and settlements is numerical rather than spatial or taphonomic.

The main point to stress at the end of this short section is that it is actually quite difficult to compare the material character of burials and settlements in the Middle

Bronze Age. Middle Bronze Age settlements and cemeteries have often been excavated at different times and/or under the different conditions; the direct contemporaneity or association of even closely located settlements and cemeteries is hard to establish (see also Johnston 2020, 97); meanwhile, in some regions, there are significant spatial separations between Middle Bronze Age settlements and cemeteries (Caswell and Roberts 2018) or substantial discrepancies in the volume and quality of material available from each context. Overall, it seems likely that the difficulties we have encountered in comparing Middle Bronze Age settlement and cemetery assemblages are not only taphonomic issues – they also tell us something about past practice. At the very least, the evidence examined here casts doubt on previous assertions about the unusually close material and ideological melding of funerary and domestic material worlds at this time.

Revisiting the 'domesticity' of Middle Bronze Age grave goods in Dorset
Alongside prominent arguments over the last 40 years that there were close overlaps in the material makeup of funerary and domestic spheres in the Middle Bronze Age of southern Britain, it is important to stress that less well-known but more detailed studies have offered an alternative perspective on this topic. Rather than viewing the difficulties involved in approaching the relationship between burials and settlements as debilitating, these studies show the interpretative potential of tackling this relationship empirically.

Needham (1987) was among the first to compare Middle Bronze Age pottery across depositional domains using excavated evidence from Surrey. In this region, he suggested, only certain types of pot from the full domestic repertoire were found in funerary contexts (*ibid.*, 111): funerary assemblages mainly comprised coarse bucket urns, occasionally accompanied by small, knobbed cups; the fineware globular vessels that often featured in settlement assemblages were generally missing from burials.

In a series of studies over the last 25 years and using the substantial corpus of Middle Bronze Age pottery from Wessex assembled for her doctoral research, Woodward (Ellison 1975; Woodward 1995, 198–201; 2009, 213–44) has cast further light on material relationships between Middle Bronze Age settlements and cemeteries in Dorset and Hampshire via detailed comparisons of the types (globular urn, bucket urn, etc.) and size of pots found in each context. Most notably, in her report on the substantial excavated Middle Bronze Age pottery assemblage from Bestwall Quarry, Dorset (Woodward and Ladle 2009, 213–44), Woodward compared the sizes/types of pots from settlement contexts at Bestwall with those of pots from graves in the major nearby cremation cemeteries at Simons Ground (White 1982) and Latch Farm (C. Piggott 1938). Woodward observed the overall small size of the pots in the cemetery at Simon's Ground and the relatively common occurrence of fineware globular vessels: 'small fine vessels which may have functioned as individual drinking or eating vessels, were relegated to the grave with their owners while ... heavy duty storage vessels were rarely selected for burial purposes' (2009, 256–7, figs 172–3). By contrast the funerary assemblage from Latch Farm incorporated a high incidence of large storage pots, including types (distinctive South Lodge-type vessels) that might indicate a slightly earlier Middle Bronze Age date for this cemetery (*ibid.*, 257). Woodward also highlighted the relatively high occurrence of fineware globular urns in the settlement assemblage from Bestwall relative to that found at other Middle Bronze Age settlement sites in Dorset.

Our own attempt to compare the pottery from settlements and burials in a different part of Dorset (the Dorset Downs) that has not previously been subject to detailed analysis reached similar preliminary conclusions. Overall, it was very difficult to compare pottery assemblages from settlements and cemeteries in the Dorset Downs area due to substantial differences in the survival of pots in both contexts and the different ways in which this material had been categorised and analysed over the 20th century. Where comparison was productive, we found that the pottery deposited in burials was, overall, distinctly different in its makeup (in terms of vessel forms, fabrics, and so on) to that from settlement deposits in the same region – the cemetery assemblages included a markedly higher incidence of small cups and of roughly-made vessels tempered with burnt flint. After this initial work, we made the decision not to continue this analysis because it was not really telling us anything new.

In summary, detailed analysis suggests that it is no longer possible to uphold the idea that Middle Bronze Age settlement and burial deposits in southern Britain are united by their inclusion of a very similar suite of pottery vessels. This observation adds an important material dimension to Caswell and Roberts's (2018) questioning of the spatial proximity of Middle Bronze Age settlements and cemeteries and to other recent attempts to nuance understandings of relationships between funerary and domestic practices at that time.

To finish this section, it is worth considering briefly how it might be possible to extend and add further subtlety to the alternative understanding of material relationships between Middle Bronze Age settlements and burials presented here. In the course of compiling this study, we became aware that there were many more qualities of Middle Bronze Age pots that might have been compared productively across depositional domains beyond traditional specialist categories like type and size, which might offer further insight into this topic. Given the sharp increase in the volume of pots being used and deposited in Middle Bronze Age Dorset, it would not be surprising if the ways that prehistoric people engaged with these objects were different to (and subtler than) our own.

One such alternative feature of Middle Bronze Age pots that stood out to us in compiling the GGDB was the occurrence of what are known as 'mend-holes' (see also Section 6.4). These are post-firing holes, made by boring or chipping from the inside and/or outside of the pot, and are typically located to either side of a fracture. Often the fracture itself occurred at the time the pot was fired; in some cases the pot was broken in use and then mended. It is generally thought that some kind of binding would have been threaded through the holes in order to hold the pot together. Mend-holes are a feature of pottery vessels throughout British prehistory but, overall, their incidence is generally low (Cleal 1988, 139). Previous studies have, however, shown that they were a particular feature of pots from certain periods and from certain depositional contexts. Mend-holes are relatively common in Early Neolithic plain bowl assemblages across southern Britain (Cleal 1988, 141) and in Late Neolithic Grooved Ware assemblages from East Anglia/Lincolnshire (*ibid.*, 140). They are virtually absent in (mostly funerary) Early Bronze Age Collared Urn assemblages (Longworth 1984, 8). However, mend-holes occur in higher numbers, once again, in Middle Bronze Age Deverel Rimbury assemblages, at least in some regions (Cleal 1988, 141; Brown 1995; 1999; see however McNee 2012, 103; see also Chapters 5 and 6 for further discussions about broken, mended and wonky vessels in graves). While evidence for the Middle Bronze Age has not previously been subject to detailed contextual analysis, Cleal's study of mend-holes in the Late Neolithic in southern Britain indicated that pots with mend-holes were specifically chosen for deposition in ritual contexts – at henge monuments and in formal deposits (1988, 143).

It is therefore interesting to note that in Dorset only one mend-hole in total was recorded and illustrated in the substantial settlement assemblages that we examined – mend-holes did not occur on any of the pots from Bestwall Quarry, only one possible example was recorded at Cranborne Chase (Barrett 1991a, 220, fig. 8.4, sherd 73), and none at all were encountered in our sample of settlement assemblages from the Dorset Downs. By contrast, a low but persistent occurrence of mend-holes was evident in Middle Bronze Age cemetery assemblages from Dorset – 17 pots with mend-holes were used as funerary containers, while two further examples were recovered from cemeteries where their direct contexts of discovery are not known. Perhaps most interestingly, rather than being distributed evenly, funerary vessels with mend-holes also appear to have occurred at only a handful of the 42 Middle Bronze Age cremation cemeteries recorded in Dorset (it is worth noting that further examples may have been discarded by antiquarian excavators). Notably, this includes a distinctive cluster of seven broken/repaired vessels in the cremation cemetery at Simon's Ground (White 1981), on one of which (the burial urn in Grave 30/31 from Barrow 7) eight separate mend-holes were bored around a single missing sherd (Fig. 4.07). In this last case, it seems likely that, unless the funerary pot was lined, the cremated remains would have spilled through the hole – quite an odd image to imagine as part of a funerary performance.

Further work is needed to investigate our initial observations – for instance by considering taphonomic issues that may have created this patterning. However, it is certainly worth considering the idea that qualities beyond form, fabric and size – pots which had been broken/mended, or with particular decorative features such as crosses on the interior of the base (another unusual feature of burial assemblages in central southern Britain throughout the Bronze Age) – were sought out specifically for deposition in funerary contexts. Regarding mend-holes in particular, it is also interesting to consider why broken/mended pots were chosen for burial purposes in

Figure 4.07 Broken/mended pots used as containers for cremated remains. Top: Deverel Barrow (Miles 1826, pls ii & v); bottom left: Bere Regis (© Trustees of the British Museum); bottom right: Simon's Ground (White 1982, pl. 13; reproduced with kind permission of Dorset Natural History & Archaeological Society).

the context of recent discussions about the parallels that may have been drawn in later prehistory between the life cycles of people and those of objects and buildings (e.g. Brück 2001a; 2001b; 2006; see also Jones 2010). One interpretative option is that Bronze Age people deposited their dead in broken/mended pots because these pots were no longer seen to be useful (Woodward 2009, 256). Another is that broken pots were sometimes actively chosen as the best funerary containers, perhaps because a metaphorical link was made between the broken (or mended) life of the pot and that of the person it was buried with or the community who interred it. Given the likely fragility of mended vessels, it is even possible that pots which cracked during firing were selected specifically for burial early on in their histories. These 'mended hole' pots 'marred and marked for death' due to their breakage in firing, may even have been set to one side for this purpose soon after firing. In this case, the repair could have been used to assert the assignation of these pots to a funerary role, the process of making the mend-holes themselves then becoming significant (Bailey 2018).

Summary

In this section we have revisited the highly pervasive ideas that there was a significant degree of cross-referencing between funerary and settlement domains, both materially and conceptually, during the Middle Bronze Age in southern Britain – the point at which settlement evidence also becomes much more visible in the archaeological record – and that this close relationship is exemplified by evidence from pottery assemblages. In so doing, we have highlighted the previously underplayed complexities involved in making direct comparisons between settlement and cemetery material repertoires. Drawing on detailed studies of the pottery from both contexts, we have argued that material relationships between Middle Bronze Age settlements and burials in southern Britain were more complicated, and arguably more interesting, than has previously been acknowledged. The pots buried with the dead in the Middle Bronze Age overlapped in character with, but were generally distinctly different from, those used and deposited in settlements. Ideas about the right kind of pots to use in funerals, and how to deposit them, varied from cemetery to cemetery. We have also highlighted the importance of looking beyond traditional analytical categories in comparing the material makeup of different depositional contexts. Overall, it is certainly possible that the pots deposited in Middle Bronze Age graves in southern Britain referred conceptually to domestic life. However, there is little direct evidence to suggest, as has previously been asserted, that Middle Bronze Age pots were necessarily derived directly from 'living' settlement contexts, or that they can be used as markers of an unusually close relationship between domestic life and funerary practices at this time. One main point to take from this exercise is that grave goods are distinctive as an evidence set, even when they are seemingly at their most 'everyday' in character. The occurrence of pottery in graves cannot be seen straightforwardly as a material reference to settlement, even when pots are the primary form of grave good. Another key finding is that material relationships between burials and settlements are complex across our study period – this should perhaps encourage us to look more closely at the specific dynamics of this relationship at different times and in different places rather than on identifying it as being straightforwardly close or otherwise mainly conceptual.

4.6. Discussion

In this chapter we have explored the connections between grave goods and the wider 'living material repertoire' (including hoards and settlement deposits) to understand how people constructed and animated meaning through their depositional practices. The character of this repertoire has rarely been explored in traditional archaeological accounts of grave goods. Perhaps one key reason for this is that researchers have, understandably, felt that there is plenty enough to say about grave goods in themselves. Where evidence beyond burials has been considered in relation to grave goods, there has been a tendency to equate the wider 'living material repertoire' too simply and too directly with settlement evidence. Our work within this chapter has shown that all three main 'categories' of material evidence – hoards, burials and settlements – need to be viewed in parallel, not asymmetrically, if we are to begin to understand something approximating to the 'full' living material repertoire of later prehistoric lives. As wide a range as possible of available contexts needs to be carefully considered together to appreciate the full complexity of how prehistoric people decided what objects to bury with the dead.

There are several methodological and interpretative challenges involved in pursuing more dynamic and contextually rich interpretations of grave goods. It is, for instance, particularly difficult to assemble data that could be compared as 'like for like' across different depositional contexts. Having gathered the datasets together, it is tempting to over-emphasise the points of similarity at the expense of difference and divergence. We have attempted to move beyond these potential shortcomings by using temporal models that illustrates the relationships between overall levels of object deposition across different contexts. Our analysis of the ebbs and flows of material deposited in different contexts in Dorset and Kent showed that peaks in the deposition of grave goods did not neatly correlate with troughs (or indeed peaks) in the deposition of objects in hoards and/or settlement. Rather, there were significant regional and chronological differences. There is, however, a clear correlation between the *volume* of material deposited in hoards and settlements at the end of the Bronze Age: the number of objects deposited in graves was consistently lower, highlighting the more particular character of grave goods. These are points of similarity and difference that we could not have confidently charted without undertaking broad brush yet empirically grounded, cross-context data analysis.

In comparing the makeup of objects deposited in graves, hoards and settlements in Middle Bronze Age Dorset, we observed the sheer diversity of objects from settlements compared to those from burials and hoards. This allowed us to question the received wisdom that settlement and burial were closely and straightforwardly connected during this period, especially in that region. Instead, we argued that the relationship between all three contexts was more complex, nuanced and interesting than previously thought. It was apparent that certain objects and materials were deposited only in certain contexts, while others – notably pots, beads and pins – transcended contexts, providing the possibility of insight into how the separate domains overlapped and were related and distinguished in people's thoughts and worldviews.

Overall, an important conclusion of this multi-stranded analysis is that grave goods possess an important and far-reaching distinctiveness and integrity as a depositional category in their own right, not only for archaeologists today but also in prehistory. There is certainly reason to believe that sometimes the objects placed in graves may have 'cited' or reflected settlement or hoarding practices. However, our analysis of some of the most telling overlaps also highlighted important distinctions. The material connections that we identified between hoards and burials over our study period were both extremely rare and mostly quite abstract. Despite persistent efforts over the last 30-40 years to seek points of association between hoards and burials, our own analysis emphasised more clearly the efforts that prehistoric people made to create hoards as a separate depositional category. For instance, in our examination of Early Bronze Age metalwork, we observed that the relationship between metalwork placed in hoards and burials was carefully negotiated. Although spearheads and daggers appear so similar in terms of their form and decoration, they were rarely deposited in the same way. Existing accounts tend to stress the overall close physical and conceptual relationship between settlement deposits and burials and the particularly close connection between these domains in certain periods. Our own consideration highlighted both the complexity of this relationship throughout our study period and the subtle, varied and sometimes surprising ways in which prehistoric people made the objects they deposited in graves stand out from everyday practice. For instance, in our examination of Middle Bronze Age pots from Dorset, it was striking to note that mend-holes – a feature that may have been redolent of 'everyday life' and the daily routines of making and mending – were more likely to end up in funerary contexts than in settlements: they may have been specially selected for the grave in a process that combined symbolism and pragmatism.

Finally, we hope to have shown that there is still a lot to learn about the makeup of traditional archaeological categories, including grave goods, hoards, settlement deposits, and so on (see also Cooper *et al.* 2020). Rather than treating them as being analytically coherent and fixed therefore, it seems very important to us that traditional analytical categories are understood as works in progress. Additionally, whatever the limits of these interpretative groups, we would argue that by using them critically, by considering them side by side, and by becoming more sensitive to the interstices and crossovers between them, these categories still have an important role to play in helping us to better understand the material dynamics of later prehistoric lives.

Chapter 5

Small things, strong gestures: understated objects in prehistoric graves

She wondered at first why it mattered so much. How could something so seemingly insignificant give comfort to someone? A ribbon in a gutter. A pine cone on the street. A button leaning casually against a classroom wall. A flat round stone from the river. If nothing else, it showed that she cared.

(Zusak 2007, 343)

5.1. Introduction

The excerpt above, from Markus Zusak's novel *The Book Thief* (2007), is taken from the chapter *Thirteen presents* in which the book's main character – a 13-year-old girl, Liesel Meminger – waits over the sickbed of the Jewish man, Max, who her adopted family have been hiding in their basement on the outskirts of Munich as World War II intensifies around them. Max becomes seriously ill in the winter of 1942; there is an unspoken feeling that the family will soon have a corpse on their hands. As Max's condition worsens, Liesel starts to glean objects which she feels 'might be valuable to a dying man' (*ibid.*, 342) or which, in case he wakes up, might be something to talk about. Beyond the ribbon, pine cone, button and stone listed above, she gathers a trampled football with flaking skin like a dead animal carcass, a feather 'lovely and trapped' in the hinges of the church door, a lolly wrapper containing 'a collage of shoe prints' (*ibid.*, 343), a piece of sky, memorised and scribbled down on a scrap of paper, an injured toy soldier, a finished novel, and a leaf 'like half a star with a stem' which somehow made its way into the school broom cupboard (*ibid.*, 345). Not exactly grave goods, these objects could easily have become so and were, in part, imagined as such. Zusak's remarkable story – from a time and context well outside prehistoric Britain – is an eloquent reminder of how the simplest things can become meaningful in times of grieving.

Deetz's (1977) manifesto for the importance of archaeology in understanding American history, *In Small Things Forgotten*, highlights another essential quality of seemingly insignificant objects. The book's title is taken from the last entry in a Massachusetts court appraiser's log of the belongings of someone recently deceased in

1658. The entry read 'In small things forgotten, eight shillings six-pence', a statement which Deetz understood to acknowledge that small things not only had value, they were also often overlooked (1977, 4). At the time Deetz was writing, such objects rarely featured in museum displays which, understandably, tended to focus on eye-catching discoveries. Rather, their lesser companions were consigned 'to the dump' (*ibid.*, 8).

The identification of small, seemingly insignificant things is one important outcome of the process we undertook on the *Grave Goods* project of logging systematically all the objects deposited formally with the dead from 4000 BC–AD 43. As discussed briefly in Chapters 1 and 2, some 19th and early 20th century excavators were diligent about retrieving and describing the humbler objects from prehistoric grave assemblages and were sensitive to the potential significance of these items to both burial parties and the dead. Due to their perceived lack of value at another level, however, many modest objects were discarded and actively destroyed by antiquarian excavators (see Chapter 6). Others were lost by collectors or in museum holdings. Many more were separated out from the 'more attractive' elements of burial assemblages in museum collections and were sometimes also deposited in different museums. These and further processes of archaeological 'conceptual sorting' have led to a situation whereby many humble objects are still missing from museum display cases and continue to be persistently overlooked in mainstream archaeological accounts. Only very recently have determined efforts been made to revisit museum stores and to reunite 'small things' with their more glamourous burial companions – the small bone point recently reunited with the Folkton Drum in the European prehistory galleries at the British Museum for the purposes of the *Grave Goods* project is a prime example.

Although modest objects dominate the GGDB numerically, therefore, we actually know very little about them – they have evaded public display, general synthesis and detailed analytical attention. For these reasons, and because we, unlike some archaeologists in the past, feel particularly drawn to these items, it is the simple, the ordinary, the often ignored, but almost certainly *not* insignificant objects from prehistoric graves in Britain that we pay specific attention to in this chapter.

5.2. A context for understated grave goods

At the outset, and particularly because this is not a well-trodden subset of evidence, it is important to explain briefly what we mean by 'understated grave goods', the extent to which these have already been considered in existing studies, and also how our own approach differs.

Defining understated grave goods

'Understated grave goods' is, of course, a subjective analytical category. These objects could be identified in multiple ways; they are often only recognisable comparatively – an object which is modest in one setting might stand out in another. Once the potentially relational qualities of 'understated grave goods' are taken into consideration – their operation as part of distributed networks of people and objects which were essential to understanding how they were valued (e.g. Fowler 2013) – these identifications become even blurrier. Importantly, the fact that we recognise these objects as being understated may well be primarily because we do not/cannot understand the values/properties that were attributed to them in prehistory. Groups of objects which might be considered as the underdogs of grave goods analyses, together with recent considerations of these objects, are listed in Table 5.01. Key points relating to these object groups, the extent to which they have been examined

Table 5.01 Summary of subsets of grave goods that might be considered as understated.

Understated prehistoric grave good category	Key recent analyses	Grave Goods project consideration
Objects missing from existing mainstream grave goods analyses (e.g. pottery and flint)	At a regional level: McNee 2012 (LBA/EIA Kent); Pouncett 2019 (Neolithic E. Yorkshire)	Chapter 6 (pottery)
Objects made from less elaborate and/or locally derived materials (e.g. animal bone, stone, clay)	Woodward & Hunter 2015	Chapter 7 & below (objects made of animal bone)
Animal bone occurrences other than objects (meat joints, etc.)	Wilkin 2011; Giles 2012; Brück 2019, 203–5	Chapter 8 & below
Diminutive objects	Waddington & Sharples 2007; Giles 2012; Jones 2012	n/a
Tools	Woodward & Hunter 2015	n/a
Old, worn and broken (biographical?) objects	Ellison and Dacre 1981; Brück 2006; 2019; Giles 2012; Woodward & Hunter 2015	Chapter 4
Burnt objects	McKinley 1997	Chapter 8
Covers, wraps and containers (mainly made from perishable materials or stone)	Brück 2004; 2019, 90; Jones 2010; Giles 2012	Cooper et al 2019
Natural objects (e.g. fossils, shells and pebbles)	Sheridan and Shortland 2003; Jones 2005, 73–122; Brück and Jones 2018; Brück 2019, 169–71	Chapter 7 & below (pebbles)
Objects from periods not known about for their grave goods (e.g. the Neolithic, the MBA)	n/a	Chapter 8 (Neolithic)
Objects that defy straightforward categorisation/identification (e.g. carved/pierced/polished stone and bone/antler objects, baked clay objects)	Woodward & Hunter 2015	
Singular grave goods	n/a	This chapter

in previous analyses and whether or not we consider them to be 'understated' in the context of this chapter are summarised below.

The exposure of various objects made from less exotic materials (bone, stone, and so on) was one major achievement of Woodward and Hunter's (2015) *Ritual in Early Bronze Age Grave Goods* project. This project examined the makeup and biographies of assorted bone and stone objects – bone points, tweezers, buttons, and miscellaneous items; stone 'sponge fingers', whetstones, etc. – from 'rich grave assemblages' that have not previously been subject to detailed analysis. By logging, analysing and describing these seemingly unassuming items in great detail, Woodward and Hunter revealed many of them to be worn, well-handled, polished, covered in nicks and scratches and, therefore, potentially valued by the communities that deposited them. Interestingly, Woodward and Hunter also used the positioning of such objects relative to the body and their occurrence in otherwise lavish burials to reinterpret them as being far from ordinary in the funerary context. Instead, pig/boar tusks, antlers and tubes and points of bone were viewed as the remains of 'elements of special costume' or 'ritual paraphernalia' (2015, 557). Although, in the light of that study, we now have a good empirical understanding of animal remain objects from materially rich Beaker/Early Bronze Age graves, this is not the case more widely for this period or for other times in prehistory. The occurrence and character of bone and stone objects beyond elaborate grave assemblages also remains obscure. Additionally, the important topic of how objects made of animal remains relate to other animal remains in prehistoric graves – animal burials, meat joints, single bones, etc. – is unexplored beyond a regional/period-specific level (e.g. Wilkin 2011; Giles 2012).

Diminutive objects – from the unique miniature polypod food vessel deposited at the right elbow of a young Early Bronze Age woman in Kent (Andrews *et al.* 2015, 52), to the miniature looped and socketed axehead found with a Middle Iron Age burial in grave W.57 at Arras, East Yorkshire (Stead 1979) – are an intriguing aspect of the GGDB. Although these objects are, literally, small and also very interesting, they are not considered in detail here, although attention is given at the end of the chapter to some 'small' and mundane things that may derive their meaning from their place in a cluster or assemblage. In many respects, miniature objects or tiny depictions of human and animal elements on objects *are* obviously visually arresting in their own right, compressing power and concentrating potency in the skill of their crafting (Mack 2007). These objects *do* regularly appear in museum displays (even if it is sometimes hard to spot them), they are often interred as part of relatively rich burial assemblages, and they *have* received recent analytical attention (e.g. Giles 2012; Jones 2012; Waddington and Sharples 2007; see Martin and Langin-Hooper 2018 for a wider consideration of miniature (and broken) objects in the ancient world).

Discussions about object histories – items that were old, worn, broken and/or repaired at the point of deposition – have proliferated in recent studies of prehistoric grave goods (e.g. Olivier 1999; Brück 2006; 2017b, 139–40; 2019; Joy 2010; Frieman 2012; Garrow and Gosden 2012; Giles 2012; Woodward and Hunter 2015; Jones 2016;

Chittock 2021; see also Chapman 2000; for wider considerations of this topic). The identification of 'heirlooms' via detailed scientific/microscopic analysis was a key agenda for the *Ritual in Early Bronze Age Grave Goods* project (Woodward and Hunter 2015, 472). Brück (e.g. 2006; 2017; 2019, 74–6) has led discussions about the potential significance of breaking things and also of depositing bits of objects in funerary and other formal depositional contexts for the Bronze Age. Joy (2010) and Giles (2012) were instrumental in developing subtle biographical approaches for Iron Age grave goods, foregrounding both specific items that were commonly broken/repaired prior to deposition (mirrors and weaponry), and worn, damaged and re-used objects in funerary assemblages more widely. One interesting feature of these studies is that, almost without exception, wear and repair are viewed as evidence of the heightened value of the grave goods concerned – people valued these objects so much that they mended them rather than throwing them away when they aged and broke (see Chittock 2021). It is also worth highlighting that wear and tear are most often sought out on durable objects that are already recognised as being valuable due to their rarity or exotic character (the Mold cape, Bronze Age daggers and jewellery, Iron Age mirrors, swords and chariot gear). Beyond these already special items, broken or damaged grave goods are thought to have been significant because they added drama to funerary performances – pots were smashed, tools were decommissioned, necklaces were split and scattered. Alternatively, fragmentary grave goods are viewed as signatures of prehistoric peoples' partible understandings of personhood – the value of the fragment(s) in this case being a property of its/ their association with unseen/unknowable (and thus archaeologically unreachable) objects or persons.

Old, worn, damaged, smashed apart, wonky, very partially represented and repaired objects undoubtedly formed a major component of the GGDB. Without examining these objects first-hand on a large-scale, however, we cannot add significantly to existing interpretations of these grave goods and they are not considered in detail here. It is worth mentioning, however, that wear, damage, wonkiness and repair are not at all specific to obviously valuable prehistoric grave goods. Perhaps the main group of repaired, wonky or damaged objects in the GGDB is pots (see also Chapter 6). Repaired pots – sometimes extensively/excessively so – occur in graves from at least the Early Bronze Age onwards. The earliest recorded examples in our case study regions are from north-west Britain – from the Early Bronze Age in Gwynedd and Orkney. Perhaps less well known are the mended pots that occur in Late Iron Age graves in south-east England – in these cases glued together with resin (Fig. 5.01). These pots were not clearly part of dramatic or destructive funerary performances. They are also easy to dismiss interpretatively as items that were no longer useful or wanted (Ladle and Woodward 2009, 256) – their potential value beyond the burial party or the deceased is not directly obvious. We might suggest, however, that a systematic search for and analysis of wonky, repaired and/or poorly finished pots (and other 'everyday' objects) could offer new insight to existing ideas about grave

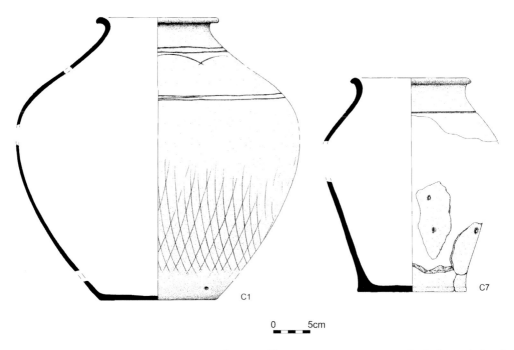

Figure 5.01 Late Iron Age cremation urns from Wickhurst Green, East Sussex; the holes and sherd edges of both vessels were covered with a resin-like substance suggesting extensive repair in antiquity (Margetts 2018, 96; © Archaeology South-East, UCL).

good biographies which, as noted above, have thus far focused mainly on wear and repair on showier things.

In contrast to the old, worn heirloom, we also note, with a few exceptions, a lack of serious attention to the 'newly made' amongst prior studies of grave goods. These objects are perhaps particularly likely to appear wonky, hurriedly finished or simply made. Boast (1995) and Law (2008) offer nuanced considerations of the possible meanings of newly made (roughly finished and decorated) pots in Beaker/Early Bronze Age graves (see also Chapter 6). The constructive and meaningful role fulfilled by mortuary craftwork – things made by the dying during palliative care or made specifically for the dead by mourners – was also a strong theme which emerged from conversations with specialist nurses, hospice volunteers and patients, in the AHRC-funded *Continuing Bonds* project (https://continuingbonds.live/). It is therefore worth rethinking whether some of the wonky, poorly made, apparently hasty craftwork seen on funerary objects beyond Beaker/Early Bronze Age pots (such as the Arras pots, Rigby in Stead 1991, 105, or the Ferry Fryston terret rings, Boyle *et al.* 2007) was not mere expediency: shoddy crafting 'for the funeral', never meant to withstand proper use. Its very appearance may have embodied the fragile last work of a life, or handiwork wrought by grief – distinguished by its appearance from everyday items.

In their detailed consideration of known occurrences of fossils (17 incidences in total) and potential fossil simulacra (e.g. fossil-like pots) in Early Bronze Age funerary contexts, Brück and Jones (2018) did not simply bring this small but important group of understated grave goods to light. They also considered briefly the significance of wider incidences of natural objects – e.g. quartz pebbles – in graves, accepting the complexities involved in identifying 'natural' objects for a period during which understandings of nature-culture relations were almost certainly very different from our own (*ibid.*, 250; see also Brück 2019, 169–71). The role played by quartz pebbles in Early Bronze Age ritual practices (including in funerals) is also a feature of interpretations of ceremonial monuments, particularly in western Britain (see Chapter 7). Within this broad category of 'natural grave goods' (stones, shells, fossils), existing analytical focus has been almost exclusively on the more alluring objects – on glittering quartz pebbles and on fossils or, as Conneller describes them, 'spirit animals emerging from stone' (2011, 253). While not 'particularly "exotic" or visually striking objects' (Brück and Jones 2018, 255), the significance of fossils as grave goods has been linked to their representation of ancestral associations (*ibid.*, 240), or of previously animate beings (*ibid.*, 254). They otherwise gained potency in burials via their 'bundling' (Paukatet 2013) with other materials and practices e.g. through their incorporation in necklaces or in collections of objects (Brück and Jones 2018, 244). Quartz pebbles, meanwhile, are thought to have been valued for their association with the moon, their bone-like properties, and their glittering luminescence (see Chapter 7 for more details). No systematic analysis has been undertaken, however, of the full spectrum of natural grave goods – decaying lumps of rock, rough flint nodules, and so on – over the duration of later prehistory.

Overall, understated grave goods do feature sporadically in studies of prehistoric grave goods in Britain (see Grajetzki 2014 for evidence of the growing recognition of the significance of small things from funerary contexts much more widely). However, substantial elements of this evidence set have not received detailed examination and understated grave goods have only very rarely been a primary analytical focus. Where understated grave goods have been discussed, researchers tend to develop ways of explaining these objects as being *other than mundane* due to their physical properties, their potential association with ritual processes or supernatural beings, their relationships with other (more glamourous) objects, or their operation as elements of distributed notions of personhood. In what follows, we hope to unveil groups of understated grave goods – animal remains, pebbles and lone objects, and small collections of rather mundane objects that gain their valence from being brought together – that have largely been overlooked analytically. These examples are deliberately assorted in their makeup, much like separate stalls in a jumble sale. Our intention is to probe more deeply the role of understated objects in all kinds of prehistoric graves and to ask if it is always necessary to seek out other-worldly associations or alternative world views in order to appreciate their value.

5.3. Animal remain grave goods

Given their prevalence, it is perhaps surprising that animal remains are one of the least widely discussed sets of prehistoric grave goods (Wilkin 2011, 64). No broad synthesis has been undertaken of animal remains as grave goods. Detailed considerations of this topic largely reside within specialist sections of fieldwork publications (e.g. McKinley 1997; Maltby 2002). Overarching reviews of later prehistoric animal remains cover the evidence from graves only fleetingly (Hambleton 2008). Relative to other grave goods, animal remains are, of course, often not particularly attractive visually. It could also be argued that interpretations of animal remain deposits (bones and objects) can be quite limited – these interpretations are easily won and also easily dismissed.

Animal remain grave goods have widely been identified potentially as the remains of funerary feasts, as food offerings for the afterlife (e.g. Brück 2019, 203–5), as amulets (Woodward and Hunter 2005, 47), or as evocations of particular understandings of human–animal/human–landscape relations (e.g. Jones 1998; Brück 2004; 2019, 208; Wilkin 2011, 75; Fowler 2013, 134). Small bones (e.g. frogs, voles) could represent residual inhabitants of chambers, cists and cairns but other diminutive creatures may well be deliberately included in the grave. Animal remain grave goods need not be complete – they include token paws and pierced teeth; claws or heads may well represent skins, furs or talismans. As Bond and Worley (2006, 89) noted for the early medieval period, however, broad explanations of animal remains in burials are often given without detailed consideration of how the evidence itself is constituted. Before presenting our own holistic study of animal remain grave goods in the GDDB, it is worth summarising briefly what has already been said in this regard.

Several authors rightly stress the complexities involved in examining animal remains from burials (see also Bond and Worley 2006; Thomas and McFadyen 2010; Wilkin 2011). Both the recovery and the recording of animal remains in burials prior to the mid-20th century was extremely patchy. Even now, animal remains are not always analysed in detail following their excavation. Animal bone from cremation burials can be particularly hard to identify, especially if only a few bone elements are represented. Certain animals – those with denser, smaller bones and those with horns/antler/teeth that were both more durable and more intriguing to antiquarian excavators – are probably better represented in graves than animals with larger bones (e.g. cattle) that are more fragile and were often broken up before burial, for instance in extracting marrow. We would add to this that only very recently have concerted attempts been made to identify the species of animal represent by animal bone grave goods (e.g. Maltby in Woodward and Hunter 2015, Appendix 3); new methods for making precise determinations (e.g. McGrath *et al.* 2019) have not yet been applied to this dataset.

Two common features characterise existing period-based/regional studies of animal remains from prehistoric burials. First, these tend to consider animal remains from *all* funerary contexts together – from burials, funerary architecture (e.g. burial mounds) and other associated deposits (e.g. pit deposits). Although multi-contextual approaches like this can be very valuable (e.g. Thomas and McFadyen 2010; Wilkin 2011), in some cases the temporal complexity of considering animal remains from different funerary site contexts has been side-lined, blurring the specific ways in which animal remains were employed at distinct points in the histories of these places. Secondly, beyond occasional high-level cross-referencing of these datasets, objects made from animal remains have been analysed entirely separately to other animal remain deposits – a distinction which, as Bond and Worley (2006, 97) pointed out, is not necessarily productive given the potential for these evidence sets to be mutually informative.

Neolithic animal remain grave goods are particularly difficult to interpret due to the 'open' character of Neolithic funerary architecture and the difficulty of establishing direct any relationships between objects and human remains (see Section 8.2). It is also widely acknowledged that detailed re-analysis of animal remains from Neolithic monuments at a wide level is required (e.g. Smith and Brickley 2009, 78; Thomas and McFadyen 2010). For these reasons, and since they are also discussed in Chapter 8, Neolithic animal remain grave goods are considered only briefly here. Animal remains in Bronze Age funerary contexts – in particular those from the Beaker/Early Bronze Age period – have received more detailed attention. Brück (2004; 2019) has offered overarching and richly-illustrated summaries of this evidence for the British and Irish Bronze Age; animal bone objects from rich burial assemblages and associated monuments were examined in detail by Woodward and Hunter (2015). Wilkin's (2011) detailed consideration of (mostly unworked) Late Neolithic/Early Bronze Age animal remains from funerary contexts in Dorset, Wiltshire and Oxfordshire is a rare example of a systematic regional study. Animal remains in Iron Age burials have been understood primarily as food offerings beyond exceptional more dramatic examples (e.g. Sharples 2010, 277; Giles 2012, 134). This contrasts with interpretations of animal remains from other formal Iron Age deposits (e.g. pit deposits) that are often viewed as specific articulations of contemporary understandings of human–animal relations (Hill 1995; Madgwick 2010; Sharples 2010, 256–7).

Our own study of animal remain grave goods covers evidence from the whole of later prehistory. We have considered objects made from animal parts alongside other animal remain deposits. Additionally, we have examined only animal remains deposited directly within graves (those immediately associated with the body or interred in the grave fill). Overall, we hope to develop a broad long-term understanding of how animal remains were involved in burials, to consider the evidence beyond well-known illustrative examples and to focus on previously overlooked animal remain grave goods. One key caveat is that we have necessarily relied on existing animal remain determinations/descriptions from published excavation reports and, where available, more detailed analyses. Close reanalysis of this evidence set would be an important next step.

Broad patterns

Animal remain grave goods make up 12% (720) of the 6044 objects in the GGDB. Of these, 236 are objects made wholly or in part from animal remains (bone/antler/ hide/sinew/shell); the remaining 484 records represent other animal remain deposits – isolated bones, fully/partly articulated and disarticulated whole carcases and articulated animal parts. There are marked differences in the incidence of animal remain grave goods between case study areas and over our study period (see, for example, Fig. 3.05).

Animal remain grave goods comprise just under 30% of all Neolithic grave goods and are a key feature of the evidence from Orkney and the Outer Hebrides. The majority of Neolithic animal remain grave goods were deposited as mixed assemblages within the chambers and cells of long barrows and chambered cairns. Dogs and sea eagles were potentially deposited as burials alongside human remains in Orkney. Occasional animal remain objects deposited directly with human remains in the Neolithic include pins/points, simple perforated objects and necklaces. The human remains from the earliest layers at Isbister chambered tomb, Orkney were accompanied by 21 limpet shells with their tops removed, potentially from a necklace (see Fig. 8.06). Another necklace from Compartment 3 at Point of Cott, Orkney was made of highly polished orca teeth (McSween and Finlay in Barber 1997, 35–6).

Just under half of all the animal remain grave goods in our dataset date to the Bronze Age. Most of these were deposited in Beaker/Early Bronze Age burials. Of these, a slightly higher incidence is recorded in East Yorkshire – an emphasis which almost certainly relates to the better preservation of bone in the calcareous soils of the Wolds. Overall, however, animal remain grave goods make up less than 10% of all Bronze Age grave goods. The make-up of this evidence set is particularly diverse. Objects include bone/antler awls, beads, dagger/knife pommels, necklaces, needles/ pins/points, pendants, picks, spatula, dress fasteners (belt hooks, toggles, buttons), tweezers and perforated objects of unknown purpose. This chimes with the evidence from rich grave assemblages (mainly from the Wessex region) examined by Woodward and Hunter (2015). Animal pelts/leather were used to line pots, to wrap other objects (e.g. daggers) and as shrouds; the pot accompanying one inhumation burial in a barrow at East Lulworth, Dorset was capped with a limpet shell (Warne 1866, 10). Animal remain grave goods were particularly sparse in the Middle Bronze Age when they mainly occurred as burnt and unburnt bone fragments in cremation burials. Although Late Bronze Age grave goods are rare overall (we have recorded just 27 examples in total), over half of these (14) were animal bone deposits – burials and fragments – or objects made of animal bone – pins and a pendant.

Iron Age animal remain grave goods are, once again, widely distributed across our case study areas (with the exception of Gwynedd and Anglesey where Iron Age burials are, in general, lacking) and are diverse in their make-up. Deposits of butchered animal bone and articulated joints are a strong element of Middle Iron Age burials in East Yorkshire and Late Iron Age burials in Dorset. Whole animals were buried as grave goods mainly in the Middle Iron Age in East Yorkshire and the Middle/Late Iron Age in Orkney and the Outer Hebrides. Animal parts were also fashioned into a range of objects deposited in Iron Age graves (see below).

Types and modes of deposition
Animal types
Where it could be determined (for 511 of the 720 animal remain grave goods in the GGDB), 31 different animal species including various types of mammals, birds, reptiles, molluscs and fish are represented in the GGDB (Fig. 5.02). Despite this diversity, almost 90% of animal remains grave goods involve five main species – sheep/goat, pig/boar, deer (red and roe), cattle or dog/fox. Based on how we might categorise these animals in modern terms, two-thirds of the animals represented overall were 'domesticated/ managed' animals (sheep/goat, pig, cattle, horse, chicken, dog, etc.); meanwhile just under one-third were 'wild'. The proportion of wild animals represented in graves also changes over time in a surprisingly non-linear way. In line with Thomas and McFadyen's (2010) re-analysis of animal remains from Cotswold Severn long barrows,

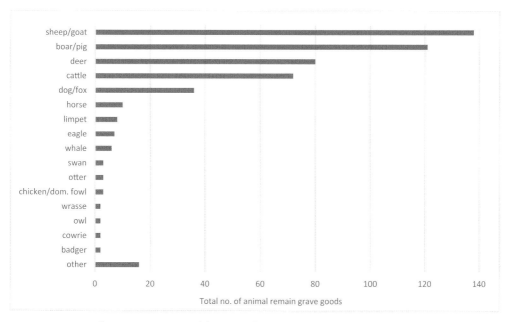

Figure 5.02 Animal species represented by animal remain grave goods in prehistoric graves. 'Other' (i.e. with only one occurrence) includes: beaver, chaffinch, cod, cormorant, crab, curlew, frog, gannet, hawk, helix nemoralis, *oyster, rabbit, seal, toad, vole, wolf.*

a low but persistent level of wild animals is represented in Neolithic graves (Fig. 5.03). Almost half of Beaker/Early Bronze Age animal remain grave goods represent wild animals, mostly deer. This pattern diverges with the evidence from southern Britain analysed by Sykes who argued that wilderness and wild animals may have lost some of their status in this period in the context of broader social changes (2014, 63). Although there is a marked shift towards domesticated species in Iron Age graves, wild animals, again mostly deer, are slightly better represented in the Late Iron Age in Kent. At the very least, this patterning offers an interesting counterpart to evidence for progressive economic dependence on a narrow set of domestic animals over later prehistory (e.g. Hambleton 2008). It is also worth noting that a recent study of animal remains in later prehistory more broadly in southern England also noted a greater emphasis on wild animal species in the Late Iron Age in Kent (Stansbie 2016).

More specifically, a particular emphasis on deer antler grave goods is apparent in the Beaker/Early Bronze Age period across all case study areas. Sheep/goat and pig remains were most commonly used for Iron Age grave goods – a pattern that is clearest for the Middle Iron Age in East Yorkshire where 79 of the 82 examples represent sheep/goat or pig; Fig. 5.03).

Wilkin (2011) also recorded a particularly high incidence of deer (and cattle) remains in his detailed study of animal remains at Late Neolithic/Early Bronze Age funerary sites in central southern England. In this context, he highlighted the possible parallels that were drawn between human and deer seasonal/life cycles, the potential value attributed to antlers as (mostly) shed then harvested objects (rather than as hunted then butchered remains), the power that antlers may have gained as tools used in the construction of funerary monuments/graves and the extent to which antlers might have been viewed as emblems of growth and renewal – themes that were potentially of key importance in funerary ceremonies (*ibid.*, 65). Wilkin also raised the possibility that cattle and deer remains took on a particular role in Early Bronze Age ritual contexts due to their representation, respectively, of farming and of wilderness at a time of major landscape change – the construction of fields and woodland clearance on an unprecedented scale. Alternatively, the significance of deer could have derived from their ambiguous status in this respect – they were neither entirely wild nor entirely managed/manageable (Sharples 2010). We might then ask how and why deer remains lost their symbolic force during subsequent waves of landscape change, such that they were no longer deemed appropriate for formal deposition in graves or more broadly.

As Wilkin, himself, pointed out (2011, 75), these ideas need to be contextualised through further analysis of animal remains and of broad-scale ecological change in the Bronze Age. What our own study makes clear is that deer antlers (and to a lesser extent deer bone) were an important aspect of Beaker/Early Bronze Age grave goods well beyond central southern England. It is also interesting to highlight the diverse ways that deer remains were involved in Early Bronze Age funerary practices. Antlers were

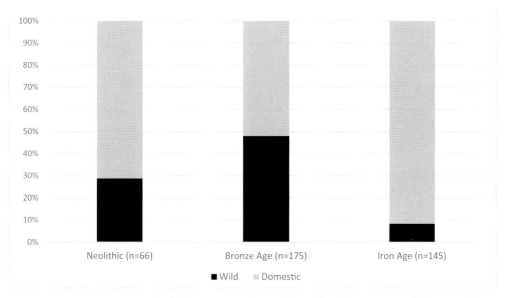

Figure 5.03 Proportions of wild/domesticated animals employed as grave goods, by period.

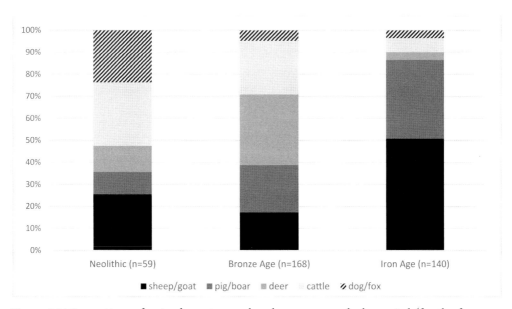

Figure 5.04 Proportions of animal species employed as grave goods, by period (for the five most common animals).

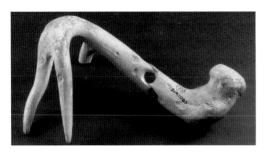

Figure 5.05 Pierced and polished roe deer tine from Oakley Down barrow 18, Dorset (Woodward and Hunter 2015, 130, fig. 4.12.6; © Wiltshire Museum, Devizes).

often deposited unworked in graves, or as 'picks', positioned variously in relation to the body (Wilkin 2011, 70). However, they were also burnt with human bodies on the cremation pyre, e.g. at Queenafjold, Orkney (Ritchie and Ritchie 1974), added unburnt to cremated human remains before being buried (e.g. at Painsthorpe Wold M201, East Yorkshire (Mortimer 1905, 120–1), and shaped into a range objects – pins, pendants, a knife and diverse pierced objects the purpose of which is difficult to determine (Fig. 5.05). Where recently excavated Middle Bronze Age cremation burials have been examined in detail, there is also evidence that deer continued to play a significant role in funerary settings beyond the Early Bronze Age (e.g. at Gwithian Site GM/X Pit 3, Cornwall; Nowakowski *et al.* 2007).

The narrow emphasis on sheep/goat and pig remains as grave goods in the Iron Age stands out from the overall diversity of animal remains found in Iron Age contexts more broadly across Britain (Hambleton 1999; 2008). While the main emphasis of animal species varies between regions and between individual sites, sheep/goat and cattle (rather than sheep/goat and pig) tend to dominate Iron Age faunal assemblages in general, including in Yorkshire (Hambleton 1999, 85; 2008, 38–9). Pigs, horses and dogs are the other main species represented, albeit at much lower levels (Hambleton 2008, 39). It therefore appears that pigs, in particular, were selected very specifically as grave goods in the Iron Age. Meanwhile cattle and horses only very rarely played a role in Iron Age funerary contexts, despite their prevalence more broadly in this period, including in other formal/ritual deposits (Hambleton 2008, 85). This overall under-representation of cattle and horses as grave goods can be contrasted with their spectacular and dramatic inclusion in a few Iron Age graves in East Yorkshire. The sheer volume of Iron Age and Roman cattle on top of the Ferry Fryston chariot burial barrow (Boyle *et al.* 2007) and the Burnby Lane and Mile chariot burials which both contained pairs of ponies – the latter buried 'in harness' in the grave (Stephens forthcoming) are key examples.

Modes of deposition
Our analysis can be taken one step further if we also consider the manner in which animal remain grave goods were deposited – broadly speaking, as wholes (burials), parts (joints and isolated elements), and/or as objects. We use the terms 'wholes' and 'parts' here as analytical devices rather than suggesting that prehistoric people necessarily understood animal remains in this way (Brück 2004; 2019; Fowler 2013).

Objects

Overall, objects made from animal remains were most common in Bronze Age graves (Fig. 5.06). Contrary to previous assertions for the Early Bronze Age (Barrett 1994, 23; Wilkin 2011, 66), however, animal remain objects in burials in our case study areas were not straightforwardly a feature of cremation burials, with other animal deposits (burials, joints and fragments) occurring more commonly in inhumation burials. For a start, animal fragments are almost certainly under-represented in Beaker/Early Bronze Age cremation burials, most of which were excavated by antiquarians and were not subject to detailed sampling. Even in the Beaker/Early Bronze Age period, animal remain objects were distributed fairly evenly between cremation and inhumation burials relative to the overall incidence of these rites in graves with grave goods. One key difference in this respect was that animal bone tweezers, potentially used directly during the funerary ceremony, were only found in cremation burials in our case study areas. In the Iron Age, animal remain objects were actually more common in inhumations than they were in cremation burials. It is also interesting to note that, overall, certain animal types were made into objects more often than others (Fig. 5.07). Where whale remains occur in graves, they are usually part of objects – notably, dagger pommels (Woodward and Hunter 2015, 102, table 3.2.2). Deer remains were also commonly made into objects albeit that many of these were minimally worked antler 'picks'. Pigs, dog and eagles, by contrast, were rarely, if ever, made into objects deposited as grave goods. The cattle-hair braided bracelet with tin-studs from the Early Bronze Age Whitehorse Hill cairn cremation burial, Devon (Jones 2016) also reminds us of

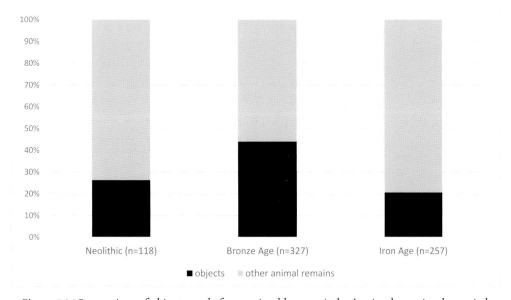

Figure 5.06 Proportions of objects made from animal bone vs 'other' animal remains, by period.

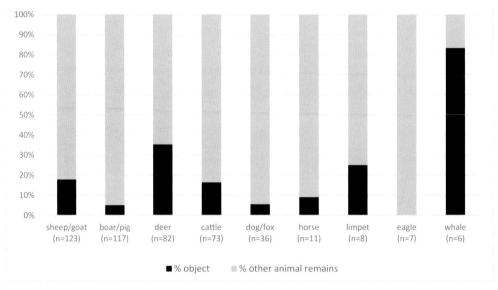

Figure 5.07 Proportions of objects made from animal bone vs 'other' animal remains, by species (for the nine most common species).

how other delicate, and thus often missing, faunal remains were used creatively in fashioning prehistoric grave goods.

Although animal remains deposited as objects in Bronze Age graves have received detailed recent attention (Woodward and Hunter 2015), those deposited in Iron Age graves are much less well known and are worth describing in more detail. The 54 Iron Age animal remain objects recorded in the GGDB show the extent to which animal parts were used both extensively and specifically in this period. Also notable is that most of these objects/object parts were simple and/or would have come into direct contact with the body/other treasured things – the protective and tactile qualities of animal remains perhaps being brought to the fore. Iron Age grave goods were rarely made primarily of animal remains – key examples from Middle Iron Age graves in East Yorkshire include simple bone points, potentially used to fasten shrouds (Stead 1979, 86) but also potentially representing spear- or lance-heads (Mortimer 1905, 151; Fig. 5.08), finger rings, toggles, pendants and beads. Just outside of our case study area, the fox metatarsal and pine martin phalanges from the Early Bronze Age Gristhorpe log-coffin burial (Melton *et al.* 2010) in North Yorkshire might well represent 'lucky' paws or colourful pelts from these wily small predators. More commonly, horn and antler were used for the handles/hilts of Iron Age knives and swords; horse/chariot gear straps and spearhead shaft bindings were made from leather; hide, fleece and animal pelts were used for sheaths/scabbards, shields and other wrappings like the pelt bag (potentially made from otter fur) holding the mirror in the Wetwang Village chariot burial (Hill 2002) – the imprint of these soft furnishings still traceable in their metal accompaniments.

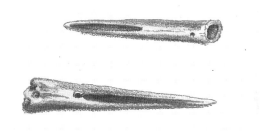

Figure 5.08 Worked bone point from Middle Iron Age grave GR1 at Grimthorpe, East Yorkshire (Mortimer 1905, frontispiece detail).

Wholes

Animal burials form a small but significant component of animal remain grave goods – there are 45 examples in the GGDB. Animal burials (and related animal bone deposits) from Neolithic chambered tombs in Orkney already have a relatively high profile (e.g. National Museums Scotland nd). The occurrence of animal burials as grave goods in the Bronze/Iron Ages is discussed much less often, however. Only dogs were buried as grave goods over the duration of later prehistory (Fig. 5.09). Young lambs were deposited in graves from the Bronze Age onwards. In the Iron Age, animal burials occur more regularly in graves and a wider range of species was deposited in this manner. Focusing on the top five animal species represented as grave goods, it is noteworthy that burials were actually the main way in which dogs were deposited in prehistoric graves. Meanwhile, deer were never deposited as burials – an interesting fact in itself given their prevalence in burials as objects and parts (Fig. 5.10).

The role of dogs as important human companions and, indeed, in shaping human histories from at least the Mesolithic onwards is widely acknowledged (Haraway 2003; Taylor *et al.* 2018; Sykes *et al.* 2020). Dogs' varied and, ultimately, possibly sacrificial role in prehistoric burials adds a novel dimension to these arguments. Interestingly, although in many cases graves that include both dog and human burials appear to convey a sense of equivalence between the dog(s) and the human(s), the specific character of the relationship portrayed varies in subtle ways – being buried with a dog was a personal matter. In the Early Bronze Age cremation burial in Cairn 1 at Porth Dafarch, Anglesey, cremated dog remains were interred along with those of a young woman and a single bronze rivet, potentially from a dagger, in a large Collared Urn (Lynch 1991, 189–90). The urn was inverted over a small ceramic cup that was lined with bracken and contained the incomplete skeleton of a very young child. The burial was capped with a flat stone slab, with pebbles set around the rim. Interesting here is the care that was seemingly taken to present the dog as a particular attribute of the woman rather than of the child or of both the woman and the child. The possible dog buried along with six goats and a man in the grave from Square Barrow 403 at Wolds/Humber (specific site location not disclosed), Yorkshire in 330–204 cal BC, was part of a very different image of death (Stephens and Ware 2019, 28). Details of this burial await publication. In this case, however, the dog was apparently presented as a working animal – a common guardian of the goat tribe. A more homely doggy image

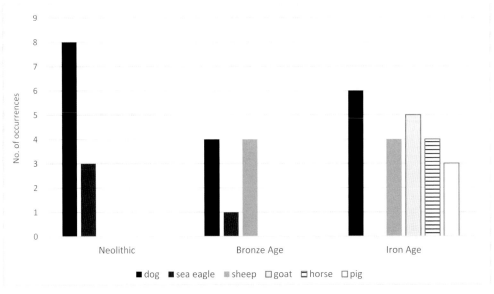

Figure 5.09 Animal burials employed as grave goods, by species/period.

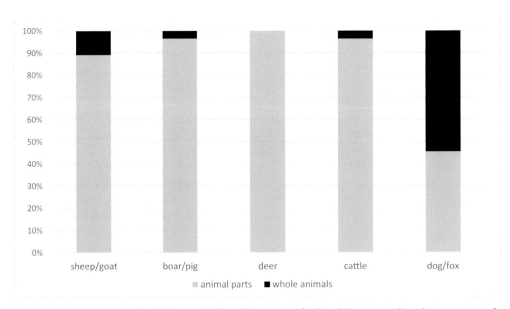

Figure 5.10 Proportions of 'whole animal' burials vs joints/isolated bones employed as grave goods, by species (for the five most common animals).

was created in the formal Middle Iron Age burial at South Dumpton Gap, Kent. Here, a dog was buried with its head resting on a stone pillow. A second stone pillow was placed above the dog upon which the head of the human burial rested (Whimster 1981, 300–1). Perhaps in this burial in particular, the often blurry boundaries between and mutual dependency of human and canine beings is emphasised (Haraway 2003). The role of the dog as guard, guide and companion in death is captured in a poignant page of notes found in a copy of Mortimer's 1905 monograph on prehistoric burials from East Yorkshire, owned by one of us (Giles): in copperplate hand-writing the anonymous note-taker cites Mortimer's observation of the prevalence for burying dogs with infants. 'With a dog', the note goes on, 'the soul can never be lost'.

It is also worth commenting further on the diversity of and the complexities involved in interpreting animal burials in Iron Age graves. Young pig and lamb burials in Iron Age graves, unlike dog burials, probably mostly represent high-end food offerings: their succulence providing a distinctive taste-memory for the funeral feast (e.g. Giles 2012, 114). Other animal burial grave goods come closer, perhaps, to Iron Age animal remain deposits found beyond formal burials. At Hornish Point, South Uist, the remains of a 12 year old boy together with several near complete young sheep and cattle were distributed between four pits cut into a substantial Middle/Late Iron Age midden. While the boy's remains were dismembered and distributed evenly between the four pits, the animals were butchered but kept broadly intact – the two cattle in two separate pits, the two sheep in a third. Not quite straightforwardly animal or human burials, deposits like this emphasise the importance, particularly for this period, of considering the full spectrum of animal remain/human deposits together in seeking to better understand Iron Age human–animal relationships. It is certainly possible that the contrast that has been drawn between meat joints in formal burials and partially/fully articulated animal remains in other formal deposits is woollier (pardon the pun) than has previously been recognised.

Parts

Identifying shifts in the character of animal part deposits in prehistoric graves is beyond the scope of this investigation since it requires detailed reanalysis of these animal remains. In line with Wilkin's (2011) study from the Late Neolithic/Early Bronze Age of central southern Britain, however, it appears that traditionally non-meat-bearing parts (skulls, feet, teeth, antler, horn) were deposited in prehistoric graves more often than meat-bearing elements (limbs, trunk). This certainly suggests that the conceptual role played by animals in funerals was at least as important as their foody role. Taking only traditional meat-bearing elements (limbs, trunk), the diversity of food offerings in Bronze Age graves – involving low numbers of a range of species – can be contrasted with the highly standardised food offerings represented in the Iron Age, particularly in the Middle Iron Age in East Yorkshire (Figs 5.11 and 5.12). While the uniformity of this last practice is already recognised (Stead 1991; Giles 2012, 70),

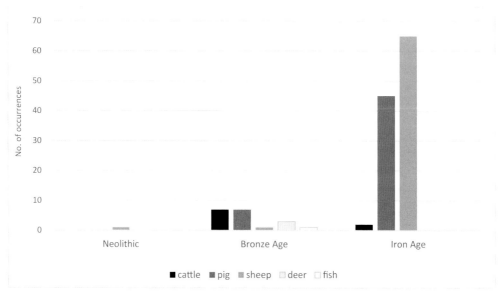

Figure 5.11 'Meat joints' in graves, by period.

Figure 5.12 Meat joint from burial R2 at Rudston Makeshift (© Trustees of the British Museum).

our own study highlights the extent to which this standardisation was also anomalous within the context of food offerings in prehistoric burials more broadly.

Summary
Numerically significant yet interpretatively underplayed, prehistoric animal remain grave goods are notable overall for their versatility. In many cases the animal remains themselves, would have been relatively easy to come by and perhaps, also, to commit to the grave. A wide variety of animals (both closely managed and less so) lived alongside humans throughout prehistory. Even more unusual animal parts like whale bones were probably gathered from beaches rather than 'won' via heroic endeavours. Nonetheless, animal

remains came to matter in prehistoric graves through their working into personally valued objects, their employment in dramatic or sacrificial ceremonies, their capacity to cite imagined landscapes and alternative states of being, and their operation as cherished companions and as food for the living, the dead and the supernatural alike.

5.4. What is in a pebble? Another thing that only people who collect pebbles will understand

In their 2018 rendition of the Radio 3 series *The Essay* exploring how geologies shape the places that matter to people, the BBC listed '29 things that only people who collect pebbles will understand' (BBC nd). Among these 'things', the myriad ways in which pebbles can be valued stands out – for their tactile and visual qualities, the way they clack or clink when collected together, their abundance or rarity – as does the fact that *why* they are valued is highly personal and often quite fleeting. For this reason, the value of pebbles is not always obvious or easily explained. Regarding the specific purpose and significance of pebbles therefore, as one of the authors of the accompanying volume *Cornerstones* put it: 'I like the fact that no one knows, that imagination is required' (Cracknell 2018).

Pebbles, unworked and crudely worked stones of unknown purpose are among the simplest objects found in prehistoric graves in Britain. They occur in just over 3% of burials (97 graves in total) in the GGDB. Rather than being mainly a signature of relatively impoverished graves, they feature in simple, dramatic and materially rich burials alike. Despite their unassuming form, pebbles and stones were often identified as grave goods by antiquarian excavators (see Chapter 2). It is partly for this reason that we are still able to discuss them here. Pebbles and stones performed a variety of roles in funerary contexts. They were used to line graves, to prop up other objects (e.g. pots, see Chapter 6), as assemblages covering the body and as part of the admixture of materials produced during and buried after cremation ceremonies. They were also deposited as objects in their own right, usually, most clearly, within inhumation burials. In some cases they were carefully placed, for instance in the hand. Where the stone type is specified this is most often quartz or flint nodules. However, beach pebbles more generally, chalk, jasper, sandstone, pumice and gypsum have also been identified. Occasionally the pebbles deposited in prehistoric graves are polished or have unusual features such as natural perforations. Often, however, they are entirely unaltered as far as it is possible to tell. Given that the ritual significance of quartz has already been widely discussed (see also Chapter 7), our emphasis here is on bringing to the fore other kinds of pebbles and rocks in prehistoric graves.

Imported quartz and beach pebbles, pumice lumps and slate fragments are a regular element of deposits from the chambers/cells of Neolithic monuments, particularly in Orkney and the Outer Hebrides. Some of these items – like the unusually round beach pebble deposited with the Early Neolithic human bone at Unival, North Uist (Scott 1950) and the quartz/greenstone ball from Curquoy,

Orkney (Davidson and Henshall 1989, 141) – resemble and may even have been seen to refer to finished, crafted objects such as carved stone balls. The one articulated inhumation burial from Grey Mare and her Colts chambered cairn, Dorset was entirely covered by a large collection of small stones (Piggott 1946). A single quartzite pebble was found with the Early Neolithic cremation burial at Kilham, East Yorkshire (Greenwell 1877, 533–6). The earliest (potentially Late Neolithic) burial from Cairn 22, Davidstow Moor, Cornwall was accompanied by a simple notched stone, similar to those that were also scattered across the initial phases of the ring cairn itself (Christie 1988, 118–9).

Examples from the Bronze Age are more abundant, varied and obvious in their operation as grave goods. Pebbles and stones feature particularly strongly in the evidence from Cornwall and Orkney and the Outer Hebrides for this period. A Beaker cremation burial from Allasdale, Barra, Outer Hebrides, was deposited with a single smoothed and polished beach pebble (Cook 2006). An urned Early Bronze Age cremation burial from Whoom Cairn 8, Orkney (Grant 1937, 77–80) was accompanied by three oval steatite objects described as plugs or, alternatively, amulets. In each case, the sides were tapered and encircled by a groove. A polished pebble and a smoothed piece of pumice (identified potentially as a polisher) were recovered from behind the head of the elderly Middle Bronze Age man buried at Pabay Moor, Outer Hebrides (Barrowman and Innes 2009). In addition to the quartz pebbles/fragments that commonly occur in Early Bronze Age burial assemblages and in ceremonial architecture more widely in Cornwall (Jones 2005; see also Chapter 7), we can highlight other assorted pebbles and stones from Cornish grave assemblages. A small pile of beach pebbles was placed at the feet of the crouched Early Bronze Age inhumation burial at Gwithian Site GM/V (Nowakowski *et al.* 2007). The richest of the cremation burials from Boscregan included a small heart-shaped pebble; a naturally perforated pebble was recovered from another burial on this site (Borlase 1879a, 201–4). Two polished pebbles identified as jasper were mixed in with the Early Bronze Age cremated bone at Bosporthenis (Borlase 1872). An assortment of stones and pebbles – including flints, white pebbles and a large quartz crystal – was recovered from the fill of the primary grave at Caerloggas 1 (Miles 1975; Jones 2005, 92).

More widely, iron pyrites nodules and haematite are found in Bronze Age graves across our case study areas. These nodules are usually identified as 'strike-a-lights' due to their association in some contexts with flint 'strikers' – most famously in the Amesbury Archer burial in Wiltshire (Fitzpatrick 2011) but also in Beaker/Early Bronze Age burials across Europe and, within our case study areas, at Wetwang Slack (Brewster 1980, 662; see Teather and Chamberlain 2016 for a detailed discussion of this evidence set). However, many pyrites nodules are not accompanied by the flint necessary for making a spark (and vice versa: one of the burials at Barrow 11, Petersfield contained a flint striker but no pyrites nodule; Needham and Anelay in press). Only 30 of Teather and Chamberlain's 52 British Bronze Age examples of strike-a-lights contained both the striker (usually flint) and the strike stone (usually pyrites). Many pyrites nodules are unworn; some occur in groups (e.g. in Grave P at Barrow 1, Bradstow School, Kent (Hurd 1911)). It is certainly possible given the wider occurrence of pebbles and rocks in graves that pyrites nodules were sometimes appreciated solely in their own right. Alternatively, the act of dissociating the striker and the striker stone in the grave may have been intentional, perhaps symbolising the fact that life's flame could no longer be sparked. Some stones from Early Bronze Age graves were roughly shaped into discs, like the 'much worn and decayed' gypsum fragments from Roke Down, Dorset (Grinsell 1959, 89–90; Fig. 5.13), the perforated chalk discs from Cobdale, East Yorkshire (Mortimer 1905, 319) and the circular pieces of greenstone and sandstone from Collared Urn cremation burials in barrows at Tarrant Keynston and Bere Regis, both in Dorset (Grinsell 1959, 88, 135). Other stones were, more simply, 'rubbed down' like the 'piece of cherty rock' from Painsthorpe Wold Barrow 4, East Yorkshire (Fig. 5.13). Perhaps the most dramatic incidence of rock in a Bronze Age grave comes from a Late Bronze Age pit burial at Cliffs End Farm, Thanet, Kent (McKinley *et al.* 2015, 96–7) where the elderly woman, thought to have been killed by a series of blows to the head, held a small chalk lump to her mouth (Fig. 5.13, right).

One striking aspect of the fewer recorded incidences of pebbles and rocks in Iron Age graves – 18 in total – is that they sometimes occur in materially rich burials. Again, quartz pebbles and flakes are the most common inclusion of this kind in Cornish burials, for instance at Forrabury, where a white, water-worn quartz pebble was the sole finding from one grave (Jones and Quinnell 2014). These basic offerings can be contrasted with the 'iron knob' (Stillingfleet 1846), probably an iron pyrites nodule, found in the sumptuous assemblage (that included gold and amber rings, a delicate blue glass necklace, an elaborate brooch, a toilet set and bronze bangles) from the Middle Iron Age 'Queen's Barrow' at Arras, East Yorkshire (Fig. 5.14): interpreted as indicative of a 'superstituous or talismanic notion' (Stillingfleet 1846, 27) but sadly not retained as a formal 'grave good'. The craniologist and antiquarian Thurnam exhibited other haematite nodules from Iron Age burials at the Danes Graves cemetery, one in the form of a 'cast of a fossil sponge' (Anon 1849). 'Raw' iron 'growing' in or harvested from the chalk may have had a special meaning for these ferrous communities. Elsewhere, the polished pebble that accompanied the fine pottery (including a pedestal urn), half a pig's skull and an iron razor in Late Iron Age Burial 2 at Malmains Farm, Kent (Philp 2014, 11) and the triangular slate plaques found in the mouths of several Middle/Late Iron Age inhumations at Harlyn Bay, Cornwall (Whimster 1981, 376) suggest a rare but under-appreciated dimension to Iron Age grave goods. All these objects probably performed quite different roles (strike-stones, burnishers, whetstones, charms or keepsakes). What is interesting here is that unaltered pebbles and roughly worked stones operated meaningfully, offering, perhaps, a sense of grounding in these otherwise lavish and performative settings.

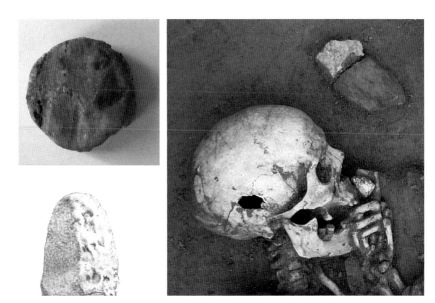

Figure 5.13 Pebbles and rocks from Bronze Age graves. Upper left: 'worn and decayed' gypsum disc from Roke Down, Dorset (© Trustees of the British Museum); lower left: 'rubbed down piece of cherty rock' from Painsthorpe Wold, East Yorkshire (Mortimer 1905, pl. 33); right: chalk lump held to the mouth of the elderly woman buried at Cliffs End Farm, Kent (© Wessex Archaeology).

Figure 5.14 Haematite nodule (and other grave goods) from the materially rich burial at Queen's Barrow, Arras, East Yorkshire (courtesy of Adam Parker and © York Museums Trust; Yorkshire Museum). Note that we have added our own the ferrous nodule (top right) since this was not retained along with the other items.

5.5. Less is more: burials with just one thing

Our interest in single grave goods – objects that were deposited alone with the body in graves – deserves a little explanation. Like Fowler (2013, 81–2) and others (see Chapter 2), we would argue that grave good quantities are not necessarily relevant for determining the wealth and status of the deceased. On the other hand, we do think that it is worth exploring if and how grave good quantities might be relevant in other ways. In the context of this chapter, we ask if things that were buried solely with the body have a particular character or strength in part because of their numerical restraint. Framed differently, if lone grave goods are viewed as objects that were prioritised over and above an array of other objects that might have been interred, could they, at least sometimes, be understood as being of particular value rather than necessarily as being signatures of impoverished graves as they are often portrayed? Accepting the possibility that the lines drawn between objects and people in prehistory were not necessarily clear-cut, we might still see lone grave goods as objects that needed to be set apart from other objects at the point of deposition (Fontijn 2019, 28). It is also possible that by depositing a single object with the deceased, particular emphasis was placed on the relationship between the object and the person, rather than also on relationships between grave goods.

Interestingly, although lone grave goods were originally omitted from Woodward and Hunter's (2015) analysis of materially rich Beaker/Early Bronze Age 'Wessex' burials, the project team later reversed this decision. This was, in part, because they felt that these objects provided important context (e.g. in terms of their spatial distribution) for objects from lavish grave assemblages. Additionally, over the course of their analysis, Woodward and Hunter came to appreciate that graves with just one object could, in some cases, be considered as being 'well-furnished' in themselves (2015, 539). In examining this evidence set, it is important, first, to bear in mind that we are unable to account for objects originally included in graves which did not survive for archaeological scrutiny. Secondly, in some cases – for instance brooch 'pairs', toilet sets, pots with lids – the definition of objects as single items is not clear-cut, even before we consider the possibility of relational understandings of people and objects in later prehistory (e.g. Fowler 2013). These issues do not, we feel, undermine significantly the value of foregrounding the particular qualities of numerically pared-down burials.

At a broad level, 1661 of the 2815 graves in the GGDB for which basic quantifications of objects/bodies is possible included only one grave good – a significant majority (59%). Although the patterning is not absolute, it also appears that burials with lone grave goods were more prevalent at certain times and in certain contexts. Seventy-one per cent of the 536 quantifiable graves with grave goods from the Middle Bronze Age (mostly in Dorset) included just one object, mostly pots. Many more burials from this period (a further 93) included only two objects – a pot and a lid – which might well have been seen to operate as one. A slighter greater emphasis on burials with lone grave goods is also apparent in the Iron Age at a wide level (60% of graves with grave goods, compared with 50% for the Bronze Age), and where cremation rather than inhumation was the primary burial rite, 64% of cremation burials included lone grave goods compared with 54% of inhumations.

More specific emphases on burials with lone grave goods are apparent within these general patterns. Sixty-five per cent of Iron Age inhumation burials in Kent, rising to 75% for the Late Iron Age, included just one object. This subset of objects arguably includes some of the most unusual and interpretatively intriguing grave goods for this period – objects that are not well known from existing grave good accounts. At Mill Hill, Deal, Kent, an Iron Age teenager with abnormal spine growth was buried with a bronze handle, probably from a cloth or leather bag, carried on his back (Parfitt 1995, fig. 56, 160; Fig. 5.15). A copper-alloy bracelet adorned with two crude rings – one pennanular, the other potentially reshaped from another bracelet – was found on the right forearm of an older teenager buried at the same site (Stead in Parfitt 1995, 108–9, fig. 48; Fig. 5.15). A horse skull covered the young baby (6–8 weeks old) buried in a small circular pit in Zone 6 of the East Kent Access Route excavations (Andrews *et al.* 2015, 129).

The seven broad grave good categories most commonly found in all prehistoric graves (pots, animal remains, coffins, jewellery, weaponry, tools and pins/brooches; see Chapter 3) correspond with those found in burials with lone grave goods. Beyond this broad resemblance, however, the character of objects buried alone in graves is markedly different to that of grave goods more widely. Objects that contained, supported or covered the body – mainly pots and coffins – were by far the commonest set of objects deposited as lone grave goods. Iron Age chariot boxes and buckets are key exceptions to this rule. However, in 61% of quantifiable graves with grave goods where the body is recorded as being covered or contained, the object involved was the sole grave good. This pattern can be seen as further evidence of the significant role of containing and covering the body in later prehistoric burials (Cooper *et al.* 2019). In the vast majority of cases (85%), tools and weaponry occurred in graves with multiple objects rather than singly. Perhaps the most unexpected pattern in this respect is that awls were almost always interred with assorted other grave goods – only three (5%) of the 62 awls recorded in the GGDB were lone grave goods. Overall, it seems to have been the case that certain objects – tools, weapons, awls, buckets, chariot and horse gear – were ideally accompanied by other things in prehistoric burials. Other items – jewellery, pins, brooches – were employed more flexibly. If only one thing was prioritised for burial, this was usually a pot or a coffin – simple things that directly covered or contained the dead. Although this could be seen as relating to the practicalities of burial, it is important to stress that the vast majority of prehistoric burials included no objects at all.

Most of all, we would like to highlight here the capacity of lone grave goods to operate not only as context for richer assemblages, but as touching, personal, and powerful assemblages in their own right, even if they are sometimes difficult to interpret specifically. None of the following examples from our case study areas is widely discussed in accounts of prehistoric grave goods. They have been overlooked either because of the overall simplicity of the grave assemblage and/or because the objects themselves are not straightforwardly spectacular or easily categorised. We hope, however, that they will serve to emphasise why we feel that it is very important not to pass by lone grave goods in our attempts to build richer understandings of prehistoric funerary practice.

The hands of the Early Bronze Age man buried in a cist at East Trevelgue, Cornwall were missing. In their place was a beautifully finished granite perforated axe (Borlase 1872, 86; Fig. 5.15). A fine flint blade was found with the Early Bronze Age inhumation burial in the shallow pit at Rudston barrow G63 (Greenwell 1877, 245–7), East Yorkshire. The sole Middle Bronze Age inhumation burial associated with the ring ditch at Down Farm, Dorset was a child with a string of pierced shells (Barrett *et al.* 1991, 214). The chalk spindle whorl accompanying the Middle Iron Age elderly woman buried in Grave R92 at Rudston, East Yorkshire was placed at the right shoulder as if worn as a pendant (Stead 1991, 94, fig. 70; Giles 2012, 162, fig. 5.20). A Middle Iron Age man with a slight spinal deformity, found in a cist on the cliff-edge at Swainbost, North Uist, had a fine iron belt buckle at his hip (Duffy and MacGregor 2007). A pierced polished cattle carpal escorted the elderly Middle Iron Age man buried on the base of a large bell-shaped pit in Zone 19 of the East Kent Access Route (Andrews *et al.* 2015, 169). A string of three blue glass beads adorned the neck of an ailing teenager (with septic arthritis in her left hip) buried in the Late Iron Age inhumation cemetery at Southdown Ridge, Dorset (Brown *et al.* 2014, 190).

5.6. Small sets and bundles

In contrast to these single items, we want to turn finally to a range of burials distinguished by small sets or suites of things. An Early Bronze Age cremation from Harlyn Bay, Cornwall, placed in an unmounded pit burial on the coast, represented portions of up to five children, ranging from *c.* 2–14 years of age (Jones *et al.* 2011). They appear to have been contained in a plant-fibre bag, then placed in a Trevisker pot incised with geometric decoration and capped with a slate slab. The pot bore traces of ruminant dairy fat and the bone was extremely

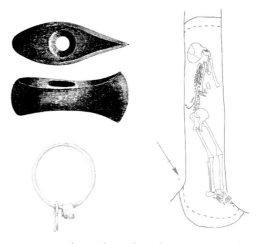

Figure 5.15 Objects buried singly in graves. In the Early Bronze Age at East Trevelgue, Cornwall (top left: axe hammer from cist burial; Borlase 1872, 86) and in the Iron Age at Mill Hill, Deal, Kent (right: Grave 26, a teenage boy with a bag; bottom left: Grave 121, composite bracelet from the right arm of another teenager; Parfitt 1995, figs 48 and 56).

'clean' of charcoal, suggesting it had been picked out or even washed, and amalgamated with a small amount of burned sheep/goat remains. In amongst these fragments of children and animals lay a flint flake knife made from a beach-cobble and other burned flint fragments (suggesting at least some had been part of the pyre), three uncalcined waterworn quartz/quartzite whole pebbles, and a small bronze object. The small wedge or axe-shaped sheet metal artefact with rolled top was old and cracked by the time it was deposited, possibly as a bag-tie or necklace tag, found 'on top' of the bag of bone. A high tin content would have made this a silvery and shiny object but it was also covered in some kind of organic 'aromatic' substance suggesting it was both polished and coated for protection (Ratcliffe in Jones *et al*. 2011, 92). The artefact is described as a 'trinket-type' pendant, capturing its diminutive and attractive nature but lest this devalues such an object, Jones *et al*. point out such items are usually found in association with other impressive grave goods in the Wessex cremation tradition and may be a compressed version of larger, exotic items (*ibid*., 94). Here, the assemblage brings together a suite of understated objects to inter amongst a variety of human and animal cremated remains at the point of burial, with no sense of individuated association.

The interpretation of the object set found in Early Bronze Age inhumation burial 2 at Langton Wold (Greenwell 1877, 138) has intrigued archaeologists for some time, most recently Woodward and Hunter (2015, 446) and Brück and Jones (2018, 244). Greenwell's original account described several 'implements and ornaments' as the accoutrements of a 'woman ... of advanced age' found 'in front of the waist, and lying close together, as though ... placed in a bag' (1877, 18). The litany of small objects includes: three bronze awls (two with tapered facets, one rounded and pointed); a tubular segment of 'shiny and orange-brown' belemnite (Woodward and Hunter 2015, 446); a pierced and worn jet disc bead (possibly a skeuomorph of a quoit-shaped faience bead, *ibid*., 447); a grooved and incised, curving boar tusk implement; a bead carved out of a polished animal tooth root (Greenwell believed it to be deer, 1877, 52); a 'bead'-like item made from a fish vertebra with a central hole; a small, perforated, periwinkle shell (once 'orange-red' in colour; Woodward and Hunter 2015, 446); a fragment of long *Dentalium* shell, which has a natural longitudinal perforation, and three small and glossy 'arctic' cowries (Fig. 5.16). (Greenwell also mentions a beaver's tooth with sharp cutting edge, over 43 mm long (1877, 138) but, strangely, this has not made its way into the British Museum's more recent catalogue of finds: Kinnes and Longworth 1985, 32–3: fig. 2, nor therefore Woodward and Hunter 2015). Bronze awls are most commonly found with adult women and have recently been interpreted as related to tattooing or scarification rather than textile or hide-work: an activity which can have therapeutic intent (as demonstrated in the coincidence between tattoo and notable arthritic joints, in the Chalcolithic 'ice man', Woodward and Hunter 2015, 95–6). Meanwhile, the five pierced objects may have been strung on 'a humble necklace' (Greenwell 1877, 52) which Woodward and Hunter estimate at *c*. 39 mm in minimum length. Their proximity to the other 'unstringable' cache of

Burial 2

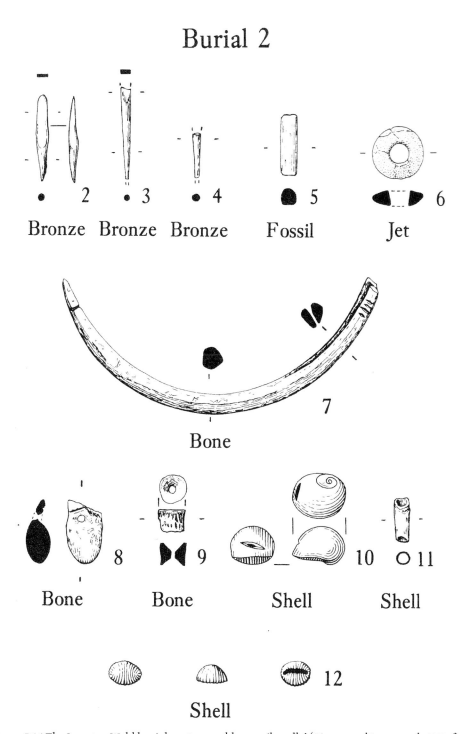

Figure 5.16 The Langton Wold burial no. 2 assemblage or 'bundle' (Kinnes and Longworth 1985, fig. 2).

objects suggests a cluster of individually unextraordinary things (which Woodward and Hunter exclude from their own discussion of 'caches' largely interpreted as tool sets, 2015, 516). How might *we* interpret them given the arguments outlined above?

By themselves, none of these objects is rare or remarkable but cached together, Brück and Jones argue that they seem to represent a perfect analogy for the sacred medicine 'bundles' of the Americas (2018, 244): 'carefully curated assemblages of powerful, elemental and mnemonic objects, or substances ... that articulated a set of larger personal, community or social relations' (Pauketat and Alt 2018, 77). Brück and Jones note that many of the small objects were pierced perhaps to be worn and discussed them as 'powerful things' with particular properties (2018, 244) but they do not elaborate on what these were. What we observe in these objects is that they were largely derived from coastal or marshy locales, both near and far: crystallising powerful connections whether acquired in person or through exchange (see Chapter 7 for a further development of these themes). A common theme of shiny, glossy tactility binds the assemblage together. The teeth, bone and shells may not just have been seen as analogous substances whose iridescence conferred animacy (see Conneller 2011 and our discussion of quartz etc. above); they shared the material character of calcium laid down as lameller growth to produce a distinctive durable 'hardness'. Whilst transformed from living organism to stone, both the belemnite and jet share a parallel kind of lithic 'ossification': material equivalences perhaps, for the other objects (Brück and Jones 2018, 256). In Pauketat and Alt's examination of pre-Columbian Cahokia, they argue that marine shells were seen as a life-giving substance, cropping up in agriculture, ceramic temper and architecture (2018). Perhaps the Langton woman's diminutive and (to our eyes) mundane 'bundle' was used to conjure properties of healing and hardening when new 'bone' had to be made or repaired. Bringing a micro-assemblage approach to this bundle challenges the notion that these were *mere* personal keepsakes by taking their material properties seriously. Once they entered the domain of grave goods, it might suggest (contrary to some of the medicine bundles discussed by Pauketat 2013) that this particular suite of things could *not* be transferred to another person without the loss of its supernatural power: it was in her hands, through her gathering of things over time, that these objects had their charge – forming what we will call an 'indissoluble bond' with the dead (after Giles 2012, 126).

Our final example comes from the collection of glass beads found in the Late Iron Age, Conquest-era mirror burial of Langton Herring, Dorset, associated with a small and gracile individual of around 19–24 years of age, whose osteology yielded 'ambiguous results', probably suggesting a 'woman with narrow android hips' (Russell *et al.* 2019, 200). She had led a fairly sedentary life, devoid of hard labour, and was not a well person: alongside periods of ill-health and malnutrition in childhood, chronic maxillary sinusitis plagued her young life with a respiratory infection active at the time of death and possible signs of scurvy (Smith in Russell *et al.* 2019, 202-3). Ironically, the relatively privileged meat-rich and fine-grained diet detected both through her isotope signature and tooth-wear might have led to dietary deficiencies that took their toll alongside these acquired infections. This may suggest a particularly acute sense of perplexed grief at her young death. Although disturbed by metal-detector discovery, the grave goods here comprise a fine bronze mirror decorated with unusual Celtic art motifs, executed in a rare 'rocked engraver' style (Joy in Russell *et al.* 2019, 208), as well as two copper-alloy brooches, a set of tweezers and a copper-alloy armlet. The burial fits the wider pattern of late 'Durotrigian' high-status inhumations, embodying an increased interest in 'individual power, identity and persona', probably deliberately exuding important cross-Channel connections during the turbulent period of final Conquest and Durotrigian resistance (the burial has been dated to *c.* AD 25–53; Russell *et al.* 2019, 226).

Clearly this is a quite spectacular burial where it is easy to be dazzled by the exceptional grave goods. Yet the objects we want to focus on here are the suite of

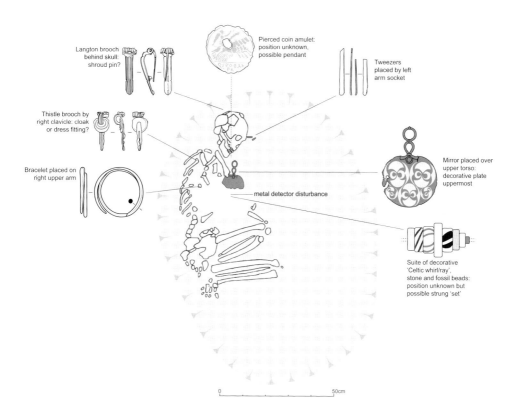

Figure 5.17 The Langton Herring burial and its grave goods. Composite image drawn by Craig Williams (based on images from 'The Girl with the Chariot Medallion', Russell et al. 2019 in the Archaeological Journal, courtesy of Miles Russell, Elizabeth Foulds-Schech and the Dorset Museum © Durotriges Project Bournemouth University).

glass beads, thoughtfully considered by Foulds in that article (numbers in our text refer to the arbitrary ordering in Russell *et al.* 2019, figs 8 and 9, and Foulds 2017) and memorably described by Clare Randall, who saw them soon after excavation, as looking like 'a bag of boiled sweets' (pers. comm.). The suite comprises eight rings of diverse material, appearance and origin. They consist of a large purple-and-white ray bead (1); a large blue-and-yellow whirl bead (2); a medium-sized opaque, slightly yellow bead (3); a small purplish-brown bead (4); a large green, white and brown ray-bead (5); a large and evenly worked Purbeck marble, white-and-grey flecked stone bead (6); a smaller, worn and pitted, white limestone bead (7); and finally, a small, fossilerous flint bead (8), its tiny crustaceans visible in shelly detail on the surface. Some of the beads, like the woman, probably come from Dorset itself (nos 6–8) and it is easy to see these as unremarkable small ornaments made from near-to-hand materials. Yet here we want to point to how their meaning and significance derived from their assembling alongside the 'Celtic whorls and rays' (nos 1–3 and 5), seen by Guido as Continental in origin (1978, 51–3 and 57–9). Two matches for nos 1 and 2 can be seen in stray finds from St Helier and St Aubin, Jersey (on display in the museum of La Hogue Bie) but the closest analogy for this 'set' comes from the sword cist burial at La Hogue au Comte, Guernsey, excavated in 1885 (Burns *et al.* 1996, 103, fig. 70). In that chamber, antiquarians discovered a variety of weapons, scabbard fittings and bracelets accompanied by a small suite of beads: one amber, one jet and five glass (with one stray purple glass fragment). Flecked blue-brown, clear yellow-green, translucent and yellow and greenish-blue: these five glass beads with their amber and jet counterparts form an attractive and tactile set of equivalent size and variety to Langton Herring. The classic signs of clacking and clinking 'Hertzian' fractures on the glass beads (Carter 2016) suggest repeated fingering. Both sets may have been used to form 'charming ties': aesthetically pleasing and apotropaic strands accompanying the twin symbols of Late Iron Age power – the sword and the mirror. Yet they were also deeply personal items: no two beads are the same. Their gathering together emphasised their role as a collection (Belk 1994; 1995, Joy 2016). Such discrete gatherings spoke of the judicious skill, taste, care and time spent in selecting, commissioning, inheriting or accumulating these sets. They did not just define something of their owners' identity: they shaped it, embodying both regional and cross-Channel connections at a time when trade, kinship ties and martial aid strengthened the bonds between these coastal communities. This may also explain why such collections could not be untied, dismantled or passed on, becoming bound to the personality of these charismatic figures. The small, local and apparently mundane thus became meaningful in its collecting and curation, standing as a metaphor for a women conjoined through her connections to a wider world.

Overall, of all the objects discussed in this chapter, collections of understated objects seem to us to signal histories that are carefully thought through and which call for interpretative attention. Gathered together, the diverse origins, memorable journeys, pivotal encounters, enduring relationships, aesthetic leanings and careful choices embodied by these objects are redolent of stories worth telling, as we hope to have shown here.

5.7. Discussion

The keepsake, the talisman, the amulet, the familiar. The small things that the dead would not be without: worn, handled, loved, protective, nurturing and given over to the dead. We hope to have shown that understated grave goods bring us closer to the personality and life or relations of the deceased precisely because they are mundane or intimate. They are much more likely than their more opulent counterparts to represent personal possessions, simple concerns and spontaneous ideas rather than grand and long-considered post-mortem statements. In this sense, as Deetz put it, they 'capture the essence of our existence' (1977, 259). At the same time, small things can be so simple, so personal, so elusive, that many of them are frustratingly hard to reach interpretatively – imagination is required.

In most cases, we have chosen not to offer detailed or elaborate explanations of the small things discussed in this chapter. Sometimes, this is because we felt it was more important to emphasise the myriad ways in which certain underexposed groups of objects (e.g. animal remain grave goods) actually mattered in graves rather than focusing on specifically *how* they mattered – a topic which would be better illuminated via detailed re-analysis and contextualisation. Elsewhere, our explanations were simple because we found it difficult to add meaningfully to existing broad interpretations of the objects concerned, for instance to add substantially to previous discussions about prehistoric peoples' potential appreciations of natural objects like quartz pebbles or fossils. Recent attempts to take the material qualities of objects more seriously and to use this evidence to explore prehistoric value systems and world views are incredibly important interpretatively. Particularly in addressing the simplest of grave goods, however, we suggest that seeking rich meanings can reach interpretative limits and may also sometimes be missing the point. It is possible that the power of some simple grave goods was directly due to their interpretative remoteness. Like Liesel, in the story we considered at the start of this chapter, funerary parties may not always have had a clear idea of why certain objects were important at the point of death: they just mattered. By collecting these seemingly insignificant things and depositing them in the grave, people showed that they cared.

In arguing for the personal, sometimes fleeting, and often hard to reach interpretative importance of understated grave goods, we do not imply that their richer meanings should be left uninterrogated. As noted above, some small sets of objects almost demand interpretative probing. Rather, we suggest, it is essential that we do not over-use existing ideas about modest offerings to the point that they become generic, that we remain alert to simple items or small sets of objects that *can* offer specific new insights and that we bear in mind the possibility that unreachable meanings may be important in themselves. During *Grave Goods* project talks and engagement events, it was often the simplest grave assemblages that evoked the greatest public interest. This highlights a further role of simple personal objects as conduits for linking prehistoric and contemporary approaches to death. It is possible that for contemporary societies in which everyday personal objects are perhaps the most common form of grave good – a pair of glasses, a cigarette, a Goss pot from Blackpool (Hallam and Hockey 2001; Harper 2012) – the placement of a polished beach pebble in the hand of a child in a prehistoric grave seems more tangible and more immediately relevant than the exuberance and the multi-layered meanings of a materially 'rich' grave. Overall, we hope to have shown that, once examined directly and framed creatively, understated objects can make their own interpretative contribution to understandings of burial practices, regardless of their specific meanings.

One unexpected and important realisation of the complexities involved in reaching specific explanations of the humblest of grave goods is that it has, for us, cast light on how little we also understand about more exuberant grave assemblages. With these latter burials, it is much easier to apply sophisticated scientific methods and to develop elaborate theories – there are more elements to work with, to describe and, arguably, to hide behind analytically. However, it is vital to ask if, after all this, we actually come any closer to understanding the specific meanings or purpose of clearly remarkable grave goods than we do of the simpler objects showcased here. Do we really know any more about the role of the Mold Cape in Bronze Age burial practices than we do about that of a polished cattle carpal in an Iron Age grave?

Understated grave goods offer new perspectives on, and an important counterpart to, more glittering objects. We should use them as prompts for seeking out the small, previously unnoticed elements of museum collections and displays. They are neither flashy, exotic, nor immediately exciting interpretatively. However, in their own quiet way they remind us of the importance of bearing in mind everything, of looking closer, and of appreciating the special role of the seemingly insignificant in mortuary contexts.

Chapter 6

Performing pots: the most common grave good of all

6.1. Introduction

Around 3700 years ago in north-west Wales, a young person died. Their body was then cremated and the remains placed in an inverted pot in a pit within a ring cairn at Moel Goedog, Gwynedd (Lynch 1984). The container of these remains was a typical Enlarged Food Vessel but the pot had cracked prior to deposition in the grave. It was mended, as indicated by two drilled holes on either side of the break (Fig. 6.01, left), possibly suggesting that the pot had fulfilled other functions before it became a grave good. The holes were neatly drilled, however, and it is feasible that the vessel cracked while drying out and was repaired before it reached its leather hard state (Frances Lynch and David Jenkins pers. comm.). Yet its rim was also abraded, implying that the pot had a lengthy biography prior to ending up in a funerary context. A more extreme example of a funerary vessel that had had been subject to use comes from Brenig 44, also in Gwynedd, where two-thirds of the rim of a Collared Urn (containing two cremated individuals) had broken off before it was buried (Fig. 6.01, right). In the latter case in particular, the pot may have been kept in circulation for some time, as a treasured possession, memento, heirloom or retained as a repository for two individuals who died years apart. The Food Vessel from Moel Goedog may have been specifically commissioned for the individual it held and was thus destined to serve this role even if it had cracked. Alternatively, it may even have been set aside for a funerary purpose following its splitting in the firing process (see Chapter 4). These examples serve to demonstrate that seemingly 'mundane' objects such as old, worn or imperfect cracked pots in graves, both mattered in the past and invite intrigue in the present.

Prehistoric pots in Britain come in a vast array of forms and sizes, and can be tall, short, squat, slender or bulbous. In stature, they range in size from less than 4 cm in height to over 150 cm. Pots can be shaped into bowls, jars, cups and dishes and exhibit barrel, beaker, bucket, carinated, flowerpot, fluted, globular, hemispherical, rounded, square or straight-sided forms. They are often described in anthropomorphic terms: they have lips, mouths, necks, bodies, bottoms and feet. Pots come in an extensive

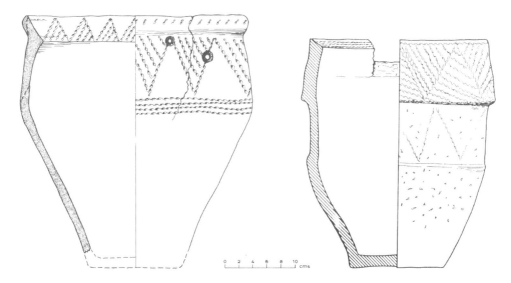

Figure 6.01 Left: Enlarged Food Vessel Urn from pit F8 at Moel Goedog ring cairn (Lynch 1984, fig. 6); right: Collared Urn, Pot B from F20 at Brenig 44 (Lynch 1993, fig. 11.9B; images courtesy of the Cambrian Archaeological Association).

variety of colours, shapes and styles and their diversity increases further when they are decorated. The malleable qualities of clay and its propensity to be moulded into myriad different forms provides potters with considerable freedom of expression to create unique objects.

Pottery grave goods are a sometimes neglected field of analysis and study. As the most common grave good (see Chapter 3), their presence can be taken for granted, and their significance in burial contexts overlooked. For example, in Woodward and Hunter's study of 'rich' graves from the Early Bronze Age, burials that contained pottery only (and/or flint artefacts) were actively excluded (2015, 8), while even the pots from those graves which were categorised as 'rich' were, unlike all other object types, not studied in detail (*ibid.*, 539). In the past, antiquarians and archaeologists relied heavily on ceramic styles to create typologies which were used to help refine burial chronologies. Unwittingly, this functional attribute has perhaps, at times, diluted critical appraisals considering *why* pots may have accompanied the dead and the varying roles they may have played in that context. As grave good finds, pots rarely trigger emotions such as awe, excitement and allure (the 'wow' factor) that many other objects buried with the dead – elaborately decorated swords or exotic necklaces, for example – conjure up. In addition, unlike certain other categories of grave good, pots are rarely considered to impart directly details regarding the gender, age, status or other identity of the deceased.

It is the intention of this chapter to showcase the modest pot: to bring it from sitting passively in the background to a more dynamic position at the forefront of burial practices. Through charting the ebbs, flows, fashions and changing traditions of pottery grave goods in later prehistoric Britain, we can elicit and reassess the various roles that the 'humble' pot may have played and performed between the Early Neolithic and Late Iron Age.

Despite being the most common grave good, pots were without doubt originally even more ubiquitous in prehistoric funerary contexts. Ceramic vessels are relatively fragile and liable to breakage. Pickaxes and mattocks were generally employed in antiquarian excavations, sadly rendering many complete vessels into sherds at a single stroke. Furthermore, pots were not always considered valuable or treated with respect by workmen digging barrows and graves in the past. Compared to a sword or necklace of jet or amber, pots were often seen as mundane or worthless objects and, if they broke, they were rarely kept. A comment by Charles Warne in the 1860s, describing the scene he encountered when visiting the recently excavated Rimbury cemetery in Dorset, provides us with one example of just how many funerary pots did not survive in the archaeological record:

> Between 30 and 40 urns, principally in a state of mouldering decay, were discovered by the labourers ... yet but two were preserved, for it is unfortunately one of the vulgar errors of the rustic, that these urns (or as they designate them, 'crocks') are the depositories of money, and it is to the consequent disappointment attendant on this belief that the destruction of almost innumerable urns is to be attributed. In this instance the men themselves admitted, that being annoyed at not finding treasure, they wreaked their vengeance on the luckless vessels, by placing them as marks at which to exercise their skill in throwing stones ... I shall not readily forget our first visit to this extraordinary spot; the surface of the adjacent ground was thickly strewn with the debris of urns – relics of the labourers' wrath. (Warne 1866, 60–1)

These were, without doubt, far from the only vessels that became casualties of poor, hurried or thoughtless past excavation practices. There are numerous other accounts of pots crumbling or turning to dust on discovery, meaning that they were not described in any detail or retained. That pots remain such an important and abundant category of grave goods is a testament to their ubiquity and resilience.

6.2. Pots in the Grave Goods database

From the moment they entered the funerary realm during the Early Neolithic, pots persisted in the burial record and became, for want of a better word, the most *reliable* grave good; ceramic vessels turn up in funerary contexts more than any other object type (see Figs 3.03–3.05). The GGDB contained a total of 6044 objects and, of these, 2643 were pots. Pots thus comprised 43.7% of all grave goods, demonstrating how prevalent they were.

The dataset collected provides us with an excellent opportunity to trace one category of grave good: to assess how the inclusion of pots in funerary contexts may have changed (or remained similar) in different regions and at different times throughout Britain. Pots were not always a constant feature as grave goods. Rather, there are peaks and troughs in their use as burial accompaniments; times when they were seemingly not relevant contrast with other periods when they were very popular indeed (Fig. 6.02). In addition, our data highlight regional variation apparent in the adoption and prevalence of pottery grave goods (see Fig. 6.05 below).

Employing a diachronic perspective, this chapter aims to pull out several overlooked or hitherto unidentified patterns tied into a range of themes. Following a summary outlining the ebbs and flows of pottery from 4000 BC to AD 43, we investigate a number of different sub-topics. In order to maintain focus and to constrain an almost infinite range of possible research areas, we conduct our investigation into pots primarily within the Beaker/Early Bronze Age period, when grave good pots were arguably at their apogee. We look at the pots caught up in graves from a temporal dimension, considering their sometimes complex pre- and peri-burial biographies, what they were used for (both before and within the grave), as well as the presence of broken pots, partial pots and sherds in burials. We then move on to investigate, in depth, the relative sizes of pots in graves, in relation to the different categories of person buried, to the burial rite involved and through time. We also look at the 'aesthetics' of pots – how decoration changes through time and ways it could potentially have been connected to the person buried. Finally, we

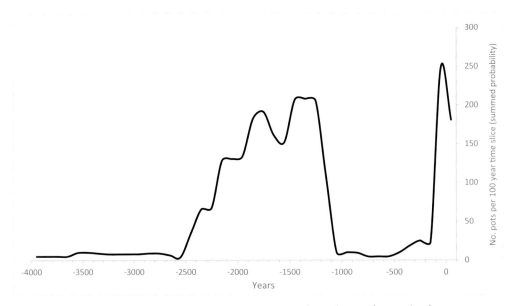

Figure 6.02 The prevalence of pots in burials through time (GGDB data).

turn to the variable ways in which pots were placed in the grave – as multiples, as stacks, and as wrapped and propped objects.

Full typo-chronological discussions of prehistoric pottery in Britain have, of course, been considered in meticulous detail elsewhere (e.g. Abercromby 1912; Simpson 1968; Clarke 1970; Cowie 1978; Gibson 1978; Longworth 1984; Kinnes and Longworth 1985; Manby 1986; 1994; Needham 1996; 2005; Cleal and MacSween 1999; Brindley 2007; Law 2008; Wilkin 2013). We do not wish to underplay the value and relevance of typological approaches. However, by moving away from them to a certain extent here, other qualities that pottery grave goods had, along with their various functions and meaning, can be explored. Detailed typo-chronological analyses tend to focus on specific periods and unwittingly create divisions that celebrate distinctions rather that strands of continuity and similarity (although see Law 2008). By releasing pots from any temporal strait jackets in this chapter, a more diachronic approach to later prehistoric pottery grave goods can be provided. Typologies can inadvertently detract from a wider appreciation of how styles emerge, develop and change through time (e.g. Lucas 2012, 201). Boozer (2015) argued that typology can reduce or even dissolve an appreciation of difference, placing artefacts into rigid schemes and thus artificially creating homogeneity. If used appropriately, however, typologies can also provide an important tool in detecting distinctiveness, difference and relationality in the past (Fowler 2017, 95).

6.3. A potted summary: pots in graves from the Early Neolithic to the Late Iron Age

In order to set the scene, we provide first of all a diachronic overview of the ways in which ceramic vessels moved into and, occasionally, out of focus as grave goods from *c.* 4000 BC to AD 43. In so doing, we also take care to provide some indications of regional variability across our six case study areas *within* periods as well – changes in relation to the styles of pots used and manner in which they were deployed occurred across space as well as through time.

Early and Middle Neolithic
During the Neolithic, pots are rarely encountered as complete vessels in funerary contexts. Most of the vessel types are bowl shaped and open. There has been relatively little consideration of how these pots may have functioned in burial contexts (see Section 8.2 for a detailed discussion). Rarely have distinctions been drawn between those vessels which may had been 'grave goods' (in the sense that they were placed with specific individuals in the tomb) and those which were likely associated with subsequent activities, including tomb closures.

In both Orcadian tombs and East Yorkshire barrows, Unstan and Towthorpe Ware respectively were sometimes encountered as complete vessels which had been placed in direct relationships with specific individual burials. The way in which some Neolithic barrows in East Yorkshire were constructed, and the burials within them 'sealed', gives us an opportunity to assess how pots may have operated as grave goods during this time (see Section 8.2 for details). For example, a Towthorpe bowl was placed upright by the head of one of the four articulated skeletons (Burial C) under the barrow of Aldro 88 (Mortimer 1905, 58–9). Another complete Towthorpe vase stood between the two degraded skeletons at Aldro 94 (*ibid.*, 82). In addition, these burials were accompanied by other objects seemingly operating as grave goods, including flint knives and animal joints. Two complete Towthorpe bowls were noted surrounding the six primary articulated inhumations, buried as a tightly clustered group, at Towthorpe 18 (Gibson *et al.* 2009; Young 2015, 58). In some Orcadian tombs, Unstan and Carinated Bowl vessels are often found semi-complete or as large sherds and were likely whole when they entered the tombs (Davidson and Henshall 1989).

A significant number of Neolithic potsherds in tomb contexts were also scorched, implying that they may have been burnt *in situ* when human remains were cremated within the tombs (often in 'crematoria' in East Yorkshire). Examples of burnt pots in Orkney include Calf of Eday Long, where portions of 34 vessels were found scorched in a large pile in the centre of the chamber floor (Calder 1937), and Isbister where numerous sherds had also been burnt, perhaps even outside the tomb, before being re-introduced (Hedges 1983, 245; see also Section 8.2). Crematoria under some of the East Yorkshire long barrows contained heat-affected fragments of Grimston Ware, often directly mixed with cremated human bone, as noted for example at Kilburn and Market Weighton (Greenwell 1877, 504, 507). As discussed in detail in Section 8.2, the often-fragmentary nature of most of the pots in Neolithic funerary contexts makes it hard to reconcile grave goods with individuals. The fact that most became broken up and fragmented could indicate that they were only relevant as grave goods for a specific snapshot in time – the moment of burial – and once they had served their purpose in burial rites, their subsequent condition, like that of the dead people they were interred with, was no longer considered important.

Late Neolithic

Formal burials are only occasionally archaeologically visible in the Late Neolithic. Grooved Ware pots are rarely found in chambered tombs and more frequently encountered from sites of a ceremonial or ritual nature such as henges and pit/stone/timber circles. While sherds of Grooved Ware pottery have been found in funerary contexts, they tend to occur in closure and demolition events and perhaps relate to activities associated with the blocking and sealing up of tombs, rather than as grave goods *per se*. In Orkney, Grooved Ware pots have been noted, again generally as broken sherds, in sealing deposits or from other secondary contexts at chambered tombs, such as at Holm of Papa Westray North (Ritchie 2009), Pierowall Quarry (Sharples 1985) or Quanterness (Renfrew 1979, 31–8). This is a pattern noted throughout most of Britain (Cleal 1999; Cleal and MacSween 1999) and implies that the deposition of pottery as grave goods during the Late Neolithic was only rarely appropriate (Willis 2019, 357).

Beaker period

The inception of the Beaker period, *c.* 2450 BC, marks the first time when pottery rises to the fore in funerary contexts and really stands out more than other types of grave good. Throughout the Beaker/Early Bronze Age period, pots remained the principal object deposited with burials, although with many regional variations and twists (Fig. 6.03; see also below). Beaker burials are predominantly represented by crouched inhumations interred in flat graves or cists, accompanied by a relatively restricted range of grave goods (Needham 2005, 205; Fitzpatrick 2011, 195–8). Data collated widely across Britain during the *Atlantic Europe and the Metal Ages* project (AEMA 2016) indicates that, while tools and weapons (such as knives, arrowheads or daggers) and ornaments (such as necklaces, toggles and pendants) accompanied the deceased, Beaker pots were the preferred grave good by far. A total of 928 Beaker pots were recorded; the next most frequent objects were knives (87 examples) and barbed-and-tanged arrowheads (80 examples).

Turning to our project case study areas specifically, Beakers are rarely encountered in grave contexts in Cornwall and were only adopted for this purpose after 2000 BC (Jones and Quinnell 2011, 210), 400 or more years later than their inception in many other regions. Just 13 Beakers have been found in burial contexts in Cornwall and

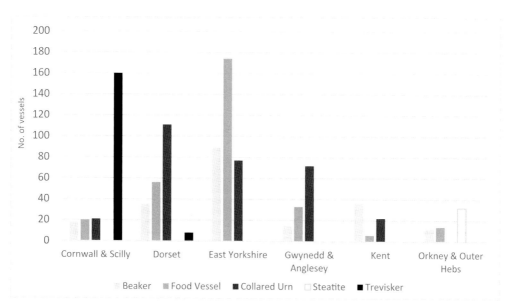

Figure 6.03 Number of Beaker/Early Bronze Age pots by study area. Note that steatite (stone) vessels have also been included for comparative purposes.

only eight of these were found in direct or close association with human remains, predominantly cremation burials. A Beaker accompanying a cremated bone deposit was recorded from Site 22, Davidstow Moor, and other examples include Denzell Down, Carvinack, Crean and Try (A.M. Jones 2005, 18–19). Some of these pots were in a fragmentary state, such as at Lousey (Christie *et al.* 1985, 54). The example from Carvinack is a rusticated Beaker, a type often restricted to the domestic sphere. Most of the Cornish Beakers were poorly made and/or decorated and motifs were often reduced to crude incision or fingernail impression. Cornish Beakers were roughly contemporaneous with Trevisker Ware, although the latter ceramic tradition endures for a much lengthier time frame and may have lasted for up to 1000 years, *c.* 2000–1000 BC (Parker Pearson 1995; Jones and Quinnell 2011, 221).

For this period, it is not only Beakers, but later prehistoric grave goods in general, that are hard to identify in Cornwall. The mainly acidic soils of the south-west peninsula do not help the preservation of unburnt human remains and, thus, direct relationships between humans and objects are difficult to discern. Furthermore, funerary contexts are somewhat different to other regions and objects were rarely deposited as obvious grave goods. Instead, they are more frequently found in broken states and sometimes deliberately fragmented and scattered in barrow ditches or mound layers, rather than accompanying the body. The evidence we have at our disposal may imply that pots (along with other objects) often represented elements of ritual activities or performative events, rather than those of a strictly funerary nature (see A.M. Jones 2005 for a detailed discussion of these issues). Several authors have suggested that Cornish Beakers may not have carried the same significance or inherent meaning that they did in other regions (Boast 1985; 1995; 2002; A.M. Jones 2005). A.M. Jones (2005, 20) stated that 'Beaker burial in Cornwall may have been more closely associated with local cosmologies which were more linked to the veneration or control of sacred places in the landscape'.

In Dorset, Beakers appear at an early date (from *c.* 2450 BC onwards) and are often noted accompanying inhumation burials. They tended to be placed at the foot of the body, bucking the trend with many other areas where they were most commonly located at the head. Examples include an adult male from Canada Farm (Bailey *et al.* 2013) and a child from Bincombe 11 (Prideaux and Payne 1944). Beakers were also relatively common in Kent, and in contrast to most other regions in Britain they were employed as grave goods for an extensive time frame, perhaps as long as 500 years. Recently discovered examples from developer-led excavations include the barrows of Thanet Earth (Rady and Holman 2019) and Northumberland Bottom (Askew and Booth 2006), where they were placed at the extremities of the body (by the feet and behind the heads respectively). Inhumation burials associated with Beaker pots are common in East Yorkshire where vessels were usually placed behind the head of the deceased or above the skull. Numerous examples could be cited, including Cowlam 67 (Mortimer 1905, 243), Garton Slack 81 (*ibid.*, 241) and Painsthorpe Wold 4 (*ibid.*, 115–16).

Only 12 Beakers are known from burial sites in Gwynedd and Anglesey, and only in four cases were these found in direct association with the body; where encountered with inhumations they were usually placed at the extremities. At Llithfaen, a Beaker had been placed at the feet of a crouched adult male (Hughes 1939), and at Merddyen Gwyn, the vessel lay behind the head of another adult male (Lynch 1970, 89–92). It is generally accepted that Beakers were adopted at a relatively late date throughout Wales, often 200 years or more after their initial uptake in parts of southern England and north-east Scotland (Burrow 2011, 75).

Beakers are rarely encountered in formal burial contexts in Orkney and the Outer Hebrides, notably despite the very strong presence of Beaker settlement sites in the latter region. Out of a total of eight examples, only one was found in direct association with an inhumation; in most cases the Beaker pots were broken and some were deliberately fragmented prior to deposition with the cremation burial. At Allasdale, Barra, several Beaker sherds were noted in the fill of one of the graves (Wessex Archaeology 2008a) and a complete Beaker was associated with a degraded adult inhumation at Ensay, Harris (Simpson *et al.* 2003).

Early Bronze Age

After the *more* uniform uptake and adoption of Beaker pottery styles from *c.* 2400 BC onwards, and following the end of Needham's (2005) 'Fission Horizon' around 2100/2050 BC, this homogeneity broke down. More choice and freedom of expression was seemingly exercised in pot making processes. The introduction of Food Vessels as grave goods also coincides with the gradual rise in cremation practices from *c.* 2150/2100 BC onwards. The transition is slow and steady in most regions, as is the switch from Beakers to Food Vessels; the two ceramic types are generally found in similar burial contexts. Occasionally Beakers and Food Vessels were found together in the same grave, such as at Wimborne St Giles 9 (Warne 1866, 16), Bishop Wilton 39 (Mortimer 1905, 140) and Goodmanham G115 (Greenwell 1877, 324–5).

There is seemingly a considerable overlap in all Early Bronze Age ceramic forms in Cornwall. Food Vessels have been recorded from barrows that also contained Beakers, Collared Urns and Trevisker Urns (Longworth 1984, 165–6; Patchett 1944; 1950). This may reflect the fact that many Cornish funerary sites were long-lived, although the activity witnessed at them was episodic rather than continuous. These multi-phased sites make it more difficult to discern individual burial events and re-use sometimes disturbed the residues of earlier activities, creating a messier and more complex picture to untangle (A.M. Jones 2005). Twelve Food Vessels associated with human remains have been recorded in Cornwall, all bar two with cremation burials. Most of these *contained* the cremated remains, as at Carn Kief (Patchett 1950, 57) and Treworrick (Patchett 1944, 38–9). Some Cornish Food Vessels, such as the examples from Colroger and Treworrick, show stylistic similarities with Irish Vase Urns (Patchett 1944, 48), potentially highlighting long-distance coastal connections between Cornwall and Ireland at this time.

A total of 55 Food Vessels are known from Dorset (compared with only 39 Beakers), and like many other parts of Britain, about half were associated with cremation burials, reflecting the steady changeover from inhumation practices after 2100 BC. Small cups often accompanied the Food Vessels, the majority placed *inside* the larger vessel which also contained the human remains. In this region, Food Vessels frequently contained the cremated bone or were placed at the head or along the body of the inhumations.

Food Vessels are markedly rare in Kent. Their scarcity may relate to the continued use of Beakers as grave goods long into the Early Bronze Age; the former were simply not adopted with any enthusiasm. An unusual example was uncovered during excavations along the East Kent Access Road at Ebbsfleet Cottages, accompanying a young adult female inhumation (Andrews *et al.* 2015); it was a unique miniature triple-conjoined Food Vessel whose form and decoration has affinities with Yorkshire vases. In Gwynedd and Anglesey, Food Vessels are more common, and here they were all associated with cremation burials, mainly acting as containers of the remains, as at Bedd Branwen (Lynch 1970, 127–9) and Treiorwerth (*ibid.*, 143–8).

More Food Vessels with burials were noted in East Yorkshire than in any other of the case study areas (a total of 169); the most common placement of these was directly in front of the face of the deceased, in contrast to Beakers which were mainly found behind the head. Compared with other areas where Food Vessels were also relatively common (such as Dorset and Gwynedd/Anglesey), the majority were associated with inhumations, rather than an approximately 50:50 inhumation/cremation split. Of further note is that more Food Vessels accompanied or covered the cremation burials than contained them and most small vessels were also placed over piles of cremated remains. These positions may signify a transitional stage in the switch from pots accompanying inhumation burials to those containing cremated bone.

While only a few Food Vessels (or Beaker/Food Vessel hybrids) are known from Orkney and the Outer Hebrides (nine in total), they were formally deposited as grave goods, all bar one containing cremation burials. They are generally large vessels and all were placed in upright rather than inverted positions, such as at Quandale (Grant 1937, 76, 83) or Sand Field (Downes 2005: 174–5), both in Orkney.

The emergence and adoption of the Collared Urn tradition is staggered throughout Britain. Modelling of the available radiocarbon dates (Sheridan 2007; Law 2008; Wilkin 2013, table 2.6 and fig. 2.5) indicates that the earliest Collared Urns come from Wales (*c.* 2150 BC), followed by Ireland (*c.* 2050), then Scotland and England at roughly the same time (*c.* 1920 BC). Eight of the 13 Welsh dates are from Anglesey, a region where the 'mixing' of Food Vessel and Collared Urn has been noted by several researchers (see Law 2008, 250–62). It has been suggested that this change to Collared Urns was in part related to wider changes in regional and social networks from *c.* 2000 BC, including a switch in copper supplies from Ireland to Wales (Wilkin 2013, 52).

The introduction of Collared Urns broadly matches the period when cremation burial rites rise to dominance and inhumation becomes increasingly rare (see

Fig. 3.13). Few Collared Urns are known from Cornwall (16 examples). All these examples are associated with cremation burials; most directly contain the cremated human remains. By this time, local Trevisker styles of pottery were much more commonly employed in burial contexts. A total of 146 Trevisker Urns have been identified in this region, most (126) in direct association with human remains. With one exception, they accompanied cremation burials and the majority (82%) actually contained the cremated bone. The Food Vessel phase is unusual in that, at this time, formal burials (and thus accompanying grave goods) become much more visible in the region, perhaps indicating a change in burial ideologies associated with the rise in popularity of Trevisker Urns. As Cornwall began to follow its own tradition with Trevisker styles of pottery, there is nonetheless some evidence for these being circulated over long distances. Trevisker pottery made from gabbroic clays has been found in Brittany and northern France and Kent (Gibson *et al.* 1997, 438–9).

Collared Urns were widely adopted in Dorset and were overwhelmingly associated with cremation burials, mainly containing them (73 examples or 72%), and less frequently covering a heaped pile of cremated remains. A few Trevisker vessels were also used in funerary contexts here, all containing cremated bone, hinting at some level of interaction with Cornwall. Compared to preceding traditions, Collared Urns were common in Gwynedd and Anglesey, along with Cordoned Urns. There is a sharp spike in the number of burials identified associated with this style of ceramics (75 compared with 31 Food Vessels); almost all of them contained the cremated bone (90%).

The adoption of Collared Urns in East Yorkshire marks the period when cremation burial finally became the dominant rite there, indicating a seemingly more rapid transition away from inhumation burial than in other regions (where it was adopted more gradually during the preceding Food Vessel phase). Fewer Collared Urns are known in East Yorkshire compared to Gwynedd, Anglesey and Dorset. It is worth stating, however, that a comparatively large proportion (16%) from East Yorkshire accompanied inhumation burials (in other areas the figure is generally closer to 3–5%). For instance, two inhumations were accompanied by Collared Urns at Goodmanham Hill G89 (Greenwell 1877, 294–300) with a further example from Cheesecake Hill (Mortimer 1905, 286–94); in all cases the urns were placed by the head. What the data from this region clearly demonstrate is that the adoption of a particular pottery style, and the adoption of any related burial practices, were not necessarily directly comparable across all regions.

Collared Urns were not adopted in either Orkney or the Outer Hebrides; notably, in the former region, steatite (stone) vessels – which were used in much the same way as ceramics and have thus been included here for comparative purposes – came into circulation at this time. Twenty steatite vessels are known from Early Bronze Age funerary contexts in Orkney, in most cases containing cremated bone and thus being employed in similar ways to Collared Urns further south. They were mainly placed upright in small stone-lined cists, such as at Knowes of Trinnawin (Fraser 1913, 420–1), Curquoy (RCAHMS 1946, 205) and Spur Ness (Sharman 2007). Several of these urns were cracked or chipped and had been repaired, such as that from Geord of Nears (Grant 1933, 72), suggesting that they were considered valuable and kept in circulation for some time prior to deposition with burials. The source of steatite is Shetland, with a principal known prehistoric quarry in Catpund, near Sandwick (Bray *et al.* 2009). This stone was likely transported in a roughly hewn form to Orkney but the distance between the quarries and the destination is at least 130 miles (*c.* 210 km) over the oft-stormy and unforgiving North Sea. This marks a significant reorientation in Orkney's networks of connection and potentially has important ramifications in terms of new influences and interactions during this period (see also Section 7.5). That such long-distance and sometimes perilous journeys from Shetland were involved to secure this material no doubt hints that it was highly valued and desirable. As to why, after *c.* 1800 BC, in Orkney it was deemed appropriate, or simply became more fashionable, to place the dead within stone rather than ceramic containers can only be guessed at.

Middle and Late Bronze Age

After *c.* 1500 BC, in many parts of Britain formal burial becomes increasingly hard to identify. It is, however, very well-attested in our case study area of Dorset; the three main styles of Deverel-Rimbury vessels (Barrel, Bucket and Globular Urns) were associated with cremation burials, often placed in small pits or cists within flat cremation cemeteries (see also Sections 4.5 and 7.6). Although Middle Bronze Age cremation burials in Deverel-Rimbury vessels, or local variations thereof, are encountered in other regions, they are mainly concentrated in Dorset, Wiltshire and Hampshire. With the exception of East Yorkshire (22) and Kent (37), there are relatively few Middle Bronze Age pots in funerary contexts in our other case study areas. That formal burial continued in Dorset and adjacent regions throughout the Middle Bronze Age is significant, as is the fact that pots were deemed the most appropriate funerary accompaniment. In this region, just over half of Deverel-Rimbury urns (a total of 644 vessels) *contained* the cremated human remains (51% of cases where the relevant details are known). A reasonable number (18%) were also inverted over the heaped or bagged pile of burnt bones and covered rather than directly contained them.

In many parts of Britain, the archaeological invisibility of formal burial continued into the Late Bronze Age. Instead, partial or 'token' quantities of cremated human remains are occasionally encountered in contexts of a more domestic nature, such as pits and settlement enclosure ditches (e.g. Brück 1995; 1999; 2019) or in watery contexts (e.g. Schulting and Bradley 2013); seemingly, grave goods were not a relevant element of funerary practice in many areas at this time. Nonetheless, of the 25 recorded Late Bronze Age grave goods in the GGDB, eight were pots (two from Dorset, two from East Yorkshire and four from Kent). In all but one case – an exceptional multiple inhumation burial at Cliffs End Farm Kent (McKinley *et al.* 2015) where one half of a finely decorated, burnished bowl was placed directly front of the face of a juvenile burial – these pots contained or covered cremated human remains.

Early and Middle Iron Age

As with the preceding Late Bronze Age, evidence for formal burial in the Early and Middle Iron Age is rare in most places and the rites afforded to the dead in many cases did not leave traces in the archaeological record. In East Yorkshire, a small number of Late Bronze Age/Early Iron Age cremation burials were inserted into Early Bronze Age monuments in small biconical jars or bowls: in Mortimer's barrow 82 at Garton Slack (Brewster 1980) and two cremated bone deposits at Riggs Farm with another at Painesthorpe 111 (Mortimer 1905, 147 and 128) and Ganton Wold (Greenwell 1877, 174). Finger-tip impressed sherds and part of a 'fine drinking vessel' were also found with an intriguing cremation burial inserted into the top of the Early Bronze Age round barrow at Aldro 108, associated with fused elements of mould-cast swords and daggers, burned, twisted and damaged, as well as two intriguing small lenses of 'glass' or discs of quartz crystal, mounted in bronze sheets (Mortimer 1905, 56). It is evident that the preceding predominant rite of cremation gave way to inhumation; both disarticulated and complete burials have been found in a variety of contexts, including storage pits within Iron Age enclosed settlements and hillforts, such as Danebury, Hampshire (Cunliffe 1984; Sharples 2010) but tracing links between these 'pit burials' and ceramics which might be considered as 'grave goods' is difficult since they are incorporated with other material culture-rich and sterile layers that confound this tight association between corporeal identity and associated artefacts. Semi-formal 'burial' is attested by the presence of flexed unfurnished inhumation burials in pit graves, such as at Suddern Farm cemetery (Cunliffe and Poole 2000) and Weston Down Cottages (Gibson and Knight 2007, 19–21), both in Hampshire. The overall pattern throughout much of Britain suggests that (outside of East Yorkshire and a few, short-lived and sporadic rites, see Harding 2016) during the Middle Iron Age, grave goods of any form, including pottery, were not considered a necessary part of the funerary ritual. Several researchers have suggested that individuals were excarnated or defleshed prior to deposition, explaining their generally disarticulated states (Carr and Knüsel 1997; Carr 2007). Recent osteological analysis of the bone has identified a more complex mortuary sequence that involved a form of protected excarnation, minimising weathering and damage from scavenging, amongst both complete human pit 'burials' and partially articulated human remains, complicating our understanding of even this rite (see Booth and Madgwick 2016).

An interesting exception to these general trends is our case study area of East Yorkshire (Giles 2012) where, out of a total of 73 Middle–Late Iron Age pots (many pots in this region were attributed only to the Iron Age), 64 were directly associated with inhumation burials. Most of these vessels were fragmentary and several lacked substantial parts of their rims. Up to two-thirds of the vessels studied by Rigby had experienced some form of deliberate damage or fragmentation and some could no longer 'stand' (in Stead 1991, 108). They mainly came from small and medium-sized cemeteries, including Cowlam (Stead 1986), Rudston Makeshift (Stead 1991, 6–15), Argam Lane (*ibid.*, 16, 208) and Wetwang Slack (Brewster 1980; Dent 1984). Most were jars, remarkably similar in form and distinguished merely by fabric and not decoration. Several had evidence of sooting or chips and cracks, indicating that they had been used prior to deposition in the grave. Much has been made of the placement of these vessels: Parker Pearson, following Piccini, argued that men were buried with a pot at their feet and women with pots in the area of their heads and hands, which 'may portray a relationship between server/provider and served/provided' helping to constitute gendered role differences (cited in Parker Pearson 1999a, 53). However, a larger study of the position of ceramics in the East Yorkshire graves does not support this model – a more nuanced understanding of body position reveals that although they *tend* to be 'in front' of the deceased, there is no statistically significant gendered pattern (see Giles 2012). The strong association of such jars with the left humeri of sheep, however, suggests the notion of a funeral feast from which a portion was set aside for the dead (Legge in Stead 1991, 143). They are not found in chariot or weapons burials which are, instead, associated with the heads and forelimbs of cooked pork: evoking the strong sense of a particular culinary rite for these more lavish or notable burials. These are not restricted to what Parker Pearson saw as a totemic association with elites (1999a, 60) since age and other attributes also seem to be a factor. In East Yorkshire then, locally made jars seem to have been the appropriate container (and 'dressing') for food for the deceased, in the Great Wold Valley cemeteries, as well as Danes Graves and Eastburn, but they were less common in the Wetwang–Garton Slack burials (Dent 2010). Funerals where a larger mourning party or more distinctive 'taste-memory' might be required opted instead for cooked pork, reminding us of the 1930s headline cited in Chapter 2, celebrating apparent evidence for Yorkshire's long-standing rite of being 'buried with ham'! The ceramic repertoire here is not involved in the structuring of 'diacritical' feasting or class-ridden dining habits – the meat itself was being used to create differences between small-scale and larger events. This forms a distinct contrast to the deployment of pots in the following period.

Late Iron Age

During the Late Iron Age, evidence for formal burial becomes more evident again, in certain areas at least, and many well-furnished burials are known. The range of grave goods is considerably more extensive than previous periods and inhumation burials were sometimes accompanied by a wide array of objects. Unambiguously Late Iron Age burials were found mainly in Dorset and Kent, of our case study areas. Only two outlier examples in East Yorkshire and Cornwall were identified; however, it is worth noting that many burials for this period have only vague (period-wide) date attributions. Not surprisingly, the different funerary practices to some extent influenced the ways that pots functioned as grave goods.

Fewer than half of the 362 Late Iron Age pots associated with burials in Kent were found in direct association with human remains due to the high level of chance discoveries and antiquarian investigations in this region. Those that were directly associated with human remains performed a variety of roles. Most contained the cremated human remains, however, others contained objects, sat alongside piles of cremated bone or accompanied other vessels (e.g. buckets) containing cremated remains. A variety of fineware Belgic-related jars, cups, pedestal urns, cups and butt-beakers were used as containers and examples include Tassells, Quarry Allington (Stead 1976; Whimster 1981, 477) and Arnold's Quarry (Kelly 1971, 74). Sometimes the ceramic vessel containing the human remains was placed inside a larger container. At Parish Field, one grave held three Belgic-related fineware vessels containing small quantities of cremated remains (and representing at least one individual) which were then placed within a large wooden bucket (Whimster 1981, 472–3); another grave from this site contained a centrally-placed bronze tankard which held the cremated bone, surrounded by five vessels arranged in a circle around it. This group of vessels included fineware jars, pedestal urns and a platter (Birchall 1965, 302). A range of vessels including a pedestal cup, butt beaker and a platter also accompanied a cremation burial at Brisley Farm (Stevenson 2013); perhaps in both instances they may represent a drinking and eating set. These Late Iron Age pots were used in life for storage, cooking, serving and drinking in settings that structured differences between guests, reproducing macro- and micro-differences in taste, class and identity. Differences in food preparation, recipes, ingredients, dining and culinary know-how did not just evidence links with Rome and its trade networks: they moulded the 'gastropolitics' of local society (Misha Enayat pers. comm. and further discussion in Chapter 8).

In Dorset, the pots accompanying inhumation burials were found in a range of positions around the body. They were noted at the head (both behind, above and in front of the face), the shoulders, torso, behind the back, alongside and on the body, and at the feet. At the Maiden Castle 'peacetime' cemetery, for example, all these positions were noted (Wheeler 1943, 349–50). Pots were generally deposited singly but two or more vessels occasionally accompanied the burial. The female inhumation from Portesham (with mirror) had a fineware decorated bowl at her feet and two shouldered jars behind her back (Fig. 6.04; Fitzpatrick 1997b).

Summary

In this section, we hope to have captured, albeit necessarily briefly, some of the ebbs and flows of pots as grave goods through time and across space (Fig. 6.05). It is clear that, even as the most prevalent grave good, pots were far from always involved in a burial. Usually, however, when archaeologically visible burial occurred, pots were there. In the remainder of this chapter, we explore a number of the most intriguing aspects of pots in graves – their sizes, their decoration, their biographies, their placement within the grave, the relationships between pots and different burial rites, and between pots and different people. In order to maintain focus and coherency, we will look almost exclusively at the Beaker/Early Bronze Age period within these more detailed analyses (though Chapter 8 gives further space to a consideration of Late Iron Age assemblages in the south-east).

Figure 6.04 Reconstruction of the burial at Portesham (drawn by Craig Williams).

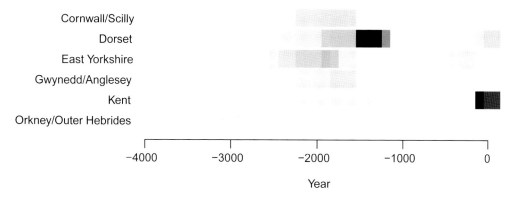

Figure 6.05 Pots in burials through time, by region (darker shading indicates greater numbers, calculated as % of all pots in all periods/regions).

6.4. New pots, old pots, fresh pots, used pots: vessels made for the moment and vessels with a biography

Some object types deposited with the dead were clearly made specifically for the act of burial or funerary performance, including, for example, coffins and perhaps ceremonial (non-functional) daggers. Pots, on the other hand, also functioned in domestic contexts and fulfilled everyday roles, thus traversing and perhaps interconnecting the three realms of life, death and afterlife (see also Chapter 4). The question as to whether pots were made for the deceased person at the moment of death or for the funeral has only rarely been addressed directly (see, however, Boast 2001).

Many categories of objects such as stone, flint and metal tools, weapons and items of adornment (such as buttons, toggles, necklaces) have benefited from detailed visual, microscopic and other scientific analysis to ascertain condition, wear/abrasion and the overall use-life of these objects (e.g. Woodward and Hunter 2015). Pottery grave goods have not usually been subject to analysis to the same extent. While many are retained within museum collections and can be re-assessed for clues of their life, such examinations are often hindered by heavy restoration and reconstruction.

Determining which pots were made for the moment of burial and which had already been circulating for some time prior to their deposition as grave goods was not feasible at a broad scale since it would require detailed further analysis. Anecdotal remarks in site reports can help to identify pots with biographies and evidence of cracks and repair holes or incidences of heavy abrasion (particularly on rims and bases) are occasionally commented on. Examples of sooted vessels or pots containing or covered with residues, however, are less clear cut, as the former could have occurred if the pot was placed on the pyre or associated with cremation rites and the latter may represent foodstuffs or offerings for the deceased.

Pots made for and during the funeral

There are, occasionally, indications that a vessel had been commissioned specially for the burial and, in some cases, even transformed from soft clay to hard ceramic on the funerary pyre. In his detailed study of Collared Urns, Law (2008, 310–22) developed a sustained and convincing argument that at least some vessels had been decorated by multiple people, sometimes possibly as part of the wider, extended funerary process. Describing the urn found inverted over a cremation burial at Kingskettle, Fife (Fig. 6.06), he suggested that

> not only have different motifs been applied to the collar and rim of this vessel, they have also been created using different materials and techniques. While the overall effect is neither haphazard nor chaotic, the juxtaposition of discrete passages, each one possessing its own unique character, serves to emphasise its piecemeal construction, making this vessel another likely candidate for having been decorated by more than one person. (Law 2008, 319)

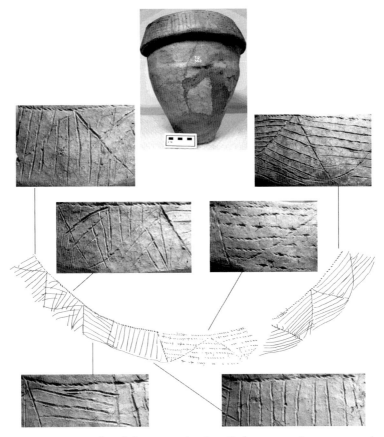

Figure 6.06 Decoration on urn [1833] from Kingskettle, Fife (Law 2008, fig. 7.13; reproduced by kind permission of Rob Law and National Museums Scotland).

In this case, damage to the pot's collar could potentially suggest an extended use-life prior to its involvement in the funeral (*ibid.*, 322), although to our minds this does not necessarily need to have been the case.

In addition to instances such as this, which may have been made specifically following someone's death, several examples of pots probably having been fired on the cremation pyre itself were noted in Early Bronze Age contexts, from Cornwall in particular. At Boscregan, cremated bones had left marks as a result of adhering to the inside of a large Trevisker Urn (Borlase 1879a, 201–4), implying that the pot was damp when the bones from a defleshed body were placed in this raw pot, with both then fired in the pyre together. At Angrouse Cliff, some of the cremated bone had stuck to the interior of a rather poorly fired and smoke-blackened ribbon-handled urn, again suggesting that the pot was fired or perhaps re-fired on the pyre (Borlase 1872, 237–9; Patchett 1944, 32–5). Human bones were also found adhering to both the inside of a Trevisker vessel at Watchcroft (Abercromby 1912, fig. 467; Borlase 1872, 247–52) and a large burnt Biconical Urn from Bosporthenis (Patchett 1944, table vi, F.15). At the opposite end of Britain, a Middle Bronze Age flat-rimmed urn from a cist on Egilsay, Orkney, had cremation slag stuck fast to its exterior, again implying it had been fired or refired on the pyre (Moore and Wilson 1995, 237). In these examples, the pot may have been in a leather-hard state and was altered from malleable clay to hard ceramic during the cremation event itself.

Pots with biographies

While it is likely that some pots were made specifically for the moment of burial, in other cases they were clearly already imbued with a biography – in colloquial terms they were 'battered and bruised'. Within the GGDB, 84 examples of 'already old' pots were identified (22 used, 31 worn and 33 repaired); this is undoubtedly a very substantial under-estimation as vessel condition is not always commented upon or recorded.

Examples of pots that were abraded and had clearly been used prior to burial include a cracked and worn Food Vessel buried with a crouched inhumation from Dover, Kent (Stebbing 1951, 150–1). A Late Bronze Age–Early Iron Age urn that contained a cremation burial from Kilnsea Warren, East Yorkshire, had also been used on several previous occasions and was extensively sooted and burnt (Manby 1980, 352). Examples of worn pots include a Collared Urn from Blanch Farm 241, which was abraded and had cracked, but then was protected with a wicker basket-work receptacle (Mortimer 1905, 327–8).

A few examples of mend-holes have been identified from Early Bronze Age funerary pots, such as a small Food Vessel with two drill-holes near the rim from Low Farm barrow 40 (Mortimer 1905, 229–30), as well as the example from Moel Goedog that we saw at the start of the chapter (Lynch 1984). When it comes to evidence for repair, however, Middle Bronze Age Dorset is the most prominent region by far (see also Section 4.5). Perhaps the most extreme example comes from Simons Ground, where

– among many others – an upright Globular Urn had at least eight mend-holes on its body (see Fig. 4.07; White 1982, 16–17).

The majority (61%) of mend-holes on either side of cracks are evident on Deverel-Rimbury Urns. This could imply that, during the Middle Bronze Age, a greater proportion of pots had lengthy biographies before they were placed in the grave, but other factors should also be considered. Without being too unkind to the potters of this period, Deverel-Rimbury vessels were not always of a comparable quality to those of the preceding Early Bronze Age. Often, they were coarse with poorly-sorted pastes and fired rapidly and unevenly. As a result, many were friable and more prone to cracking. This may, in itself, say something about how funerary pots during this time were perceived. Perhaps they were chosen for the moment and as long as there was a pot containing or accompanying the deceased, it did not always matter if it was not well made. It is likely pertinent that the Middle Bronze Age marks the first time that domestic pots and funerary vessels show little difference in style overall (although see Chapter 4). It is possible that some of these pots had been mended after suffering a minor mishap while being used to prepare or cook food and then later repurposed as grave goods; equally, it is also conceivable that broken vessels were deliberately sought out to accompany the dead (see Section 4.5).

Broken pots, partial pots and sherds

Although incomplete and broken pots in graves are often considered to result from accidents (such as during excavation), or from post-depositional factors, there are certain patterns which suggest that sometimes the deposition of fragmentary pots was deliberate (see also Chapman 2000). Many inverted urns missing their bases and rimless upright urns were likely casualties of the plough, but other fragmentary vessels suggest intentionality. For instance, the majority of Beakers in Cornish funerary contexts were broken but the sherds were sometimes arranged to suggest that they were fragmented and scattered over the bodies deliberately, as at Tregiffian (Borlase 1872, 107–10) and Lousey (Christie *et al.* 1985, 46–60; Jones and Quinnell 2006, 42–3). At the latter site, the sherds from two broken Beakers had been carefully placed in a circle around the human remains. This tradition also seems to have continued into the Early Bronze Age. At Treligga Common 7 a small undecorated and rimless Food Vessel (containing food residues) was placed next to a degraded child inhumation (Christie *et al.* 1985, 62–6). As the vessel was inverted, the rim cannot have been removed by post-depositional ploughing/erosion, suggesting it was intentional. At Largin Wood, a Trevisker Urn containing cremated bone had been neatly chopped in half, again possibly on purpose (Trudigan and Apsimon 1976, 112–14).

A similar tradition of deliberately breaking pots can be identified in the Outer Hebrides. At Geirisclett, North Uist (Callander 1929; Henshall 1972, 515–17) and possibly also at Bhaltos, Lewis (Cormack 1973), burials were accompanied by only partial or fragmentary Beaker vessels. It could be posited that, in these cases, only part of the vessel was required to represent the whole and the rest of the Beaker may have been retained by the mourners. Similarly, it was considered that the Beaker from Kewing, Orkney, was broken prior to being placed in the grave fill of the cist (Ballin Smith 2014a, 152). As the date from the cremation burial was Early Bronze Age (*c.* 1960–1690 cal BC; SUERC-817), it is feasible that this vessel had been kept in circulation for some time and was an heirloom or curated item. That Beakers were rarely found in funerary contexts in these regions may be of significance here.

The steatite urn from Oram's Fancy, also in Orkney, was considered to have already been baseless and broken prior to becoming a container for the cremated remains (Petrie 1871, 347–51). It was placed upright and thus some of the cremated remains fell out of the bottom and were then raked into a pile around the vessel. Another Orcadian steatite urn, this time from a cist at Balfour, was also broken prior to burial, but in this instance, it was repaired first with two visible mend holes (RCAHMS 1946, 278). Fragmentary vessels have been noted in other regions, although it is the northern- and southern-most case study areas where the practice seems to be more pervasive. Examples from elsewhere include an incomplete plain Food Vessel placed directly under the body of a child in the barrow of Dewlish 6, Dorset (Grinsell 1959, 104).

The broken and partial conditions of these pots may have been enacted for a variety of different reasons. Pots may have been purposefully transformed at the point of burial – perhaps they were smashed to take them out of circulation or to destroy their power. Some of these vessels may have been in circulation for lengthy periods of time prior to deposition in the grave. Steatite urns in particular, given that they were made from a source of stone that required long-distance exchange to procure, may have been highly prized. Their more fragmentary and worn states may be a testament to their previous biographies. In certain cases, the missing part of the vessel may have been broken off by a mourner and taken as a token memento. Recounting Leslie Grinsell's instructions for his funeral, Chapman and Gaydarska provide a pertinent anecdote about fragmentation. Grinsell's cremated remains were to be placed in a replica Collared Urn and to be scattered after the pot was smashed at the summit of a hill overlooking one of his favourite landscapes (bringing to mind the Lincolnshire rite of 'deading' a pot that Grinsell himself recorded, see section 2.7). Each of his twelve closest friends were to retain a large sherd to remember Leslie by; as such, each sherd symbolised a linkage in a larger network that could be brought together again and made whole (Chapman and Gaydarska 2006, 1–2).

6.5. Size matters

While the last section considered the often complicated 'lives' of pots themselves, we now investigate the intersections between pots and people, and pots and funerary practice. In some older archaeological accounts, just as burial position within a barrow was often seen to reflect social status, vessel sizes too were assumed to relate to particular kinds of person. There was, in some people's minds at least, an unspoken supposition that big pots equate with big men (see, for example, Needham 2005, 207), whilst smaller vessels were assumed to go with infants or children. Similarly, it was generally assumed that urns would, naturally, need to have been made to be large enough to contain the cremated remains of the individual concerned, whilst those vessels merely accompanying an inhumation had no such function and thus could have been both smaller and more variable (Mortimer 1905, liv–lv; Cowie 1978, 20–4; Longworth 1984, 34, 49–52).

More recent analyses have investigated such pot–person–rite relationships from a more critical perspective. Hanley and Sheridan (1994), for example, building on the discovery of a 'pair' of Beakers (one very small, one large) at Balblair, Inverness, considered the possibility that small Beakers, both on this site and more widely, may often have been associated with children. Additionally, Barclay's research on Collared Urns from the Upper Thames region suggested that smaller vessels were often found in secondary contexts within barrows not in direct association with the burials, while it was larger vessels that usually contained cremation burials (Barclay 2002). Law's study of Collared Urns in East Anglia suggested a similar pattern, also indicating that different sized pots were decorated in different ways (Law 2008, 174). These studies alone – all three of them regionally focused and specific only to one ceramic type – suggest that interesting patterns and person–pot relationships may lie behind the excavated evidence. In the study set out below, we build on these early indications, looking at a much wider sample geographically, as well as across different typological categories of pot, to investigate whether and how pot sizes related to different people and different burial practices.

It is important to point out that, in compiling the GGDB, sufficient information about specific pot dimensions was only rarely available (i.e. it was not reported in most original primary sources). Therefore, to provide a larger, representative quantity of pots for this detailed analysis, a random sample of 900 additional vessels from formal burials was collated (300 each for Beakers, Food Vessels and Collared Urns) from the following sources: Beakers: Clarke (1970); Food Vessels: Cowie (1978), Gibson (1978), Manby (1994; 2004) and Wilkin (2013); Collared Urns: Longworth (1984) and Kinnes and Longworth (1985). Including those that were sufficiently documented in the GGDB, the dimensions (height, rim diameter and base diameter) for 1113 vessels in total (389 Beakers, 368 Food Vessels and 356 Collared Urns) were recorded.

This information was then used to explore whether any relationship could be discerned between the funerary rite employed in a given burial and the size of the pot concerned. When associated with cremation practices, it is often presumed that the vessels were containers for the cremated remains, but this is far from always the case. In this study, three different associations between cremation burials and pots were identified for the Early Bronze Age (Fig. 6.07). As well as containing the cremated remains, vessels were often placed over them, or beside them. Even with the inverted examples, there is often good evidence to indicate that the remains had not originally been placed in the urn and then subsequently spilled out, especially as many of these relate to *in situ* cremations that were raked up. For example, at Kiplingcotes

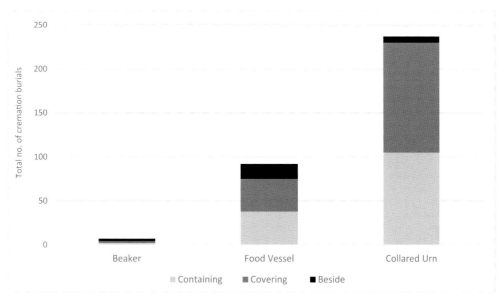

Figure 6.07 The roles of urns in Beaker/Early Bronze Age cremation burials (GGDB data).

Station, East Yorkshire, the *in situ* cremation of a tightly crouched male was covered by a number of objects including a Collared Urn (Longworth 1984, 207). In other cases, cremated bone was placed in bags or other organic containers in shallow pits and only later protected, covered or accompanied by the pot (see also Cooper *et al.* 2019). With Food Vessels in particular, the pot was frequently placed next to a pile of cremated remains. These distinctions are likely to have been meaningful in symbolic, metaphorical and practical terms, suggesting that pots may have functioned in different capacities: accompanying, covering, hiding or protecting the person interred.

Pot sizes and funerary rites
Overall, as noted above (Sections 3.2 and 6.3), over the course of the Beaker/Early Bronze Age period, burial rites shifted broadly from inhumation to cremation. Over the same period, we see an overall chronological shift from Beakers to Food Vessels to Collared Urns. As might be expected, therefore, we also see general differences in the associations between these pot styles and the burial types they accompany (Fig. 6.08).

Turning our discussion to pot *sizes* (Table 6.01 and Fig. 6.09), we see that Beakers, which much more commonly accompanied inhumation burials, generally fall within a restricted size range; larger vessels are uncommon. Although rare, a few Beakers were observed to contain cremated remains, a practice particularly noted in Scotland; unfortunately, none of these had been published with measurements and therefore it was not possible to demonstrate whether they were significantly different in size to those that accompanied inhumation burials. Food Vessels were commonly associated with both inhumations and cremation burials; they often accompanied

Table 6.01 Size variation amongst Beaker, Food Vessel and Collared Urn pots (data from 1113 randomly sampled vessels, as detailed above).

Pot style	Height (mm, mean)	Rim diameter (mm, mean)	Height (mm, range)	Rim diameter (mm, range)
Beaker	166	132	70–380	65–235
Food Vessel	186	186	45–460	50–450
Collared Urn	240	208	40–560	50–460

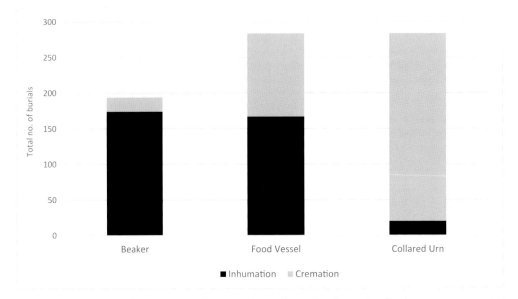

Figure 6.08 Associations between vessel types and burial rites for the Beaker/Early Bronze Age period (GGDB data).

or covered, rather than contained, the latter. Food Vessels demonstrate a greater variety in vessel size compared to Beakers, likely reflecting that these pots fulfilled roles in both cremation and inhumation burials. Most Collared Urns were associated with cremation burials, and principally *contained* the human remains. This pot style exhibited a similar size range to Food Vessels, but Collared Urns were generally significantly larger on average overall.

Overall, we have two clear patterns. Over the course of the Beaker/Early Bronze Age period, cremation became more prevalent and pots became larger. It might therefore be posited that, at a macro- level, the practice of cremation – associated with a need to *contain* rather than accompany the human remains – drove up pot sizes. In putting forward that argument, however, it is important to ascertain whether this is a meaningful relationship and not simply the result of two essentially separate trends co-occurring.

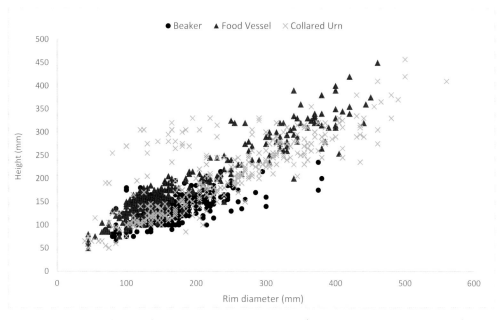

Figure 6.09 Beaker, Food Vessel and Collared Urn sizes (data from 1113 sampled vessels).

Importantly, adding weight to the argument that pot sizes and burial rite were connected, it is possible to discern significant differences *within* each category of pot as well. As mentioned above, very few Beakers were buried with cremation burials and unfortunately measurements were not published for these. However, with Food Vessels, the vast majority (71%) of small pots (<190 mm in height and 190 mm in rim diameter) were associated with inhumation burials (Fig. 6.10). Conversely, 100% of the large Food Vessels (generally 'Enlarged Urns' >400 mm in height and >340 mm in rim diameter) either contained or were placed on top of/inverted over heaped piles of cremated bones. This shows a clear-cut distinction between the overall size of Food Vessels and their association with inhumation or cremation burials. This division becomes even more apparent with Collared Urns (Fig. 6.11). A significant number of small vessels (<190 mm tall and 130 mm in rim diameter) either accompanied inhumations (12%) and cremation burials (15%) or covered rather than contained the cremated remains (36%). In addition, several of these smaller vessels came from funerary contexts but lacked direct associations with human remains, although they often contained burnt soil, pyre debris or were seemingly empty. Exactly what roles they played in funerary rites is open to consideration, but it may be that the smaller vessels which were associated with cremation burials had been integral to the cremation process.

It has been suggested that little cups, particularly incense burners (which had often been subject to burning), were used to carry the flame to light the pyre (e.g. Colt Hoare 1812, 25; Ferguson 1893, 276), although these observations have been challenged

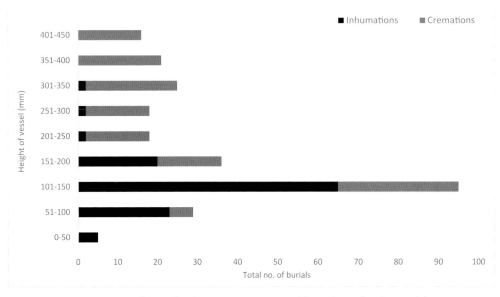

Figure 6.10 Relationship between pot sizes and burial rite (Food Vessels).

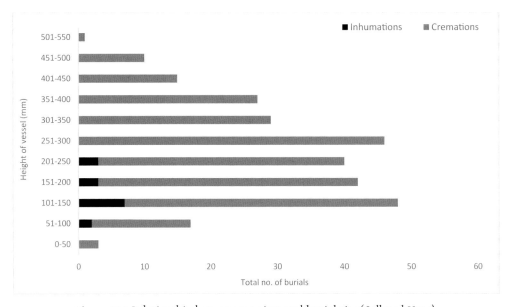

Figure 6.11 Relationship between pot sizes and burial rite (Collared Urns).

in recent decades (Gibson and Stern 2006; Hallam 2015; Copper 2017). At Brett's Pitt, Herne Bay, Kent, a small burnt incense cup accompanied the larger cremation urn (Canterbury Archaeological Trust 1994). Several examples are also known from East Yorkshire, such as a heat damaged biconical cup from Bishop Burton 262 (Mortimer 1905, 167; Hallam 2015, 327). On occasions these small cups were placed directly on top of *in situ* cremation burials such as at Cheesecake Hill (Mortimer 1905, 286–94), or immediately adjacent to them as at Goodmanham barrow 86 (Kinnes and Longworth 1985, 81). In addition to the patterns described above, it is also interesting to note again Barclay's research on Collared Urns from the Upper Thames region. Small cups were often found as secondary deposits within barrows in this region (Barclay 2002, 95). A number of these vessels showed evidence of overfiring or vitrification; some were brittle and warped as a result exposure to extremely high temperatures (*ibid.*, 93–4). These small burnt vessels may not only have been used to carry the flame to the pyre but were then also burnt together with the body on the pyre. Notably, all Collared Urns above 280 mm in height and greater than 250 mm in rim diameter, either contained or covered cremated bone.

Noting these discrepancies of pot size in relation to inhumations and cremations – even *within* pot types – a stronger argument can be made that the burial rite involved did indeed have an overall effect on the size of pot employed. As discussed in more detail below (within our 'exceptions to the rule' section), this would not of course have been the case in every single burial. However, at a very broad scale, it might well be argued that changing burial rites affected the kinds of pot people were making (Fig. 6.12).

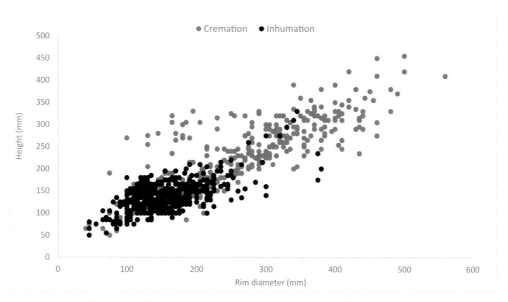

Figure 6.12 Vessel sizes and burial rites for Beakers, Food Vessels and Collared Urns (data from 1113 sampled vessels).

Size of pots in accordance with age of the deceased

The number of Early Bronze Age small cups from our case study areas was limited and thus any analysis of GGDB data alone proved inconclusive. Both children and adults were associated with miniature or pygmy cups in roughly equal numbers. One pattern of note, however, is that these small vessels more frequently accompanied or contained cremation burials. In order to examine the role of these 'miniature' pots in more detail, a wider comparison was undertaken, using detailed information provided in two Master's dissertations on Bronze Age funerary cups (Hallam 2015; Copper 2017). Many of these vessels were discovered by accident or in antiquarian investigations and thus lack contextual details. Where information about the age of the deceased was provided, in northern England Hallam (2015; appx 1 and 5.3) noted that at least 16 small cups were associated with children and a further three with young people or adolescents; a total of 26 funerary cups were identified with adults, and where sex was discerned, most were associated with females (ten as opposed to only two males). In southern England, Copper (2017, appx 8) identified a minimum of 31 small cups associated with children or infants and a further nine with young people or adolescents; the majority of these were cremation burials. By comparison, only 29 adults were associated with these vessels. In brief, these two studies demonstrate that, in northern England, miniature cups were associated with both children and adults and, in the case of the latter, more frequently with women; and in the south they were more commonly associated with young people than with adults.

To extend our investigations of the relationship between pot size and different categories of people we gathered further data for our case study area of East Yorkshire. There, when vessel size (for Beaker/Early Bronze Age pots) was charted against the age of the deceased, it could be demonstrated that almost all infants and children were buried with smaller vessels <170 mm in height. While adolescents and adults were associated with both small and large vessels, only one example of a pot taller than 170 mm accompanying a child was identified, implying that large pots were almost never deemed appropriate grave goods for children during this phase. To supplement this observation, an overview of small Collared Urns (under 140 mm in height) was undertaken, using Longworth's (1984) corpus as the primary reference. A total of 106 small vessels were identified and, in the limited number of examples for which age details were supplied, eight were associated with adults while 17 were associated with infants, children or 'young people', further supporting the suggestion that smaller vessels were more commonly paired with small people.

In summary, as far as it is possible to tell from the data collected, smaller pots were more likely to be associated in burial with children and younger people and larger pots with adults. There is a touching intimacy in the tailored provision of capacious and diminutive vessels which we would not think twice about in relation to coffin size but is worth drawing attention to in relation to these analogous mortuary vessels.

Exceptions to the rule: size of vessel sometimes does not matter
The above analysis has demonstrated that the size of a vessel often did relate directly to the age of the deceased and that larger vessels were predominantly associated with cremation burials. Nonetheless, there are a few interesting instances where the size of the vessel did not reflect the volume of contents it held. A Trevisker urn found upright in a cist eroding out of the cliff at Harlyn Bay, Cornwall, contained the cremated remains of a minimum of five individuals (one adult, one juvenile, two children and an infant). The urn also held a number of other grave goods, including ten flint and stone tools and a copper-alloy pendant in a woven bag (as discussed in Chapter 5). Yet the vessel was not overly large (330 mm in height, 220 mm in diameter) and was full almost to the brim, with some materials spilling out (Jones *et al.* 2011). One of the cists from the cemetery of Blowes, in Orkney contained an urn (made of steatite rather than clay); it was only 200 mm tall and 180 mm in diameter, and again so much bone and associated pyre material had been crammed into this small vessel that a quantity had dropped out and lay in a large pile next to the urn (Grant 1933, 34).

At the other extreme, some sizeable vessels contained only 'token' quantities of human remains. For instance, only a few scraps of cremated bone were noted within a tripartite Enlarged Food Vessel Urn from Hilton Coombe in Dorset (Ashburnham 1918, 76). A large upright Enlarged Food Vessel Urn (with a rim diameter of 450 mm) from Bincombe 13, Dorset, only contained *c.* 200 g of bone (Best 1964) and a large undecorated Food Vessel from Blomuir in Orkney only held 135 g of burnt bone. Of further interest was that most of the bone came from the head and torso of a young adult male (Lamb 1981). Perhaps specific element selection of cremated bone could indicate that these large vessels functioned as repositories for human remains from which bones could easily be removed or, indeed, added at various times, suggesting an extended temporality and potential storage dimension to these vessels. Intriguingly, two small Collared Urns from Bedd Branwen, Anglesey, contained nothing except the ear bones from two new-born babies at their bases, covered with dark unctuous earth and stone chips (Lynch 1970, 148–9; 1972). In Dorset, a particular practice of covering inurned cremation burials with flint chips, sometimes calcined, has been observed. Examples include Scrubbity Handley 6 (Longworth 1984, 186) and Winklebury Camp (Pitt-Rivers 1888, 34). Their presence at the latter site was explained as being either to hold the cremated bone down or to sterilise or purify the burial (*ibid.*) but it could be posited that white and often burnt chips acted as a substitute for human remains that were removed from the urn for re-appropriation in a different context.

Summary
In short, it appears that size did matter. While the patterns are complex to unpick, the evidence suggests that the broad shift from inhumation to cremation, and the broad shift to larger vessels, over the course of the Beaker/Early Bronze Age period *were* related trends. Even within individual pot types, vessels were much more likely to be larger if found with a cremation burial than with an inhumation. The logic of

this relationship between pots and burial rite is clear – pots got bigger as their role as containers of burial increased – and perhaps might have been expected. Nonetheless, our analysis, which transcended sub-period boundaries and incorporated over a thousand pots, has demonstrated this on the basis of substantial evidence for the first time. Similarly, it has now also been possible to demonstrate that smaller pots were deposited preferentially with children and younger people. While this suggestion has been made before, in drawing together the evidence from a number of recent studies in combination with our own substantial dataset, we hope to have placed our understanding of this relationship between pots and people on a much firmer footing.

6.6. The aesthetics of pots

From the Early Neolithic onwards, most pots encountered in funerary contexts were decorated. Undoubtedly a variety of reasons governed the decision to decorate or not to decorate, and the type, location and arrangement of ornament may have conferred specific meanings to these vessels. To appreciate this more fully we need to consider both the motifs and motives of pottery decoration. During certain periods, the reduction of decoration is notable, such as between *c.* 1750 and 1200 BC when Collared Urns and Deverel-Rimbury Urns were either plain or decoration was limited to specific zones on the vessel. During this phase the range of motifs was reduced and limited mainly to geometric ornament, predominantly focused around the rim, collar and shoulder of the vessel. This contrasts with the preceding traditions of Beaker and Food Vessel pots, which were often covered from rim to base in profuse and elaborate motifs. That vessel decoration decreases in tandem with the increasing popularity of cremation burial practices may not be coincidental, a point that will be returned to below.

Decoration seemingly became more important – and perhaps more symbolically relevant – during certain periods. For instance, in earlier Neolithic Orkney, Unstan vessels were often covered in complex design schemes, frequently suggestive of basketry or wickerwork. Equally, the designs observed on Food Vessels have also been considered to represent interwoven organic material such as basketry and rushes, while the schemes on Grooved Ware may also have been skeuomorphs of wooden vessels. It is in the Beaker and, especially, the Food Vessel phases of the Early Bronze Age that decoration rises to an apogee. Generally, Beakers are decorated almost all over the vessel body exterior from rim to base, although they are rarely decorated internally (see for example Boast 1995). Sometimes the lower zone of the vessel body is undecorated, or some horizontal panels on the body are left plain, perhaps to accentuate adjacent panels of decoration. Some Beaker pots have profuse and dense zones of ornamentation that can comprise intricate and even conflicting areas of decoration – metopes – to dazzle and entrance the eye. During the Beaker period, decoration is normally tightly bounded and compartmentalised, constrained within incised horizontal bands. Overall, the regular forms of Beaker pots and standardised decorative schemes applied to their body exteriors suggest that the repertoire of pot design and style for these vessels was quite prescriptive. The emergence and floruit of Food Vessels stands in stark contrast to Beakers in this regard. Some of the shapes and motif designs, particularly on the bowls, could be described as experimental, playful and highly innovative. Food Vessel decoration sometimes breaks boundaries, resulting in the creation of original and spectacular pieces of art and decoration flows across the vessel rather than being constrained within linear divisions (Fig. 6.13). As Sheridan astutely observed, 'Food Vessels were not designed for the convenience of twenty-first-century ceramic classification' (2004, 246).

The ingenious use of excision and incision on Encrusted Food Vessel Urns created a three-dimensional effect. Additional features on vase urns, such as cavetto zones, stops, pierced ears or lugs and handles, play not only on visual but also sensual qualities. The pronounced humps and bumps covering the pots are reminiscent of braille, providing them with an additional tactile element. Decoration on Food Vessels also departs from other prehistoric pottery traditions in that motifs extend to the interior of the vessel and the internal rim bevels of most pots are covered in herringbone, zigzag or slashed line motifs. Generally, the motifs covering the internal rim clash and compete with the external decoration. For instance, at Folkton G243, North Yorkshire, the external motifs were two rows of herringbone, while the internal

Figure 6.13 Left: Food Vessel urn from Rosborough, Northumberland with (right) detailed image showing elaborate moulding and decoration between shoulder and rim (photographs: Neil Wilkin © Trustees of the British Museum).

rim bevel was covered in a row of herringbone, with a row of hanging reserve triangles beneath (Greenwell 1890, 12, fig. 4). The exterior of the rim of a Food Vessel from Goodmanham G115 in East Yorkshire comprised a row of short, vertical incisions on the exterior with zones of fine-twisted herringbone on the interior (Simpson 1968, fig. 45.1; Kinnes and Longworth 1985, 88). This desire to decorate both the inside and outside of the rim, employing competing motifs to create a stunning visual effect, could indicate that the pots were meant to be viewed from above, perhaps when looking down into the grave (see also Law 2008, 296–308). This may be one reason why most of these vessels were placed in the grave upright rather than inverted.

A recurrent pattern noted is that Food Vessels associated with cremation burials are generally more sparsely decorated and often plain below the shoulder; on the other hand, those accompanying inhumations are more often all-over, or at least more extensively, decorated (e.g. Wilkin 2013, fig. 5.12 for north-east Yorkshire). This observation can be taken further, and there is a compelling evidence to indicate that smaller and un-/minimally decorated Food Vessels more often accompany infants or children. With few exceptions focused on specific regional areas (Pierpoint 1980; Shepherd 2012; Curtis and Wilkin 2019), there has been little detailed investigation of whether different styles of decoration could possibly have been an indicator of age or sex.

Shepherd (2012) undertook a detailed analysis of Beaker pots from north-east Scotland and East Yorkshire and was able to discern distinctions in pots that accompanied adult females and males. In north-east Scotland, vessels with sharp and exaggerated necks, further accentuated by distinctive horizontal grooved or banded decoration, more commonly accompanied male burials (*ibid.*, 268). Curtis and Wilkin (2017; 2019, 227) confirmed this observation and demonstrated that slender vessels in this region were predominantly associated with adult/elderly males, while vessels with less pronounced neck/body distinctions, and with a less elaborate range of decoration, tended to accompany younger individuals. Shorter and squatter Beaker shapes, on the other hand, more frequently accompanied female burials (Shepherd 2012, 268–71; Curtis and Wilkin 2017). There was less of a clear-cut sexual distinction amongst Yorkshire Beakers, with both female and male burials being accompanied by a variety of different Beaker types (Shepherd 2012, 271).

Wilkin also offered a compelling interpretation regarding the shifting significance of decoration in the Early Bronze Age. He suggested that:

> Changes in ritual practice may help to explain the connection between burial mode and decoration. The restriction of decoration may relate to the time and effort spent on decorating vessels once funerary practices had become more protracted with the introduction of cremation followed by formal deposition. More speculatively, 'all over' decoration may have had significance in terms of the inhumation as a 'whole', fleshed, body. The undecorated surfaces below the shoulder of vessels associated with cremation burials may have related (symbolically) to the transformation of the body associated with the breaking down of the body on the pyre. (Wilkin 2013, 201)

Collared Urns, after the 'blip' with Food Vessels, generally demonstrate more uniformity in shapes, styles and decoration on a similar scale to those of Beakers. There is much repetition in the execution of decoration, and geometric motifs overwhelmingly dominate, mainly created using corded techniques (Longworth 1984, 8; Law 2008, 63–6). Compared to the preceding Food Vessel tradition, there is far less 'experimentation' in evidence, and the margin for innovation was apparently narrow, implying a renewed conservatism in pot-making akin to that during the Beaker phase.

An assessment of the overall quantity of decoration present on Beakers and Food Vessels was undertaken, using East Yorkshire as a case study. While the percentage of decoration on vessels was collated simply into two groups (>50% or <50%), it served to illustrate that younger people were more often accompanied by undecorated or only partially decorated vessels in this region (Fig. 6.14). This pattern would benefit from more detailed and extensive analysis (see also Pierpoint 1980, 45–123). One (at present largely anecdotal) observation made while undertaking this analysis was that some of the vessels associated with children or infants were not only sparingly decorated, but often this was through 'naïve' or organic motifs. Decoration was often executed using fingerprints and fingernails. Perhaps these vessels were made by children, either the siblings or friends of the deceased, or even more poignantly by the child prior to death. Examples include a child (Burial 16) buried with a haphazardly decorated Beaker behind the head at Rudston and an irregularly made and fingernail decorated

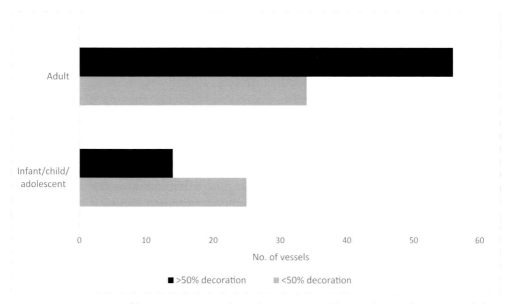

Figure 6.14 Percentage of decoration on vessel in relation to age of deceased. Data from East Yorkshire for Beakers, Food Vessels and Collared Urns.

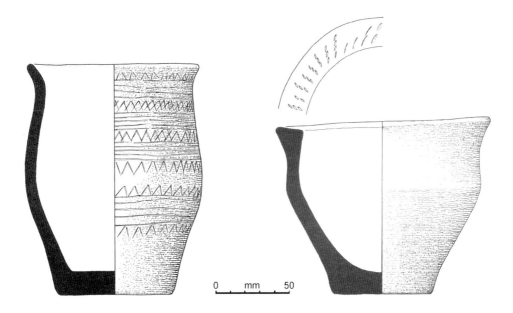

Figure 6.15 Left: Beaker from Rudston; right: Food Vessel from Flixton 2, both buried with children (Kinnes and Longworth 1985, figs 67.12 and 70.1).

small Food Vessel accompanying an infant (Burial 1) from Folkton (Flixton 2) (Fig. 6.15; Kinnes and Longworth 1985, 74 and fig. 67.12, 78 and fig. 70.1).

6.7. Positions, grouping and arrangement of pots in the grave

Placement of vessels

Pots were no doubt placed with the deceased for a variety of different practical and ideological reasons. However, most past interpretations have focused primarily on their roles as containers for food and drink (offerings from the funeral feast, or to sustain the deceased in the next life) and as repositories for the body itself (after cremation on the pyre). The placement of the pot in relation to the deceased was almost certainly often deliberate and meaningful. Pots can be found above or below the body, they can cover or contain the body, and they can be placed in front or behind the body. They are noted in upright and inverted positions. When associated with inhumations (usually in a crouched position during the Beaker/Early Bronze Age period), they were often placed at the extremities of the individual (with head and feet being the most common locations). Food Vessels were frequently placed directly in front of the face of the deceased, close to the mouth, and may have had connotations that they held sustenance for the afterlife.

The placement of grave goods in relation to the deceased has been the subject of some interest in recent years (Sørensen 1997, 104; Fitzpatrick 2011, 212–22; Brück

2019, 80–1). Brück suggested that different parts of the body may have been ascribed specific cultural meanings or may have symbolised interpersonal relationships. The Amesbury Archer, for example, had numerous objects placed around his crouched body, including two Beaker pots in front of his head near his hands, and three vessels positioned behind his body. Fitzpatrick (2011, 212-22) suggested that the clustered assemblages of objects around him may have been gifted by different members of his family or wider kin group, thus expressing different trajectories and biographies. In a similar manner, the three chalk 'drums' from Folkton, North Yorkshire had also been arranged behind a tightly crouched young child, buried on the edge of barrow G245 (Manby 1974, 122; Kinnes and Longworth 1985, 115; see also front cover image). It could be postulated that in certain circumstances objects placed in front of the deceased may have been intended to reference and point to the future, whilst those positioned behind the body may have related to the past. If this line of interpretation is broadly correct, it might be argued that any pots placed on the body or held in the hands may have related to the present, the moment of burial. In support of this idea, the pots behind the body of the Archer were old and chipped and may have been heirlooms, while those in front of his head were fresh and likely made for the moment of the burial (Cleal 2011).

Multiple vessels

When pots are encountered as grave goods during the Beaker/Early Bronze Age, the *general* rule is a ratio of one vessel per person; exceptions to this are of interest, as we have already seen with the Amesbury Archer. Sometimes a single pot is shared by two or more individuals and, on other occasions, a single individual was buried with two or more pots. The supplementary vessels were not always smaller (as is generally inferred by terms such as 'accessory' or 'miniature' cups) and occasionally several standard size vessels were placed in the grave with a single individual. A crouched inhumation of an aged male, Burial No. 2 at Garrowby Wold barrow 104 in East Yorkshire, was surrounded by three similarly sized Beaker pots. One was placed directly in front of the face, likely at the moment of burial; the other two were possibly added some time *prior to* the burial (Fig. 6.16; Mortimer 1905, 134–6 and fig. 345). In certain instances, therefore, the presence of two or more pots in the

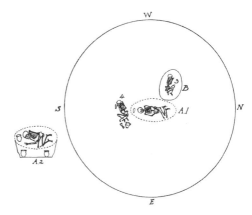

Figure 6.16 Mortimer's original plan of Garrowby Wold Barrow 104, showing the burial with multiple Beakers (A2); burial A2 was found underlying A1 (Mortimer 1905, 135).

grave may suggest a lengthy temporal span to the funerary processes, and a more complicated sequence of funerary rituals. This leads to the question of whether objects added later by mourners should be considered funerary offerings rather than grave goods. Like bouquets of flowers left by relatives and friends at graves today, these pots may have been deposited some time after the burial, and therefore have different connotations (Brück 2019, 74–8).

The occurrence of single pots with more than one individual was noted mainly in our Dorset and East Yorkshire case study areas. In the former region, for example, two crouched adult inhumations in the same grave at Oakley Down barrow 4 were accompanied by a small polypod or four-footed vase placed equidistantly between the heads of both individuals (Parke 1951, 91–2; Grinsell 1959, 165). In a cist at Worth Matravers 3, one articulated and two semi-articulated inhumations of females were buried with a small Collared Urn (Grinsell 1959, 160). The central primary grave under Eweleaze Barn barrow 46 contained four individuals, including three infants (all under 3 years of age) who shared a small plain Food Vessel. This vessel was already old when it was placed in the grave and had an ancient break and its handle was missing (St George Gray and Prideaux 1905). In East Yorkshire, a double burial of two adolescents in Blanch barrow M265 also shared a polypod vessel (Mortimer 1905, 330), and a small Food Vessel was positioned equidistantly between two adult males at Cowlam G56 (Greenwell 1877, 214; Kinnes and Longworth 1985, 55–6)

Inter-pot relationships
Smaller accessory vessels (including miniature cups, incense cups and polypod bowls) sometimes accompanied Food Vessel and Collared Urn burials but the ways in which the pots were arranged in association with each other varies. The smaller vessel(s) was sometimes contained or nestled within the larger urn which usually also held the cremated human remains. Often the larger urn contained the cremated remains and the smaller urn held pyre debris or other burnt material but sometimes the human remains were noted in the smaller vessel or distributed between both pots. This is the case with Hawold Sheepwalk barrow C94, East Yorkshire, where the smaller upright incense cup was placed within a larger Collared Urn and both contained cremated human remains (Mortimer 1905, 324). A large urn containing the cremated remains at Linkinhorne, Cheesewring, Cornwall, also held a polypod pot, but the smaller vessel was empty (Patchett 1950, 52).

Smaller pots inside larger vessels in Cornwall include an inverted Food Vessel within a large handled Trevisker Urn, also inverted, at Poulhendra (Patchett 1950, 58), and a small Biconical Urn inside a large Trevisker Urn from Trevelloe (Patchett 1944, 33); these were also both inverted. Only the larger urns from Poulhendra and Trevelloe contained cremated bone but at the latter site, the smaller one inside held 'dust'. A pair of inverted Collared Urns from Port Dafarch, Gwynedd, were arranged so that the larger one containing the cremated remains was placed over a miniature empty one, with charcoal filling the gap between the two (Stanley and Wey 1868).

At Bridlington Bay Sand Pit, East Yorkshire, the cremated remains of a young child were deposited in a miniature pot (70 mm tall) that was then placed inside a much larger, but otherwise empty, Collared Urn, both placed upright (Sheppard 1949, 1–4). Sheppard posited (1949, 3):

> The reason for these miniature cinerary urns found inside larger ones, suggests that ... a mother has been buried with the remains of her child – the very small vase indicating that probably the mother died in child-birth, the cremated remains of the baby being enclosed in the small urn, and placed with the bones of the parent, so that when they both awoke in the next world they would be together.

Although an interesting hypothesis, in this instance no human remains of an adult female were noted in the larger urn.

A secondary burial at Bishop Wilton MC70 comprised an urned adult cremation burial placed within a Food Vessel that was accompanied by a small upright incense cup placed next to it (Mortimer 1905, 169–70). Nearby, at Garton Slack C62, an upright Food Vessel containing an inverted miniature Food Vessel was placed behind the head of a young child (Mortimer 1905, 212–14). A similar arrangement was identified in the central grave at the barrow of Kirkburn Garton Slack C41. Here an incense cup was placed in an inverted position in front of the face of an older adult female while a Food Vessel was deposited upright behind her head. There are several other examples where pairs of pots are encountered, with one pot inverted and the other one upright – playing on oppositional juxtapositions. The potential connotations associated with inverted and upright positions are intriguing and it

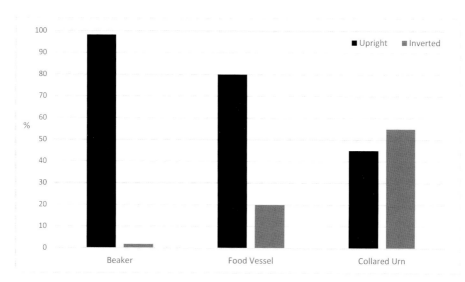

Figure 6.17 Percentage representation of upright and inverted position for Beaker/Early Bronze Age pottery.

may be no coincidence that the practice of inversion began in tandem with the introduction of cremation rites. While Food Vessels were sometimes inverted over cremated remains, the majority of Collared Urns were found in inverted positions. An overview of pots where the positions were documented shows that while 20% of Food Vessels were inverted, the popularity of this position rises to 55% for Collared Urns (Figure 6.17). The burning of the body on the pyre resulted in smoke and ash being released upwards into the sky. Perhaps if a pot was subsequently inverted over the heaped cremated bone, it helped harness and secure the human remains back into the ground. Using 'conceptual metaphor theory', a recent investigation of the potential reasons for inverting not only pots but other elements associated with Early Bronze Age barrows has explored this practice further (Wiseman *et al.* 2021).

Sometimes pots were carefully stacked within or on top of other vessels. In Cornwall, an upright Collared Urn at Cairn Kief was covered by an inverted Enlarged Food Vessel Urn (Patchett 1950, 57; Longworth 1984, 166). At Towednack, one inverted Trevisker Urn was placed directly on top of another inverted vessel, with a thin slab separating the two: a 'double-decker' arrangement (Douch 1962, 98). An undecorated Trevisker Urn from Trannack Down was completely encased inside another decorated urn. The outer urn tightly fitted the inner one, almost like a glove, with a tiny gap between the two, but calcined bones were found at the bases of both vessels (Borlase 1872, 209). Also of interest, the Rillaton gold cup was also found inside a larger ceramic vessel (possibly to protect or hide it), prior to being placed on the chest of an adult male inhumation (Borlase 1872; Needham 2006).

Wrapping pots

Sometimes, like the cremated human remains which were often put in bags or wrapped in textiles prior to deposition (Cooper *et al.* 2019), the pots themselves were also wrapped up or contained in organic material. Here the pots did not form the outer container but rather a liminal membrane that was then subsequently further encased, like a Russian doll. Examples include a Collared Urn from Wimborne St Giles 23, Dorset, which had 11 pierced holes along the rim, allowing a textile to be attached to the pot and completely wrap it (Longworth 1984, 192). A Collared Urn containing a child cremation burial from Blanch M241, East Yorkshire, was itself contained within a small wicker basket (Mortimer 1905, 327–8), while a Trevisker Urn from Rosecliston, Cornwall, was wrapped in some form of textile and then placed within a small oak casket; a double containment (Dudley and Thomas 1965). A Food Vessel containing cremated bone from Sand Fiold in Orkney was wrapped in linen (Dalland 1999), although in this case the pot was slightly cracked, and the organic wrapper may have been used as a bandage to prevent the pot from breaking apart.

Propping pots

The use of stones in particular ways within graves often helped keep pots in position, without falling over. Pots containing cremation burials were sometimes covered by flat stone slabs (probably used to protect the vessels and the remains within) but there are many cases of pots being placed on top of large flat slabs. This would have afforded them a stable and even surface and perhaps suggests an element of display. These include Denne's Brickfield in Kent, where five urned cremation burials of uncertain Bronze Age date were surrounded by large flints, seemingly holding them in position (Payne 1911, lxxxiii). Sometimes the pots were boxed in by upright slabs set on edge such as a Bucket Urn from Limekiln Hill (Greenfield 1959), and a Food Vessel from Ridge Hill, Bincombe both in Dorset (Acland 1916; Grinsell 1959, 92). In the latter example, the pot was set into its own compartment (like a photo frame) and quite separated from the adult male burial it accompanied. Vessels were not only propped by orthostats but dense piles of stone chips were occasionally used to harness the vessel in place. In Dorset, a cremation burial in an upright Deverel-Rimbury urn at Askerswell Down 2 was surrounded with tightly packed large flints, some of which were burnt (Wacher 1959, 170), and a similar observation was made of the Collared Urn from Bere Regis 8a, which was securely kept upright and protected by carefully arranged flints, some of them again burnt (Grinsell 1959, 88).

Many examples of the use of stones to prop, support or exhibit pots have been identified in our case study areas, mainly dating to the Early and Middle Bronze Ages. It is likely than many more incidences were once present but were not recorded in antiquarian excavations. Their presence indicates that keeping pots in place and stopping them from toppling over was sometimes important. Through these customs, vessels were framed and put on display, presenting a static and perhaps ideal image of a burial.

6.8. Discussion

In dissolving ceramic typologies and their associated constraints to some extent and focusing more on what pots overall were *doing* in burial contexts across sub-period boundaries, we can begin to appreciate much more completely the various roles they were asked to fulfil. Detailed typo-chronological categorisations of prehistoric pots have predominantly focused on burial derived assemblages, as this is the context in which they tend to survive best as complete vessels. This has, at times, unwittingly had the effect of wringing out the agency and purpose that pots had as grave goods. This chapter has attempted to demonstrate that a more investigative, trans-typological approach to pottery grave goods in later prehistory can shine light on the multitude of different reasons that pots were buried with the dead. Pots had personalities and were imbued with meaning. In the long-term, there has arguably been a tendency to view pots functionally – for example, as containers for either the cremated body or associated food. It is clear, however, that they had many attributes in addition to these.

Long-term analysis across multiple regions has enabled us to demonstrate very clearly the 'natural' ebbs and flows seen in pottery grave goods across the board. Different pot styles were adopted (or not) at different times and/or to different degrees in different regions (Fig. 6.05). They were also used differently as well with, for example, Collared Urns regularly accompanying inhumation burials in East Yorkshire but being found almost exclusively with cremation burials elsewhere. In exploring the biographies of pots and their placement in the grave, it has become clear that these vessels were very commonly used to convey meanings. While some might argue that aged pots (such as those from Moel Goedog and Brenig mentioned right at the start of the chapter) may have been employed simply as convenient vessels that were to hand at the time, it is very likely that such pots were also employed strategically and intentionally to convey messages about the person buried. Similarly, some pots may have been specifically made for the funeral, their particular character relating equally strongly to the individual within the grave. Although it is perhaps especially hard to access the meanings of containing, covering and accompanying pots, it seems very likely that this placement related in some way to the deceased too.

On the basis of our substantial dataset, we have also been able to demonstrate clear relationships between the sizes of pots, the 'type' of person buried and the rite of burial employed. In the case of the former, the association between larger pots and adults, and smaller pots and children, does not seem to have been strictly functional – it suggests simply that certain kinds of pot were viewed as 'fitting' particular kinds of people. The relationship between burial rite and pot size is complicated to unpick. It is possible that the 'evolutionary pressures' associated with an increased need for vessels which contained cremation burials over time ultimately led to larger vessels. However, clearly it is not quite so simple – other factors such as changes in the way pots were viewed during the funeral and the importance of decoration may well also have influenced pot size. Towards the end of our analysis, we also considered the possible metaphorical statements made with pots – multiple vessels standing for different groups of people, upright pots referencing the flow of smoke from funeral pyres, stacks of pots 'hiding' certain messages from view.

The fact that pots are by far the most prevalent grave good – present throughout most of our study period and found in large numbers in most regions – ensures that they offer us a unique perspective. Through them, for this reason, it is possible to gain insights that are relevant to, but perhaps not as visible within, other grave goods as well. Arguably the key realisation to emerge from the above overview is that pots *did* and *meant* many, many different things. We may see them as one type of object but it is abundantly clear that they were not straightforwardly one thing. Just as ceramic types come and go through time, so too did pots' functions and meanings in the grave. They are, after all, both materially and conceptually the most 'plastic' of grave goods, with numerous roles to play in the context of a death and the ensuing burial. Throughout our periods, until some of the latest Iron Age examples, their hand-made form also gave them a potency which was perhaps particularly poignant, whether made locally by known hands or evoking distant lands. It is to the ways in which other grave goods embodied distance that the next chapter turns.

Chapter 7

Material mobility: grave goods, place and geographical meaning

7.1. Introduction

We begin this chapter by looking at two Early Bronze Age burials – separated by hundreds of kilometres and characterised by very different materialities – which both have something to tell us about grave goods, place and meaning. Our first burial is relatively well known. Excavations at Rameldry Farm near Kingskettle in Fife revealed a short cist within which was found a crouched inhumation of a man aged 40–50 (Baker *et al.* 2003). The man had been buried during the Early Bronze Age (*c.* 2280–1970 cal BC) with a bronze dagger and a garment which incorporated six V-perforated buttons (Fig. 7.01); five of these were made from jet, the sixth was made from 'lizardite' stone. The jet was ultimately derived from Whitby in North Yorkshire, 250 km away to the south-east as the crow flies. The best-known source of lizardite is in Cornwall, 700 km to the south, but other outcrops are known somewhat closer in specific areas of Scotland (*ibid.*, 93). One of the jet buttons (Button 1) was decorated with an incised cross and zigzag pattern that had been inlaid with tin; this material was almost certainly sourced in Cornwall, making a south-western origin for the lizardite more likely. The copper

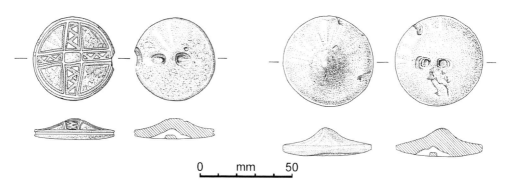

Figure 7.01 Buttons 1 (jet/tin) and 2 (lizardite) from Rameldry Farm (after Baker et al. *2003, illus. 3). Illustration by Sylvia Stevenson.*

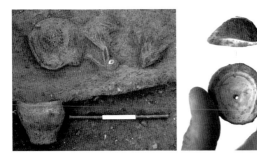

Figure 7.02 Left: The child burial and associated limpet shell from Bar Pasture Farm, Thorney (Richmond et al. 2010, pl. 7); right: detailed photograph of shell (© Phoenix Consulting Archaeology Ltd).

incorporated within the dagger was, at this time, probably derived from Wales or north-west England (see Section 7.2), 350 km to the south-west. The materials buried with this man embody long-distance networks extending right across Britain. Button 1 alone, in its tiny 40 mm diameter form, connects the south-west tip of England to the north-east coast to southern Scotland. It is possible that the hard work of travelling and complex web of social relations which lay behind this collection of materialised geographies leant these buttons, and the garment they adorned, value, significance and meaning.

Our second burial is less well known and its key object somewhat less travelled. Excavations at Bar Pasture Farm near Thorney in Cambridgeshire revealed a neonate inhumation, buried within a round barrow during the Early Bronze Age (Richmond *et al.* 2010; see also discussion in Evans 2015). The baby had been placed on a length of birch bark and was accompanied by a complete Food Vessel and a single perforated seashell; the position of the shell, by the child's elbow, suggests that it may well have been dangled from the wrist (Fig. 7.02, left). The shell appears to be common limpet (*Patella vulgata*), although concretion prevents certain identification. Evans (2015), in discussing this find within a wider study of Fenland shell jewellery, notes that limpets are only found on rocky coasts and that, at this point during the Early Bronze Age, the nearest suitable location would have been Hunstanton, 60 km to the north-east of where the burial was found. He goes on to suggest that – at this time of significant environmental change and marine inundation in the Fens – the child's family may have moved directly to Thorney from the north Norfolk coast, bringing the shell with them as a memento of their old home as they relocated inland (*ibid.*, 1117). Even though it had not travelled very far, this tiny and simple shell may have materialised significant journeys, emotions and meaning, just as did the somewhat better travelled and fancier objects from Rameldry Farm. Near-local materials, objects and substances, we suggest in this chapter, have not been given sufficient attention compared with more far-away exotics. Yet they can be equally significant in terms of connections with people, places or journeys which are not 'everyday' and thus distant enough to stand-out, to be memorable and thus form significant grave goods for a variety of reasons. In the rest of this chapter, we investigate the geographical origins of objects placed in graves, focusing on the meanings of those that had travelled far but also on the often-considerable significance of those that did not.

7.2. 'Exotic' materials and mobility in prehistoric Europe

Objects moved widely across later prehistoric Europe, sometimes over very large distances. During the Neolithic, for example, we see the movement of jadeitite axes from their Alpine source as far as northern Scotland, western France and Scandinavia (Pétrequin *et al.* 2012). During the Bronze Age, it has been argued that a system comparable to modern globalisation – 'Bronzisation' – emerged (Vankilde 2016), largely driven by the need to move bronze's component parts, copper and tin, but also other materials; as a result, amber necklaces, for example, most likely sourced in Scandinavia and manufactured in southern England, ultimately ended up in Mycenaean shaft graves at the other end of Europe (Harding 1984, 77–81). During the Iron Age, certain Celtic art objects moved extreme distances leading to a Europe-wide art 'style' (Megaw and Megaw 1989), whilst 'Roman' items (many of which were in fact made in Gaul), such as amphorae and ceramic dinner sets, found their way into non-'Roman' elite mealtimes and grave deposits in southern England (Fitzpatrick 2007). Lying behind most previous discussions of these material mobilities is a notion of *value* relating to 'the exotic', to artefacts that had travelled long distances and/or had come from specific, known locations. Langdale stone axes from Cumbria in northern England, for example, are thought to have been intentionally quarried from a specifically notable and dangerous mountain-top location, accruing extra value or meaning because of this (Bradley and Edmonds 1993, 134). Equally, the specific origins and life-histories of certain Bronze Age weapons and other metalwork items appear to have been well known, with knowledge of these influencing the locations of their deposition (Fontijn 2019). In the Late Iron Age, 'Roman' products such as wine or imported spices are thought to have been employed strategically in elite contexts because of their foreignness and associated 'worth' (Fitzpatrick 2007).

Specifically, in relation to the study of grave goods, the notion of 'exotic' materials, associated with wealthy or otherwise powerful individuals, has operated as a dominant trope within interpretations for many years (see Chapter 2). In British prehistoric archaeology, this has been the case especially with regards to Early Bronze Age material where discussions of 'Wessex culture' graves in particular are concerned. 'The exotic' has featured in accounts from as far back as the early 19th century, when Colt Hoare (1812) noted the similarity between faience beads from Wiltshire and Egypt (cited in Sheridan and Shortland 2004, 268). The innately conservative views of British prehistoric society held by most Culture-Historians during the early 20th century, and the broad acceptance of a way of thinking that artefactual (and other) change was generally *introduced* from continental Europe, ensured that 'exotic' objects were essentially to be expected and thus little remarked upon. Piggott, for example, in coining the term 'Wessex culture' saw these burials as directly introduced from France against a native culture that was 'uninteresting and unenterprising' (S. Piggott 1938, 52), hardly problematising the importation of exotics like amber and faience at all.

By contrast, processual archaeologists such as Renfrew viewed this wealth, political power and status as internally generated and saw the objects caught up in 'rich' or 'exotic' graves as an inevitable and necessary expression of those – 'the recognized means by which leaders communicated their eminence and their power to those in the group inferior to them in status' (Renfrew 1973, 224).

Building upon these ideas, early post-processual, often structural Marxist, approaches evoked the notion of a 'prestige goods economy' (e.g. Shennan 1982; Thorpe and Richards 1984) whereby 'exotic' items represented a form of 'currency' within gift-exchange networks through which hierarchical social relationships were both created and consolidated (see also Fowler 2013, 85–6). Even in more recent years, the notion of prestige 'exotic' goods exchanged between elite members of society often over long distances has persisted to a considerable extent. As Sheridan and Shortland put it: 'the wealthier the grave and the more exotic, rare and well-crafted the possessions, the more powerful the individual is said to have been. It has become almost a commonplace of archaeological thinking' (2003, 18). Linked to this set of assumptions, Fowler has noted a wider tendency for interpretations to treat as equivalent, or blur, what are actually quite separate concepts or values – such as 'prestige', 'exotic', long-distance exchange and cosmology (2013, 89). Similarly, Jones has pointed out the circular reasoning in some of the arguments put forward: 'the assumed value of the substances and their context in single burials is mutually satisfying: value is conferred on the 'individual' by the association with exotic substances, and value is conferred on the substance since it is found in distinct and 'special' graves' (2002, 159).

As discussed in Chapter 2, over the past 20 years or so, some people have sought to shift interpretation away from the simplistic equation of 'exotic grave goods = wealth = power' – to a certain extent, at least. There has, for example, been a notable shift towards understanding certain materials (including amber, jet, faience, fossils, etc.) as having had, in themselves, supernatural or magical powers (e.g. Sheridan and Shortland 2003; Giles 2013; Woodward and Hunter 2015; Brück and Davies 2018). In most of these interpretations, however, these 'magical' materials are nonetheless seen to have been employed strategically by those who were important enough to possess them. Linked to many of these discussions, Mary Helms's anthropological work on objects, travel and value – most notably *Ulysses' Sail* (Helms 1988) – has been particularly influential, with numerous archaeological studies drawing on her examples for inspiration. Helms investigated artefact movement amongst contemporary non-western societies, moving her interpretive emphasis away from straightforwardly economic terms such as 'exchange' or 'trade' towards the idea of 'acquisition'. Her focus was on artefacts that came from beyond the directly comprehended social and cosmological realm of a given society, and the ways in which those objects accrued 'value' and even supernatural powers as a result of their origins in these 'mythical' places that were not immediately recognised and understood (see Needham 2000, 188 for an excellent summary of Helms's ideas and examples of their application to archaeology). Finally, it is important to note that in addition to these accounts which, arguably, have maintained the view of 'exotic' items as directly reflective of, or having provided, some kind of power held by the individual buried with them, some have sought to deconstruct the relationship between exotics in graves and powerful people in life more completely, building on arguments first clearly articulated by Brück (2004; see also Chapter 2, above). Fowler attempted to create a meaningful difference between the objects and the specific person buried in stating that 'the burial of a person may constitute a gathering, or bundling, of things, materials, and relations at the scale of the community but temporarily focused on a specific body and place' (2013, 100). Giles (2012, 250 following Sharples 2010, 95) has thus evoked the Iron Age chariot with its Celtic art horse-gear as one of the 'sacred items' probably owned by a whole community: an 'extravagant object' which become indissolubly and finally attached to a distinctive individual perhaps only in death. In this scenario, the burial becomes a lens through which the wider community – *not* the individual *per se* – expresses itself whilst adorning or equipping the deceased. We explore this idea, as well as the 'construction of the exotic', in further detail below.

Alongside these discussions of 'exotic' object movements, human mobility has risen again to become a key topic for debate within archaeology over the past 20 years, first as a result of the application of isotopic analysis and more recently also through the analysis of ancient DNA. Within our study period, the latter has thus far been particularly influential in relation to discussions of the arrival of the Neolithic in Britain and Ireland *c.* 4000 BC (Brace *et al.* 2018) and to the apparently large-scale immigration of 'Beaker people' *c.* 2500–2200 BC (Olalde *et al.* 2018). Material mobility is by no means a direct correlate for human mobility – objects can be passed 'down the line' and equally the movement of some people will not have resulted in the archaeologically visible movement of objects. However, as we shall see, especially at a fairly coarse level and large geographical scale, material mobility can provide significant insights into wider social processes and connections, as well as into past people's understandings of objects and what they meant. Importantly, to our minds, a detailed understanding of object movements can also offer a *parallel* – i.e. not necessarily competing, but not necessarily straightforwardly compatible – narrative to those told of human mobility through isotopes and aDNA. All these strands of evidence must necessarily be brought together to construct a holistic and effective understanding of process in the prehistoric past. The substantial geographical scale of most recent aDNA studies, combined with their targeted 'big picture' publication strategies, has – some have complained – led to a return of overly large trans-continental grand narratives, re-awakening – some have argued – age-old and outmoded Culture-Historical discussions. It must be said, however, that prior to these recent, hard science driven developments, a significant amount of artefact focused work in Britain had itself aimed to resolve comparable 'big picture' questions such as the introduction of 'the Neolithic' (e.g. Sheridan 2010) or the processes of Beaker adoption (e.g. Needham 2005).

It is notable that, even after the Culture-Historical interpretive focus on both people and materials arriving from continental Europe receded in the 1960s, the majority of accounts addressing 'big picture' change in British later prehistory have focused on *cross-Channel* material mobility. Connections across the Irish Sea, for example, or simply across the land, have not been considered nearly as much; the draw of international mobility in itself and of the associated international-scale discussions remains considerable. In contrast, accounts focusing on specific materials such as jet (Sheridan and Davis 2002) and stone (Woodward and Hunter 2011) have tended to investigate and emphasise the *internal* terrestrial movement of objects throughout Britain much more. As we discuss below, in reality, it is likely that cross-Channel interaction occurred throughout later prehistory but this would have occurred in differing intensities at different times and would have come to be expressed materially to differing degrees, with the latter potentially varying entirely independent of the former. Similarly, cross-land, insular interaction was doubtless always also a constant, with similar ebbs and flows that were again potentially independent of one another. This chapter on material mobility seeks to interrogate further the geographical movement of objects and the nature of the relationship between distance and value in contexts where, arguably, object life histories and people's life histories came to be most directly intertwined: the grave.

7.3. Material mobility from the Neolithic to the Iron Age: a brief outline

To set the scene for the analysis of material mobility (and immobility) among grave goods that forms the bulk of this chapter, in this section we explore briefly the character of object exchange and human interaction more generally throughout later prehistory in Britain.

Neolithic

The materials of the Early Neolithic (*c*. 4000–3300 BC) have long been recognised as having come from the European continent. Domesticated animals, cereals and pottery, and – perhaps two to three centuries later – long barrows and causewayed enclosures provide a clear link with earlier precedents across the Channel (Whittle *et al.* 2011). Recent aDNA studies indicate significant immigration of people from the Continent, probably along with these materials (Brace *et al.* 2018), suggesting that the latter's adoption by the existing indigenous population of Britain was less significant than previously suggested by many. Despite the *apparently* increasingly simple picture that is emerging of the process of 'transition' – at least at this one level – it is important to stress that significant material complexities nevertheless remain to be untangled. For example, although convincing parallels for Early Neolithic carinated bowl ceramic assemblages have been observed amongst the

Michelsberg and Chasséen complexes in northern France, the latter assemblages also contain ceramic forms, such as 'bottle-shaped' vessels and 'vase supports', which simply do not appear in the British assemblages supposedly derived from them (Anderson-Whymark and Garrow 2015, 69–70); lithic typologies on either side of the Channel are also characterised by significant differences as well (*ibid.*, 70). Equally, the relationship between continental funerary monument forms and those – again supposedly derived from them – in Early Neolithic Britain and Ireland is far from straightforward, leading Scarre (2015, 80) to suggest that a complex process of 'transmission and translation' occurred as the idea(s) of monumental architecture crossed the Channel during the early 4th millennium BC. As mentioned above, the relationship between genomic (and indeed isotopic) accounts, and those constructed in relation to artefacts and materials, is rarely straightforward – both parallel evidence-sets need to be combined in order to produce overarching narratives of change. Turning to terrestrial (as opposed to cross-Channel) material connections during the Early Neolithic, the picture also appears to be one of high connectivity. Neolithic things and practices spread rapidly across much of Britain and Ireland in the centuries around 3700 BC (Whittle *et al.* 2011, 836), for example, whilst the wide distribution of stone axes, sometimes over very long distances (Bradley and Edmonds 1993, 37–58) also suggests strong networks of connectivity and exchange.

In contrast to the previous phase, the Middle–Late Neolithic (*c.* 3300–2450) has generally been viewed as a period during which Britain and Ireland were not closely connected to the Continent. Ceramic styles (Impressed and Grooved Wares) and monument types (cursuses and henges) that were exclusive to Britain and Ireland emerged at this time. In contrast to the cross-Channel picture, strong connections across the Irish Sea and around the north-western seaways of Scotland are indicated materially through the movement of actual materials, as well as material styles and monument types (e.g. Ballin 2009; Wilkin and Vander Linden 2015). The fact that Grooved Ware pottery, for example, is found across Britain from Orkney to south-west England suggests that terrestrial connections remained strong. As with the previous phase, however, complex parallel narratives run alongside these simpler ones, with the 'Atlantic rock art phenomenon', for example, seemingly indicating an element of connectivity right across coastal north-western Europe (e.g. Bradley 1997) at some level.

Beaker/Early Bronze Age

The Beaker period, *c.* 2450–1600 BC, has long been viewed as representing clear evidence that continental connections were renewed – the immigration of 'Beaker people' into Britain has arguably been the most robust survivor of Culture-Historical narratives. The issue of 'Beaker culture' in Britain has been seen variously over time as a result of the arrival of Beaker-using *people* or of indigenous adoption of the *concept/package* (Vander Linden 2013; Parker Pearson *et al.* 2019, 2–15). Again, recent aDNA analysis has substantially transformed the debate, suggesting significant replacement of the indigenous gene pool by arriving Beaker-using people from the continent (Olalde *et al.* 2018; Parker Pearson *et al.* 2019, 435–6). Needham's (2005) influential model of Beaker adoption in Britain assumed relatively large-scale immigration from the outset and as a result remains widely cited and relevant today (e.g. Parker Pearson *et al.* 2019, 14–15). Needham suggested that the long-term process of Beaker use was characterised by three phases: Beaker as 'circumscribed culture' amongst a limited group of people *c.* 2500–2250 BC; Beaker as 'instituted culture' amongst the wider population in general *c.* 2250–1950 BC; and Beaker as 'past reference' when only a minority of communities still referred materially to that ceramic style *c.* 1950–1700/1600 BC (Needham 2005, 209–10).

The relationship between Beaker 'culture' and the implementation and subsequent wider spread of metalworking technologies is a complex one. The earliest known copper mine in Britain and Ireland is Ross Island in south-west Ireland. This site is known to have been in use from *c.* 2400 BC and is directly associated with substantial quantities of Beaker material culture (O'Brien 2004), leading some to suggest that Beaker-using prospectors specifically moved from continental Europe to Ireland in search of copper (see O'Brien 2014, 217–18). From around 2200 BC, there was an apparent wave of exploration further afield, which gave rise to copper mining in north and mid-Wales and north-west England (Timberlake 2009; Williams and Le Carlier de Veslud 2019). Almost all these sites appear to have gone out of use *c.* 1700 BC, around the same time as the large-scale, sub-surface copper workings at Great Orme in north-west Wales, took off. This site subsequently operated for *c.* 800 years with a particularly intense phase *c.* 1600–1400 BC (Williams and Le Carlier de Veslud 2019). During the main periods of their operation, both Ross Island and Great Orme are thought to have supplied the vast majority of all copper used in Britain (Bray 2012, 60; Williams and Le Carlier de Veslud 2019), indicating wide-ranging material exchange networks throughout much of the Bronze Age. A certain amount of European copper was imported during the early 'Ross Island' phase, while continental sources provided most of the raw material used in Britain from *c.* 1400 BC following the demise of Great Orme (Williams and Le Carlier de Veslud 2019, 1193). It is likely that tin from south-west England was a key source for north-west Europe as a whole, especially from *c.* 1600 BC when bronze (as opposed to copper) fully took off on the continent (*ibid.*, 1192). Similarly, gold from south-west England also appears to have been widely exchanged, apparently providing the raw material for most Early Bronze Age gold artefacts known from Ireland (Standish *et al.* 2015) and, consequently, probably Britain as well.

In terms of the wider use of materials other than metal, we see a particularly significant rise in 'Wessex culture' burials *c.* 1950–1500 BC, especially in central southern England but also more widely across Britain (see also Section 7.5). Various material types that must have been exchanged over long distances – including amber, jet and stone – are found in significant quantities during this period (Woodward and Hunter 2015). The 'Wessex culture' was initially viewed by Stuart Piggott as 'an actual ethnic movement' (1938, 52) from Brittany, but more recent accounts have sought to tone down and complexify his original arguments:

> the difficulty facing interpretation of the Armorican-Wessex links is then that, on the one hand, there are undeniable connections, the passage of certain material goods and ideas and, therefore inescapably, the movement of people to and fro, whilst on the other hand, there is little evidence that many of the travellers stayed on in foreign lands and little sign of any elements of convergence in burial practice and general belief structure. (Needham 2000, 188)

Needham suggests, drawing on Helms (1988), that a system of 'cosmological acquisition' was in operation that worked in both ways, with societies in Wessex and Armorica both keen to import objects from beyond '"real" human existence' and which thus had supernatural powers or cosmological significance (Needham 2000, 188).

The cross-Channel sea routes in operation throughout the Bronze Age have been discussed at length by Needham in particular (e.g. 2005; 2009; 2017). Needham's concept of the 'maritory' (a combination of *mare*, or sea, and territory) has been influential. In coining the term, he sought to move beyond the simply mechanical and physical aspects implied in the notion of a 'maritime interaction network' to include the beliefs and practices shared across that zone as well (Needham 2009, 13). Needham saw the Early Bronze Age Channel maritory as having been characterised, and given longevity, by a particular ideological and organisational infrastructure which also incorporated key 'ritual' objects such as precious cups (*ibid.*, 31–2). Interestingly, the results of large-scale multi-isotopic analysis conducted on 286 Beaker period burials across Britain indicates a pattern of fairly widespread but relatively low-level mobility (perhaps from region to region) of people, but only occasional, clear indications of very long-distance or cross-Channel movement (Parker Pearson *et al.* 2019, 404–5). It is important to emphasise that significant Early Bronze Age material connections and indications of exchange can be identified across the land as well as the sea. Jet from Whitby, North Yorkshire and stone from Langdale, Cumbria, were certainly transported long distances and apparently used to create 'special' artefacts – argued by some to have had particular ritual and/or magical powers – throughout the Early Bronze Age as well (Sheridan and Davis 2002; Sheridan and Shortland 2003; Woodward and Hunter 2015). Similarly, following on from the main period of use for Beaker pottery, ceramic styles unique to Britain and Ireland (Food Vessels and Collared Urns) emerged, extending right across those islands but not into continental Europe (Wilkin and Vander Linden 2015).

Middle/Late Bronze Age
The Middle and Late Bronze Age are characterised by continuing significant and strong material connections across the Channel. From the final Early Bronze Age onwards

(*c.* 1700–1500), some similarities across wide areas are evident in ceramics, house architectures and land allotment (Needham 2009, 20; Bradley *et al.* 2015, 171–212). However, by far the clearest evidence of mobility and long-distance relationships is seen in shared metalwork forms, leading Needham to describe the Channel as 'a super-highway facilitating connections' (2017, 45) during that period and many to discuss the existence of an 'Atlantic Bronze Age complex' extending from Iberia to eastern England (O'Connor 1980; Matthews 2017). Fontijn (2009, 131) has noted that 6% of all Bronze Age metal artefacts from the Netherlands and western Belgium are direct imports from Britain. In discussing these finds, he also makes an excellent point relevant to discussions throughout this chapter (i.e. beyond the specific period he is concerned with) – that the precise 'origin' point(s) (in our terms) of those objects may not actually have been known by the people ultimately using and depositing them. It is likely that many of those bronze artefacts were imported 'from' Britain via France, and thus would perhaps have been understood as having come 'from the south' rather than from across the sea (Fontijn 2009, 141; see also Fontijn and Roymans 2019). Notably, from the British perspective, the directionality of metal supply changed significantly *c.*1500/1400 BC, following the end of the main supply from the Great Orme mine in north Wales; at this point, European sources of metal became much more important.

Two probable shipwreck sites off the south coast of England at Salcombe, Devon and Langdon Bay, Kent shed further light on both the physical transportation of objects around north-west Europe (including across the Channel) and on people's understanding of 'foreign' artefact forms. The Langdon Bay assemblage, recovered from the sea bed, has produced large numbers of objects that are virtually unknown from terrestrial contexts in Britain, leading to the suggestion that metal must often have been transported across the Channel in artefactual form but then melted down and turned into locally acceptable object types (Needham *et al.* 2013, 91; Needham 2017, 38). Beads from the Late Bronze Age site of Must Farm, Cambridgeshire were potentially imported from as far away as the Middle East (Must Farm 2019), whilst four small turquoise glass beads from a Late Bronze Age or Early Iron Age upland roundhouse at Gardom's Edge, in Derbyshire, may have had a European or a Near Eastern origin (Jackson 2016 and Jackson in Barnatt *et al.* 2017, 177–81), demonstrating long-distance connections comparable to those known in the Early Bronze Age.

Ultimately, it might be said that the very high visibility – in metalwork at least – of long-distance exchange networks extending across wide areas of Europe during this period, and the academic discourse surrounding these, has to a certain extent overwhelmed our understanding of more local movements of people and things. It is assumed, probably correctly, that such large-scale movements especially of metal must have been underlain by smaller-scale, terrestrial mobility. Certainly, shared artefact types and similarities in many other elements of the material world suggest significant connectivity along these lines right across Britain.

Iron Age

The 'collapse' of Bronze Age metal exchange networks at the end of that period has long been seen as leading to a cessation of cross-Channel contact that essentially lasted until the Late Iron Age (Webley 2015, 122). However, it has more recently been pointed out that this view arises largely from a continued focus only on metalwork (especially 'Celtic art') and, later on, on 'Roman' imports. Webley has argued that, once our focus is shifted away from metal to 'domestic' material culture, numerous close similarities across the Channel are discernible (for example in iron tools, triangular loom weights and long-handled weaving combs):

> the material culture of the communities on either side of the Channel and North Sea from the 8th to 2nd centuries BC thus presents a complex picture. Often we see an emphasis on distinctive local identities expressed through media such as styles of personal equipment and decoration on pottery. At the same time, cross-regional connectivity throughout the period is implied by the sharing of new technologies and artefact types. This was not a time of isolation for Britain, nor were contacts limited to elite levels of society. (Webley 2015, 128)

As Joy has pointed out, within the sphere of 'elite' metalwork, the development of an 'insular' style of Celtic art in Britain and Ireland that was distinct from continental material does not necessarily indicate an absence of connections and could in fact have resulted from increased social contact (2015, 162).

We do not yet have the detailed aDNA and isotope data from Middle Iron Age populations to examine these connections further through individual and population level mobility, in the ways now possible for the Neolithic and Bronze Age (though the current COMMIOS aDNA project will assist greatly here). Whilst we have moved beyond the coarse-level equation of 'Arras' and 'Aylesford-Swarling' burials with large folk invasions we need not dismiss movements of 'first generation' migrants or rare and influential incomers as well as small groups into otherwise quite stable populations, as has been posited for East Yorkshire (Stead 1979, 93; Hunter 2019; Fernández-Götz 2019): a model which fits the current isotope data well (e.g. Jay and Richards 2006). Alongside affinities in domestic material culture, the sporadic exchange of finished objects (such as torcs, bracelets or anthropoid swords) as well as raw substances (coral, amber and gold) suggests a continuing interest in portable 'exotica', sometimes recycled from an earlier object (such as the Danes Graves wheel-headed pin, Giles 2013): customised and 'worked up' locally. The tiny iron pin from the Wetwang Slack female chariot burial, with its bead of coral and dot-and-circle impressed slip of gold, shows how local people compressed the power of the exotic into miniature form. As with the vegetal tendrils of La Tène art, designs and substances were idiosyncratically deployed amongst avian and aquatic, or bovine and equine imagery, to create locally *affective* art from this wider Continental 'grammar' (Giles 2008; Garrow and Gosden 2012, after Fox 1958).

Figure 7.03 The Wetwang Slack female chariot burial pin (© Hull and East Riding Museum: Hull Museums).

Cross-Channel exchange networks become much more clearly visible during the last two centuries BC, with wine amphorae, Armorican pottery and Gallo-Belgic coinage circulating on both sides of the Channel, facilitated by the establishment of a number of 'ports-of-trade' along the south coast of England (Fitzpatrick 1992; Cunliffe 2009a; 2009b; Webley 2015; Bradley *et al.* 2015, 302–4). Materials going in the other direction are less easy to spot but, certainly, Kimmeridge shale from Dorset appears to have been exported into northern France (Webley 2015, 129). In the second half of the 1st century BC, from around the time of the Roman conquest of Gaul, exchange links to south-east England became even more prominent, with wine and olive oil amphorae and subsequently Gallo-Belgic and Mediterranean tableware pottery imported, along with some elaborate Italian metal vessels; technologies such as wheel-turned pottery and coin minting also came in (Webley 2015, 129–30). A pulse of mid-1st century BC 'weapons burials' along the south coast, interred with continental designed shield umbos, swords and unique artefacts, such as the North Bersted helmet, have been linked to classical texts as evidence either of returning British mercenaries from Caesar's Gallic wars (laden with trophies or gifts for their service) or as actual immigrants – resistance figures or political asylum seekers – absorbed into British tribes at a time of crisis and buried in ways that often then reflect a fusion of cultural identities. Less tangible 'imports' from the continent, such as political centralisation and social hierarchy, are also evident – the dynamics behind these have been much debated (Creighton 2000; Haselgrove 2001) and although they are too complex to get into detail about here, we discuss their impact in relation to Late Iron Age grave goods in Chapter 8. As we also saw for the Middle/Late Bronze Age, the significant long-distance connections and relatively high population densities visible throughout the Iron Age have to some extent led to a presumption of internal, terrestrial mobility as well. The picture is certainly one of connectivity but equally of significant localism and regionality at many different scales (Cunliffe 2009a; Sharples 2010).

Summary

The picture of material (and human) mobility throughout later prehistory into and across Britain is thus a complex one characterised by ebbs and flows of *archaeologically visible* connections which, presumably, sometimes at least, must have reflected accurately the intensity of actual contact as well. From the start of the Neolithic onwards, the picture is broadly one of substantial flow of materials both across the Channel and around Britain and the Irish Sea – jadeitite, Langdale tuff, copper, gold, tin, amber, jet, shale, olive oil, wine. The movement of object *styles* is more difficult to grasp interpretatively, since these can of course travel as ideas; nonetheless, the movement of concepts and styles does represent material mobility of a sort. The non-movement of certain things – Grooved Ware or cursus monuments across the Channel for example – is harder to interpret still since the *absence* of take-up of a concept or practice does not necessarily indicate an absence of connections or material mobility in other spheres. As Culture-Historians were well aware, the relationship between the movement of materials, people and ideas is a tricky one to untangle. In the remainder of this chapter, therefore, we stick primarily to objects that we *know* – geologically – moved (or stayed put), investigating what they can tell us about objects, place and geographical meaning from the Neolithic to the Iron Age.

7.4. Grave goods and material mobility

This book is about the relationship between objects and people, but also between people and people, and objects and objects. Objects that had travelled far, and objects that had stayed broadly local, found in graves, have a great deal to tell us about all those things. The geographical mobility of grave goods has certainly been commented on before, but primarily in relation to the Early Bronze Age and usually only with reference to a single material (e.g. Beck and Shennan 1991; Sheridan and Davis 2002; Hunter and Woodward 2011; 2015; Standish *et al.* 2015). The very long-term perspective offered by the GGDB provides us with a unique insight into the mobility, perception and use of materials over the course of later prehistory which, as we will see below, enables us to present a subtly different account to the broader narrative outlined above. This, in turn, potentially provides us with insights into the shifting directionality of social and 'economic' relationships, enabling – where appropriate – a shift away from the overly-dominant discourse of cross-Channel connections towards terrestrial ones, and shedding new light on perceptions of 'value', 'place' and 'the exotic'. We have already discussed the tendency within archaeological narratives concerned with material mobility to focus on 'exotic' (and thus it is usually assumed 'special') objects whose value was assigned to them for this reason. In line with one of the *Grave Goods* project's key aims – to bring to the fore those grave goods that do not always see time in the limelight – in this chapter we also focus substantially on objects that had travelled only a short distance and on those which appear to reflect directly a geographically immediate sense of place.

Methodology

The following analysis of mobile materials divides into two parts. In the first, we investigate what we have termed 'exotic' materials – those whose source area can be determined with confidence and which, therefore, can often be demonstrated to have moved long distances before being buried in a grave. It is important to stress that in using the word 'exotic' ourselves, we simply mean geologically/geographically exotic (in a contemporary sense), not necessarily symbolically exotic (in the past) as well. This analysis enables us to assess the nature of connectivity across Britain (and beyond) through time, and thus also to start to consider the reasons how and why certain raw materials may have been moved so far. In the second part, we investigate the deployment of 'local' materials in burials – focusing on objects which appear likely to have been sourced in or close to the area in which they were deposited. An understanding of 'the local' is a crucial counterpart to any interpretation of 'the exotic' – both are determined relationally – and to a full understanding of the materiality of grave goods throughout later prehistory.

The materials we have included in our study as 'exotics' are amber, coral, gold, jet, shale, steatite and tin. It is crucial to state at the outset that the process of establishing precise origin points, even for these materials, is not totally straightforward. Nonetheless, as we explain below, their sources can usually be ascertained with sufficient confidence to undertake a meaningful spatial study. Amber in later prehistoric Britain is likely to have been imported from across the North Sea. Amber occurs naturally across the Baltic region and at this time was widely used, closest to Britain, in Scandinavia (Beck and Shennan 1991, 16). While it is possible to collect pieces of amber washed up on the coastline of eastern England and Scotland, the relatively low levels available there make it probable that most later prehistoric amber in Britain was imported from Scandinavia (*ibid.*, 37). Prehistoric coral is most likely to have been traded from the western Mediterranean region (Skeates 1993): Pliny's *Natural History* xxxii: 11 particularly mentions the area of the 'Gallic Gulf' (off the coast of Provence) as well as Sicily, as highly prized sources and it is the pinkish-red, less brittle form (*Corallium rubrum*) which appears to have been favoured in prehistory (Champion 1976; Stead 1979, 87). Yet as Adams (2013, 159) has pointed out, cold water coral (*Lophelia pertusa*) washed up from the Atlantic waters around Scotland, represents the nearest source: she cites the Roman author Ausonius, who described both the 'red corals and the white berries, fruit of the shell' found in these waters. Whilst degradation and discolouration in the prehistoric examples makes them difficult to compare with modern coral sources (*ibid.*, 157), Raman spectroscopy on brooch inlays from Iron Age East Yorkshire identified a parrodiene component consistent with *Corallium* species (*ibid.*, 314).

In our spatial mapping (Fig. 7.06, below) we have thus indicated 'coral connections' towards the Mediterranean as the most likely source. Gold is, on the basis of the evidence currently available, most likely to have been sourced in Cornwall, at least during the Early Bronze Age, though Late Iron Age gold use may owe more to recycled, imported coinage (Webley *et al.* 2020, 12). Mineralogically, gold sources are found more widely, including in Wales and Ireland. However, recent chemical analyses of later prehistoric gold artefacts from Ireland strongly suggested that these were sourced in south-west England despite the availability of gold closer by (Standish *et al.* 2015). Consequently, it is likely – if not yet demonstrated for certain – that at least some, and possibly all, the raw material used to make prehistoric gold artefacts (especially during the Bronze Age) in Britain was also sourced in Cornwall. In our spatial visualisations, in order not to complicate the images too much, we have used *only* Cornwall as the source area for gold; however, it should be borne in mind that other regions – also in the west – *could* have supplied the raw material as well.

Jet is well known to have been sourced primarily from Whitby, North Yorkshire, from the Neolithic through to the modern day. While other sources of jet are known, in Dorset and Scotland, it has been argued that even objects found in those regions were nonetheless often from Whitby (Sheridan and Davis 2002, 816). Shale is closely associated with the well known source at Kimmeridge, Dorset on the south coast of England. Geologically, shale is widespread across Britain, and as a consequence we have included only artefacts specifically identified as having come from Kimmeridge in our study of 'exotic' materials; other possibly 'local' shales are discussed in the next section. Steatite can be specifically located – it is known to have been quarried only in Shetland during later prehistory (Bray *et al.* 2009) and, of our six study areas, ended up only in Orkney. The single tin object recorded (from the Isles of Scilly) is very likely to have been sourced from Cornwall. Finally, it is worth noting that, purely by chance, the main known or likely source areas for four of our seven 'exotic' materials (gold, tin, shale and jet) are actually situated within, or very close to, three of our case study areas (Cornwall, Dorset and East Yorkshire). As will become clear below, this represents a substantial bonus in that it enables us to look at 'exotic' materials in their local area, where they were not necessarily geographically 'exotic'.

Our analysis of 'local' materials focuses on artefacts made from a wide variety of stone types: chalk, gneiss, granite, greenstone, limestone, pumice, quartz/quartzite, sandstone and slate; jet, shale and steatite are also included in this analysis. All of the former are found in disparate areas of Britain and thus cannot be attributed confidently to one specific source area. Our case study areas are widely distributed and, of course, as a result, have their own specific and distinctive geologies. In the analysis that follows we have simply investigated the uses of 'local' and 'non-local' stone on the basis of whether a given material is known, geologically, within or close to that case study area. It is theoretically possible that, for example, a chalk item buried on the Wolds of East Yorkshire could actually have come from the chalklands of Dorset, and so on, but for understandable reasons we have elected to run with the most parsimonious explanation unless there are clear indications that we should not do. Our aim has been to establish which objects were *probably* local in origin and which were *almost certainly* not; as will become evident, in most cases, this was abundantly clear.

There are, of course, certain biases inherent within our data which need to be borne in mind. First, as with almost every analysis in this book, we are talking about objects in graves, *not* all objects, meaning that those periods with fewer burials or with less of a tendency for grave goods to be deposited are under-represented. This does not represent a 'total' study of material mobility but a partial one undertaken on the substantial – and certainly significant – sample of later prehistoric objects recovered in graves. We are also limited within our broad-scale analyses to material recovered in our case study areas. It is also important to note that, in presenting our data, we have generally counted the total number of 'occurrences' of each material (meaning that several different objects made from one material in one burial will usually have been counted multiple times), as we considered that the most accurate method of assessing the intensity of material mobility and exchange. It is also worth stating that two very common grave good types, copper-alloy and pottery objects, may well often have been, or viewed as being, 'exotic' in addition to those listed above. However, their geographical origins were too complicated to approach in the context of this chapter (and indeed this project more generally).

7.5. 'Exotic' materials

In total, 175 artefacts made from the materials we have defined as 'exotic' in this chapter were recorded within the GGDB. As might be expected, their prevalence varied considerably both through time and across space (Figs 7.04 and 7.05). In temporal terms, the Neolithic is conspicuous in having no 'exotics' – as defined here. It is worth noting that artefacts which had moved long distances but were not made from those materials specified as 'exotic' here – such as the gneiss macehead from Orkney which is likely to have been imported from the Outer Hebrides (Anderson-Whymark *et al.* 2017, 12), or the chisel/whetstone from Cowlam G59, East Yorkshire made from Lake District stone (Kinnes and Longworth 1985, 58–9) – were occasionally identified. Meanwhile, the Middle/Late Bronze Age is represented only by amber – three beads from three different graves on one site, Margett's Pit in Kent (Wessex Archaeology 2010). The Beaker/Early Bronze Age and Iron Age periods, in contrast, stand out markedly as having significant numbers of 'exotics'. The widely perceived Beaker/Early Bronze Age rise in both materials and material mobility (discussed in Section 7.2) is very clearly reflected in our data. Similarly, it is also evident that the Iron Age saw significant, if lesser, quantities of 'exotic' artefacts buried with the dead as well. Thus, whilst Collis has memorably referred to the lack of exotic imports in 4th–3rd century BC burials across Britain and the near Continent as an 'ebbing tide' (1984), our data supports his argument that this lull is transcended by portable substances like coral, amber and some marine shell (Collis 2001, building on Champion 1976 and 1982). Steatite is found exclusively in the Beaker/Early Bronze Age period (although it should be noted that some steatite objects could only be attributed to the Bronze Age as a whole and thus were not included in this temporally specific study), whilst coral and tin appear only in Iron Age graves. Jet and gold, while found in both periods, occur much more commonly in the Beaker/Early Bronze Age phase.

In terms of the spatial distribution of 'exotics' across our case study areas, clear differences are also found. Figure 7.05 illustrates the geographical locations of our selected 'exotics' across all periods. Interestingly, those bars that stand out most clearly in the chart are jet in East Yorkshire and steatite in Orkney. Although Whitby is located in modern day North (not East) Yorkshire, the proximity of this source has clearly influenced strongly the kinds of material deposited in that region (see also Section 7.7). While jet certainly made it much further afield (with a notable peak on the

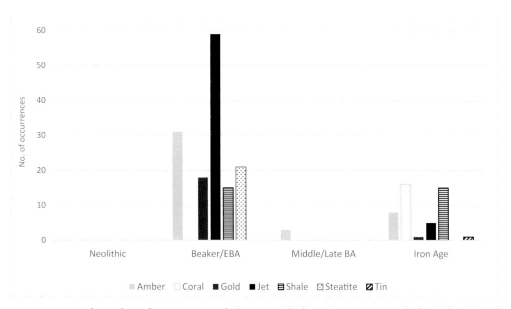

Figure 7.04 Total number of occurrences of objects made from 'exotic' materials (as defined here) within the GGDB, by period.

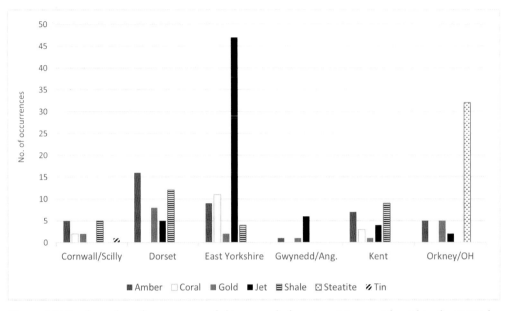

Figure 7.05 Total number of occurrences of objects made from 'exotic' materials within the GGDB, by case study area.

opposite side of Britain in Gwynedd, as well as in Wiltshire which is not represented in our data), it was most often placed in graves close by: a 'local' exotic acquired from very specific coastal sources which might nonetheless represent significant and memorable journeys of acquisition. Steatite presents us with an interesting local/non-local dynamic to unpick. The quarries, for what then usually became steatite 'urns', were located in Shetland (Bray *et al.* 2009, 7), which while local in comparison to all of our other case study areas is nonetheless situated a considerable distance, over often very difficult seas, away from Orkney. While 'local' at the scale of Britain, these objects may well have been viewed as 'exotic' at the regional scale (see also Sharman 2009, 47). Given the substantial material connections between Orkney and other parts of Britain (and beyond) which are clearly visible in other materials (Fig. 7.05), it is interesting that steatite urns did not end up further afield as well. Dorset, the source of Kimmeridge shale, also has the highest number of artefacts made from that material but this peak does not stand out nearly as much. Other notable material peaks include that of amber in Dorset, a pattern that fits comfortably with the prevalence of Early Bronze Age 'Wessex culture' burials, and coral in East Yorkshire, an exclusively Iron Age material that, again, sits relatively comfortably with expectations given the high numbers of recorded burials in this region at that time. Amber and gold were the only materials to be recovered in all six of our case study regions; as noted above, amber was also the only 'exotic' to feature in each period from the Beaker phase to the Iron Age.

In order to represent the material mobility of our 'exotics' more fully, this time including the directionality and intensity of movement as well, Figure 7.06 maps the extent and quantity of these connections, by period. While the lines necessarily extend *straight* from source area to point of deposition, needless to say it is likely that the objects/raw materials themselves travelled less directly in reality – these images are intended to represent material mobility networks *schematically*, not to show the 'true' paths that objects and/or raw materials took, which would be impossible.

Give the numbers of 'exotics', by period, discussed above, it is no surprise that the Beaker/Early Bronze Age and Iron Age phases again stand out in Figure 7.06. In the case of the former, the connections are substantial in both number and distance, extending right across the UK and beyond. Notably, for this phase, lines can be seen connecting every case study area with all the others, either directly or via one additional step. This indicates substantial flows of material right across the country at this time. Notably, even the Outer Hebrides, which produced low amounts of material culture generally within our study and thus had less potential to feature strongly from the outset, would be integrated into this visualisation if we had opted to include the gneiss macehead found in a small cist at Dounby in Orkney, mentioned above, which was probably imported from north-west Scotland or the Outer Hebrides (Anderson-Whymark *et al.* 2017, 12). The Middle/Late Bronze Age phase features only as a consequence of the amber beads from Kent mentioned above. The map of Iron Age connections is quite different to the Beaker/Early Bronze Age period, with a notable and exclusive emphasis on the south-east. The absence of clear terrestrial connections is also striking – our arrows extend almost entirely across the Channel and around the coast. Even those which, in our schematic diagram, do extend visibly across the land are depicting links – between Scandinavia and Cornwall, and Whitby and Kent – that are arguably more likely to have occurred by sea as well. In both Dorset and Kent, burials of the Late Iron Age contain direct imports showing links to the Channel Islands and the near Continent, especially Gaul. The seaboard may have been the preferred route of movement for all of these connections – journeys of 'middle' as well as longer distance that were still challenging and dangerous, freighting these materials with significance.

In summary, as far as our 'exotic' materials are concerned, clear, extreme variability is in evidence. This patterning was certainly affected, but equally not totally dictated, by raw numbers of burials and the character of grave goods during any one phase. The total absence of exotics (as defined here) during the Neolithic comes as a bit of a surprise, revealing perhaps in relation to the perception of materials at that time rather than the actual mobility of people (which is generally assumed to have been significant). It is also interesting how the patterns revealed for the Beaker/Early Bronze Age and Iron Age reflect to a considerable extent those expected, although the network diagram for the former phase is arguably even more extensive and impressive than predicted. The final key pattern observed is the *local* prevalence of certain 'exotics', most notably jet in East Yorkshire but also shale in Dorset and

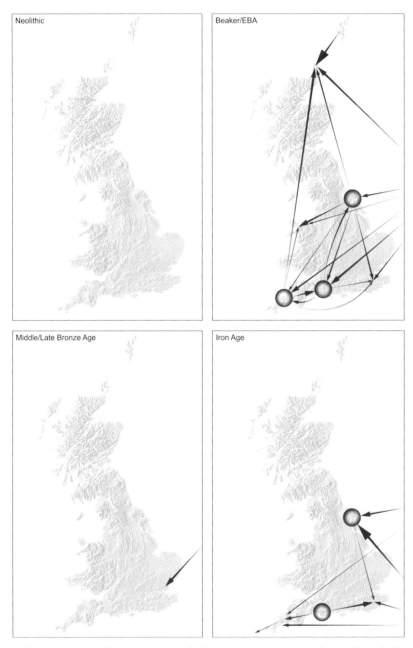

Figure 7.06 The movement of 'exotic' materials, by period. Arrows are drawn directly between the material's most likely source and the case study area where it was deposited; the size of the arrows represents the strength of connection (i.e. number of objects in that material deposited in a given case study area); the raw material source locations relevant to each period are indicated with circles (image: Craig Williams).

(possibly) steatite in Orkney as well. These 'local exotics' are explored in more detail below.

7.6. Local materials

In this section, we explore the deployment of local materials as grave goods. The materials considered, as geologically locatable stone types, are: chalk, gneiss, granite, greenstone, jet, limestone, pumice, quartz/quartzite, sandstone, shale, slate and steatite. In total, 293 objects made from these stone types were recorded in the GGDB. As part of our analysis, each individual item was characterised as probably 'local' or 'non-local' according to whether or not its specific material(s) could be found, naturally, within or close to the case study area concerned.

Figure 7.07 shows the number of local and non-local stone objects recorded across space and through time. It is immediately apparent that local objects dominate the picture, with the most notable peaks in Cornwall and East Yorkshire during the Beaker/Early Bronze Age period and in Dorset during the Middle/Late Bronze Age. The significant peak of 'non-local' objects in Orkney during the Beaker/Early Bronze Age period reflects the high number of steatite urns imported from Shetland (discussed above). Interestingly, Kent is the only other region to see a predominance of non-local items, in both the Beaker/Early Bronze Age period and the Iron Age; the earlier of

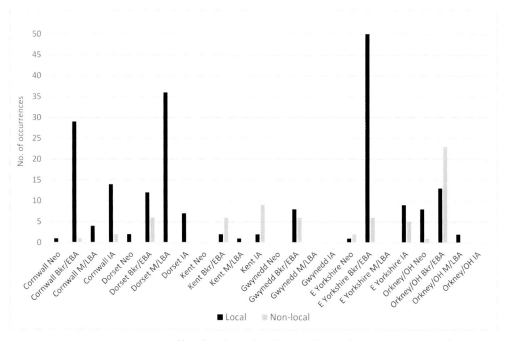

Figure 7.07 Occurrence of local and non-local stone objects, by region and period.

the two is not dominated by any particular material/item, the latter is primarily a reflection of abundant shale armlets most and possibly all of which would have been imported from Dorset.

The process of drilling down into the notable peaks amongst 'local' objects is revealing, not least because it often reflects a very specific, localised practice involving those local materials. Some of the peaks are simply the result of a variety of local objects combining to produce a high total (e.g. Orkney Neolithic/Early Bronze Age, Gwynedd Early Bronze Age, Cornwall IA). However, others are caused by a very strong preponderance of one particular thing. The Cornwall Beaker/Early Bronze Age peak, for example, is created by high numbers of quartz pebbles, which were identified in 16 out of the 26 graves included in this analysis. The Dorset Middle/Late Bronze Age peak is the result of high numbers of sandstone pot 'lids' having been recorded, especially at the Simon's Ground barrow group but also at a number of other sites. The East Yorkshire Beaker/Early Bronze Age peak reflects high numbers of jet items, including buttons, necklaces and beads. The Dorset Beaker/Early Bronze Age and IA peaks (albeit low ones relatively) are both caused mainly by the presence of shale bracelets. Finally, the peak of local objects during the East Yorkshire Iron Age is mainly a consequence of the presence of chalk objects – in the form of worked blocks (4/14 graves) and spindle whorls (4/14 graves).

The significance of the local: quartz, sandstone and chalk
To investigate the significance of the 'local' in a little more detail, in this section we drill down further into the specific details of a selection of the 'local' object types regularly placed in graves. The case study examples we have selected cover a range of periods and geographical regions and focus on a series of objects/materials that have not always been much discussed: quartz in Early Bronze Age Cornwall, sandstone in Middle/Late Bronze Age Dorset and chalk in Iron Age East Yorkshire.

Quartz in Early Bronze Age Cornwall
The quartz objects found in Early Bronze Age burials in Cornwall were exclusively unworked stones – sometimes representing quartz in its translucent crystalline form, sometimes simple pebbles or stones. These were recorded within the GGDB in a wide variety of positions within those burials: surrounding and supporting an urn ('Shepherd's House' barrow: Patchett 1944; 1952); singly inside an urn, along with a small quantity of 'comminuted' burnt bone (Crigamennis barrow: Christie 1960); with several more traditional grave goods, including a Trevisker urn and a sheet bronze pendant, buried with five cremated individuals within a cist (Harlyn Bay, Site 32093: Jones *et al.* 2011); forming a cobble lining at the base of a cist (Trelowthas: Nowakowski 1995); and so on.

It is important to stress that, while quartz pebbles already stand out as a significant regional element within the GGDB, the presence of quartz within Bronze Age burial contexts in Cornwall is actually far more significant than our recorded evidence alone suggests (see for example Jones 2005, 73–122). Quartz features prominently on many mortuary sites, performing roles beyond being clearly definable 'grave goods'. Numerous barrows and cairns included quartz as a key element of their funerary architecture: for example, as a white kerb for the dark slate cairn at Treligga 1; as part of the make-up of the barrow mounds at Treligga 2 and Carvinack (Fig. 7.08); as a scatter of stone and Trevisker pottery within the mound at Davidstow 16; as cist linings and as a large block adjacent to a cist within a larger pit at Harlyn Bay sites 21705, 21769 and 57953 (A.M. Jones 2005, 76–7, 100; Jones *et al.* 2011, 97; Jones and Mikulski 2015). Equally, quartz also features very strongly as an element of wider depositional practice – not directly centred around human remains – at many funerary sites: for example, being scattered (along with dagger fragments, flint and tin slag) across the central area of the ring cairn at Caerloggas 1; placed with deposits of charcoal in three pits under the mound at Cocksbarrow; and forming part of a massive deposit of over 100 blocks within the eastern quadrant of the barrow ditch at Davidstow 3 (A.M. Jones 2005, 92–3, 106). The deposition of quartz appears to have continued to be significant into the Middle Bronze Age as well, being included in relatively rare burials, as at Constantine Island where the person's skull was resting on a 'pillow'

Figure 7.08 Internal quartz 'core' clearly visible within the main soil mound at Carvinack, Cornwall (photograph originally in colour © Cornwall Council).

Figure 7.09 A selection of quartz pebbles from the Middle Bronze Age cist burial at Constantine Island, Cornwall (photograph: Andy M. Jones © Cornwall Archaeological Unit).

of quartz-rich stone and a series of quartz pebbles were the only 'grave goods' (A.M. Jones 2010, 74; Fig. 7.09), and in various significant settlement contexts (*ibid.*, 92–3).

Quartz was clearly significant to people during the Early Bronze Age in Cornwall, and especially so, it seems, within the mortuary sphere. Notably, this also appears to have been the case – if to a slightly less visible extent – in our other quartz-rich case study areas, the Outer Hebrides and Gwynedd/Anglesey, as well as further afield (Brück 2019, 169–70). The reason(s) why this was the case are impossible to establish with any degree of certainty. Nonetheless, in exploring the significance of local materials, it is nonetheless worth considering some possibilities. The symbolism of quartz in prehistory (and later) has been discussed previously, not least because it is widely employed in various Neolithic ritual contexts across Britain and Ireland (Darvill 2002; see also Gilchrist 2019, 110–44 for a review of quartz's use in the medieval period). Especially in certain circumstances, the 'whiteness' of quartz appears to have been a key emphasis, providing visual effects in contrast to other, darker materials and as a reflective substance. Darvill (2002, 74) notes the symbolic meanings that the colour white has in many different cultures, often being associated with concepts such as purity, peace, happiness, newness, etc. Quartz is also luminescent, reflecting both moonlight and firelight, and when struck or rubbed together has triboluminescent properties making it glow (Jones and Goskar 2017, 288). Past discussions have linked the use of quartz to both solar and lunar symbolism, for example in recumbent stones circles and passage graves, and consequently also to associations of death more widely (Darvill 2002, 84; see also Warren and Neighbour 2004, 9; Bradley 2005, 112). As Burl put it:

> it may not be too fanciful to think that they saw, in the litter of quartz that glittered so brilliantly in the moonlight, fragments of the moon itself. The same connections between quartz, moon and death may have led to the frequent deposits of quartz and white pebbles with burials in prehistoric Britain. (Burl 1980, 196)

Taking this argument further, Tilley has explored the notion that the white of quartz may have been metaphorically linked to the white of human bones, with the stone perhaps even being viewed as 'the bones of the land' (1995, 48). Darvill also discussed the fact that prominent quartz features in the landscape may have formed part of people's 'sacred geography' (2002, 86), which would then have been referenced when the rock was deposited within a particular context elsewhere. Owoc (2002) has viewed quartz as one portion of a spectrum of prehistoric colours employed within burial mounds in south-west England, all of which held particular meanings and significances, and which may have referenced the parts of the landscape from which they came. Tilley too has suggested that the process of bringing different clays and stone types together on one site may have created and symbolised the landscape in microcosm (1995, 48; see also Brück 2019, 170–1). At the slightly more mundane end of the interpretive spectrum, Warren and Neighbour (2004) have suggested that quartz's 'deep' symbolism but also its 'everyday' significance to people (as a workable raw material that people encountered throughout their lives) may have been drawn upon in combination within funerary contexts. Equally, Jones *et al.* (2011, 101) suggested that, at Harlyn Bay, the high incidence of quartz within many of the numerous Early Bronze Age pits and cists found in the vicinity may have been a means simply of referencing past mortuary acts and thus of binding the community together through shared memories and practices.

Ultimately, it is impossible to know which, if any, of these possible significances lay behind the use of quartz in Bronze Age burials (and practices associated more widely with mortuary activity) in Cornwall. Entirely different meanings could have been relevant at different times and different places, and certainly the wide variety of uses to which quartz was put might be seen as indicating a spectrum of significance. Quartz is undoubtedly one of the key materials found on sites of this date in the region. The prevalence of this locally available material – not just as grave goods in burials but as part of these sites' wider architecture and depositional events – suggests that it was regularly important to people to incorporate the associations it had. In contrast to many of the 'exotic' substances we discussed in the previous section, which had come from afar, quartz would have been a material that people in Cornwall during the Bronze Age encountered regularly and, presumably, often as part of their everyday routines (see also Warren and Neighbour 2004). The fact that, on a number of sites, quartz was combined with other local minerals (such as slate, yellow clay, killas and tourmaline) may indicate that other aspects of the local landscape were evoked in burial as well. It is possible that people wished to reference familiar landscape locations and routines in the context of burial and other 'ritual' activities at mortuary sites through their deposition. Quartz's meaning or 'value' clearly was significant, but it was arguably derived through everyday encounter and the regularities of life.

Sandstone in Middle Bronze Age Dorset
The presence of sandstone in Middle Bronze Age burials in Dorset is significant. The GGDB records a total of 33 sandstone lids, all of them associated with cremation urns. It is in fact likely that the actual total should be much higher, since an additional 68 lids made from 'stone (unspecified)' dating to the Middle Bronze Age were also recorded in Dorset and it is likely that many of these too were sandstone; equally, many more of these essentially unworked stones are likely to have been discarded, unrecorded, by antiquarian excavators and others. Interestingly, three ironstone, one limestone, one ceramic (with a handle) and one possible wooden lids, and one shell 'lid' (found to be capping an urn), were also recorded from Middle Bronze Age Dorset. Stone lids were employed in a variety of ways – they were usually used to cap the top of upright urns which contained cremated bones but were also sometimes placed on the upward-facing bases of inverted urns or on the downward-facing rims of inverted urns (i.e. almost 'holding in' the cremated bone against gravity). A small number of the capstones/lids had previously been used as quernstones, but most were simple, large slabs (Fig. 7.10). At the site of Simons Ground, where the lids are particularly well recorded, small 'cairns' of multiple stones had also been employed as a kind of 'lid' (White 1982, 20; see also below).

The site of Simons Ground, excavated in 1967–9, is worth exploring in some detail, not just because it contributed 29 of the total of 33 certainly identified sandstone lids within the GGDB, but also because of the depth of thought given both to these objects and to the wider use of sandstone in the site report (White 1982). Simons Ground was a substantial Deverel-Rimbury cremation cemetery, focused on five excavated barrows. Only one of the barrows contained a central burial; notably this too had an impressive sandstone lid capping the urn (Fig. 7.11). Altogether 'about 300 cremation urns were found, containing a minimum of 138 cremated individuals' (*ibid.*, 1); these extended in a broadly linear spread over an area of *c.* 250 m between the barrows. White clearly considered the 'missing' cremation burials to be the result of post-depositional processes (*ibid.*, 42-43), but it is also possible that burial-like deposits which never contained any human bone had been made on the site (Cooper *et al.* 2020, 146).

The Simons Ground report details 29 sandstone lids altogether, spread across the four main clusters of cremation/urn burials (White 1982, 22). The majority (19) of these 'usually occurred in the form of lumps piled, as a small cairn, on top of

Figure 7.10 Urn B28 at Simons Ground (foreground), with its capstone/lid clearly visible (White 1982, pl. 9; reproduced with kind permission of Dorset Natural History & Archaeological Society).

the rims of upright urns' (*ibid.*, 20), but five such cairns, placed on the bases of inverted urns were also noted, along with five large sandstone slab lids (which occurred only on upright urns) (*ibid.*, 22; Figs 7.10 and 7.11). Most (19/29) of the 'lids' were identified close to Barrow B but small numbers were found elsewhere across the site. Sandstone was also used in variety of other ways. White noted the presence of 'empty' pits (i.e. those that did not contain urns or cremated bone) which sometimes contained sandstone pebbles and occasionally

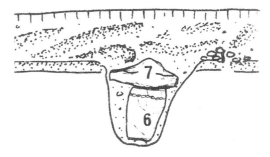

Figure 7.11 '6. Primary urn F48 and 7, its capstone' at Simons Ground (White 1982, fig. 11 detail; reproduced with kind permission of Dorset Natural History & Archaeological Society).

large slabs; the latter he suggested might have acted as packing for isolated 'marker or ritual posts' (1982, 20). Similarly, he also suggested a specific use for the spreads of sandstone 'lumps' observed in one area of the site: 'these were found directly under the heather turf and extended in a long line over the pots in the Linear Urnfield [around Barrow F]. The lumps were about 8 inches apart and clearly marked the position of the urnfield' (*ibid.*, 22). Scatters of large sandstone lumps were also found in distinct concentrations in some of the ring-ditches as well (*ibid.*, 8).

The theme of the Simons Ground burials having been marked – and clearly identifiable to people during the Middle Bronze Age – is one that White emphasises throughout his report: 'in the vast majority of instances the pots were incomplete; upright ones lacked their rims and inverted ones their bases. This seems to indicate that urns were only partially buried to mark their position clearly' (*ibid.*, 20; see also 43). This image of an urnfield with some pots poking out of the ground, and others marked by stone cairns, slabs and scatters of pebbles, is intriguing, and one which certainly fits well with recent narratives of the period which have suggested that burials were commonly revisited, and that cremated bone may have been a 'resource' distributed amongst the living (e.g. Brück 2019). It may be the case that White did, to some extent, under-estimate the effects of later truncation (although he certainly considered them (1982, 3)); but even if so, equally, it does seem clear that many of the burials were marked – even if only just under the surface – in various ways. The notion that our sandstone lids were actually visible above ground facilitating later access – both 'in' and 'out' – to the cremated bone is a really interesting scenario to ponder; the identification of a single, ceramic-handled lid on one urn (*ibid.*, 31) is also notable in this regard.

White's report is also very helpful with regards to the geological sourcing of the sandstone employed at Simons Ground. He notes the use of 'brown ferruginous sandstone' on the site (1982, 20) and suggests that the presence of these stones:

> has one very important implication. They were brought from early lower levels of the Bagshott Series which are exposed in the Star Valley below Simons Ground. Sandstone is found in the fields of the valley below the site, but not commonly. Thus for the Bronze Age community at Simons Ground to have had a source of sandstone, they must have consistently practised agriculture and ploughed land in the river valleys. (*ibid.*, 43)

While we may not ourselves choose to place quite so much emphasis on the intensive agriculture implied, it does seem clear that the sandstone employed directly (as lids) in approximately 10% of the burials, and across the site in a variety of other ways, has to have been specifically acquired from elsewhere and brought perhaps a couple of kilometres to Simons Ground specifically for use in the cemetery.

As with the inclusion of quartz in the Cornish burials discussed above, it is difficult to ascertain exactly what the inclusion of sandstone in these burials *meant* to people. At one level, it played a simple, functional role, providing a facility for marking and/ or ensuring continued access to cremation deposits within urns. However, sandstone was identifiably used for this purpose in only a small percentage of the total buried population. As White discusses at various points within his report, this patterning, as with other variables in the burial rite, may, of course, be a consequence of temporal patterning or some other cultural variation that is hard to access. It could be that certain people's bones were, on burial, considered more likely to require continued access than other people's, and thus stones were specifically incorporated to facilitate this in certain cases. Equally, it could be that, as with quartz (above), elements of the local landscape were being included – and metaphorically referenced – within certain burials, potentially those of people associated most directly with the nearby sandstone-bearing valleys discussed by White (above).

While we have focused substantially on Simons Ground in this section, it is worth reiterating that many other Middle Bronze Age sites across Dorset were also recorded as having produced stone lids in association with cremation burials. This suggests that the practice of enabling continued access to the bones after initial burial, and potentially also that of referencing the local landscape in burial (whether these others were sandstone or another of Dorset's geologies), may well have been widespread at this time.

The white and the red: chalk in Iron Age East Yorkshire

The white chalk found in East Yorkshire graves takes two main forms. First, worked and shaped blocks are found either supporting or covering the corpse, e.g. Garton Slack 1/2 (Barrow 1, Burial 1) and Garton Slack 7 (Barrow 1, Burial 1 (the 'mirror grave') and secondary Burial 2) as well as Caythorpe (Burial 5B). In the latter case, roughly hewn blocks were placed 'cairn like' around the body whilst in the mirror burial from Garton Slack, 'flinty chalk blocks' were tipped over the remains of two suckling piglets placed at the woman's back, covering part of her torso (Brewster 1980, 228). We have written elsewhere of the importance of considering these stone 'wrappings' of the corpse as part of funerary technologies of care and concealment, covering the body with a substance extensively used in roundhouse daub and flooring, as well as field marl, yet such hefty spreads also conjure a 'weighting down' of what might have been feared as a potentially restless body (Cooper *et al.* 2019, 243–4). In the mirror grave, an additional 'roughly trapezoidal smoothed slab of chalk' was placed in front of the woman's abdomen on the base of the grave, close to where the mirror was propped. Brewster drew parallels between its blank form and the slightly later Iron Age/early Roman chalk figures found in nearby settlements (1980, and see Stead 1988) but if so, this would be a unique funerary object which appears very early for this phenomenon. The second category of chalk object found in graves is the spindle whorl: often biconical (with one conical example from Arras A18), sometimes marked with a central groove. Three were found at Rudston (R92, R145, R183: all probable or definite women) and one at Danes Graves (DG62). This 'female' artefact association is so strong that it led Stead to question the interpretation of the chalk spindle-whorl found in the 'Whitcombe warrior' male grave from Dorset, suggesting it might instead be a 'flywheel' for a 'pump drill' (Stead 1991, 94), rather than countenance any sense of gender fluidity or doubling (see Jordan 2016). All but R145 (found at the right-hand side of the waist) were discovered close to the face/head or above the shoulders on the right-hand side, suggesting they might have been worn around the neck of the deceased as 'tool-pendants' (Giles 2012, 162). Meanwhile at Wetwang Slack, the only pure chalk or limestone grave good appears to be a simple bead, once again found above the right shoulder (WS26, Dent 1984).

From this brief outline, we can note two things. First, chalk objects in Yorkshire burials are rare but the cluster of blocks in Garton graves and spindle whorls at Rudston confirm the importance of small, local traits or preferences in grave goods – one element of mortuary 'micro-traditions' that can often be seen between burials close together in space, time and perhaps relatedness (Giles 2012, 172). This should not surprise us: the antiquarian Mortimer first proposed that such similarities might represent family or group based funerary rites (even arranging his museum to reflect this; Sheppard 1900, 7). We could read this as part of the way in which 'neighbourhood' identity was symbolised and performed, with funeral fashions playing a key part in such practices. Second, the origin of the substance itself is telling. Worked chalk blocks, discs, plaques and tablets of unknown function (some elaborately carved with circular or geometric designs), spindle whorls and loomweights (including a 'miniature loomweight pendant') were found in the contemporary settlements of Wetwang and Garton Slack just above the cemetery (Brewster 1980, 70). The grave goods thus used a substance redolent with the realm of the domestic and as Brewster notes, they also showed a clear preference for 'local chalk' despite the fact that it had a 'platey' and glossy texture which was 'fairly hard and difficult to work' (*ibid.*, 71). Here we see the polar opposite of the exotic and the distant: a preference for the material which was literally their bedrock – the bone of their land.

One of the inherent problems we acknowledge with our archaeological data on exotic and local materials is that we unavoidably describe objects on the basis of their dominant substance. We are also bound by modern categorisations: dividing the white, Cretaceous chalk from other 'materials' whilst recognising it as cognate with other 'lithics'. However, our ways of dividing up substances (key as this is to our database) will never quite capture Iron Age conceptions of the material world. For example, tiny elements of copper-alloy and iron brooches, bracelets and horse-gear from the East Yorkshire burials used applied decorative materials ranging from red glass and true enamels to sandstone, porphyry, haematite colourants, ferruginous and vitrified dolomitic clay 'pastes' to bone and coral (Stead 1979; 1991). The simultaneous power of red to conjure fertility *and* violence (Giles 2008) may lie behind its use on brooches (in terms of apotropaic value) and weapons (intimidating in its intimation of spilled blood), as Pliny describes for coral (see above). However, Adams' research on a selection of East Yorkshire brooches using Raman spectroscopy has identified a previously unknown 'haematite and calcium carbonate' inlay, interpreted by the British Museum analysts as derived from 'coloured quartz, red limestone or marble' (Adams 2013, 157; Fig. 7.12). This combination of minerals might more reasonably be sourced to the rare beds of red chalk – the Hunstanton formation – which outcrop in thin but distinctive pink to brick-red bands across the High Wolds and down their western side (Sumbler 1999). Its 'marly seams' (*ibid.*,

6) may have been the perfect place to obtain a red chalk that could be carved into pre-formed beads. Were these merely imitations of exotic coral or rare red glass, effectively creating a value laden hierarchy or economy of substances (e.g. Stead 1991, 167)? Or could we instead follow Conneller (2011) in arguing that materials cannot be interpreted independently of the practices through which their meaning was constituted and propose that we are seeing a homology of 'red matter'

Figure 7.12 The haematite and calcium carbonate (red chalk?) adorned brooch from Burton Fleming (Burial BF10; brooch no. 10175 in Adams 2013; © Trustees of the British Museum).

(irrespective of chemical composition) deployed across such inlays? In the absence of large-scale quarries and geological surveys, knowledge of where to find this hyper-localised, rare red material may have given it special meaning to the inhabitants of the Wolds, whilst materialising powers or properties seen in substances from afar. When placed on a corpse, such inlaid objects may have been used both to adorn the dead and perhaps to 'charm' or 'bind' them with powerful substances (see Gilchrist 2008). Yet they also worked alongside the Celtic art that often enfolded or gripped this matter: simultaneously alluding to distant connections whilst grounding the deceased in the local world.

7.7. Discussion

The process of investigating material mobility through the lens of grave goods is not straightforward. Certainly, at least two layered processes need to be taken into account: the first is the mobility of materials in the world at large and the second is the tendency of people to deposit those materials in graves in a given period/region. In attempting to get at the first set of processes, the biases of the second set, of course, have a considerable effect. Beck and Shennan (1991, 80), for example, demonstrated that despite the high overall amounts of amber in Early Bronze Age burials in Wessex, the actual prevalence of that material there, as a proportion of all burials, was no higher than in many other regions – it was simply more visible because there were more burials (both deposited and excavated). The complexities of high archaeological visibility relative to the actual prevalence of materials in the past are crucial to consider but ultimately impossible to resolve. It is therefore important to bear in mind that, despite these complications, the glimpses that grave goods allow us, of that first set of processes, is certainly significant and thus worth exploring. When combined with the broad-scale picture set out in Section 7.3, interesting patterns of ebb and flow – in both 'layers' of the process – do emerge.

As discussed in Section 7.3, terrestrial mobility during the Neolithic was substantial, with the movement of Neolithic things and practices in general, as well as specific material/object types (such as stone axes) which can be sourced, both suggesting significant connectivity. Our GGDB dataset reveals that this mobility was not, however, emphasised – or even clearly visible at all – in grave goods at this time. For the Beaker/ Early Bronze Age period, past narratives have focused primarily on 'Wessex culture' burials and the 'foreign' artefacts they contain, including amber and certain specific objects from Armorica. Our evidence, by contrast, suggests that perhaps too much emphasis has been placed on cross-Channel material mobility and that significant terrestrial movement of materials has been overlooked within this 'big picture' discourse. For the Middle/Late Bronze Age, the wider metalwork evidence in particular suggests significant connectivity; again, this has been discussed especially across the Channel, which has been described as a 'super-highway' at that time (Needham 2017). However, our evidence makes clear that, as with the Neolithic, this undeniable material mobility *in some spheres* is not reflected in the burial evidence. The relative decrease in archaeologically visible burials by the end of this phase, and apparent decrease in emphasis on depositing grave goods (especially beyond pottery) at all, will undeniably have contributed to this. However, equally, it is also clear that 'exotics' were rarely buried and that local materials (e.g. Dorset sandstone lids) sometimes, by contrast, were emphasised markedly. During the Iron Age we have seen that the coastal flow of artefacts and materials represented in graves in southern England was significant (a picture that chimes well with the broader patterns of strong cross-Channel connections and major links around the south coast of England) but that comparable links were not as much in evidence between those zones and the north and west. Overall, it is clear that, while most of the later prehistoric period covered within our study was characterised by significant material mobility in general (as outlined in Section 7.3), this was not always reflected in graves. 'Exotic' materials are prevalent in burials during some phases, notably the Early Bronze Age and Middle–Late Iron Age but not in others. In is interesting to note that exotics are prevalent during those periods when grave goods generally appear to have been given more emphasis (see Section 3.2). However, other factors – such as hoarding and depositional practice more widely – also need to be taken into account (see also Cooper *et al.* 2020). 'Exotic' gold, for example, features fairly prominently in Middle Bronze Age hoards, if not in graves. These are complicated matters that cannot easily be resolved here but we might posit that at certain times, curation, inheritance or recycling were important principles that ensured objects and substances continued to 'flow' among the living instead of being dedicated to the dead. Their eventual deposition was on a different trajectory.

In the first part of our broad-scale analysis, we considered objects made from materials that have often been considered to have been perceived during prehistory as 'exotic' and highly valued as a result (e.g. S. Piggott 1938; Needham 2000; Sheridan and Davis 2002; Woodward and Hunter 2015). Importantly, these materials can, with some confidence, usually be attributed to specific geographical areas. Our finding that the Beaker/Early Bronze Age phase was especially 'rich' in exotics can hardly be claimed as a revelation. As discussed already at various points in this chapter, the key role that 'exotic' grave goods played at that time has been central to most narratives of the period. Nonetheless, a number of interesting insights relating to these exotics have emerged as a result of the particular viewpoint that the large-scale data collection behind the GGDB affords. Our plotting of the movement of exotic materials during the Beaker/Early Bronze Age period indicated significant material mobility, with networks of connectivity extending right across Britain in multiple directions. The fact that our selected case study regions – and thus the depicted endpoints of this mobility – are very widely distributed, makes clear the extensiveness of material exchange at that time. It is very likely that many of the areas in between would also have been connected into this network. The intense movement of materials during this phase – arguably driven by long-distance bronze exchange (Vankilde 2016) that was facilitated by relatively high levels of, in fact, probably only short- and medium-distance human mobility (Parker Pearson *et al.* 2019, 404–5) – apparently led to the significant movement of many other materials as well.

The distribution and directionality of Iron Age 'exotics' is significantly different to those in the Beaker/Early Bronze Age period. It is notable that amber continues to feature, whilst a new foreign exotic, coral, also comes into view as well; it suggests pre-Roman cross-Channel, and beyond that wider European, connections which sit comfortably with the existing picture of a strongly connected southern and eastern England over the course of the later 1st millennium BC (see Section 7.3). Equally, the apparently maritime movement of materials along the south coast of England also fits well with the existing picture. Again, our selection of 'exotics' found in graves provides significant insight into the 'higher level' process of material (and social) mobility as a whole. Fontijn (2019) has recently coined the notion of rare and extraordinary *mappa mundi* objects to describe artefacts whose design and materials evoked the expanse of the 'known' world, whether personally experienced or apprehended through things that came from afar. In Late Iron Age graves in Kent, this extended to whole assemblages of related objects, especially concerned with drinking and dining (as we discuss in Section 8.4). From our regional datasets, we can certainly see moments – and individuals – where those wider connections were given greater prominence, whether or not these individuals personally blazed such trails or navigated seaways. When such designs and elements crystallised in the form of a funerary vehicle, as with Bronze Age coffin 'vessels' or Iron Age chariots, there may even have been an attempt to transform the deceased into an ancestral voyager (Giles 2012; Parker Pearson *et al.* 2013).

We hope to have demonstrated very clearly by now that it is also vitally important to consider the local as well. It should probably come as no surprise that, as we saw in Section 7.6, local materials came to be caught up more often in burials than those not from the local region – common sense dictates that this is likely. However, the picture is not always quite so simple. Certainly, in some periods/areas it was not possible to identify any clear trends among the dominant 'local' materials and so an argument can be made that these local stone types simply came to be caught up in those burials because they were near and/or more readily available. However, in a number of other cases the use of a particular stone, and sometimes a specific set of objects made from it, suggested that the presencing of 'the local' in the grave – in the form of 'everyday' materials or familiar landscapes – may have had a clear and meaningful purpose. In contrast to Helms's work (see above) which considers the potential potency of material culture whose origin 'beyond the horizon' was *unknown*, the power of these local objects lay in their familiarity and everyday, *known* locations. We can thus draw a distinction between grave good assemblages which embody an 'extensive' network of relations and connections, with those that condense 'intensive', local ones.

In addition to these, on the one hand 'exotic' and, on the other, locally significant objects/materials, it is also revealing to look at those materials which seem to have fallen within both categories. Jet and shale are usually categorised as 'exotic' materials within the Beaker/Early Bronze Age period. We have highlighted the fact that they were also, clearly, locally significant as well. Jet in particular has been characterised as a special, exotic material that was transported over long distances and worn by powerful people: 'aside from faience, Whitby jet – and of course gold – were the materials of choice for the elites who indulged in power dressing during the early part of the Bronze Age' (Sheridan and Shortland 2003, 21; see also Woodward and Hunter 2015). Kimmeridge shale has for various reasons played a lesser role in these discussions, but nonetheless has also been viewed as a special raw material that was transported over long distances acquiring 'value' as a result. Certainly, this may well have been true for both materials in some circumstances, but it is not the whole story. These materials – in their local regions at least – were not valued simply because they were 'exotic' or had travelled from afar. They may have been keepsakes or gifts from *near* local places that nonetheless commemorated significant moments in someone's life, giving them special resonance in a grave. Judged on the basis of the raw quantities of objects deposited (see Fig. 7.04), jet and shale were most 'valued' in Yorkshire and Dorset respectively. Given what we have learnt from quartz in Cornwall, sandstone in Dorset and chalk in East Yorkshire, this should probably come as no surprise. Although our understanding of the chronology of their deposition is not sufficiently fine-tuned to investigate the matter with any confidence, it seems possible that these *local* significances potentially accrued around these two materials first, ultimately leading to their movement much further afield (as we saw with the buttons from Rameldry Farm at the start of this chapter). It could well, in fact, have been local significance that ultimately led to the creation of the distant 'exotic'. It is also possible that, subsequently, once they were valued further afield for their 'exoticness', their local meanings and worth may have changed. These are complicated matters to pin down. What is, however, very clear is that, as discussed above, it is vital to consider the local as well as the exotic in our accounts – these concepts are very much intertwined.

Chapter 8

Time's arrows: the complex temporalities of burial objects

8.1. Introduction: time and burial

At the start of this chapter, in order to explore the complex, overlapping temporalities that can sometimes be caught up in burial sites (and in the artefacts interred upon them), we return to a grave good already encountered in Chapter 6, excavated at Kingskettle, Fife (Callander 1921, 37–45): a Collared Urn, probably decorated by several people (Law 2008, 317–22). Law's detailed description of the decoration on the pot (Fig. 8.01; see also Fig. 6.06, above) expertly brings out both the personal, intimate details and the potentially very extended temporality of decorating such a pot. The scene he describes becomes even more poignant if we see the vessel as having been created specifically for this funeral, a possibility that Law considered but – because part of the rim was missing – could not be totally sure of (*ibid.*, 322).

> Looking at the drawing of the collar decoration [Figure 8.01], moving from left to right, we can see the remains of four triangles: two filled with incised vertical lines the rest with vertical and parallel lines sloping from left to right and right to left. The outline of the triangles was drawn in the wet clay causing little ridges to form either side of the incision. Next to this we find a section composed of incised horizontal lines, the top and bottom of which cut through the first of 12 incised vertical lines which make up the fourth section

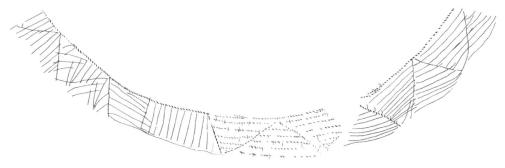

Figure 8.01 Line drawing of the decoration on Urn 5 [1833] from Kingskettle, Fife (Law 2008, fig. 7.13, detail). Reproduced by kind permission of Rob Law.

of the decorative scheme. The remaining horizontal lines are cut by the first vertical line, indicating the upper and lower ones were later additions. The 12 evenly spaced incised vertical lines are followed by three triangles, each filled with horizontal lines made using twisted cord. It appears the same piece of cord was used to produce many of the in-fill lines due to the recurring impression of a cord segment comprised of slightly thicker beads. Notice too the number of finger-nail impressions left as the maker pushed the cord into the soft clay. This may have been the result of a small piece of cord, held between thumb and forefinger, being placed onto the surface of the clay and then impressed from right to left. The thumb of the right hand rests on the surface pressing one end of the cord against the forefinger, while the left hand pulls the cord straight. The closeness of each nail impression reveals the points at which the cord was pressed into the clay. Finally, when the end of the cord is reached the thumb presses down causing the nail to leave yet another impression. These in-filled triangles are followed by five more which are also filled with horizontal lines, though here they are incised. Although part of the collar is missing, and there is an area of plaster obscuring the point at which the two motifs abut, it is clear that the outline of the first incised triangle was formed using twisted cord, perhaps at the same time as those to the left. Finally, on the vessel's rim, we find a number of short diagonal lines contrasting with sections of zigzag which in turn mutate into a lattice style pattern. (Law 2008, 317)

In addition to the deep insights into the *chaine operatoire* of decoration that such a detailed study can provide, we also encounter a number of other, overlapping *layers* of temporality at Kingskettle through Callander's original report on the excavations at the site (1921, 37–45). At one end of the chronological spectrum we can infer that this place had acted as a focus for burial over an extended period, potentially many years: potato digging and subsequent follow-up investigations revealed five Early Bronze Age vessels in total, associated with three (or possibly four) cremation burials. At a different chronological scale, the presence of charred wood in amongst some of these reminds us to consider the pyre-burning phase of the mortuary process – an event potentially conducted some distance in space and time from the final burial. Similarly, the fact that a pair of barbed and tanged arrowheads found with one of the burials were themselves burnt (*ibid.*, 44) also reminds us of this extended process – these had presumably been placed with the individual on the pyre, gathered up along with the bone and subsequently taken to the burial site. At the opposite end of the temporal spectrum, other aspects of the archaeological evidence at Kingskettle allow us almost to see single moments in time: cremated bone was found both within and alongside the urn described above, leading Callander to suggest that 'it would appear that they had fallen out of the urn when it was tilted into its inserted position' (Callander 1921, 40) – that momentary act captured as an archaeologically visible snapshot. As Olivier (1999), Fowler (2013, 46–7) and others have discussed, burial sites represent perhaps an especially good place in which to observe the complex 'multi-temporalities' or 'lines of becoming' into which archaeological evidence sometimes gives us insight.

In this chapter we will explore the often highly complex temporalities of grave goods in a series of different contexts. In order to establish a temporal baseline for that discussion, we will return briefly to the 'ideal' burial-with-grave-goods first considered in Section 3.1. In that case, we described a clearly defined grave containing a single, articulated inhumation, within a wider cemetery of similar graves, accompanied by a few items which had been both worn and placed around the body on the base of the grave. Barrett (1991b), Gilchrist and Sloane (2005), Appleby (2013) and others have demonstrated the significant value of investigating the sequential process(es) of burial even in apparently 'simple' cases. In this example, the potential temporalities involved in the burial were, relatively, fairly short. We might assume – in fact, given that this is an ideal, fictional example, we can clearly state – that the person, a woman, died; that shortly afterwards a grave was dug for her in her family's cemetery; that she was promptly dressed specially for the funeral and placed in the ground; that the objects with her were either worn on the body (the necklace around her neck, the brooch fastening a shroud) or deposited around it immediately after she had been lowered into the ground (a pot and a joint of meat placed on her left-hand side, according to local tradition); and that the grave was then backfilled straight away and never re-opened – until our fictional archaeologists dug it up.

Elsewhere, we have already considered the fact that many burials and the deposition of grave goods with them were not nearly as temporally 'neat' as this example (Cooper *et al.* 2020): bodies and objects could be 'curated', sometimes for centuries, before deposition; bodies and objects could follow fairly similar, or quite different, paths into the grave; graves could be re-visited, with bones removed or objects added (either directly with the corpse or perhaps on top of a cist lid); and so on. In this chapter, we want to investigate ways in which this temporal complexity can be embraced interpretively in order to develop a full and richer account of prehistoric burial practices in such 'multi-temporal' situations. Our first two case studies focus on scenarios in which the temporality of the mortuary process could often be highly extended. The first investigates objects deposited in Neolithic chambered tombs (and related monument types), within which activity could last for centuries and a relationship between specific bodies and specific artefacts is often impossible to establish. Our second study looks at 'pyre goods', most of which were artefacts caught up in the wider process of cremation which, in itself, generally extended the funerary/ mortuary process considerably more than our 'ideal' scenario above; this example foregrounds the Bronze Age material in our database. Our third case study examines the contrastive temporalities of Late Iron Age burial rites in Kent and south-east England more generally.

8.2. 'Multi-temporal' mortuary material culture in the Neolithic

The difficulties of incorporating material culture from many Neolithic contexts into our study have already been discussed in Chapter 3. The GGDB, by the very nature of the core topic at hand, had to be set up to record burials that were more akin to our 'ideal' situation above, where a relationship between the different objects and (usually) one person could be established with relative ease and certainty. This kind of burial scenario is only rarely encountered in Neolithic contexts, since at that time human bodies often came to be mixed together over extended periods within large, collective tombs and the formation processes responsible for the inclusion of much material culture with them are often uncertain. These were 'permeable structures' as Bradley (2019, 101) put it.

Interestingly, within academic discourse more widely, there has been a notable tendency to downplay or even ignore the presence of material culture, and certainly of objects that might have been 'grave goods', within Neolithic tombs. This approach can be traced back as far as Thurnam in the mid-19th century, who stated that in long barrows 'the rarity of objects of flint and other stone, and of those of bone, as well as pottery, is also very remarkable; and leads to the inference that those which have been met with have seldom been deposited intentionally, or as a necessary part of the funerary rites' (1869, 193). This way of seeing things persists in many accounts up to the present day. Cummings, for example, states that Early Neolithic chambered tombs 'seem to ubiquitously contain the remains of the dead … sometimes accompanied by small amounts of material culture, usually pottery and stone tools, but rarely in any quantity' (2017, 107) and Bradley that 'artefacts are not common at most of these monuments [in southern England]' (2019, 63). Equally, Field describes deposits of cultural material in earthen long barrows as 'meagre' (2006, 143), while Darvill states that 'in general, finds other than human bones are rather rare in the chambers of long barrows in the Cotswold-Severn region, as indeed in long barrows generally' (2004, 165).

Oddly, especially in the case of Darvill's study (see below) but also more generally, these statements have by and large been made despite a clear understanding that the material culture deposited at some – if by no means all – sites was both plentiful and significant. It is our contention that a generally pessimistic approach to finds within Neolithic burial contexts first developed and still persists today as a result of several factors which have combined to ensure that those objects are consistently (and unfairly) underplayed: the impressiveness of the human bone assemblages found on most sites (amongst which artefacts can get lost or seem incidental); the spectacular and generally cohesive character of many grave good assemblages from the Beaker/Early Bronze Age (against which Neolithic material is, even unconsciously, compared); the fact that many Neolithic tombs were excavated by antiquarians (and thus contextual details about the relationship between bodies and objects have been lost); and, finally, the temporal complexity through which Neolithic 'grave goods' accumulated (which we consider in detail below).

In this section, the key idea that we wish to explore is that the uncertainty which has developed about the relationship between people and objects in Neolithic burial contexts results from two subtly different, but related, kinds of temporal 'extendedness'. If we are open-minded in embracing this chronological depth – a site's 'multi-temporal' qualities, as Olivier (2001) has termed it – when considering what a grave good is, or should be, artefacts can potentially become a much stronger and more visible feature within our interpretations of Neolithic burial practice.

Our first suggestion is that, in many Neolithic contexts, the extended use-life of and activities within tombs have had the effect of making objects that actually conform to our core notion of what a grave good should be less visible archaeologically; often, they *were* there and *are* visible as occasional glimpses. Our second suggestion is that, if we are to understand 'grave goods' in most Neolithic burial contexts, we need to extend the chronological brackets that are usually applied to their recognition (as in the 'ideal' scenario above) and embrace a vaguer relationship between 'individual' and 'object' than traditionally we wish to see in conceptualising that term. This takes us back to some of the conceptual ideas considered in Chapter 2, around mortuary material culture as complex embodiments not just of the person but their wider relationships, involved in ongoing acts of remembrance extended across generations, even centuries.

While our primary focus in this section is on material culture within Neolithic chambered tombs (and related monuments), it is important to state at the outset that the GGDB dataset included a wide variety of burials – including crouched inhumations within the causewayed enclosure ditch at Hambledon Hill in Dorset, pit burials covered by stone slabs in proximity to the henge at Llandegai in Gwynedd, various isolated inhumations in Kent, and many more. The nature of local soils, the original prevalence and subsequent survival of tombs and the extent and character of antiquarian excavations – in various combinations – in Cornwall/Scilly, Gwynedd/ Anglesey and Kent, has resulted in the survival of only fairly limited evidence sets for Neolithic grave goods in those three case study areas. In Cornwall and Kent in particular, many Neolithic tombs were completely ransacked and/or destroyed, resulting in almost total loss of human remains and the objects associated with them. Even in Dorset, situated as it is beyond the core Cotswold-Severn long barrow distribution, relatively few Neolithic sites with grave goods were recorded. Our best evidence without doubt comes from our East Yorkshire and Orkney/Outer Hebrides case study areas, whose traditions of constructing Neolithic chambered tombs and round/long barrows respectively are well known and rich to explore.

Figure 8.02 depicts the types and quantities of material culture found in each of our study regions. In is worth noting again here that *only material found in direct association with human remains* was recorded within the GGDB for Neolithic sites (see Section 3.1), and so this graphic should be viewed as only a partial representation of the entirety of material culture found in Neolithic burial contexts. It is also worth noting that some of the best-known Wolds Neolithic round barrows are located in *North* Yorkshire and thus are not included in our detailed dataset (we do, however, discuss them all together at a more general level below). Despite these caveats, the kinds of artefacts recorded in the GGDB map closely onto the broader picture of Neolithic mortuary material culture that it is possible to glean from wider surveys (e.g. Henshall 1972; Manby 1988; Davidson and Henshall 1989; Darvill 2004, 165–72): mainly pottery, animal bones, flint and stone tools and personal items (such as beads/ necklaces and pins).

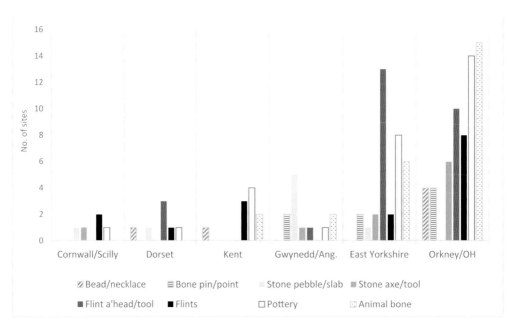

Figure 8.02 Occurrence of key object types found in direct association with human remains on Neolithic sites in our case study areas. Given the complexities often involved in quantifying this material, we have elected to indicate the prevalence of finds types by site (not as total finds numbers).

Within our dataset, Orkney in particular stands out as having substantial quantities of material culture deposited in tombs, with East Yorkshire also prominent – as might be expected given the character of sites involved, but perhaps more significantly the number of excavations at relatively undisturbed tombs and graves undertaken in those regions. Notably, a fairly wide range of artefact types is seen even in those regions with low total numbers overall; it is also interesting to note the apparent lack of consistency across those study regions which suggests that there was not a clear, widespread concept of 'a grave assemblage' at this time.

The 'temporal extendedness' of sites and the visibility of grave goods
Unival
Our primary focus in this first section is on the chambered cairn at Unival, North Uist in the Outer Hebrides, excavated by Scott in 1935 and 1939 and also described in detail by Henshall (Scott 1948; Henshall 1972, 143–52; Fig. 8.03). Despite substantial Iron Age activity at the site and the relatively dilapidated state of the tomb, it nonetheless proved possible to gain significant insight into the processes of material culture (and to a lesser extent human bone) deposition there during the Neolithic, apparently over the course of multiple, successive visits. On the basis of careful excavation and recording, great attention to detail, thoughtful reporting and a bit of creative archaeological imagination, it proved possible for first Scott (1948) and

Figure 8.03 Scott's photo of the façade and excavated chamber at Unival (Scott 1948, pl. 1)

then Henshall (1972) to create a richly textured narrative of the activities – including 'grave good' deposition – witnessed at the tomb. The following description is drawn from a combination of both of their accounts.

Unival, a stone-built 'square' or 'wedge-shaped' chambered cairn, is situated on the shoulder of a prominent hill in the local landscape of North Uist. Internal to the main chamber, and integral to the monument from the start, was a small, stone cist-like structure, interpreted as having been the initial container of multiple, successive bodies over the course of the site's use (Fig. 8.04). Although bone preservation is generally poor in the Outer Hebrides due to the strongly acidic soils, on excavation, the articulated 'upper half' of a mature female skeleton was recovered within the cist, mixed with the partial remains of a second, younger person; several other small clusters of human bone were found adjacent to the northern and western walls of the wider chamber, suggesting the burial and subsequent re-arrangement of multiple individuals. Fires had clearly been introduced to the tomb and, as a result, charcoal was abundant in places and especially within the cist; all of the bones had probably only survived the acid soils because they had been burnt. An estimated minimum of 22 pots was recovered from the tomb; these were in varying states of completeness, ranging from whole vessels to small sherds. Additionally, two flint and nine quartz flakes were recovered from the 'funerary levels', along with a broken, axe-shaped pumice

pendant from the upper levels and a stone ball from the lowest layer, interpreted as
a foundation deposit.

Henshall's interpretive description of this activity is worth repeating in detail:

> It was clear that the ritual involved placing one or more vessels in the cist with each burial
> and probably another vessel outside the cist against the chamber wall, and that as each
> burial was subsequently moved from the cist the accompanying pottery was moved to the
> side of the chamber. Once the pots had been placed against the wall of the chamber they
> had not been disturbed: one pot was found unbroken, and two more, though broken, were
> unscattered. The centre of the floor was much trampled, and the relatively few sherds were
> small, probably dropped whilst moving broken vessels from the cist. In the cist were two
> broken, but nearly complete, vessels, which it was assumed had accompanied the last burial.
> There were also a few sherds of two more pots, presumably from vessels accompanying
> earlier burials, and accidentally left behind when these were moved from the cist. There
> was also evidence that other pots, found by the chamber walls, had formerly been in the
> cist. One, for instance, was found mainly in a well-protected position where it was unlikely
> to be disturbed, but a few sherds (which had presumably been left behind in the cist and
> later shovelled out) were found on the chamber floor. Another was heavily reburnt, which
> was likely to have happened whilst in the cist. Yet another was found with the two halves,
> reduced to sherds, in two places, presumably having been removed from the cist in two
> pieces. (Henshall 1972, 145–6)

The placing of one or two ceramic vessels in the tomb to accompany each inferred
burial can certainly be viewed as the deposition of grave goods. Henshall's account
of the processes behind the particular assemblage at Unival – directly building on
Scott's detailed excavation report – is convincing both in terms of its explanation of

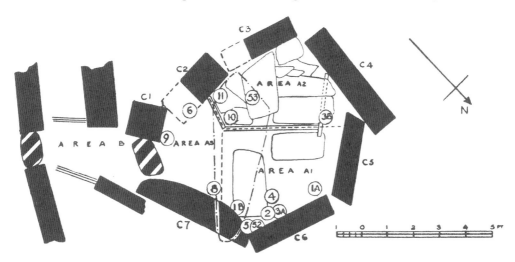

*Figure 8.04 Scott's original 'pottery find plan' detailing the locations of many of the different vessels
(numbered, in circles) found within the chamber at Unival (Scott 1948, fig. 5). The internal stone 'cist'
is located at the top of the plan (marked 'Area A2').*

the dynamics behind the finds and its creative, but still reasoned, interpretation of these. In our opinion, a key reason why it proved possible to construct such a richly textured account is the unusual balance of 'temporal extendedness' seen at this site. On the one hand, similar activities appear to have occurred there for a sufficiently long period of time for them to be rendered visible archaeologically as a meaningful and sustained practice – 22 vessels, perhaps one or two placed in the tomb with each body, represents the grave goods for say 10–15 different people. Due to the extended temporality of burial at the site, these vessels had come to be in quite different states of preservation, those placed last in the cist remaining complete or near-complete, while others that had been there longer sometimes became more fragmented, having been left for a while, moved, burnt, moved again, and so on. Conjoins identified by Scott between sherds in the cist and semi-complete vessels elsewhere in the tomb (Pots 3 and 9) demonstrate both the fragmentation and movement of these vessels. As Henshall points out, the pots placed close to the edges of the chamber were protected to an extent (sometimes even remaining complete) whilst those vessels found towards the centre were highly fragmented having been subject to trampling and other attritional processes. Equally, as Scott (1948, 33) suggests, it is possible that missing sherds and incomplete vessels may indicate that pieces of pots, much like pieces of human bodies, were removed from the tomb and distributed amongst the living, following their fragmentation. The practice at Unival of depositing introduced soil (often containing high levels of burnt material) helped to preserve the archaeological visibility of these material dynamics, doubtless facilitating the survival of those substantially complete vessels by 'burying' them; moreover, the three-dimensional resolution that this introduced stratigraphy provided enabled Scott to investigate and understand the site's chronological depth, or 'temporal extendedness' as we have termed it here (see Scott 1948, 23–4 and fig. 5, upper image). Subsequent Late Neolithic/Beaker activity within the tomb appears to have sealed the original Neolithic deposits further, rather than disturbing them; the survival of all of this earlier archaeology, despite the construction of an Iron Age house and other substantial activity on the site, is also very fortuitous.

Ultimately, the particular character of the Neolithic activities at Unival and the 'ideal' temporal length of their duration – plus their remarkable survival despite later activity and their careful excavation – all combined to result in deposits where we *can* infer that specific grave goods probably were deposited with specific people. On other sites, even if the original mortuary practices were similar, such preservational conditions are rarely forthcoming, with the result that attritional processes would subsequently have rendered those practices impossible to see in that way – much like the vessels at Unival that were not protected from damage having been placed at the side of the tomb. We have dealt in substantial detail with the material dynamics in evidence at Unival to demonstrate, through this case study, that similar processes may well have occurred on many other sites but, without this particular set of circumstances, will not been made visible. Even in the 'exceptional' case of Unival, a great deal has to be inferred and many gaps have to be filled with imagination. Nonetheless, arguably, having explored the visibility of grave good deposition there, other glimpses elsewhere do become a little more apparent and insight into comparable practices can be gleaned.

Clettraval and The Chestnuts

Interestingly, at the nearby site of Clettraval, 6 km south-east of Unival, similar mortuary practices were inferred on the basis of directly comparable evidence despite the very different architecture of the two tombs (Scott 1935; Henshall 1972, 79–90). However, the more complex format of the tomb at Clettraval (a 'Clyde-type') which consisted of five separate chambers arranged in a linear grouping, and less benign later activity (including stone robbing to construct an Iron Age wheelhouse), meant that those processes were rather less clearly visible. Nonetheless, the presence of a similar stone cist and 29 different vessels in varying states of completeness (with sherds in different chambers that conjoined) along with a few scraps of human bone suggested to both Scott and Henshall that mortuary practices at both sites may have been similar.

At the extreme opposite end of Britain, on the basis of the presence of pots in different conditions in different parts of the site, Alexander also inferred very similar practices at The Chestnuts chambered long barrow in Kent: 'in this tomb a number of bodies, of which 10 have been identified, were placed – some inhumed, some cremated. The earlier burials were accompanied by Windmill Hill pottery. These [vessels] were later thrown into the forecourt when new burials ... were placed in the eastern compartment' (Alexander 1961, 13). In this case, later disturbance of the site was substantial, and – due to the much vaguer impression we have of the distribution of specific artefacts within the tomb and generally fragmented state of the ceramics – Alexander's interpretation comes across as much less firmly grounded in the material dynamics of the evidence. Nonetheless, the fact remains that numerous Early Neolithic vessels – which quite possibly had been 'grave goods' that ultimately came to be fragmented and scattered – were recovered from the site, and Alexander's interpretation of what had happened *could* certainly be correct.

Orkney

The rich and wide-ranging evidence of mortuary material culture from Orkney is especially tricky to interpret. As Hedges simply put it: 'the difficulties in interpreting the deposits in chambered tombs is generally recognised, for chambers are likely to have been in use for a very long time ... Thus the apparent association of objects can be misleading' (Hedges 1983, 43) – these were 'multi-temporal' sites. It is, however, not just the temporal extendedness of Orkney tombs that makes their contents difficult to interpret – the complexity of the practices which occurred, even within apparently relatively narrow chronological windows, was significant. Equally, the relatively low recording standards of many, if not all, antiquarian excavations often frustrate our understanding of the material dynamics within the tombs and thus inferences about any specific associated practices. According to numerous antiquarians and archaeological accounts, the bodies and objects encountered within many of these tombs were found in different states. This may indicate that these monuments were subject to different trajectories within their cycles of construction, use, episodic re-use, abandonment and final closure and sealing, highlighting the complex, multi-phased, temporal sequences of death, burial and 'reactivation'. In some cases, the sequence of funerary activity seemingly resulted in the near total removal of all material culture once contained within the tomb. It reminds us that grave goods themselves, like parts of bodies, were not simply 'done with' after interment but had afterlives that reflected not just continuing but *new* bonds with the dead, some of whom would have been well beyond living memory. Cairns that were almost completely empty include Calf of Eday NW and SE (Calder 1937), Holm of Papa Westray South (Wilson 1851) and the Dwarfie Stane on Hoy (Calder and MacDonald 1936); these tombs appear to have been cleared out in Neolithic times, prior to final closure and blocking. The nuances of the treatment of human bodies in some Orcadian tombs have recently begun to get much clearer as a result of modern analysis, with the fragmentation and disarticulation of bodies generally now thought to have occurred *in situ*, as a result of repeated entry by humans (and perhaps also animals) into the tombs, and bodies being increasingly broken up through later manipulation and handling (e.g. Crozier 2016). The deposition and manipulation of human bone nonetheless remains characterised by tremendous variety – bodies were left whole, placed on benches, piled up as disarticulated bones, burnt, partially burnt, separated into different body parts (notably skulls), potentially even moved between different tombs, and much more besides (e.g. Chesterman 1979; 1983; Richards 1988; Jones 1998; Reilly 2003).

An extensive range of animal remains ended up in Orkney tombs – from cattle and sheep to voles and frogs to white tailed eagles, deer, otters and dogs (e.g. Hedges 1983, 226–42; Davidson and Henshall 1989, 55–6; Jones 1998). As far as it is possible to tell, these animals were introduced through a wide variety of cultural (as well as natural) mechanisms – within midden material, as deposits of food, as whole 'offerings' or 'totems', *etc*. In many cases, the temporality of the relationship between human burials and those animal bones is complicated to unpick. In certain cases, animal bones had clearly been intentionally mixed in with human remains. At the Knowe of Ramsay, for example, the disarticulated and scorched remains of an adult male were interleaved with wild birds, including sea eagle, bitterne, curlew, duck and swan (Davidson and Henshall 1989, 135–6); as each bird species was only represented by a single bone, this suggests they were carefully and deliberately selected to accompany this individual. Equally, at Holm of Papa Westray North, Petrie's original account describes comparable intermixing of multiple animal species and humans:

> In the compartment A ... were fragments of deer's horns, the horn core of the ox, and a jawbone of the boar, resting on top of a human skull. In the compartment B ... 10 pairs of deer's horns were found intermixed with bones of the ox, deer, sheep, &c., the wing-bone

of a swan, and the bill of the curlew. And underneath this and a layer of deer's horns, was part of a human skull, face downwards. Another human skull, was lying on its side, resting on a portion of a deer's horn. (Petrie 1859, 62)

Although the temporal relationships between animal and human remains can be complex, in certain cases their contemporaneity has been demonstrated through radiocarbon dating (*e.g.* at Point of Cott; Barber 1997). In other cases, however, for example at the well-known sites of Isbister (the 'Tomb of the Eagles', where the remains of at least 14 white tailed eagles were deposited) and Cuween (where 24 dog skulls were found), the deposition of these specific animals appears, on the basis of present dating evidence at least, to have occurred centuries later than the main phase of human bone deposition (Schulting *et al.* 2010, 26; Griffiths 2016, 295). Here, partial bodies of both wild and domesticated animals were apparently deliberately introduced during much later acts of reconvening with what were perhaps, by now, 'ancestral' remains.

In terms of other categories of material culture deposited in Orcadian Neolithic tombs, we see a relatively restricted range – pottery is the most numerous artefact type, followed by flint and stone tools and then bone pins/points. Yet again, the temporal dynamics of the deposition of this material culture are usually complex. In comparison to the situation observed at Unival and Clettraval (above), the quantities of complete and/or relatively complete pots found within tombs in Orkney are low. In their holistic survey of the evidence, Davidson and Henshall noted only two complete vessels from the 'miniature chamber' (which was physically separate to the main burial chambers) at Taversöe Tuick and two probably complete but smashed bowls from Unstan, pointing out that on most sites partial and highly fragmented vessels are more common (1989, 57). In relation to the substantial assemblage of at least 45 pots recovered from Isbister, Hedges developed a sustained argument that most of the pottery had been introduced from outside the tomb in an already fragmented and burnt state (1983, 245), suggesting that a similar situation could be observed on other sites in Orkney as well (*ibid.*, 259); Davidson and Henshall broadly agreed with this suggestion for Isbister (1989, 57). In coming to this interpretation, Hedges considered a wide range of possibilities as to how the burials within tombs and the ceramics (that were often dumped in one specific area which did not contain human bone) may have been related (1983, 259–62; Fig. 8.05). To our minds, one potential interpretation – which takes account of the coherence of several key assemblages and the presence of actually quite sizeable fragments of individual vessels – is that, originally, whole vessels may well have been placed with individual burials in a tomb, as in North Uist. Subsequently, these could have been cleared out of the tomb, along with the rest of its contents, burnt (perhaps for some ceremonial reason), and then replaced back inside the tomb. This is, of course, just one possible interpretation of many, but it does also provide a parsimonious explanation of the formation processes behind the large dumps of material culture seen in several tombs.

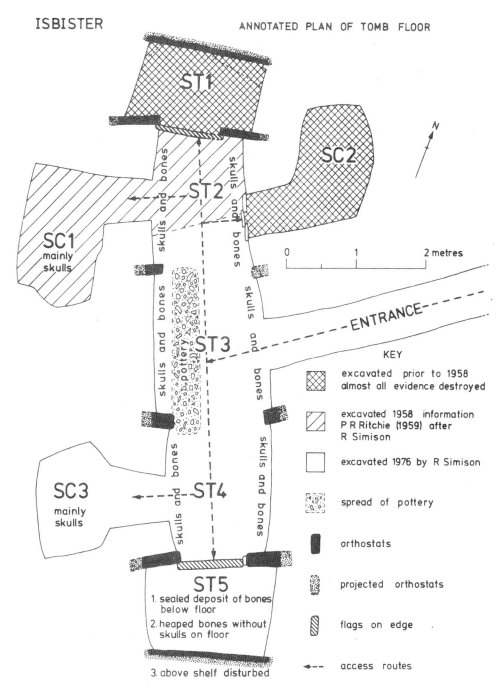

Figure 8.05 Annotated plan of the deposits at Isbister (Hedges 1983, illus. 4). The 'dump' of burnt pottery can be seen towards the centre of the image (adjacent to the 'ST3' label).

Various other sites have produced evidence for episodic, small-scale conflagrations, apparently *within* the tombs, during which human and animal bones, along with potsherds and flints, were sometimes scorched. Evidence of burning has, for example, been recovered at Blackhammer, Knowe of Craie, Knowe of Rowiegar, Calf of Eday Long and Knowe of Yarso (Callander and Grant 1937, 306–8; Davidson and Henshall 1989, 131–2; Henshall 1963, 214–15; Calder 1937, 125; Callander and Grant 1935).

In addition to these ceramic finds, Davidson and Henshall list a number of other artefacts which they see as potentially having been 'intentional inclusions' within Orkney tombs. These include two axeheads placed on one of the benches at Calf of Eday Long and axes found on the floor of four other sites; several finely flaked flint knives and arrowheads at Blackhammer, Calf of Eday Long, Midhowe and Unstan; and a probable limpet shell necklace at Isbister (Davidson and Henshall 1989, 78; Fig. 8.06). As ever, the multi-temporal nature of these sites prevents us from being certain that these items were placed in the tomb with a body as 'grave goods' rather than being introduced subsequently for any number of other reasons. However, it does remain a distinct possibility.

In summary, it is clear that large quantities of material culture were deposited in Orcadian tombs, probably as a result of many different processes. Due to the multi-temporal character of most of these sites, the relationship between the ultimate location and condition of these artefacts (when recovered archaeologically) and their

Figure 8.06 Nine of the 21 limpet shells, which may have formed a necklace, found under a shelf in the tomb at Isbister (Hedges 1983, illus. 64).

original context(s) of deposition is usually difficult to determine. This is especially so as, often, subsequent mortuary practices within many tombs appear to have involved the intentional mixing together – and perhaps even blurring of the conceptual boundaries between – humans, animals and objects. Nonetheless, we have argued that it is possible that many items, if not necessarily the majority, could have entered a given tomb as 'grave goods' in something approaching the traditional sense. It is just that, often, time and post-(original) depositional processes have intervened to make this uncertain.

Cotswold-Severn region
The Cotswold-Severn region spans multiple counties in south Wales and south-central England. It is characterised by sometimes dense concentrations of long barrows, many of them chambered (Darvill 2004). As in Orkney, numerous excavations have taken place at many sites over the years, ensuring a rich resource to draw upon in discussing Neolithic mortuary material culture. Our case study area of Dorset lies to the south of the core Cotswold-Severn region, and while it did contain a small number of excavated long barrows, these produced few well understood grave goods. As with many of the tombs described above, the fact that burials (and other deposits) within Cotswold-Severn long barrows usually appear to have been placed in the tombs successively, over several decades or centuries, ensures that essentially all the same issues apply when trying to assess the relationship between bodies and material culture.

Human bodies generally appear to have been placed into Cotswold-Severn tombs complete and then allowed to decompose, as was the case in Orkney; their bones were often subsequently rearranged within, or removed from, the tombs, perhaps during the process of adding in further bodies (Smith and Brickley 2009). In his wide-ranging study of long barrows in the Cotswolds region, Darvill considered the non-human bone deposits found at these sites in some detail, outlining what he saw as all of the key patterns (2004, 132–72). Generally speaking, the kinds of deposit made within them are comparable to those described for Orkney, although Cotswold-Severn long barrows perhaps contain fewer objects overall.

Animal bones have been found on many sites, with domesticated species usually dominant (Darvill 2004, 171; Thomas and McFadyen 2010). Few sites stand out for their animal bone assemblages in the way that certain Orcadian tombs do, and the animal bone deposits are difficult to interpret: there is little evidence that they were feasting remains or 'standing in' for humans; and there is an enigmatic pattern of articulated and disarticulated foetal and young animals being deposited within the primary chambers (Thomas and McFadyen 2010, 108–10).

On a small number of Cotswold-Severn sites, originally complete (but subsequently fragmented) Early Neolithic ceramic vessels have been found within the primary chamber deposits (Darvill 2004, 165), including a 'Windmill Hill' style pot from West Kennet long barrow (Fig. 8.07), one of nine Early Neolithic pots represented within the four chambers (Piggott 1962, 35–6). Larger assemblages representing multiple vessels have also been recovered from several sites, including six within the same chamber at both Gwernvale and Ty Isaf (*ibid.*, 154–5). Notably, Darvill himself promotes a 'grave goods' focused interpretation of these, suggesting that:

> most [of the pots within long barrows] were probably introduced into the chamber[s] with particular individuals, subsequent activity within the chambers and the movement and reorganization of body-parts accounting for the breaking and scattering of the pots, which gradually became dissociated from specific individuals and the rituals associated with them. (Darvill 2004, 167)

Worked flint has also been recovered from many tombs, with both generalised flint-working debris and specific tools represented. Intriguingly, the long barrow at Hazelton North produced a rare (but often-cited), fairly complete burial that has subsequently come to be known as the 'flint knapper' since he had a flint core by his right elbow and a quartz hammerstone by his left knee (Saville 1990, 103–4). Elsewhere,

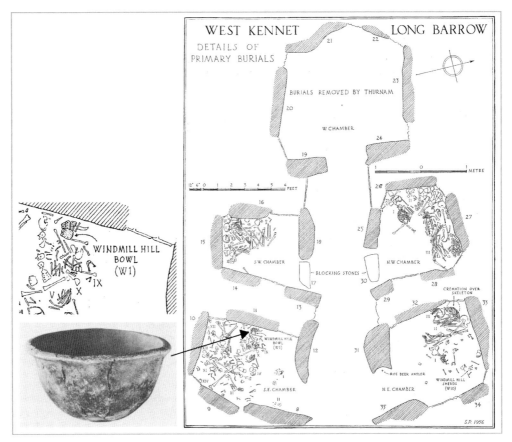

Figure 8.07 The complete but fragmented bowl, found within the south-east chamber at West Kennet (Piggott 1962, fig. 8 and pl. 20a).

tools recovered include knives from Penywyrlod, Burn Ground and Lanhill and a complete flaked and polished flint axe from Ty Isaf (Darvill 2004, 168). Notably, at Ascott-under-Wychwood, a small cache of flints including a broken scale-flaked knife, a leaf-shaped arrowhead and a flake from a polished implement was the only set of artefacts thought potentially to be 'grave goods' within the whole monument (Benson and Whittle 2007, 310). Darvill also discusses the relatively common occurrence of leaf-shaped arrowheads within Cotswold-Severn long barrows: intriguingly, one or two of these have actually been found embedded within skeletal material, leading him to suggest that those found within primary chamber deposits on a dozen or so other sites could themselves represent the cause of death, brought into the tomb embedded within a body (Darvill 2004, 168–9). Beads made from shale, seashells and even perforated boars' tusks have been recovered from a number of sites, as well as bone rings and pins/points (*ibid.*, 170).

Overall, the picture of mortuary material culture – potential 'grave goods' – that it is possible to build on the basis of the evidence from Cotswold-Severn long barrow sites is comparable to Orkney. Certainly, a case can again be made for the deposition of specific items *probably* with specific individuals on many sites: ceramic vessels in particular, but also flint tools, occasional necklaces and bone pins. As with Orkney, it is just that the temporal extendedness of these tombs' usage, and the substantial knock-on effects this had on the survival and integrity of material culture previously deposited there, ensure that you have to look especially hard at the evidence and be creative in interpreting it in order to begin to 'see' them as significant.

Yorkshire Wolds

The Yorkshire Wolds, unusually, saw the construction of both long and round barrows during the Neolithic. The vast majority of sites relevant to our study were excavated during the 19th century by Greenwell (1877) and Mortimer (1905). As a consequence, the details we might wish to have relating to these burials and the material culture associated with them are, sadly, not always forthcoming (see, for example, individual site summaries in Gibson and Bayliss 2010). The architecture of these Wolds sites differs significantly from the tombs we have already looked at in the Outer Hebrides, Orkney and the Cotswold-Severn regions. Those regions are characterised predominantly by chambered tombs, which could be – and, as we have seen, often were – entered and essentially used as 'rooms', sometimes for centuries. In contrast, both long and round barrows in the Wolds were predominantly made from chalk rubble and mostly did not have large, permanent chambers (although putative non-megalithic chambers have been suggested on some sites – Kinnes 1979). Rather, burials were usually cut into the subsoil or pre-existing mound (Fig. 8.08). This is by no means intended to imply that Neolithic burial in the Wolds region was in some way 'simpler': both cremated remains and inhumations are common, multiple burials and disarticulated body parts are regularly found, and the sequence of burial on some sites can be extremely complex and very long-lasting. However,

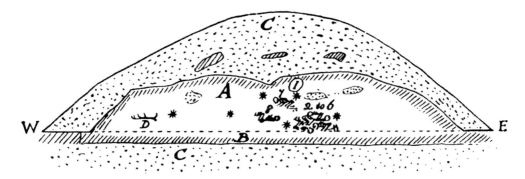

Figure 8.08 Mortimer's schematic section through Wold Newton barrow No. 284 (Mortimer 1905, fig. 1015).

the geologically determined architecture of the Wolds sites arguably has led to them being characterised by a subtly different extended temporality.

Modern radiocarbon dating programmes have enabled a hugely improved understanding of the temporality of burial at several key sites (Gibson *et al.* 2009; Gibson and Bayliss 2010). This work has demonstrated that, at many, burials were deposited over the course of several centuries, sometimes in sporadic 'bursts' with significant gaps in between. The earliest analysed burial, a child from Wold Newton found within a deposit of multiple bodies placed on the ground surface (see Fig. 8.08), dates to *c.* 3910–3705 cal BC; while those around it were of roughly similar date, Burial 7 appears to have been inserted into the mound sometime later *c.* 3645–3520 cal BC (Gibson and Bayliss 2010, 83–4). The sequence of burial seen at Duggleby Howe is even more complex, with multiple burials added *c.* 3500–3300 cal BC, followed by a gap of 150–350 years, and then another series of burials *c.* 3100–2800 cal BC, followed by yet more, sporadically, throughout the 3rd millennium (Gibson *et al.* 2009, 67–70; Fig. 8.09). The mound there appears only to have been added quite late in the sequence *c.* 2900 cal BC, and thus the earlier burials are interpreted as having been deposited successively within a single pit over an extended period (*ibid.*, 72). In total 53 cremation burials were also recovered mostly towards the upper part of the mound but unfortunately these could not be traced within the archive and thus could not be dated.

Duggleby Howe is well known for its grave goods. Burial K in 'Grave B', the lowest burial in the sequence, was associated with fragments of decorated bowl, nine flint flakes, two flint cores, and may have been contained within a wooden coffin (Gibson *et al.* 2009, 48); Burial G, also a relatively early burial according to the radiocarbon dates, was accompanied by an antler macehead, a polished stone axe and a finely-worked 'diamond-shaped' arrowhead; Burial C, later in the sequence within 'Grave A', was buried with a series of flint flakes, two beaver incisors and 12 boars' tusks as well as a large bone pin; and Burial D, close by, had 'in front of the face ... a beautiful flint knife of almost transparent glass-like [polished] flint' (Mortimer 1905, 28).

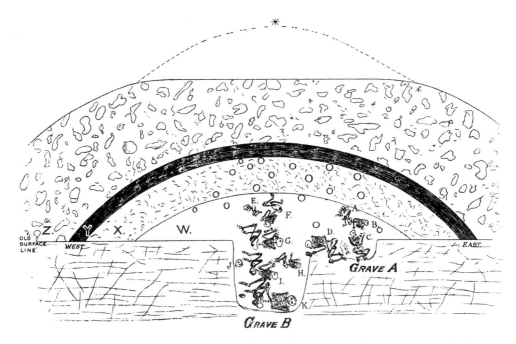

Figure 8.09 Mortimer's schematic section through Duggleby Howe. Each inhumation is labelled with a letter, cremation burials are represented by circles (Mortimer 1905, fig. 45).

Elsewhere on the Wolds, similar grave goods are identifiable. Two complete Grimston bowls and a selection of finely worked flint arrowheads were found around the six primary inhumations at Towthorpe 18 (Mortimer 1905, 9–11; Gibson and Bayliss 2010, 85; Fig. 8.10). Whole pots are also known from Aldro 88 and 94 (Mortimer 1905, 58 and 82), while pottery sherds (some quite possibly deposited as fragments) have been found accompanying burials at several other sites. Flint tools are also common (see Pouncett 2019, appx F), notably often being placed in what appears to be a slightly 'odd' relationship with the body: a flint knife at the shoulder at Aldro 94 (Mortimer 1905, 82); arrowheads at the hip and knees of two individuals at Calais Wold 275 (*ibid.*, 162); a scraper behind the head at Cowlam 57 (Greenwell 1877, 218); and a scraper close to the skull at Garton Slack 81 (Mortimer 1905, 238; Fig. 8.11). Intriguingly, with this burial, flints had been employed elsewhere as well:

> the [human] remains were in excellent preservation, and all the bones in position, except those of the left foot ... It was clear that the other portion of this foot had been amputated previous to burial, as not a trace of the missing bones could be found; but where they ought to have been were two worked flints [a knife and a flake]. (Mortimer 1905, 238)

At Sherburn 7, the body of a young woman had been laid in a slight depression of the surface, with her hands up to her face; near the body were six flakes and a knife,

FIG. 14.   ¼

FIG. 17.   ½

FIG. 15.   ¼

FIG. 18.   ½

Figure 8.10 Some of the finds from the central burial deposit at Towthorpe 18 (after Mortimer 1905, pl. 2).

whilst the 'the head was protected by two large blocks of flint, placed roof-fashion over it' (Greenwell 1877, 146).

Much like Orkney and the Cotswold-Severn region, animal bone deposits from Yorkshire Wolds tombs are fairly frequently encountered and often directly associated with human bone deposits; the antiquarian reporting of these often makes it difficult to be confident about the species recorded. Beads and bone pins have also been found in small numbers and an amber pendant was recorded close to a woman's neck at Whitegrounds (Brewster 1984, 13).

Overall, the evidence for 'grave goods' recovered from Wolds Neolithic barrows, whilst often still enigmatic and difficult to fully grasp, is arguably more clear-cut than in other regions due to the fact that they were simply less 'multi-temporal'. Complete pottery vessels and, often, flint tools are commonly found in clear, direct spatial association with specific, articulated human remains. At least one key reason why this is so is the nature of the burials and burial sites themselves: the general absence of constantly accessible chambers and presence of chalk-filled graves combining to ensure that these 'original' grave goods survived as archaeologically visible (and intact) deposits that were not subsequently dispersed around a tomb, or cleared out and burnt, as was often the case elsewhere.

Summary

At the beginning and end of this section we have focused on archaeological examples where, due to the particular character of those sites' temporal extendedness, the integrity of the original relationship between burial and artefact(s) was relatively well preserved. At Unival, while a great deal still had to be inferred, it was possible to envisage the deposition of pots with individuals in the tomb and their ongoing 'processing' (and fragmentation) around the chamber. At Duggleby Howe and many of the other Wolds sites, the specific nature of burial – in chalk-cut graves which were then infilled – meant that person–artefact relationships were often even more clearly preserved. On many

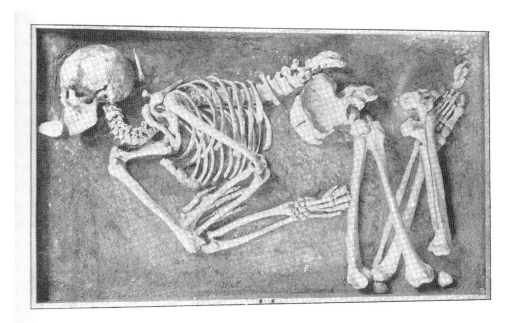

Figure 8.11 Burial 1 from Garton Slack 81, showing scraper in front of the teeth and bone pin (possibly worn in the hair or fastening a shroud) at the back of the skull, and flints by the remaining foot (Mortimer 1905, fig. 602).

of these sites, the cumulative deposition of human remains (and artefacts) was just as complex as elsewhere, and sometimes extremely long-lasting, but did not usually occur in an open chamber; consequently, ongoing activities at the site had less of an impact on both artefacts and bodies. The process of reflecting on the material culture deposited in tombs in Orkney and the Cotswold-Severn area with these examples in mind allows us to envisage what might also have been on those sites. In these cases, the character of activities within most tombs ensured that the integrity of any original person-artefact relationships was mostly lost. Nonetheless, in drawing out *potential* comparisons between them and other clearer examples, the possibility of original 'grave good' deposits on those sites could also be recognised (if not established with certainty). Our review of the evidence from all these Neolithic tombs suggests that artefacts often were drawn into mortuary practice and can provide significant insights into what happened on those sites. It is important that we do not write-off the possible prevalence of 'grave goods' at this time, even if they can be hard to 'see' and the processes behind their ultimate deposition tricky to untangle. Our understanding of what these were and how they were understood by people is complicated both by Neolithic mortuary practices (which were temporally extended) and by the character of Neolithic mortuary architecture in many regions (which created multi-temporal sites). Despite a prevailing discourse which downplays their presence, grave goods clearly were deposited in many mortuary contexts in the Neolithic.

Discussion: 'dissolving' bodies and person-artefact relationships

To finish this section looking at Neolithic tombs, we wish to explore one further aspect of these sites' temporality. Many of the sites we have considered so far have contained disarticulated human remains. As already discussed, these often visually and numerically impressive – and undeniably intriguing – assemblages have generally taken centre stage, rather than material culture, in discussions of those monuments' functions. Since Thurnam's consideration of the Neolithic 'mode of burial', including a recognition that certain body parts were missing on some sites (1869, 184–5), human bone assemblages have dominated accounts of these sites and the societies that constructed them – from mid-20th century considerations of primitive cannibalism (Piggott 1954, 47–8) through to Renfrew's (1979) discussion of segmented societies and Shanks and Tilley's (1982) argument that 'equality' in death served to mask inequalities in life. As discussed briefly in Chapter 2, over the past 20 years or so, considerations of identity and personhood have dominated interpretation. Many writers have pointed out that Neolithic concepts of 'the body' and what constituted 'a person' may have been very different to our own (e.g. Thomas 2000; Brück 2001b; Fowler 2001; A. Jones 2005; Harris 2018). Specifically with reference to the human remains found in Neolithic monuments, it has on the one hand been suggested that human bone could essentially have 'lost' its personhood to some extent as specific individuals became generalised ancestors; as a result, human bone, like artefacts, may have been circulated amongst the living as part of wider systems of exchange (e.g. Thomas 2000, 662). Equally, on the other, it has been argued that Neolithic societies may not have directly distinguished between 'living people', 'the dead', 'animals' and 'material culture', applying a highly fluid view of what constituted 'a person' who could act in the world at that time (e.g. Fowler 2001, 144). In this scenario, what we see as 'the dead' in long barrows and chambered tombs may not have been clearly distinguishable from 'the living' and it was quite possible for people to move from one state to another at different points in time (*ibid.*). Whichever of these lines of reasoning is preferred, the rearrangement, intermingling and apparent broad equivalence of different people's remains (and objects) in tombs strongly suggest that, at some level, concepts of 'the individual' – assuming they existed amongst the living in the first place – were broken down in some way upon 'death'.

Our reasons for revisiting these discussions of human remains and the personhood they embody is that this discourse has significant implications for our understanding of the mortuary material culture deposited in those tombs. At the start of the chapter, we revisited our 'ideal' burial-with-grave-goods – where one individual had been buried with specific things – in order to highlight the fact that, in most Neolithic contexts, the artefact–person relationship was *not* like that. We then described the evidence from several key regions, ultimately suggesting that material culture *is present*, and perhaps more importantly *was significant*, in many tombs. We have also suggested that, on many sites, even those where the body-artefact relationships are unclear, it is *possible* that specific objects were placed in there with specific people, as we see with the 'flint knapper' at Hazelton North or various burials from the Yorkshire Wolds, for example. However, in many other cases, especially given the arguments about the dissolution of the individual in death considered above, it is perhaps likely that the relationship between object and person was somewhat looser, even when a specific artefact *was* placed in a tomb with a specific body. The pots we have discussed at Unival, for example, or the joints of meat in Orcadian tombs, may have gone in with one person but been intended for all of those buried in the tomb. Equally, in other contexts, 'human' bodies and 'non-human' objects/animals could apparently blend into one another – 'animal' bones specifically and intentionally intermingled with 'human' ones; 'flint' artefacts substituted for 'human' limbs; pots, bones, stone and wood fragmented all together through burning.

Ultimately what we are suggesting is that, especially in the Neolithic, the body-artefact relationship – and our conceptualisations of this – potentially needs to be stretched in two related ways. First, in space – it is possible that an object placed in a tomb with one body was actually a 'grave good' for the community of the dead rather than that specific 'individual'. Secondly, and directly related to this, in time – it is also possible that people could continue receiving 'grave goods' for centuries after their initial burial, with objects being placed both in direct association with bodies inside the tomb (as we have discussed) and also in forecourts, ditches, mounds, etc. (deposits we have not investigated in detail here). Theoretically, these possibilities may also be true for later period burials as well, including even our 'ideal' example above; the point that grave goods were not straightforwardly 'for' the person buried has been made many times, and certainly some later burials were revisited with objects potentially added or taken away (Brück 2019, 24–7). However, a temporal extendedness between objects and bodies is especially evident and clearly prevalent in Neolithic contexts, creating a particular kind of archaeological record where it is very tricky to define grave goods in the traditional ('ideal') sense, as we have discussed above. Consequently, as well as an open-mindedness about 'personhood', etc., we arguably also need to maintain a confidence in first allowing, then working with (not against), and finally embracing a loose definition of 'grave goods' during the Neolithic. We have argued throughout this chapter that the artefacts in many Neolithic burial contexts have been ignored or underplayed because of the various complexities we have described. However, we hope to have highlighted the fact that, actually, the temporal extendedness of mortuary material culture is interesting and absolutely worthy of exploration, providing significant insight into the complex and sometimes enigmatic practices that characterised these sites.

8.3. Pyre goods, cremation and the temporalities of funerary process

The different temporal rhythms of inhumation and cremation

At the start of this section, it is helpful to revisit our 'ideal' burial-with-grave-goods to demonstrate, again, what we are *not* dealing with. In that fictional example, the person died, their body was inhumed quite quickly in the grave and not revisited until our hypothetical archaeologists dug it up. The objects found in the grave had also been removed fairly speedily from the world of the living – in some cases because they were directly associated with the person who had died (her necklace and perhaps also the brooch), in other cases because the mourners felt it appropriate to 'give up' certain things for the burial (the pottery vessel and the joint of meat) at that moment. In this section, we will be investigating cremation burials and objects – 'pyre goods' – that came to be burnt along with the person, and then also buried with them in the cremation 'grave'.

The fact that cremation – as opposed to inhumation – has the capacity to extend the funerary process in both space and time has been acknowledged and discussed by archaeologists for some time (e.g. Barrett 1991b; McKinley 1997; Appleby 2013; Williams 2015; Brück 2019). To illustrate our point, this time we might imagine a hypothetical cremation burial – a collection of burnt human bones (those of an adult and those of a young child) gathered together in a pot which they fill to the brim. In amongst these bones are a number of sheep/goat bones, also burnt; and on top of all this is a single, unburnt amber bead. This collection of things was buried, pot upright, in a small, circular pit at the edge of a barrow mound. In relation to the spatial location(s) of the mortuary process, in this example it is possible that earlier phases of the sequence – the construction of the pyre, the burning of the bodies, the collection of the burnt bones and their placement within the pot – happened in totally different places, far removed from the barrow. In relation to the temporal extendedness of the process, it is also possible that those events happened a long time, perhaps even many years, before the ultimate burial of the urn and its contents in the ground. In this particular case, it is conceivable that the two people died a long time apart, with the cremated remains of the first awaiting the death of the second before their burial together. The bones of the sheep/goat may have been burnt with the second person but intended as 'food' for both. The amber bead is unlikely to have been on the pyre with either person (amber is readily destroyed by fire) but other beads may have been (these could have been completely destroyed or left *in situ* on the funeral pyre). The single amber bead may have been worn by the adult or child in life, removed by the mourners for the cremation process, and then replaced back with that person on burial; or could have been unstrung from someone's existing necklace, placed with the burial as a material instantiation of that social relationship.

Our point will be clear by now – that the process of cremation burial, and the incorporation of grave and pyre goods along with it, can be a complicated temporal affair. The examples of different burials that we have outlined above are, of course, at fairly extreme ends of what would in fact have been a much broader temporal spectrum of processes for both inhumations and cremations. We have chosen to illustrate a rapid inhumation burial and a temporally extended cremation(s) burial to make our point clearly. Appleby, however, has pointed out very effectively that the *chaînes opératoires* of both cremation and inhumation can be highly complex (2013, 87–91). Interestingly, she argues that, broadly speaking, each rite presents opportunities for extended engagement with the funerary process, but at different times, ultimately suggesting that cremation is likely to extend the *pre-burial* temporality of mortuary practice more often than inhumation. We explore these ideas further below.

Pyre goods

Turning specifically now to grave goods, it might be said that cremation also, on balance, adds temporal complexity, increasing not only the length of time over which material culture could be introduced into the overall mortuary process but also the potential range of contexts involved. All objects, burnt and unburnt, associated with cremation burials that were included in our study must, by definition, be *grave* goods as well, since they had to have been placed with human remains in a 'formal' burial context. However, some of these were also identifiable as potential *pyre* goods – objects which were clearly burnt and thus likely to have been placed on the pyre with the body, collected up along with the burnt human bone and ultimately deposited along with it in the cremation burial or 'grave'. As our hypothetical example illustrated, it is possible that some pyre goods did not ever become grave goods, either because they were left or destroyed on the pyre or removed from the mortuary process prior to the burial event; only in very unusual cases would these objects be archaeologically visible. It is also important to acknowledge that unburnt grave goods could also be introduced into the process of cremation burial as well; some of these could actually have been included on the pyre but not visibly burnt (McKinley 2006, 82), but equally many may well have been exempted from the cremation process entirely.

Interestingly, pyre goods have not been subject to sustained investigation as a category in themselves for later prehistoric Britain. With occasional, brief exceptions (e.g. McKinley 1994), they have only really been discussed in passing as part of broader studies either of cremation practice (e.g. Brück 2019, 75; Willis 2019) or of grave goods more generally (e.g. Wilkin 2011; Woodward and Hunter 2015, 516–17), or on a site-specific basis (e.g. Fitzpatrick 1997a). Equally, the fact that a grave good had been burnt does not always invite comment, or the label 'pyre good', even within contemporary burial reports (McKinley 1994).

Pyre goods in the GGDB

The GGDB enabled us to undertake a long-term analysis of pyre goods across our six study regions, since we took care to note systematically when grave goods were, or perhaps more accurately *had been recorded* as being, burnt. Before outlining the character of pyre goods within the GGDB, it is important to note a few biases which may have affected the results of our study. The complex processes associated with cremation in general, and pyre goods in particular, ensure that dataset biases are potentially more significant here than in many of our other analyses. First, it is critical to note that, especially in the early days of archaeology, cremation burials themselves were not always necessarily thought significant and so often were not recorded or analysed (McKinley 1997, 129); no doubt many burnt objects associated with these were similarly ignored. Even when cremation burials have been recognised, not all burnt objects with them will necessarily have been noted and/or recorded as being burnt. Overall, pyre goods are thus likely to be significantly under-represented in the contemporary archaeological record (see also McKinley 1994). Following on from these biases in archaeological reporting, it is also important to acknowledge the potential biases created by past practice. As discussed above, some pyre goods may never actually have gone on to become grave goods (because they were left on the pyre or subsequently removed from the mortuary process) and so, strictly speaking, not all pyre goods are captured either in the archaeological record or in our dataset. Equally, certain objects placed on the pyre would not have survived the cremation – organics such as wood or leather, but also friable materials such as amber, jet and flint, and objects that could melt such as those made from copper-alloy or glass. Alternatively, as mentioned above, not all objects that were on the pyre would show any signs of burning, perhaps because they were placed towards the edge of the fire or were not readily heat-affected. Since it is initially subject to substantial heat during manufacture, pottery that was burnt subsequently on a pyre can be especially hard to identify; equally, some pots were noted as having been subject to secondary burning, but only on the inside, usually because hot ashes and burnt bones had been tipped into them, and so had not been on the pyre at all.

In the analysis that follows, to get directly at pyre goods, we investigate all objects associated with cremation burials; as we saw in Section 8.2, burnt objects are sometimes identified with inhumation burials but since these are unlikely to have been 'pyre' goods as such, we have omitted them from analysis here. We have, however, included *unburnt* objects deposited with cremation burials in order to facilitate meaningful comparison with, and to enable wider contextualisation of, our potential pyre goods.

Temporal variability
In total, the GGDB included 3110 objects found with cremation burials, 211 (6.8%) of which had been recorded as being 'burnt'. As discussed, due to under reporting and a lack of recognition, the 'real' total is likely to have been higher. Table 8.01 outlines the prevalence of these burnt objects through time. Interestingly, while the total number of objects found with cremation burials varies considerably by period (largely reflecting the relative prevalence of that rite), the proportion of those objects that were burnt is remarkably constant. If we exclude the Neolithic period (where the sample size is small and there are various other complicating factors – see Sections 3.1 and 8.2), the percentage of all objects placed with cremation burials that were burnt

ranges from 4–8%; if we exclude pots from the count, which were only very rarely recorded as burnt and constitute 64% of all cremation-associated grave goods, this range changes to 8-16% (Iron Age-Beaker/Early Bronze Age).

Regional patterning

The prevalence of burnt grave goods with cremation burials also varies considerably by case study region (Fig. 8.12). Clearly, one key variable that will have influenced this patterning is the significant broader variability in terms of overall number of cremation burials during a given period in each area (Fig. 8.13). However, regional patterning beyond this, in pyre goods specifically, is also in evidence. Kent in particular stands out as having especially high numbers of burnt objects during the Iron Age (although it must be noted that Kent had by far the most cremation burials at this time as well), and by contrast very low numbers during the Beaker/Early Bronze Age phase. East Yorkshire has very high numbers for the Beaker/Early Bronze Age phase. As might be expected, the regularity with which objects were included on the pyre during cremation appears to have varied considerably both by period and by region.

Table 8.01 Burnt/unburnt objects deposited directly with cremation burials, by period, in the GGDB. Note that not all objects could be assigned to a specific sub-period.

	Burnt (no.)	Unburnt (no.)	Burnt (%)	Unburnt (%)
Neolithic	9	48	16	84
Beaker/EBA	113	1281	8	92
MBA/LBA	30	817	4	96
Iron Age	18	492	4	96

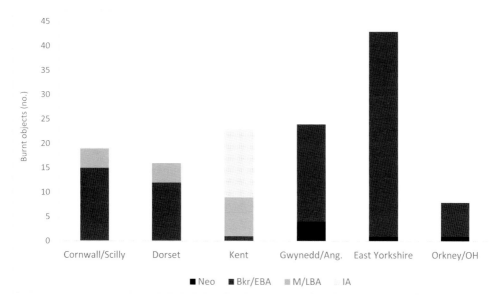

Figure 8.12 Total number of burnt objects with cremation burials by case study area/period.

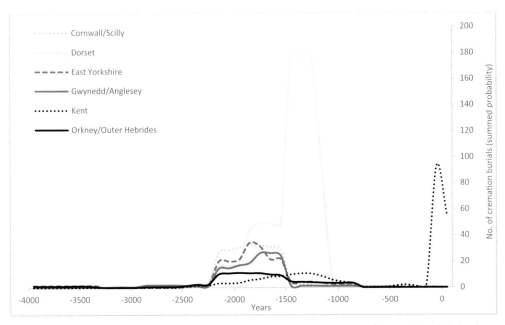

Figure 8.13 No. of cremation burials through time, by case study area (summed probability).

Table 8.02 Occurrence of burnt objects in cremation burials, by period.

	Neolithic	Bkr/EBA	M/LBA	Iron Age
Animal bone	•	•	•	•
Axe/macehead		•		
Flint tool		•		
Flint flake	•	•	•	
Dagger/pommel		•		
Awl/pin/point/brooch		•	•	•
Bead/necklace		•		
Stone		•		
Lid			•	
Pot	•	•	•	•
Other		•		

Object variability

Variability in terms of the object types included as pyre goods with cremation burials (Table 8.02) was actually fairly restricted, with the exception of the Beaker/Early Bronze Age period (discussed in more detail below). Burnt animal bones and pots/ sherds were found in all four periods, burnt flints in all but the Iron Age. During the Middle/Late Bronze Age, bone pins/points stand out, with six out of the total of eight having been burnt – interestingly, these all came from three graves on a single site, Waterbrook Park, Ashford in Kent (Wessex Archaeology 2008b), suggesting a very specific local practice. During the Iron Age, the only other pyre good object type (beyond animal bone and pots) is brooches, of which five out of 81 are burnt; interestingly, four of these were found in one pit on one site (Leysdown Road, Kent; Margetts 2012), apparently again representing a specific, localised tradition, and potentially even a one-off event.

Pyre goods in the Beaker/Early Bronze Age period
Unsurprisingly perhaps, given the fact that the Beaker/Early Bronze Age period has the largest numbers of cremation burials (1392 = 45%) and greatest variability of object types (see Fig. 3.03), that period produced the most evidence for and widest range of pyre goods: 96 artefacts representing 12 different categories of object (Fig. 8.14). As a result of the relatively high numbers of objects and clearer variability between them, it is possible to undertake somewhat more detailed analyses for this sub-period.

Animal bone is the most commonly occurring pyre good throughout our study period. During the Beaker/Early Bronze Age phase, 60 cremation burials were identified as containing animal bone (out of a total of 1393 = 4.3%); 24 of these contained burnt animal bone, 36 contained unburnt remains. It is important to note that, in reality, this figure is likely to have been much higher since burnt animal bone especially is difficult to recognise amongst burnt human bone and will not regularly have been recorded until recent decades (McKinley 1997, 132): McKinley, for example, records that 16% of cremation burials contain animal bone in her own sample analysed to

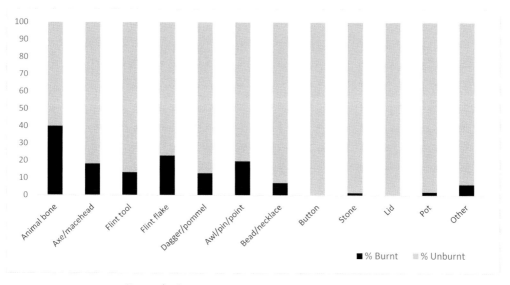

Figure 8.14 Proportion of burnt/unburnt objects associated with Beaker/Early Bronze Age cremation burials.

modern standards (*ibid.*) and Wilkin noted a directly comparable proportion of 15% in his survey of both inhumations and cremation burials during this period (2011, 65).

Within our own dataset, where species identifications had been carried out, a wide range of animals was represented in Beaker/Early Bronze Age cremation burials: cattle, pig, sheep/goat, dog, deer (antler and bone), fox/badger, wolf, bird and fish (see also Section 5.03). While sample sizes are very small, and it is important to remain mindful of the complexities of animal bone survival and recognition (especially when it is burnt), one notable pattern emerges immediately from the data: domestic species that are commonly eaten (cattle, sheep/goat and pig) dominate in terms of those that were burnt on the pyre, whilst wild species predominate in terms of the inclusion of unburnt animals (Fig. 8.15). While we do not have access to specific body part information in most cases, it seems likely that food (joints of meat, etc.) was regularly included on the pyre along with the body when it was burnt *and*, importantly, then collected up and buried along with the cremated human bone. Deer, the most common animal found, were represented primarily by antlers (11/13), a pattern consistent with Wilkin's (2011) study of animal remains in Beaker/Early Bronze Age burials in Wiltshire, Dorset and Oxfordshire. No significant patterning was apparent in terms of the geographical location of different animals within the GGDB – most regions appear to have seen a fairly wide range of animal species, burnt and unburnt, deposited.

Stone/flint tools and flakes were also commonly included in Beaker/Early Bronze Age cremation burials. In total, there were 168 occurrences of these object types – 17% burnt, 83% unburnt. As we saw in Chapter 3, flints and stone tools are a common grave good generally during this period. It is interesting that, in a substantial number of

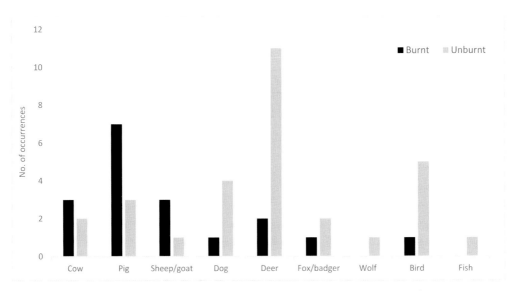

Figure 8.15 Occurrence of different animal species, burnt and unburnt, in Beaker/Early Bronze Age cremation burials.

cases, mourners elected to include these objects on the pyre as well as in the burial. Notably, certain objects were preferentially treated in this way – 23% of flint knives, for example, were burnt, in contrast to 7% of other flint tools. This could potentially suggest that significant personal possessions (such as flint knives) may have been seen as appropriate to accompany people onto the pyre, whereas other flint tools were perhaps added, unburnt, by the mourners during the burial ceremony.

Metal daggers (and associated pommels) also featured as Beaker/Early Bronze Age pyre goods – five (13%) were burnt and 34 (87%) unburnt. Four of the five burnt examples were from Gwynedd/Anglesey suggesting a strong regional practice in this case; three of those four were pommels only (not whole daggers) – two from Bedd Branwen (Baynes 1914, 10) and one from Rhiw (RCAHMW 1964). The significance of dagger pommels, in themselves, has been discussed at some length by Woodward and Hunter (2015, 47–52). Interestingly, these objects often seem to have been made from cetacean bone/ivory and, in many cases, were heavily worn when deposited – sometimes, elsewhere too, without the rest of the dagger (*ibid.*). With our examples from north-west Wales, it is possible to imagine that, because of the significance and meaning of these objects, each one was first separated from the rest of the dagger and then included along with the human body on the cremation pyre. In light of the treatment of flint knives discussed above, which often were burnt, it is notable that in all of our other regions (with the exception of a single example from Cornwall) metal daggers were included in cremation burials *without* having been burnt on the pyre first.

When it comes to items that may have been worn on the body, during life and/ or in death, the picture is variable. Our category of awl/pin/point covers a range of items (including tools as well as possible hair-pins) and a range of these were burnt; it is possible that some of these were worn on the body, or fastening a shroud around it, on the pyre (Cooper *et al.* 2019). Notably, not one of the seven buttons was burnt and only four of the 55 occurrences of beads/necklaces (= 7%) showed signs of burning. Those beads noted as having been burnt included faience, bone and shell examples. As mentioned above, materials such as jet and amber would not necessarily have survived a pyre and thus even if such beads had originally been included in the cremation event, they would not have been available for deposition with the burial. People in the past would have been aware of this too and so may well have kept those beads they wanted to bury to one side during cremation.

Discussion: fragmented people, coherent objects?

At the end of this consideration of pyre goods throughout later prehistory, it is interesting to note that, actually, beyond animal bone, there was very little patterning within this subset of grave goods in any period. Notably, where certain object types did stand out in the data as having been burnt, it was usually a consequence of a specific, localised practice – the inclusion of Early Bronze Age dagger pommels in Gwynedd/Anglesey, of Late Bronze Age bone pins/points at Ashford, Kent, and of

Iron Age brooches at Leysdown Road, Kent. The patterning evident within animal bone deposits during the Early Bronze Age, suggesting that edible meat dominates those placed on the pyre, is intriguing. More detailed specialist analysis of the bones themselves, right across our study period, would likely be highly beneficial (see, for example, Bond and Worley's (2006) study of early medieval material).

Overall, as with our study of Neolithic material in Section 8.2, there is a definite sense that the extended temporality of the funerary process associated with cremation has led to a certain haziness of vision – a feeling that we are not seeing all the objects that were, at some point, caught up in the funerary process. In many respects, this situation is comparable to that of the cremated human remains where often only a small proportion of the 'expected' total is present. As McKinley succinctly put it 'since all the human bone was apparently rarely included in the burial, inevitably all the pyre goods probably were not either' (1994, 133). It is quite possible that, as has been argued for cremated human bone, some pyre goods were intentionally left on the pyre or distributed among the mourners. Appleby's (2013) notion of an extended *pre-burial* emphasis with cremated human bone would also have affected mortuary material culture, in some respects making the deposition of *grave* goods less likely.

Given these insights into pyre goods, it is perhaps especially notable that so many unburnt grave goods – of many different kinds – were included in cremation burials. This demonstrates that, even when the pre-burial process was extended to incorporate the burning of the body (and other associated events), the inclusion of 'coherent' objects during the burial was, in the majority of cases (around 90% on average), still key. The fragmentation, through burning, of human bodies clearly was important, but the fragmentation of objects was apparently not always desired or was achieved through other means (such as the deposition of a single bead or button). Cremation may have 'stretched' mortuary practice, chronologically and spatially, well beyond the grave, but *grave* goods in the traditional sense (then and now) had persistence as an idea.

8.4. Living in the moment: cremation burials of the Late Iron Age

Our final case study builds on two important points raised above – that cremation can extend the funerary process for mourners and that it helps archaeologists pull apart the intimate temporalities of the funeral – distinguishing between those objects on/close to the body which were immolated from those placed later in the grave (whether complete or fragmentary *pars pro toto*). This in turn helps us think about the images of the dead being actively shaped when they were dressed, adorned or armed (perhaps for last viewings of the deceased) compared with those objects arranged later in the grave-pit by mourners. This distinction will not map neatly onto a distinction between 'possessions' versus 'gifts' or 'equipment for the afterlife' but it does enable us to show the temporally extended process involved in the assembling of grave goods. We will argue this helps us understand the importance of extending the funeral process as a strategy of power, augmenting the material affects of grave assemblages associated with feasting and dining in Late Iron Age cremation burials of the south-east: both the 'small-scale' cultural politics of taste and distinction, as well as the larger scale politics of emerging concepts of sovereignty.

The Aylesford style of burial (Stead 1976; Whimster 1981), once known as the Aylesford-Swarling culture after the two early type site cemeteries (Evans 1890; Bushe-Fox 1925) covers the phenomenon of Late Iron Age, peri-Conquest funerary traditions found in south-eastern Britain (Fitzpatrick 2007). Focused on the counties of Kent, Hertfordshire, Essex and Cambridgeshire, outliers are also known in Bedfordshire and Buckinghamshire with affinities to cremation burials in West Sussex (such as Westhampnett, Fitzpatrick 1997a). It is perhaps best characterised by urned cremation burials or un-urned cremation burials with pots, accompanied by fairly small numbers of ancillary grave goods, buried in pits that often cluster in small cemeteries. It is generally now interpreted as an indigenous rite which nonetheless conveys growing cross-Channel links with the Roman world through both mortuary custom and material culture (Harding 2016, 88). This does not preclude the movement of small, influential groups or individuals but neither does this model rely upon innovations wrought by a larger-scale migration (see Hamilton 2007). Allied to this phenomenon are the more spectacular 'Welwyn' style burials of the Aylesford rite c. 50–10 BC, with a late 'Lexden' phase c. 10 BC–AD 50 (Stead 1976). These traditions morph into the post-Claudian conquest era of fully recognisable Romano-British cremation rites (*ibid.*, 125), including the Folly Lane cremation chamber and shaft (Niblett 1999) and the site of Stanway which spans the late 1st century BC–mid-1st century AD (Crummy *et al.* 2007). These larger-scale burials with more diverse grave goods fall outside of our immediate study area (and the latest burials transcend our study period), but the example of Welwyn Garden City is discussed below to complement the simpler cremation burials which dominate our case study region of Kent.

Haselgrove (1984) distinguishes between three kinds of cremation burials: first, the high-end elaborate rectangular grave-pits or shafts (Welwyn, Lexden, Folly Lane, some of the Stanway burials) which represent the interred aftermath of the most sumptuous funerals. As Stead noted, these can be additionally distinguished by the presence of amphorae and, usually, imported metal or glass vessels (1967), hearth-furniture such as firedogs, cauldrons, suspension chains and drinking horns (Pearce 2015). Second, there are a range of burials interred with wood-and-metal bound 'buckets' or decorated bronze 'mirrors' (though as Fitzpatrick (2007) notes, there is some overlap between the Welwyn fashion of burial and these distinctive grave goods, just as some smaller burials may contain the odd amphora). In Kent, this includes bucket burials at Swarling, Alkham and Aylesford, and the mirror burial of Chilham. An increased emphasis on the importance of repertoires of feasting equipment may indicate an absorption of exotic objects, food and drink within existing feasting cultures (Fitzpatrick 2007): what Harding has (perhaps a little reductively) called 'the comforts of hearth and home' (2016, 151). Rare weapons and mirrors burials also show traits of continuity in creating 'signal' burials that stood out from the surrounding community (*ibid.*). Hamilton rejects the notion that such burial diversity or bricolage across the 'British Eastern Channel Area' is evidence either of 'backwardness, impoverishment or remnant archaism' (2007, 98) or even (as Pearce puts it) 'manifest resistance to Rome' (2015, 224). Creighton vociferously criticises a visualisation which shows the Folly Lane burial, for instance, as that of a 'barbarian surrounded by trinkets' (2006, 154, 156). The degree of cultural choice exercised here between continental and south-eastern rites is, Hamilton argues, indicative of 'a highly individualistic and dynamic society … [where] power and status was maintained as much through cult authority as economic control' (2007, 98). Pearce goes further: these grave goods need to be contextualised not just within Late Iron Age mortuary traditions but the changing material and social world of Conquest-era Britain, particularly in the south-east. The cremation burials in particular hint at a new form of 'political theatre' mobilised by those inculcated into Roman tastes and mores: mercenaries or auxiliaries, ambassadors, favoured client kings showered with prestige gifts and comestibles, or their offspring – the returning youthful hostages known as *obsides*, raised in Rome, who had 'come of age' (Creighton 2006). Their proclivities must have rubbed off on their peers. These burials thus foreshadow the emergence of an 'urbane sociality … Roman *savoir-faire*' in Pearce's terms (2015, 224), seen in full-blown early Roman cremations: a use of diacritical consumption habits and cultural distinctions in dress and sociality both in life *and* death that reshaped micro- and macro-politics in powerful ways. How was the temporality of cremation key to this process?

Rendering the dead: cremation, mobility and mourning

It has already been noted above that while cremations can extend the funerary process in both space and time, they accelerate corporeal transformation: contracting the time of bodily decomposition, making it a more rapid affair compared with excarnation (open or protected), inhumation or corpse curation. The manner in which this is achieved has, as Williams (2006) points out for the Anglo-Saxon period, the added *affect* of spectacle as well as its material effect: using fire to radically transform matter though it requires a more protracted performance of laying out, preparing the pyre, tending the cremation and gathering up fragments for interment, dispersal and/or curation. It was certainly not, as McKinley argues, the 'cheap option' (2006) but it did make it a more public and theatrical performance. Once transformed, mortuary time then slowed, rendering the deceased's remains not just more durable but mobile. What we might call 'mourning time' was from this moment on extended by cremation, since the *final* ritual of interment could be drawn out or even deferred. It also (as many other archaeologists have pointed out) enabled the dead to become not just more mobile but partible, with portions of the cremated body potentially interred in different places, some deposited and other bits curated or even composed into new objects (e.g. Brück 2019; Johnston 2020).

Following the deceased's rendering by flame, depositional temporalities were now drawn out. The following case studies argue this mortuary technology was strategically useful when more time in the liminal phase was needed, allowing the bereaved to gather attendees from a distance and/or accrue and acquire the paraphernalia of grave goods needed for feast and funeral. It also helped stagger secondary mortuary rites: perhaps to scatter the dead in many places, finally bringing what was usually only a small portion to a particular place of interment, possibly associated with a closing 'wake'. In the following discussion there is a strong sense of the creation of final, aesthetically pleasing *tableau* or *mise-en-scène* (Pearce 2015) that allude to the importance of objects in this final stage of mortuary performance: strategic placement and artful ordering before points of stillness and show. Such 'frozen frames' were of course part of a more dynamic, ongoing performance but materialised a particular poetic moment where symbolic or metaphorical relations were made manifest to others (see Carver 2000): eulogies delivered not just through words but gestures with treasured things.

'Brimful' burials: the performance of largesse

The majority of Late Iron Age grave goods associated with cremation burials in the GGDB come from simple pit burials in Kent characterised by variable amounts of cremated material interred with fine-wares associated with storing or serving, dining or drinking. At their simplest these consist of a single vessel: the Whitehall Close cremation burials were literally 'cupped' in locally made butt beakers (Frere *et al.* 1987). Burial AAB (Zone B) on the A249 bypass contained mere fragments of a grog-tempered platter along with burned human bone and charcoal flecks, with a pair of Colchester brooches (CgMs 2008, 42). In the small cemetery of Glebe Land, Harrietsham, nine cremation burials contained a variety of 'Aylesford' type pots and bronze vessels, paired brooches, small personal items (an iron pin, a bronze ring) and joints of meat represented in the faunal remains (Canterbury Archaeology 1988). Malmains Farm, Alkham contained similar cremation burials, often accompanied by copper and iron rings and an iron knife or razor (Philp 2014) but two 'bucket burials' stand out: both containing cremated bone and copper-alloy brooches, one with a toilet set, and other grave goods placed in the burial pit, including ceramic vessels, copper-alloy and iron rings and iron knives. In Grave 4298 at Site B (part of the A2 Pepperhill to Cobham road scheme) heavy truncation by ploughing had removed the upper halves of ceramic vessels but 284 g of cremated bone survived in the centre of a pit, placed with six (unburned) brooches (four bronze – two conjoined by a delicate chain – and two iron) and decayed pieces of wood (possibly a box or capping board; Allen *et al.* 2012, fig. 3.85). A pedestal urn was placed adjacent to this capped or boxed heap, inside of which were found fragments of copper-alloy strip clamps or clips – possibly associated with a hide or textile item. Another pedestal urn was placed to the north of the cremated bone deposit, accompanied by two small bowls filled with unburned faunal remains that seem to represent token food offerings (pork in one, mutton/goat or beef in the other), while a notched copper-alloy disc with almost serrated edge and scored surface (rather like a pizza wheel, perhaps a small cutting knife or razor) was placed in a final bowl.

In Grave 4312 nearby, a larger quantity of cremated bone was contained within a bronze-bound yew wood bucket which had raised feet punched with circle-and-dot 'ray' designs (Allen *et al.* 2012, fig. 3.89). This was again associated with two pedestal jars and a probable bronze cup. Here we see the themes of personal bodily care and adornment coupled with an enjoyment of food and drink as key themes in the context of death (Hill *et al.* 1999): conjuring the persona of the welcoming and well-prepared host/hostess-organiser (Fitzpatrick 2010, 398). Harding has argued there is little here that is 'genuinely personal' (2016, 278) but there are exceptions: the Chilham Castle cremation burial was contained in a grog-tempered vessel, and in the other half of the pit an unburned mirror of idiosyncratic 'three roundel' design had been laid decorative plate downwards, feasibly wrapped in a cloth or bag associated with paired brooches (Parfitt 1998).

Yet most of the cremations were not being used to create such 'charismatic' figures (see Giles *et al.* 2019). Instead, they conjured a particular riposte to mortality and the brevity of life, with novel, small-scale adornments and intimate pleasures. Caesar's reflection on Gaulish cremations is salient here, that they 'consign[ed] to the pyre everything … that they consider as having been pleasurable to the deceased in life' (*De Bello Gallica* VI, 19). Ever so subtly, such burials also began to speak of new tastes, new fashions, new regimes of bodily care and new tropes of hospitality (Hill 1997, 29–30) even where they blended local and exotic objects (Garrow and Gosden 2012, 245). Perhaps this is why so few of these British Late Iron Age grave goods were actually singed in the pyre: funerals were becoming important arenas where family and community groups gathered at a larger scale, and where 'distinction' and 'taste' needed to be materially performed and signalled, to rewrite old customs. As Garrow and Gosden point out in relation to the Baldock bucket burial, 'the decision was taken to bury her or him in a style that, quite possibly, simply had not been seen before by many of those taking part' (2012, 241).

The early date (*c.* 100–50 BC) of the Baldock bucket burial (Fitzpatrick 2007) and the distinctive appearance of this individual wrapped in a bear-skin before their cremation on a pyre would have made this funeral especially memorable. As with the more mundane cremations, some 'time lapse' unfolded before these raked remains of bear-and-man were scattered into the mouth of the central cauldron and backfill of the pit (see Garrow and Gosden 2012, 242–3, imaginatively reconstructing the depositional sequence gleaned from Stead and Rigby 1986). This was the last gesture of a 'busy' burial, after a large wine amphora had been placed on its side against the cauldron, then two heavy iron fire-dogs angled over these giant vessels, with two bronze basins or dishes stacked inside each other and placed in the interstices alongside two small wooden buckets with bronze bands slotted in at the edges (indeed, a slight extension to the pit seems to have cut to fit in one bucket: Stead and Rigby 1986, fig. 20). Garrow and Gosden draw attention to something key here: the objects completely dominate the show, with a 'packed assemblage of prestigious symbols' (2012, 247) which were almost hoard-like in their compression. This pattern echoes funerary deposition at Swarling itself, where several suites of ceramic vessels were 'propped up', packed around or positioned on top of flints (Bushe-Fox 1925). The original report notes how tightly clustered some of the vessels were, 'touching each other' in a pit cut just big enough to hold the stacked-together assemblages, or compressed into a sector of the grave pit, as if jostling for space (e.g. burials 15 and 18). 'Containment' of the actual cremated bone (in bags, boxes and buckets) is an additional motif that magnifies the allure of these funerary heaps: at Bridge, Canterbury, the cremated bone of an adult, possibly female, was contained within an inverted bronze Coolus-style burial, alongside a bronze 'spike' (a possible helmet plume holder) and brooch (Farley *et al.* 2014). These performative tropes of propping, stacking, nesting and filling created a temporal rhythm to this final interment. It was clearly designed to extend the 'palaver' of graveside performance, enhancing the mortuary roles of those tasked with placing objects in the pit and deciding on their arrangement. Such graves often have the feel of only *just* being big enough to hold everything: they were 'brimful', using tight clustering that suggests a need to gather and compress – magnifying their intimate largesse.

Bowls, bear-skins and board-games: Welwyn Garden City

We now turn to one of the most elaborate suites of 'grave goods' from this tradition. Within our project case study areas there are no examples of the Welwyn type and so we discuss the Welwyn Garden City burial here (Figs 8.16 and 8.17) to build upon those ideas of extended temporality achieved through cremation. The burial was that of an adult male, probably over 25 years of age (Powers in Stead 1967, 40). As with the smaller Baldock bucket burial, amongst the remains were the *burned* phalanges of a bear-skin: its paws and claws usually left intact on such a hide both to prevent spoiling the fur and accentuate its evocation of ferocity. Powers (*ibid.*) suggests the body may have been 'wrapped' in it on the pyre but it is equally possible he was 'wearing' the cured fur as a cloak or mantle – creating the image of a 'bear' of a man, as with Baldock. Amongst the cremated bone were tiny fragments of distorted bronze which had also 'spotted' some of the smaller long bones – possibly from a brooch (*ibid.*, 41). These were the only evidence of pyre goods, associated directly with the body.

As with the smaller graves described above, the funeral pit was clearly divided into clusters of objects (Fig. 8.17). At the far eastern side someone stacked five Dressel type 1 (wine) amphorae, spanning the long axis of the grave. At the far southern end was a quite large wooden vessel with iron fittings: the presence of four 'ring handles' suggests two maple-wood buckets stacked inside each other (*ibid.*, 38). At least two other wood and bronze-bound containers (one a fairly shallow dish, and both with 'swing' bronze handle for hanging up on one side; *ibid.*, 31) sat in the midst of the next suite of grave goods – an extensive range of ceramic vessels. These were characterised by a mix of both traditional funerary/cinerary urns (perhaps acting here as storage vessels?) and those clearly designed for serving and consumption, largely related to drink. Most of the pots were local products – grey-black and red-buff wares, once burnished in part or whole, many with worn rims and damage to their pedestal feet. The assemblage comprised: seven pedestal jars or urns (clustered towards the south), five bowls, two tazza, five pedestal cups (one large) and six beakers, one tripod vessel (perhaps for burning incense), four flagons (one imported, three local 'copies') and one flagon lid. The flagons and wooden dishes were located close to the amphora, alongside a noticeable clustering of cups. There were a few direct imports – one of the flagon 'jugs' with white-slip and the two platters, alongside an elegant imported Mediterranean silver cup (with Latin script possibly suggesting an earlier, Roman owner). Close to this was a shallow bronze dish which Stead interpreted as a kind of 'tray': containing at least one wooden ash block which may have formed a stand for two small bowls (one grey-black and one buff-red). The form of the bronze dish is interesting, mimicking the 'ox-hide' shields of the Middle–Late Iron Age, found in burials such as the Mill Hill Deal 'warrior' in Kent buried at least 100 years earlier (G113, Parfitt 1995). Once again, it had a 'hanging handle' on one side only, and the dish/tray had sat on a woven organic 'mat' (or even a shallow basket) made with stake-and-strand construction. In between the clusters of platters, bowls and urns, and the flagons, cups and amphorae, is a solitary bronze nail cleaner: possibly part of a disturbed toilet-set that may have included a now-lost ear scoop and tweezers (Stead 1967, 27). There is also a sense of colour to these arrangements: red, white and silver in the centre of the grave assemblage close to the cremated bone deposit, with reduced-ware urns, cups and tubs towards the south. This may not have any other meaning than a sense of aesthetic clustering, although the grey-black wares do appear to be larger and less intimate than the smaller drinking cups and personal bowls located around the 'tray'.

At this point, the grave-pit seems to have been divided by some form of wooden ash board, decorated with 46–8 bronze-domed studs whose iron shanks were soldered by lead-tin alloy. These had decayed and fallen over grave goods on the south side of the funeral pit, suggesting they adorned only one side of this object. Such studs have been found in other burials, used on a variety of box-fittings, boards, small 'tables' and other furniture (Allen *et al.* 2012). Shields with large domed rivets are known from this period (e.g. North Bersted) and as the most common weapon found in such Late Iron Age cremation burials (such as Snailwell and Standfordbury), it is worth considering whether this 'partition' was in fact a decorated shield board. A uniquely designed iron 'umbo' was found on the far northern side of the grave: interpreted by Stead as the central 'cup' for a gaming board (potentially 'repurposed' from a trophy). Since the deliberate destruction

Figure 8.16 The Welwyn Garden City burial and grave goods assemblage on display in the British Museum (Room 51) (photograph: Neil Wilkin).

and tearing of shield fittings is a common theme in weapons burials of this era it is not unthinkable it has ended up on the far side of the grave as a final dramatic gesture. Yet burials at Stanway certainly made use of oak boards to cover parts of the grave-pit and it is possible that such funerary furniture was used to both partition and conceal or protect the elegant arrangements of bone and objects, perhaps creating a void or cavity into which these decaying studs collapsed. Regardless of the original form, this partition creates a much more open-looking northern zone where someone might have stood and orchestrated events as the other grave goods were slowly laid out.

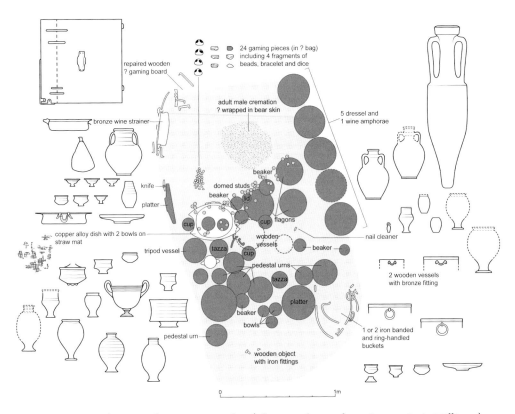

Figure 8.17 Welwyn Garden City grave plan (after Stead 1967, fig. 4; image: Craig Williams)

To the north of the partition was the impressive pile of cremated bone *commingled* with the burned bear 'skin' and small fragments of fused brooch. It may have been 'tipped' out here to form a heap (Stead 1967, 5) or it may have been loosely contained in an organic wrapper or basket. To the side of this was a tight cluster of 24 decorated glass gaming pieces, which seem to comprise 'sets' for four players (based on colour/design) that were probably kept in an organic bag. Classic signs of Hertzian impact fractures – small, crescent-moon shaped 'ring cracks' (Carter 2016) – support this notion of clashing beads knocking against each other not just on the board but in a cloth or hide bag. An adjacent cluster of six worn yet characterful fragments of beads and bracelets (broken long before the burial) were imaginatively interpreted as a sub-set of 'dice' kept in their own 'pocket'. The pieces were linked to an iron-hinged and framed wooden gaming board located in the far north side of the grave and the nature of the pieces suggests four competitors using six gaming pieces of equal importance, engaged in some form of 'race' game akin to *Ludo* (Stead 1967, 19): distinctively different to the two-player Roman-era games found at Stanway and King Harry Lane, among others (Schädler in Crummy *et al.* 2007, 359-75).

As well as the decayed fittings of this board, on the far west side of the grave were two sets of grave goods, interestingly turned on their sides as if 'propped' against the edge of the pit. One of the massive, imported platters was found with a rare triangular iron 'knife' apparently in a wooden case, with a delicate, duck-head handle cast in bronze – bringing to mind the other small knives and discs from smaller cremation burials. Such knives may have had a culinary purpose, slicing choice cuts of meat perhaps, if not one related to personal care. In another small stash, a bronze strainer pan seems to have been customised by a local craftsperson from an original bronze bowl with omphalos base: punching in an anthropomorphic 'snout-like' lip and adding an internal ornamented strainer panel with a lid to cover the 'pouring' end. Once again, the vessel has a single 'swing' handle for hanging. The 'stacked' or propped appearance of these two final groups of objects appears odd, given the way that the other grave goods lie flat upon the grave floor. It is possible then, that further organics – baskets, stacks of textiles, furs or even perishable food – once filled the significant voids at this northern end of the grave and the platter and knife, strainer and gaming board, were all 'propped' in, on their ends or sides, as if held in place by now-decayed objects. In support of this idea, a folded patch of furred rawhide – possibly from a stoat – was found next to the strainer pan (Stead 1967, 34).

Men of the moment – making a king?

The trope of hospitality and of death as something to be marked with feasting (evoked even in the lone ceramic vessel or bucket cremation burials) is magnified here to a novel degree. Yet the burial itself (regardless of the wake which may have occurred alongside it) was *not* meant to conjure or equip the dead for a commensal feast in the afterlife but for diacritical drinking and dining (see Dietler 1996; 2001). For Fitzpatrick it is this theme that dominates the Welwyn and Baldock burials (2007): paraphernalia such as 'paired' vessels or foursomes suggest equipment for a privileged 'dining club'. Actual joints of meat are rare but burnished cups are common: some purpose-made for the funeral, some, like Welwyn, well-worn. Other vessels allude to the ritualised customs of hand washing (perhaps complementing Welwyn's nail cleaner: making sure that the hands that serve or cup a vessel were distinctively clean and manicured). The Baldock cauldron and fire-dogs with their elegant 'sniffing nostrils' (Jope 2000, 319) or the Standfordbury A tripod stand and chain, created similarly exclusive 'inner circles' around the hearth: rails, guards, stands and spits that framed figures and encouraged them to draw close but simultaneously created more exclusive spaces. Distinction here was managed through spatial organisation, framing of figures and taste: dining manners and culinary customs. Such exclusivity required restricted, hard-to-obtain suites of objects – distinctive material props to structure performative cues. Even within this chosen drinking band, a leader-figure might be further distinguished by a special form of vessel (such as the Welwyn silver cup, a prestige gift for a client king from the world of Rome?) from which they alone might drink or eat. For Helms, this setting apart of a group not just by *what* but *how* they eat, who serves them or was co-present at the feast, is a crucial feature of how a community creates an aristocratic group, particularly the figureheads of chiefs or kings (1998, 116). Denying their 'ordinariness', exaggerating their 'suprahuman' abilities and creating the notion of particular 'needs' for sustenance (perhaps not just the local beer but heady, imported wine) established them as new categories of person. Creighton adds another dimension here by seeing some of this paraphernalia as the specialist equipment of sacrifice and offering to divine forces (2000, 201–4), later augmented by medico-religious objects as in the Doctor's burial at Stanway (Crummy *et al.* 2007). This would bestow upon such characters a sacral, as well as a socio-political, power.

In the Welwyn Garden City burial and in later, mid–late 1st century AD cremation burials we can see how this new elite personage was marked not just by appearance, manners and accoutrements (increasingly, items of furniture: cupboards, stools and boxes) but also their ability to join in games of strategy. At Welwyn, the board-game suggests a competitive race among supposed 'equals'. It speaks not just of a class with leisure time and access to luxury (Harding 2016, 151): gaming is often thought to evidence the skills, fortune and special virtues thought necessary in leadership (Schädler in Crummy *et al.* 2007, 374). The competition between client kings and their ascent to dominance was a 'game' of skilled rivalry, vying for both Roman and local support. Once such games entered the funeral realm, they may even have acted metaphorically: life was itself a gamble with death. In the Doctor's burial at Stanway, the counters were on the board as if in play for an afterlife: a new game was 'afoot' (*ibid.*).

We can appreciate the special value of such assemblages in the social ferment created by living under the terms of Rome following Caesar's campaigns of 55 and 54 BC, as Fitzpatrick notes (2007, 134) and the battles over supremacy, succession and descent amongst the client kings played out very visibly through Late Iron Age coinage (see Creighton 2000). This was a new, vibrant and exciting 'middle ground' not of mere emulation but innovation. These funerals captured and promoted the idea that power lay not just in connections and alliances and skilled hybridity in local and exotic customs (the order, sequence and manners of the feast; culinary know-how and acquired tastes – heady, salty, sharp and bitter; the topics of hearth-side discourse; equine and martial skill) but domains of more esoteric knowledge such as gaming. All of this had to be learned and then performed reiteratively through *substances* (organic consumption largely invisible to us in funerary assemblages), *things* (which emphasised difference and rank) and *performative moments* (being seated and served, or indeed doing the serving, being invited to play at the board or called to arms). Death became an arena where individuals who personified these skills were eulogised: the burial was part of the making of a 'sovereign' figure. Which brings us back to time.

Olivier has questioned the 'illusion' of synchronicity embodied in the sumptuous 'sealed' contexts of Early Iron Age 'princely' burials such as Hochdorf (Olivier 1999). At that moment in the 1st millennium BC, he argues, grave goods from such

Continental burials embodied 'multiple temporalities': power was presaged on relations which were extensive in *space* by 'amalgamat[ing] materials of different origins' (*ibid.*, 112) but also extended in *time* (through inherited and long-lived items), effectively 'stretching' the power of the individual beyond the present moment. Yet what is interesting with many of the Aylesford style cremation burials is that beyond rare 'ancient' items, such as Lexden's 'found object': a Late Bronze Age palstave or axehead, (Laver 1927, pl. lx, fig. 3) such assemblages (even when worn with use) rarely reached back more than a generation. The rest of Lexden's grave goods appear as novel, imperial gifts tied to an individual: the medallion of Augustus, a griffon adorned couch, gold brocade, chainmail and 'folding stool' (Fitzpatrick 2007, 135). This is very different to old swords with repairs or cobbled-together chariots which speak of time mapped by lineage and a concern with the longevity of 'belonging' to a land and a community (as in the East Yorkshire Middle Iron Age, Giles 2012). The Aylesford, Welwyn and Lexden type grave goods are usually 'of' the reign or era of the dead: close object companions with the deceased. We argue that this was not just due to swift-changing fashions in taste: Garrow and Gosden have conjured this as a 'cooling down' of once vibrant objects which had had their 'moment' in this intense but short-lived era of competition (2012, 248). There is something 'poignant' in such objects: fleeting, brief and swiftly waning. This sets our final 'temporal' case study apart from our earlier Neolithic and Bronze Age ones. As the 'oil' of social power, such objects had lived dynamically in the hands, the gestures, the unique connections and the very *largesse* of the original person marking them out as special. That relationship was indissoluble because it did not just make the man, it made the king. Heavily 'materialised mourning' is often at its most vigorous during times of social crises. Successors were moving out of the shadows, using the burial to shape a sovereign figure to which they could lay a claim of kinship or alliance, but it may have been unthinkable they could simply adopt the symbols or media of that figure's power since this line of descent was (as we know from the classical authors) by no means clear (Creighton 2000): in order to earn their place, it was something they had to do anew, for themselves. They too had to play the game.

8.5. Discussion

In this chapter, we have explored contrastive temporalities that were enabled not just by funerary technologies and mortuary rites but the grave goods associated with the dead. We have examined the multi-temporal rhythms of Neolithic burials in chambered tombs, where rites of re-arrangement with both bones and objects extended the temporalities of people and objects but bonds between individuals and things were characteristically weak or loose. In the second section, we explored the extension of time facilitated by cremation in general but noted the localised and idiosyncratic customs of what went into the flame. Yet we also note a weakness in terms of our archaeological ability to see the whole, pre-pyre funerary assemblage due to the unique way in which cremation drew out time at this stage in the burial. Finally, we examined the contradictory effects of extended cremation rites strategically deployed for political and strategic reasons, yet whose grave goods speak of a short-lived temporality embodied in person and assemblage. We end this chapter then with a sense of the deeply contrastive role of objects in mortuary time: some glossed by the patina of age value, others shimmering with a more evanescent transience.

Chapter 9

Discussion: grave choices in a material world

9.1. Representing people and ideas

The process of writing a final discussion for this book is – in some ways – analogous to the gathering together of grave goods for deposition following the death of a loved one. The book overall has presented us with an ebbing and flowing narrative, certain elements of its unique character coming into focus at particular stages. We now need to represent that book, those ups and downs, in just a few words. Which elements do we choose to stress? Which are the most important, and what can (or should) be left unsaid? Do we select its more unusual aspects to emphasise, or focus on the more standard, everyday ones? To what extent do we need to highlight connections between this book and others related to it (its ancestors and relations)? What did it do that other works did not, and is it possible to convey that specialness textually in just a few words? Where to begin?

As discussed in Chapter 1, the *Grave Goods* project's title was always intended as an intentional play on words. These are objects in burials; but they are also goods, material culture, that must be taken seriously. We hope that this primary driving force behind our work has been very clear throughout the book that has resulted. This is the first ever long-term, wide-scale study of objects and death in later prehistoric Britain. We hope therefore that it will have made a substantial contribution to broader narratives of this period beyond mortuary practice as well.

9.2. Democratising grave goods and exploring conceptual boundaries

In taking grave goods seriously, we had two central aims for the project in mind from the start: to investigate *all* material culture found in formal burial contexts (i.e. not just the 'fancy' objects) and to demonstrate empirically the character of ebbs and flows in mortuary practice in the long-term, through large-scale data collection. In relation to the latter aim, we have been able to demonstrate 'known' (or expected) patterns empirically for the first time, and to recognise exciting new ones (such as the prevalence of female-related grave goods during the Iron Age). In relation to the former aim, we had two aspects in mind. The first was to 'democratise' our understanding of later prehistory – to let all grave goods have some representation in our narratives not just certain classes or 'qualities' of them. In doing this, our focus immediately shifted onto the full range of people buried in the prehistoric past not just a sub-set (whether 'elite' or not) of them. Underlying this approach was our feeling that a slight disconnect has developed in academic studies between theoretical perspectives – which have, by and large (if not totally), moved away from the 'materially rich = powerful person' assumption (see Chapter 2) – and studies of the grave goods concerned, which have often remained focused on exceptional material (e.g. Garrow and Gosden 2012, 194–255; Woodward and Hunter 2015). We hope to have initiated a greater degree of alignment between theoretical perspectives and material culture studies by considering all grave goods as equal. In this book, we have also sought to challenge such simplistic assumptions ('rich' = powerful) not on theoretical grounds (this has been done very well already, e.g. Brück 2004; Fowler 2013) but through prehistoric material culture, allowing past practice to speak for itself. That material record – if we choose to look at it *all* – has something very different to tell us. Some readers of this book might even feel that we have given too much weighting to the understated, the unremarkable and the everyday. It is important to state, however, that we have done this intentionally and, we feel, with the justifiable aim of trying to redress the biases of the past in mind. As argued in Chapter 5, studying the understated objects actually allows us to understand the fancier ones better as well.

Our inclusion of all objects found in formal burial contexts has also forced us to consider the boundaries of what a 'grave good' (and indeed a 'burial context') actually is. As discussed in Chapter 3, it is sometimes difficult to know where to draw the line – is a coffin a grave good but a cist lid part of the grave architecture? How is a deposit of axes in the make-up of a burial mound meaningfully different to those items placed immediately adjacent to the corpse? Should some of the pots in a chambered tomb be considered grave goods but others the residue of what might be termed 'subsequent mortuary activity'? The list goes on. In all these cases, it is difficult to draw a line logically and intellectually, yet it has to be done. In an earlier paper (Cooper *et al.* 2020), we explored these issues in depth by looking at what we termed 'bodyless object deposits' at funerary sites. There, we argued for an approach that considers the full 'spectrum' of depositional practice, emphasising that, sometimes, clear-cut divisions between grave goods and hoards, for example, cannot be seen in the present, quite possibly because they did not exist in the past. In Chapter 4 of this book, in considering other elements of this argument by addressing the material relationships between graves, hoards and settlements, we chose to maintain these context types for analytical purposes. One main conclusion from this exercise was that it is very difficult to assess the material relationships between them. Past practices dictated that these different sub-sets of evidence very rarely co-exist at the same moment or spatial scale. What did become clear, however, is that settlement evidence cannot straightforwardly be taken as the closest proxy for what we have termed the 'living material repertoire'. Each 'separate' contextual area (burials, hoards, settlements, and so on) represents an *equal* part of the material jigsaw we must link together when trying to understand the materiality of the prehistoric past.

9.3. Grave goods and the wider picture

As discussed in Chapter 1, in this book we did not set out to write a straightforward, diachronic account of grave goods through time. Rather, we have opted to investigate a series of issues (relating to grave goods, of course) that we feel (a) are interesting and (b) needed to be addressed. In so doing, we have also been able to shed light on other wider narratives relating to later prehistoric Britain. We have, for example, looked at material mobility through time (Chapter 7); again, what became clear in this part of our study is that the movement of objects that was visible in graves was not necessarily the same as that visible in, for example, hoards and other metalwork deposits. We have also been able to bring to the fore important regional differences, improving our appreciation of the full gamut of prehistoric practices across Britain. Our case study areas sometimes peaked in burial activity at very different times (Chapter 3). We have also seen how they varied materially, for example, in terms of the kinds of object placed in graves (Chapter 3) or the uptake of different pot styles (Chapter 6). We have been able to chart ebbs and flows in cremation and inhumation burial in the long-term (Chapter 3) and even gained insight which joints of meat were considered appropriate or best for the dead in different places and at different times (Chapter 5).

It has also proved possible to recast traditional debates and to shed additional light on current wider theoretical discussions. 'Exotic' objects and materials have often been foregrounded in considerations of mortuary (and wider) material culture (e.g. Needham 2000; Sheridan and Shortland 2003; Woodward and Hunter 2015). In making these arguments, archaeologists have at times drawn very effectively on the work of anthropologist Mary Helms (especially 1988), who considered the potency of objects brought from areas beyond the 'known world'. Our study (Chapter 7) has suggested, in line with some other work (e.g. Fontijn 2009), that the exotic may have been constituted in a variety of complex ways. In considering the mutually constitutive nature of 'exotic' and 'local' substances, and the potentially local origins of the former's significance (in some cases), we hope to have shaken up these discussions: some 'exotics' were actually much more numerous in graves local to the area where they were obtained. Similarly, non-'exotic' stones and other materials were clearly valued greatly for their localness as well (Chapters 5 and 7).

As discussed in some detail in Chapter 2, post-humanist approaches in archaeology over the past 20 years or so have begun to deconstruct the boundaries between people and things, the 'living' and the 'dead', and so on. Our consideration of the material culture deposited in Neolithic chambered tombs has, we hope, contributed substantially to such debates which, so far, have drawn largely on human bone evidence in trying to understand partible identities, fractal persons, and so on. Our own study (Section 8.2) indicated that a more temporally extended notion of 'grave goods', and perhaps also a more fluid understanding of the relationship between 'individuals' and objects are required if we are to start to comprehend these burials and the mortuary practices associated with them fully. An incorporation of the extended temporalities of burial and notions or relational personhood were vital to our interpretations of Bronze Age pyre goods and Late Iron Age 'kingly' burials as well (Sections 8.3 and 8.4).

The notion of 'object agency' runs – often implicitly, in the background – throughout this book. Grave goods clearly had power, meaning, vibrancy, and could 'do' a lot of work in (and well beyond) the grave. We have seen (in Chapter 6, for example) how, arguably, grave goods may themselves have actually influenced mortuary practice – the increasingly large urns seen throughout the course of the Early Bronze Age a consequence, but perhaps also a cause, of the increase in cremation seen throughout this period. The properties of those pots – storage capacity, decoration, ability to evoke social relations, etc. – must certainly have influenced the kinds of mortuary practice that occurred. Importantly, it was not just the special, the valuable or the unusual objects that were asked to do this work. All sorts of things were allocated the task of speaking or acting from the grave.

The nature of our dataset (detailed empirical evidence from over 3000 graves featuring more than 6000 objects) has influenced the analytical routes we have taken to a considerable degree, underlying everything that we subsequently did and the stories we have ended up telling. It goes without saying that there remain many, many more stories to tell. The evidence set we have created, we hope, will provide a very firm foundation upon which anyone can build these.

At the end of this book, and at the very end of the process of gathering and analysing all that information about them, it still fascinates and intrigues us that people put those objects in the ground within graves. Remarkably, these items included weapons and jewellery, pots of all kinds doing all sorts of different things, but also quern-stones, flint-knapping waste, animal bones, stone lids, pebbles and more. The full panoply of life really was captured in death. We hope to have shown that, once you consider them *all*, grave goods have an even more amazing story to tell.

Appendix: objects recorded within the Grave Goods database

Object type	Object category	No.
Animal Bone (Other)	Animal bone	176
Animal Burial (Specified type)	Animal bone	48
Animal Joint/Part (Tooth/Tusk/Horn/Antler)	Animal bone	48
Animal Joint/Part (Limb)	Animal bone	88
Animal Joint/Part (Head)	Animal bone	71
Animal Joint/Part (Trunk)	Animal bone	13
Animal Joint/Part (Other specified part)	Animal bone	35
Animal Joint/Part (Unknown/Unspecified)	Animal bone	7
Anklet	Jewellery	1
Ard	Tool	1
Arm Guard/Bracer	Weaponry	5
Armlet	Jewellery	19
Arrowhead (Barbed)	Flint tool	2
Arrowhead (Chisel)	Flint tool	1
Arrowhead (Leaf-shaped)	Flint tool	23
Arrowhead (Barbed and Tanged)	Flint tool	32
Arrowhead (Unknown/Unspecified)	Flint tool	12
Assemblage	Other	89
Assemblage (Mixed)	Other	3
Awl	Tool	64
Axe/Axehead (Perforated)	Axe	15
Axe/Axehead (Polished)	Axe	15
Axe/Axehead (Unknown/Unspecified)	Axe	17
Bag	Container	37
Basket	Container	6
Bead(s)	Jewellery	89
Bier	Coffin	12

(Continued)

Object type	Object category	No.
Blade	Flint tool	19
Bowl	Container	2
Box	Container	8
Bracelet/Bangle (Specified type)	Jewellery	36
Bracelet/Bangle (Unknown/Unspecified)	Jewellery	37
Bracket	Other	1
Brooch (Specified type)	Pin/point/brooch	251
Brooch (Unknown/Unspecified)	Pin/point/brooch	45
Bucket	Container	8
Buckle	Clothing	2
Button	Clothing	33
Chainmail	Clothing	1
Chariot/Cart	Chariot/horse gear	14
Chariot/Cart Fitting (Unknown/Unspecified/Set)	Chariot/horse gear	14
Chisel	Tool	2
Clasp	Other	1
Coffin	Coffin	366
Coin	Other	5
Collar	Other	2
Comb	Other	2
Core	Flint tool	8
Cosmetic Set	Other	6
Cover	Cover	25
Cramp	Other	1
Crown/Diadem	Clothing	2
Cup	Container	4
Cushion Stone	Tool	3
Dagger [Armorico-British]	Weaponry	1
Dagger [Arreton]	Weaponry	1
Dagger [Camerton-Snowshill]	Weaponry	13
Dagger [Flat Riveted]	Weaponry	25
Dagger [Tanged Flat]	Weaponry	1
Dagger (Unknown/Unspecified)	Weaponry	30
Disc	Other	18
Dress Fastener	Clothing	3

(Continued)

Object type	Object category	No.
Ear scoop	Other	1
Ear/Hair Ornament (Other)	Jewellery	9
Ferrule	Tool	1
File	Tool	2
Flake	Flint tool	117
Floral Offering	Other	7
Food Residue	Other	13
Footwear	Clothing	1
Fossil	Natural object	7
Gouge	Tool	1
Hammer	Tool	3
Hammerstone	Tool	4
Helmet	Clothing	1
Horse Gear (Unknown/Unspecified/Set)	Chariot/horse gear	7
Jug	Container	2
Knife	Tool	147
Lid	Other	145
Liner	Grave furnishing	36
Loom Weight	Tool	1
Lozenge	Jewellery	1
Lunula	Jewellery	1
Macehead	Axe	11
Mirror	Mirror	13
Mortar/Pestle	Other	3
Nail	Tool	1
Necklace	Jewellery	50
Needle	Tool	7
Palstave	Axe	1
Pan	Container	2
Pebble	Natural object	49
Pendant	Jewellery	17
Pick	Tool	8
Pillow	Grave furnishing	7
Pin (Specified type)	Pin/point/brooch	26
Pin (Unknown/Unspecified)	Pin/point/brooch	86

(Continued)

Object type	Object category	No.
Point (Unknown/Unspecified)	Pin/point/brooch	35
Pot [Beaker]	Pot	196
Pot [Biconical Urn]	Pot	43
Pot [Cordoned Urn]	Pot	4
Pot [Collared Urn]	Pot	286
Pot [Beaker/Food Vessel Hybrid]	Pot	15
Pot [Belgic-Related Tradition (Unknown/Unspecified)]	Pot	74
Pot [Carinated Bowl]	Pot	6
Pot [Deverel-Rimbury (Unknown/Unspecified)]	Pot	278
Pot [Deverel-Rimbury (Bucket Urn)]	Pot	212
Pot [Deverel-Rimbury (Globular Urn)]	Pot	76
Pot [Encrusted Urn]	Pot	1
Pot [Food Vessel]	Pot	286
Pot [Grimston Ware]	Pot	7
Pot [Grooved Ware]	Pot	12
Pot [Incense Cup]	Pot	40
Pot [Miniature/Pygmy Vessel]	Pot	56
Pot [Plain Bowl]	Pot	3
Pot [Polypod Bowl]	Pot	4
Pot [Post-Deverel-Rimbury (PDR) (Unknown/Unspecified)]	Pot	3
Pot [Post-Deverel-Rimbury (PDR) (Fineware)]	Pot	1
Pot [Post-Deverel-Rimbury (PDR) (Coarseware)]	Pot	1
Pot [Post-Deverel-Rimbury (PDR) (Other specified type)]	Pot	1
Pot [Towthorpe Ware]	Pot	1
Pot [Trevisker]	Pot	152
Pot [Unstan Ware]	Pot	72
Pot [Windmill Hill Ware]	Pot	1
Pot [Urn (Unknown/Unspecified)]	Pot	46
Pot [Belgic-Related Tradition (Pedestal Urn)]	Pot	62
Pot [Belgic-Related Tradition (Other fineware vessel)]	Pot	91
Pot [Belgic-Related Tradition (Coarseware)]	Pot	8
Pot [Belgic-Related Tradition (Other specified type)]	Pot	72
Pot [Gallo-Belgic Ware (Specified type)]	Pot	46
Pot [Deverel-Rimbury (Barrel Urn)]	Pot	109
Pot [Deverel-Rimbury (Miniature vessel/cup)]	Pot	28

(Continued)

Object type	Object category	No.
Pot [Scillonian Bronze Age vessel]	Pot	14
Pot [Durotrigian Tradition]	Pot	55
Pot [Gaulish Tradition (Unknown/Unspecified)]	Pot	2
Pot [Bipartite Urn]	Pot	1
Pot [Accessory Cup]	Pot	8
Pot (Unknown/Unspecified)	Pot	270
Pounder/Rubber (Unknown/Unspecified)	Tool	7
Quernstone	Tool	5
Razor	Other	3
Ring (Hand/Toe/Ear)	Jewellery	44
Ring (Hand/Toe/Ear) [Ring (Ear)]	Jewellery	8
Ring (Hand/Toe/Ear) [Ring (Finger)]	Jewellery	26
Ring (Hand/Toe/Ear) [Ring (Toe)]	Jewellery	14
Rivet	Other	3
Saw	Flint tool	3
Scabbard	Weaponry	19
Scraper	Flint tool	71
Shears	Tool	1
Shell	Natural object	13
Shield	Weaponry	20
Shroud	Cover	12
Slag	Other	1
Sling Shot	Weaponry	5
Spearhead	Weaponry	74
Spindle Whorl	Tool	23
Spoon/Spatula	Other	5
Staple	Other	3
Strainer	Other	1
Strap fitting	Clothing	18
Strike A Light	Tool	9
Stud	Clothing	6
Sword	Weaponry	30
Tag	Other	2
Tankard	Container	1
Toggle	Clothing	8

(Continued)

Object type	Object category	No.
Tongs	Tool	1
Tool (Specified type)	Tool	5
Tool (Unknown/Unspecified)	Tool	27
Torc	Jewellery	1
Tweezers	Other	10
Unknown Object	Unknown	89
Vessel (Unknown/Unspecified)	Container	27
Weight	Other	1
Whetstone	Tool	26
Wire	Other	3
Worked Stone	Unknown	25
Wrap	Cover	7

Bibliography

Abercromby, J. 1904. A proposed chronological arrangement of the drinking-Cup or Beaker class of fictilia in Britain. *Proceedings of the Society of the Antiquaries of Scotland* 38, 323–410.

Abercromby, J. 1907. The relative chronology of some Cinerary Urn types of Great Britain and Ireland. *Proceedings of the Society of Antiquaries of Scotland* 41, 185–274.

Abercromby, J. 1912. *A Study of the Bronze Age Pottery of Great Britain and its Associated Grave Goods.* Oxford: Clarendon.

Acland, J. 1916. List of Dorset barrows opened by Mr E. Cunnington or described by him. *Proceedings of the Dorset Natural History and Antiquarian Field Club* 37, 40–7.

Adams, S. 2013. The First Brooches in Britain: from manufacture to deposition in the Early and Middle Iron Age. Unpublished PhD Thesis, University of Leicester.

AEMA 2016. *Atlantic Europe and the Metal Ages project.* Available at http://www.aemap.ac.uk/ (accessed 26 February 2021).

Alexander, J. 1961. The excavation of the Chestnuts megalithic tomb at Addington, Kent. *Archaeologia Cantiana* 76, 1–57.

Allen, T., Donnely, M., Hardy, A., Hayden, C. and Powell, K. 2012. *A Road Through the Past: archaeological discoveries on the A2 Pepperhill to Cobham road-scheme in Kent.* Oxford: Oxford Archaeology.

Ambers, J., Boast, R., Bowman, S., Gibson, A.M., Kinnes, I. and Morven, L. 1991. Radiocarbon dating and the British Beakers: the British Museum programme. *Scottish Archaeological Review* 8, 35–68.

Anderson, J. 1886. *Scotland in Pagan Times: the Bronze and Stone Ages. The Rhind Lectures in Archaeology for 1882.* Edinburgh: David Douglas.

Anderson-Whymark, H. and Garrow, D. 2015. Seaways and shared ways: imaging and imagining the movement of people, objects and ideas over the course of the Mesolithic–Neolithic transition, *c.* 5000–3500 BC. In H. Anderson-Whymark, D. Garrow and F. Sturt (eds), *Continental Connections: exploring cross-channel relationships from the Mesolithic to the Iron Age.* Oxford: Oxbow Books, 59–77.

Anderson-Whymark, H., Clarke, A., Edmonds, M. and Thomas, A. 2017. Process, form and time: macheads in an Orcadian context. In R. Shaffrey (ed.), *Written in Stone: function, form, and provenancing of a range of prehistoric stone objects.* Southampton: Highfield Press.

Andrews, P., Biddulph, E. and Hardy, A. 2011. *Settling the Ebbsfleet Valley: Highspeed 1 excavations at Springhead and Northfleet, Kent: the Late Iron Age, Roman, Saxon and medieval landscape. Volume 1: the sites.* Oxford: Oxford Wessex Archaeology.

Andrews, P., Booth, P., Fitzpatrick, A.P. and Welsh, K. 2015. *Digging at the Gateway. Archaeological Landscapes of South Thanet: the archaeology of East Kent Access (Phase II).* Oxford: Oxford Wessex Archaeology Monograph 8.

Annable, F.K. and Simpson, D.D.A. 1964. *Guide Catalogue of the Neolithic and Bronze Age Collections in Devizes Museum.* Devizes: Wiltshire Archaeological & Natural History Society.

Anon, 1849. Yorkshire Naturalists Club. *York Herald* 6 October, 5.

Anon, 1862. 'A Druid's cove'. *Driffield Times and General Advertiser* 6 December, 3.

Anon, 1937. Buried with ham. *Yorkshire Evening Post* 24 April, 10.

Appleby, J. 2013. Temporality and the transition to cremation in the late third millennium to mid-second millennium BC in Britain. *Cambridge Archaeological Journal* 23, 83–97.

Appleby, J., Boughton, D., Knight, M., Northover, P., Wiseman, R. and Uckelman, M. forthcoming. Metalwork. In M. Knight, R. Ballantyne, A. Cooper, D. Gibson, and I. Robinson Zeki (eds), *Must Farm*

Pile-dwelling Settlement. Volume 2. Specialist reports. CAU Must Farm/Flag Fen Basin Depth & Time Series. Cambridge: McDonald Institute.

Armit, I. 1994. Archaeological field survey of the Bhaltos (Valtos) peninsula, Lewis. *Proceedings of the Society of Antiquaries of Scotland* 124, 67–93.

Ash, J. 1996. Memory and objects. In P. Kirkham (ed.), *The Gendered Object.* Manchester: Manchester University Press, 219–24.

Ashbee, P. 1960. *The Bronze Age Round Barrow in Britain.* London: Pheonix House.

Ashbee, P. 1978. *The Ancient British.* Norwich: Geo Abstracts.

Ashburnham, C. 1918. Opening of the round barrow at Melcombe Bingham. *Proceedings of the Dorset Natural History and Antiquarian Field Club* 38, 74–80.

Askew, P. and Booth, P. 2006. The Prehistoric, Roman and Medieval Landscape at Northumberland Bottom, Southfleet, Kent. Oxford: Oxford Wessex Joint Venture. Unpublished client report. Available at: doi: https://doi.org/10.5284/1008830 (accessed 19 September 2021).

Bailey, D.W. 2018. Incomplete: the uneasy power(s) of holes, cut surfaces, and Neolithic pit-houses. In S.R. Martin and S.M. Langin-Hooper (eds), *The Tiny and the Fragmented: Miniature, Broken, or Otherwise 'Incomplete' Objects in the Ancient World.* Oxford: Oxford University Press, 170–87.

Bailey, L., Green, M. and Smith, M. 2013. Keeping the family together. Canada Farm's Bronze Age burials. *Current Archaeology* 279, 20–6.

Baker, L., Sheridan, J.A. and Cowie, T. 2003. An Early Bronze Age 'dagger grave' from Rameldry Farm, near Kingskettle, Fife. *Proceedings of the Society of Antiquaries of Scotland* 133, 85–123.

Ballin, T. 2009. *Archaeological pitchstone in northern Britain: characterization and interpretation of an important prehistoric source.* Oxford: British Archaeological Report 476.

Ballin Smith, B. 2014a. *Between Tomb and Cist: the funerary monuments of Crantit, Kewing and Nether Onston, Orkney.* Kirkwall: The Orcadian.

Ballin Smith, B. 2014b. Beakers and bunkers; investigations at Rothes Golf Club. Glasgow: GUARD, *Archaeology Reports Online 7.* Available at: https://archaeologyreportsonline.com/PDF/ARO7_Rothes.pdf (accessed 13 September 2017).

Barber, M. 1997. *Excavation of Stalled Cairn at Point of Cott, Westray, Orkney.* Loanhead: Scottish Trust for Archaeological Research.

Barclay, A. 2002 Ceramic lives. In A. Woodward and J.D. Hill (eds), *Prehistoric Britain: the ceramic basis.* Oxford: Prehistoric Ceramics Research Group, Occasional Paper 3, 85–95.

Barnatt, J., Bevan, B. and Edmonds M. 2017. *An Upland Biography: landscape and prehistory on Gardom's Edge, Derbyshire.* Oxford: Windgather Press.

Barrett, J. 1988. The living, the dead and the ancestors: Neolithic and early Bronze Age mortuary practices' In J.C. Barrett and I.A. Kinnes (eds), *The Archaeology of Context in the Neolithic and Bronze Age: recent trends,* Sheffield: Department of Archaeology and Prehistory, University of Sheffield, 30–41.

Barrett, J. 1991a. Bronze Age pottery and the problem of classification. In J. Barrett, R. Bradley, and M. Hall (eds), *Papers on the Prehistoric Archaeology of Cranborne Chase,* Oxford: Oxbow Monograph 11, 201–30.

Barrett, J. 1991b. 'Mortuary archaeology'. In Barrett *et al.* 1991, 120–2.

Barrett, J. 1994. *Fragments From Antiquity: an archaeology of social life in Britain, 2900–1200 BC.* Blackwell: Oxford.

Barrett, J. 2016. The new antiquarianism? *Antiquity* 354, 1681–6.

Barrett, J., Bradley, R. and Green, M. 1991. *Landscape, Monuments and Society.* Cambridge: Cambridge University Press.

Barrowman, R. and Innes, L. 2009. *A Bronze Age Burial from Pabay Mor, Isle of Lewis, Western Isles.* Edinburgh: Society of Antiquaries of Scotland.

Bateman, T. 1848. *Vestiges of the Antiquities of Derbyshire, and the Sepulchral Uses of its Inhabitants, from the Most Remote Ages to the Reformation.* London: John Russell Smith.

Bateman, T. 1855. *A Descriptive Catalogue of the Antiquities and Miscellaneous Objects Preserved in the Museum of Thomas Bateman, Lomberdale House, Derbyshire.* Bakewell: James Gratton.

Bateman, T. 1857. Discovery of Saxon graves at Winster, Derbyshire. *Journal of the British Archaeological Association* 12, 226–8.

Bateman, T. 1861. *Ten Years' Digging in Celtic and Saxon Grave Hills, in the Counties of Derby, Stafford, and York, from 1848 to 1858; with notices of some former discoveries, hitherto unpublished, and remarks on the crania and pottery from the mounds.* London: John Russell Smith.

Baynes, E. 1914. Prehistoric man in Anglesey. *Transactions of the Anglesey Antiquarian Society and Field Club*, 1–18.

BBC n.d. *29 things that only people who collect pebbles will understand.* Available at: https://www.bbc.co.uk/programmes/articles/3G8N1xzn75l7YZM8gNzZp94/29-things-that-only-people-who-collect-pebbles-will-understand (accessed 7 June 2021).

BBC 2018. Exploding coconut 'sent fear' through crematorium staff. Available at: https://www.bbc.co.uk/news/uk-england-manchester-42920984/ (accessed 14 July 2021).

Beck, C. and Shennan, S. 1991. *Amber in Prehistoric Britain.* Oxford: Oxbow Books.

Belk, R. 1994. Collectors and collecting. In S. Pearce (ed.), *Interpreting Objects and Collections.* London: Routledge, 317–26.

Belk, R. 1995. *Collecting in a Consumer Society.* London: Routledge.

Bennett, J. 2010. *Vibrant Matter. A Political Ecology of Things.* London: Routledge.

Benson, D. and Whittle, A. (eds) 2007. *Building Memories: the Neolithic Cotswold Long Barrow at Ascott-Under-Wychwood, Oxfordshire.* Oxford: Oxbow Books.

Berger, J. 1984. *And our Faces, My Heart, Brief as Photos.* New York: Vintage.

Best, E.M. 1964. Excavation of three barrows on the Ridgeway, Bincombe. *Proceedings of the Dorset Natural History and Archaeology Society* 86, 102–3.

Beswick, P. and Wright, M.E. 1991. Iron Age burials from Winster. In R. Hodges and K. Smith (eds), *Recent Developments in the Archaeology of the Peak District, Sheffield Archaeological Monuments 2.* Sheffield: J. R. Collis Publications, 45–56.

Binford, L.R. 1971. Mortuary practices: their study and their potential. In J. Brown (ed.), *Approaches to the Social Dimensions of Mortuary Practices.* Washington DC: Memoir of the Society for American Archaeology, 6–29.

Birchall, A. 1965. The Aylesford-Swarling culture: the problem of the Belgae reconsidered. *Proceedings of the Prehistoric Society* 31, 241–367.

Bloch, M. and Parry, J. 1982. *Death and the Regeneration of Life.* Cambridge: Cambridge University Press.

Boast, R. 1985. Documentation of prehistoric style: a practical approach. *Archaeological Review from Cambridge* 4, 159–70.

Boast, R. 1991. The Categorisation and Design Systematics of British Beakers: a re-examination. Unpublished PhD thesis, University of Cambridge.

Boast, R. 1995. Fine pots, pure pots, Beaker pots. In I. Kinnes and G. Varndell (eds), *'Unbaked Urns of Rudely Shape': essays on British and Irish pottery for Ian Longworth.* Oxford: Oxbow Monograph 55, 55–67.

Boast, R. 2002. Pots as categories: British Beakers. In A. Woodward and J.D. Hill (eds), *Prehistoric Britain: the ceramic basis.* Oxford: Oxbow Books, 96–105.

Bond, J. and Worley, F. 2006. Companions in death: the roles of animals in Anglo-Saxon and Viking cremation burials in Britain. In R. Gowland and C. Knüsel (eds), *Social Archaeology of Funerary Remains* Oxford: Studies in Funerary Archaeology 1, 89–98. Oxford: Oxbow Books.

Booth, T. and Brück, J. 2020. Death is not the end: radiocarbon and histo-taphonomic evidence for the curation and excarnation of human remains in Bronze Age Britain. *Antiquity* 94, 1186–203 (doi:10.15184/aqy.2020.152).

Booth, T.J. and Madgwick, R. 2016. New evidence for diverse secondary burial practices in Iron Age Britain. *Journal of Archaeological Science* 67, 12–24.

Boozer, A., 2015. The tyranny of typologies: evidential reasoning in Romano-Egyptian domestic archaeology. In R. Chapman and A. Wylie (eds), *Material Evidence: learning from archaeological practice.* London: Routledge, 92–109.

Borlase, W.C. 1872. *Naenia Cornubiae: a descriptive essay illustrative of the sepulchres and funereal customs of the early inhabitants of the county of Cornwall.* London: Longmans.

Borlase, W.C. 1879a. Archaeological discoveries in Sennen. *Journal of the Royal Institute of Cornwall* 6, 201–4.

Borlase, W. 1879b. Archaeological discoveries in the parishes of St-Just-in-Penwith and Sennen. *Journal of the Royal Institute of Cornwall* 21, 190–212.

Bowler, P. 1994. *The Invention of Progress: the Victorians and their past.* Oxford: Blackwell.

Bowker, G.C. and Star, S.L. 2000. *Sorting Things Out. Classification and Its Consequences.* Cambridge MA: MIT Press.

Boyle, A., Evans, T., O'Connor, S., Spence, A. and Brennand, M. 2007. Site D (Ferry Fryston) in the Iron Age and Romano-British periods. In F. Brown, C. Howard-Davis, M. Brennand, A. Boyle, T. Evans, T. Evans, S. O'Connor, A. Spence, R. Heawood, A. Lupton and J. Carver (eds), *The Archaeology of the A1(M) Darrington to Dishforth DBFO road scheme.* Lancaster: Oxford Archaeology North, 121–60.

Brace, S., Diekmann, Y., Booth, T. *et al.* 2019. Ancient genomes indicate population replacement in Early Neolithic Britain. *Nature Ecology & Evolution* 3, 765–71.

Bradley, R. 1981. 'Various styles of urn' – cemeteries and settlement in southern England. In R. Chapman, I. Kinnes, and K. Randsborg (eds), *The Archaeology of Death.* Cambridge: Cambridge University Press, 93–104.

Bradley, R. 1997. *Rock Art and the Prehistory of Atlantic Europe.* London: Routledge.

Bradley, R. 1998. *The Significance of Monuments: on the shaping of human experience in Neolithic and Bronze Age Europe.* London: Routledge.

Bradley, R. 2005. *Ritual and Domestic Life in Prehistoric Europe.* London: Routledge.

Bradley, R. 2017. *A Geography of Offerings. Deposits of Valuables in the Landscapes of Ancient Europe.* Oxford: Oxbow Insights in Archaeology 3.

Bradley, R. 2019. *The Prehistory of Britain and Ireland* (2nd edn). Cambridge: Cambridge University Press.

Bradley, R. and Edmonds, M. 1993. *Interpreting the Axe Trade: production and exchange in Neolithic Britain.* Cambridge: Cambridge University Press.

Bradley, R., Haselgrove, C., Vander Linden, M. and Webley, L. 2015. *The Later Prehistory of North-West Europe: the evidence of development-led fieldwork.* Oxford: Oxford University Press.

Bray, P. 2012. Before 29Cu became copper: tracing the recognition and invention of metalleity in Britain and Ireland during the third millennium BC. In M. Allen, J. Gardiner and A. Sheridan (eds), *Is there a British Chalcolithic? People, Place and Polity in the Later 3rd Millennium.* Oxford: Prehistoric Society Research Papers 5, 6–70.

Bray, I., Forster, A. and Clelland, S.-J. 2009. Steatite and Shetland: a geological introduction and gazetteer of sites. In V. Turner and A. Forster (eds), *Kleber: Shetland's oldest industry.* Lerwick: Shetland Amenity Trust, 4–17.

Brewis, P. 1928. A Bronze Age cist at Kyloe, Northumberland. *Archaeologia Aeliana* 4 ser. 5, 26–9.

Brewster, T. 1980. *The Excavation of Wetwang and Garton Slacks.* Malton: East Riding Archaeological Research Committee (microfiche).

Brewster, T. 1984. *The Excavation of Whitegrounds Barrow, Burythorpe.* Malton: East Riding Archaeological Research Committee.

Brindley, A.L. 1999. Irish Grooved Ware. In Cleal and MacSween (eds) 1999, 1–8

Brindley, A.L. 2007 *The Dating of Food Vessels and Urns in Ireland.* Galway: Bronze Age Studies 7.

Bristow, P. 2001. Behaviour and belief in mortuary ritual: attitudes to the disposal of the dead in southern Britain 3500 BC–AD 43. *Internet Archaeology* 11 https://doi.org/10.11141/ia.11.1.

Brown, L., Hayden, C. and Score, D. 2014. *'Down to Weymouth Town by Ridgeway'. Prehistoric, Roman and Later Sites Along the Weymouth Relief Road.* Dorchester: Dorset Natural History and Archaeological Society Monograph 23.

Brown, N. 1995. Ardleigh reconsidered: Deverel Rimbury pottery in Essex. In I. Kinnes, G. Varndell, and I. Longworth (eds), *'Unbaked Urns of Rudely Shape': essays on British and Irish pottery for Ian Longworth.* Oxford: Oxbow Monograph, 123–44.

Brown, N. 1999. *The Archaeology of Ardleigh, Essex: Excavations 1955-1980.* Chelmsford: Essex County Council.

Browne, T. [1658] 2010 reprint, with preface by W.G. Sebald. *Hydriotaphia, or Urn Burial, with an account of some urns found in Brampton, Norfolk.* New York: New Directions Publishing.

Brück, J. 1995. A place for the dead. The role of human remains in Late Bronze Age Britain. *Proceedings of the Prehistoric Society* 61, 245–77.

Brück, J. 1999. Houses, life cycles and deposition on Middle Bronze Age settlements in southern England. *Proceedings of the Prehistoric Society* 65, 145–66.

Brück, J. (ed.) 2001a. *Bronze Age Landscapes: tradition and transformation.* Oxford: Oxbow Books.

Brück, J. 2001b. Monuments, power and personhood in the British Neolithic. *Journal of the Royal Anthropological Institute* 7, 649–67.

Brück, J. 2004. Material metaphors: the relational construction of identity in Early Bronze Age burials in Ireland and Britain. *Journal of Social Archaeology* 4, 307–33.

Brück, J. 2006. Fragmentation, personhood and the social construction of technology in Middle and Late Bronze Age Britain. *Cambridge Archaeological Journal*, 16(3), 3, 297–315.

Brück, J. 2017a. Gender and personhood in the European Bronze Age. *European Journal of Archaeology* 20(1), 37–40.

Brück, J. 2017b. Reanimating the dead: the circulation of human bone in the British later Bronze Age. In J. Bradbury and C. Scarre (eds), *Engaging with the Dead: exploring changing human beliefs about death, mortality and the human body.* Oxford: Oxbow Books, 138–48.

Brück, J. 2019. *Personifying Prehistory: relational ontologies in Bronze Age Britain and Ireland.* Oxford: Oxford University Press.

Brück, J. and Davies, A. 2018. The social role of non-metal 'valuables' in Late Bronze Age Britain. *Cambridge Archaeological Journal* 28, 665–88.

Bruck, J. and Fontijn, D. 2013. The myth of the chief: prestige goods, power and personhood in the European Bronze Age. In H. Fokkens and A. Harding (eds), *The Oxford Handbook of the European Bronze Age.* Oxford: Oxford University Press, 197–215.

Brück, J. and Jones, A. 2018. Finding objects, making persons: fossils in British Early Bronze Age burials. In E. Harrison-Buck and J. Hendon (eds), *Other-Than-Human Agency and Personhood in Archaeology.* Denver CO: University of Colorado Press.

Brudenell, M. 2012. Pots, Practice and Society: an investigation of pattern and variability in the post-Deverel Rimbury Ceramic Tradition of East Anglia. Unpublished PhD Thesis, University of York.

Brudenell, M. and Cooper, A. 2008. Post-middenism: depositional histories on Later Bronze Age settlements at Broom, Bedfordshire. *Oxford Journal of Archaeology* 27, 15–36.

Burgess, C. 1976. Burials with metalwork of the later Bronze Age in Wales and beyond. In G. Boon and J. Lewis (eds), *Welsh Antiquity: essays mainly on prehistoric topics presented to H.N. Savory upon his retirement as Keeper of Archaeology.* Cardiff: National Museum of Wales, 81–104.

Burgess, C. 1980 *The Age of Stonehenge*, London: Dent.

Burgess, C. 1986. 'Urnes of no Small Variety': Collared Urns reviewed. *Proceedings of the Prehistoric Society* 52, 339–51.

Burrow, S. 2011. *Shadowland. Wales 3000-1500 BC.* Oxford: Oxbow Books and Amgueddfa Cymru/ National Museum Wales.

Burl, A. 1980. *Rings of Stone: the prehistoric stone circles of Britain and Ireland*. Boston MA: Ticknor & Fields.

Burns, B., Cunliffe, B. and Sabire, H. 1996. *Guernsey: an island community of the Atlantic Iron Age*. Oxford: Oxford University School of Archaeology.

Burstow, G., Holleyman, G. and Helbaek, H. 1958. Late Bronze Age Settlement on Itford Hill, Sussex. *Proceedings of the Prehistoric Society* 23, 167–212.

Busby, C. 1997. Permeable and partible persons: a comparative analysis of gender and the body in South India and Melanesia. *Journal of the Royal Anthropological Institute* 3(2), 261–78.

Bushe-Fox, J. 1925. *Excavation of the Late-Celtic urn-field at Swarling, Kent*. London: Society of Antiquaries of London.

Byrne, S., Clarke, A., Harrison, R. and Torrence, R. (eds) 2011. *Unpacking the Collection: networks of material and social agency in the museum*. New York: Springer.

Calder, C.S.T. 1937. A Neolithic double-chambered cairn of the stalled type and later structures in the Calf of Eday Long. *Proceedings of the Society of Antiquaries of Scotland* 71, 115–54.

Calder, C. and MacDonald, G. 1936. The Dwarfie Stane, Hoy, Orkney: its period and purpose; with a note on 'Jo Ben' and the Dwarfie Stane. *Proceedings of the Society of Antiquaries of Scotland* 70, 217–36.

Callander, J. and Bryce, T. 1921. Notices of (1) cinerary urns from Kingskettle, Fife, and (2) an Early Iron Age Cist on Kippit Hill, Dolphinton. With a report on the human remains found therein. *Proceedings of the Society of Antiquaries of Scotland* 55, 37–52.

Callander, J. 1929. Scottish Neolithic pottery. *Proceedings of the Society of Antiquaries of Scotland* 63, 29–98.

Callander, J. and Grant, W. 1934. The Broch of Midhowe, Rousay, Orkney. *Proceedings of the Society of Antiquaries of Scotland* 68, 444–516.

Callander, J. and Grant, W. 1935. A long, stalled cairn, the Knowe of Yarso, in Rousay, Orkney. *Proceedings of the Society of Antiquaries of Scotland* 69, 325–51.

Callander, J. and Grant, W. 1937. Long stalled cairn at Blackhammer, Rousay, Orkney. *Proceedings of the Society of Antiquaries of Scotland* 71, 297–308.

Canterbury Archaeological Trust 1994. A28 Sturry Bypass: an interim review of the archaeological resource and historic landscape. Canterbury: Canterbury Archaeological Trust, unpublished client report.

Canterbury Archaeological Trust 1998. *An Archaeological Investigation at Glebe Land, Harrietsham: Interim Report*. Unpublished Report. Canterbury: Canterbury Archaeological Trust.

Canterbury Archaeological Trust 2008. A prehistoric and Anglo-Saxon cemetery at the Meads, Sittingbourne. Canterbury: Canterbury Archaeological Trust, unpublished client report. Available at: http://www.canterburytrust.co.uk/news-2/projectdiaries/meads/ (accessed 15 March 2018)

Canterbury Archaeological Trust 2010. Excavations at Thanet Earth 2007–2008. Assessment Report Volume 1. Unpublished client report, Report No. 2635. Canterbury: Canterbury Archaeological Trust.

Carlin, N. 2020. Haunted by the ghost of the Beaker folk? *The Biochemist* 42, 30–3.

Carr, C. 1995. Mortuary practices: their social, philosophical-religious, circumstantial, and physical determinants. *Journal of Archaeological Method and Theory* 2, 105–200.

Carr, G. 2007. Excarnation to cremation: continuity or change? In C. Haselgrove and T. Moore (eds.), *The Later Iron Age in Britain and Beyond*. Oxford: Oxbow Books, 446–55

Carr, G. and Knüsel, C. 1997. The ritual framework of excarnation by exposure as the mortuary practice of the Early and Middle Iron Ages of central southern Britain. In A. Gwilt and C. Haselgrove (eds), *Reconstructing Iron Age Societies*. Oxford: Oxbow Monograph 71, 167–73.

Carter, A.K. 2016. Circular or half-moon marks on old beads. *Bead Forum* 69, 1–2.

Carver, M. 2000. Burial as poetry: the context of treasure in Anglo-Saxon graves. In E. Tyler (ed.), *Treasure in the Medieval West*. York: York Medieval Press/Boydell and Brewer, 25–48.

Case, H. 1995. Beakers: Loosening a stereotype. In I. Kinnes and G. Varndell, (eds), *Unbaked Urns of Rudely Shape: essays on British and Irish pottery for Ian Longworth.* Oxford: Oxbow Books, 55–68.

Caswell, E. 2013. Bodies, Burnings and Burials. Analysing Middle Bronze Age Cremations in Britain. Unpublished MA dissertation, University of Durham.

Caswell, E. and Roberts, B. W. 2018. Reassessing community cemeteries: cremation burials in Britain during the Middle Bronze Age (*c.* 1600–1150 cal BC). *Proceedings of the Prehistoric Society* 84, 329–57.

CgMs Consulting. 2008. A249 Iwade Bypass to Queenborough Improvement, Isle of Sheppey: report on the archaeological strip, map and record excavation. Unpublished report. London: CgMs Consulting.

Champion, S. 1976. Coral in Europe. In P.M. Duval and C.F.C. Hawkes (eds), *Celtic Art in Ancient Europe.* London: Seminar Press, 29–37.

Champion, S. 1982. Exchange and ranking: the case of coral. In C. Renfrew and S. Shenann, S. (eds), *Ranking, Resource and Exchange: aspects of the archaeology of early European society.* Cambridge: Cambridge University Press, 67–72.

Chapman, J. 2000. *Fragmentation in Archaeology.* London: Routledge.

Chapman, J. and Gaydarska, B. 2006. *Parts and Wholes: fragmentation in prehistoric context.* Oxford: Oxbow Books.

Chesterman, J. 1979. Investigation of the human bones from Quanterness. In C. Renfrew (ed.), *Investigations in Orkney.* London: Report of the Research Committee of the Society of Antiquaries of London 38, 97–111.

Chesterman, J. 1983. The human skeletal remains. In Hedges (ed.) 1983, 73–132.

Childe, G.V. 1929. *The Danube in Prehistory.* Oxford: Oxford University Press.

Childe, G.V. 1937. The antiquity of the British Bronze Age. *American Anthropologist* 39(1), 1–22.

Childe, G.V. 1944. *Progress and Archaeology.* London: Watts.

Chittock, H. 2021. *Arts and Crafts in Iron Age East Yorkshire: a holistic approach to pattern and purpose, c. 400 BC–AD100.* Oxford: British Archaeological Report 660.

Christie, P. 1960. Crig-a-mennis: a Bronze Age barrow at Liskey, Perranzabuloe, Cornwall. *Proceedings of the Prehistoric Society* 6, 76–97.

Christie, P. 1988. A barrow cemetery on Davidstow Moor, Cornwall. Wartime excavations by CK Croft Andrew. *Cornish Archaeology* 27, 27–171.

Christie, P., Healey, F., Roe, F., Stead, S., Cartwright, C. and Evans, J. 1985. Barrows on the north Cornish coast. Wartime excavations by CK Croft Andrew 1939–1944. *Cornish Archaeology* 24, 23–122.

Clark, P., Shand, G. and Weekes, J. 2019. *Chalk Hill: Neolithic and Bronze Age discoveries at Ramsgate, Kent.* Leiden: Sidestone Press.

Clarke, D. 1970. *Beaker Pottery of Great Britain and Ireland.* Cambridge: Cambridge University Press.

Clark, D.V., Cowie, T. and Foxon, A. 1985. *Symbols of Power at the Time of Stonehenge.* Edinburgh: National Museum of Antiquities of Scotland.

Cleal, R. 1988. The occurrence of drilled holes in later Neolithic pottery. *Oxford Journal of Archaeology,* 7(2), 139–45.

Cleal, R. 1999. Introduction: the what, where, when and why of Grooved Ware. In Cleal and MacSween (eds) 1999, 23–35.

Cleal, R. 2011. Pottery. In Fitzpatrick 2011, 140–54.

Cleal, R. and MacSween, A. (eds) 1999. *Grooved Ware in Britain and Ireland.* Oxford: Neolithic Studies Group Seminar Papers 3.

Collis, J.R. 1984. *The European Iron Age.* Abingdon: Routledge.

Collis, J. 2001. Coral, amber and cockle shells: trade in the Middle La Tène Period. *PAST* 38. Available online: https://www.le.ac.uk/has/ps/past/past38.html#Coral. (accessed 24 July 2021).

Colt-Hoare, R. 1812. *The Ancient History of Wiltshire.* London: William Miller.

Conneller, C. 2011. *An Archaeology of Materials: substantial transformations in early prehistoric Europe.* London: Routledge.

Cook, M. 2006. Allasdale, Barra, Western Isles (Barra parish), excavation and survey. *Discovery and Excavation in Scotland 2006,* 7.

Cooper, A. and Green, C. 2016. Embracing the complexities of archaeological 'big data': the case of the English Landscape and Identities project. *Journal of Archaeological Method and Theory* 23, 271–304.

Cooper, A., Garrow, D. and Gibson, C. 2020. Spectrums of depositional practice in later prehistoric Britain and beyond: grave goods, hoards and deposits 'in between'. *Archaeological Dialogues* 27, 135–57.

Cooper, A., Garrow, D., Gibson, C. and Giles, M. 2019. Covering the dead in later prehistoric Britain: elusive objects and powerful technologies of funerary performance. *Proceedings of the Prehistoric Society* 85, 223–50.

Copper, C. 2017. The Bronze Age Funerary Cups of Southern England. Unpublished MPhil Dissertation, University of Bradford.

Cormack, W. 1973. Lewis, Valtos, Traigh na Beiridh, pottery and cists. *Discovery and Excavation, Scotland 1973,* 43.

Cowie, T. 1978 *Bronze Age Food Vessel Urns,* Oxford: British Archaeological Report 55.

Cowie, T. and MacSween, A. 1999. Grooved Ware from Scotland: a review. In Cleal and MacSween (eds) 1999, 48–56.

Cracknell, L. 2018. Quartz. In M. Smalley (ed.), *Cornerstones: subterranean writings.* Toller Fratrum: Little Toller Books.

Creighton, J. 2000. *Coins and Power in Late Iron Age Britain.* Cambridge: Cambridge University Press.

Creighton, J. 2006. *Britannia: the creation of a Roman province.* London: Routledge.

Crellin, R. 2017. Changing Assemblages: tracing vibrant matter in burial assemblages. *Cambridge Archaeological Journal* Special Edition 27(1): 111–25.

Crellin, R. 2020. *Change and Archaeology.* London: Routledge.

Croucher, K.T. and Richards, C. 2014. Wrapped in images: body metaphors, petroglyphs and landscape in the island world of Rapa Nui (Easter Island). In S. Harris and L. Douny (eds), *Wrapping and Unwrapping Material Culture: archaeological and anthropological perspectives.* Walnut Creek CA: Left Coast Press, 209–28.

Croucher, K., Büster, L., Dayes, J., Green, L., Raynsford, J., Comerford Boyes, L. and Faull, C. 2020. Archaeology and contemporary death: Using the past to provoke, challenge and engage. *PLoS ONE* 15(12): e0244058. https://doi.org/10.1371/journal.pone.0244058

Crozier, R. 2014. Exceptional or conventional? Social identity within the chamber tomb of Quanterness, Orkney. In V. Ginn, R. Enlander and R. Crozier (eds), *Exploring Prehistoric Identity in Northwest Europe. Our Construct or Theirs?* Oxford: Oxbow Books, 22–33.

Crozier, R. 2016. Fragments of death. A taphonomic study of human remains from Neolithic Orkney. *Journal of Archaeological Science: Reports* 10, 725–34.

Crummy, N., Shimmin, D., Crummy, P., Rigby, V. and Benfield, S.F. 2007. *Stanway: an elite burial site at Camulodunum.* London: Society for the Promotion of Roman Studies.

Cummings, V. 2017. *The Neolithic of Britain and Ireland.* London: Routledge.

Cunliffe, B. 1984. *Danebury: an Iron Age Hillfort in Hampshire, Vol. 2: the Finds.* London: Council for British Archaeology Research Report 54.

Cunliffe, B. 2009a. *Iron Age Communities in Britain* (4th edition). London: Routledge.

Cunliffe, B. 2009b. Looking forward: maritime contacts in the first millennium BC. In P. Clark (ed.), *Bronze Age Connections: cultural contact in prehistoric Europe.* Oxford: Oxbow Books, 80–93.

Cunliffe, B. and Poole, C. 2000. *Suddern Farm, Middle Wallop, Hants., 1991 and 1996.* Oxford: English Heritage and Oxford University Committee for Archaeology Monograph 49.

Curtis, N. and Wilkin, N. 2012. The regionality of Beakers and bodies in the Chalcolithic of north-east Scotland. In M.J. Allen, J. Gardiner and A. Sheridan (eds), *Is There a British Chalcolithic? People, Place and Polity in the Late 3rd Millennium*. Oxford: Prehistoric Society Research Papers 5, 237–56.

Curtis, N. and Wilkin, N. 2017. Beakers and bodies: north-east Scotland in the first age of metal. *British Archaeology* 52, 36–42.

Curtis, N., and Wilkin, N. 2019. Beakers and bodies in north-east Scotland: a regional and contextual study. In Parker Pearson *et al.* (eds) 2019, 211–52.

Dacre, M. and Ellison, A. 1981. A Bronze Age urn cemetery at Kimpton, Hampshire. *Proceedings of the Prehistoric Society* 47, 147–203.

Dalland, M. 1999. Sand Field: the excavation of an exceptional cist in Orkney. *Proceedings of the Prehistoric Society* 65, 373–414.

Darvill, T. 2002. White on blonde: quartz pebbles and the use of quartz at Neolithic monuments in the Isle of Man and beyond. In A. Jones and G. MacGregor (eds), *Colouring the Past*. Oxford: Berg, 73–91.

Darvill, T. 2004. *Long Barrows of the Cotswolds and Surrounding Areas*. Stroud: Tempus.

Davidson, J. and Henshall, A. 1989. *The Chambered Cairns of Orkney*. Edinburgh: Edinburgh University Press.

Davies, D.J. 2015. *Mors Britannica. Life-Style and Death-Style in Britain Today*. Oxford: Oxford University Press.

Davis, J.B. and Thurnam, J. 1865. *Crania Britannica. Delineations and Descriptions of the Skulls of the Aboriginal and Early Inhabitants of the British Islands: with notices of their other remains*. London: Taylor & Francis.

Davis, R. 2012. *The Early and Middle Bronze Age Spearheads of Britain*. Munich: Prähistorische Bronzefunde 5(5).

Deetz, J. 1977. *In Small Things Forgotten: the archaeology of early American life*. London: Doubleday.

Delanda, M. 2016. *Assemblage Theory*. Edinburgh: Edinburgh University Press.

Deleuze, G. and Guattari, F. 1987. *A Thousand Plateaus: capitalism and schizophrenia* (trans. B. Massumi). Minneapolis MN: University of Minnesota Press

Dent, J. 1982. Cemeteries and settlement patterns of the Iron Age on the Yorkshire Wolds. *Proceedings of the Prehistoric Society* 48, 437–57.

Dent, J. 1984. Wetwang Slack: an Iron Age cemetery on the Yorkshire Wolds. Unpublished MA Thesis, University of Sheffield.

Dent, J. 2010. *The Iron Age in Eastern Yorkshire*. Oxford: British Archaeological Report 508.

Dietler, M. 1996. Feasts and commensal politics in the political economy: food, power and status in prehistoric Europe. In P. Wiessner and W. Schiefenhövel (eds), *Food and the Status Quest*. Oxford: Berghahn Books, 87–125.

Dietler, M. 2001. Theorizing the feast. Rituals of comsumption, commensal politics and power in African contexts. In M. Dietler and B. Hayden (eds), *Feasts. Archaeological and Ethnographic Perspectives on Food, Politics and Power*. London: Smithsonian Institution, 65–144.

Downes, J. 2005. Cremation Practice in Bronze Age Orkney. Unpublished PhD thesis, University of Sheffield.

Douch, H. 1962. Archaeological discoveries recorded before 1855. *Cornish Archaeology* 1, 91–9.

Dudley, D. and Thomas, C. 1965. An Early Bronze Age burial at Rosecliston, Newquay. *Cornish Archaeology* 3, 10–16.

Dudley-Buxton, L.H. 1929. *The Pitt-Rivers Museum, Farnham*. Farnham: Farnham Museum.

Duffy, P. and MacGregor, G. 2007. An Iron Age burial from Swainbost, Isle of Lewis. *Scottish Archaeological Journal* 29(2), 155–66.

Earle, T. (ed.) 1991. *Chiefdoms: power, economy and ideology*. Cambridge: Cambridge University Press.

Earle, T. 2002. *Bronze Age Economics. The Beginnings of Political Economies*. Boulder CO: Westview Press.

Ekengren, F. 2013. Contextualising grave goods. In S. Tarlow and L. Nilsson-Stutz (eds), *The Oxford Handbook of Death and Burial.* Oxford: Oxford University Press, 172–92.

Ellison, A. 1975. Pottery and Settlement of the Later Bronze Age in Southern England. Unpublished PhD Thesis, University of Cambridge.

Eogan, G. 1984. *Excavations at Knowth* (1). Dublin: Royal Irish Academy.

Evans, A. 1911. The Welwyn find (letter). *The Times* 28 February, 15.

Evans, J. 1881. *The Ancient Bronze Implements, Weapons, and Ornaments of Great Britain and Ireland.* London: Longmans, Green & Co.

Evans, J. 1890. Late-Celtic urn-field at Aylesford, Kent, and on the Gaulish, Illyro-Italic, and Classical connexions of the forms of pottery and bronze-work there discovered. *Archaeologia* 52, 315–88.

Evans, C. 2015. Wearing environment and making islands: Britain's Bronze Age inland North Sea. *Antiquity* 89, 1110–24.

Fabian, J. 1983. *Time and the Other: how anthropology makes its object.* New York: Columbia University Press.

Farley, J., Parfitt, K., Richardson, A., Antoine, D., Pope, R. and Sparey-Green, C. 2014. A Late Iron Age helmet burial from Bridge, near Canterbury, Kent. *Proceedings of the Prehistoric Society* 80, 379–88. doi:10.1017/ppr.2014.5.

Ferguson, C. 1893. Incense cup found at Old Parks, Kirkoswald. *Cumberland and Westmorland Antiquarian & Archaeological Society*, Old Series, volume 12, article XXVIII: 275–6.

Fernández-Götz, M. 2019. Migrations in Iron Age Europe: a comparative view. In P. Halkon (ed.), *The Arras Culture of Eastern Yorkshire.* Oxford: Oxbow Books, 179–99.

Field, D. 2006. *Earthen Long Barrows.* Stroud: Tempus.

Fitzpatrick, A. 1992. The roles of Celtic coinage in south east England. In M. Mays (ed.), *Celtic Coinage: Britain and beyond.* Oxford: British Archaeological Report 222, 1–32.

Fitzpatrick, A. 1997a. *Archaeological Excavations on the Route of the A27 Westhampnett Bypass, West Sussex, 1992.* Salisbury: Wessex Archaeology Report 11.

Fitzpatrick, A. 1997b. A 1st-centruy AD 'Durotrigian' inhumation burial with a decorated Iron Age mirror from Portesham, Dorset. *Proceedings of the Dorset Natural History and Archaeological Society* 118, 51–70.

Fitzpatrick, A. 2007. The fire, the feast and the funeral. Late Iron Age burial rites in southern England. In V. Kruta and G. Leman-Delerive (eds), *Feux des morts, foyers des vivants. Les rites et symboles du feu dans les tombes de l'Âge du Fer et de l'époque romaine.* Lille: Revue de Nord Hors série, Collection Art et Archéologie 11, 123–42.

Fitzpatrick, A. 2009. In his hands and in his head: the Amesbury Archer as a metalworker. In P. Clark (ed.), *Bronze Age Connections: cultural contact in prehistoric Europe.* Oxford: Oxbow Books, 176–88.

Fitzpatrick, A. 2010. The champions portion: feasting in the Celtic pre-Roman Iron Age. In G. Cooney, K. Becker, J. Coles, M. Ryan and S. Sievers, (eds), *Relics of Old Decency; archaeological studies in later prehistory. Festschrift for Barry Raftery.* Dublin: Wordwell, 387–402.

Fitzpatrick, A.P. (ed.) 2011. *The Amesbury Archer and the Boscombe Bowmen: Bell Beaker Burials at Boscombe Down, Amesbury, Wiltshire.* Salisbury: Wessex Archaeology Report 27.

Fontijn, D. 2002. *Sacrificial Landscapes. Cultural biographies of persons, objects and 'natural' places in the Bronze Age of the southern Netherlands, c. 2300-600 BC.* Leiden: Analect Praehistorica Leidensia 33/4.

Fontijn, D. 2009. Land at the other end of the sea? Metalwork circulation, geographical knowledge and the significance of British/Irish imports in the Bronze Age of the Low Countries. In P. Clark (ed.), *Bronze Age Connections: cultural contact in prehistoric Europe.* Oxford: Oxbow Books, 129–48.

Fontijn, D. 2019. *Economies of Destruction. How the Systematic Destruction of Valuables Created Value in Bronze Age Europe, c. 2300-500 BC.* London: Routledge.

Fontijn, D. and Roymans, J. 2019. Branded axes, thrown into a pool? The Hoogeloon Hoard and the shape-based bronze economy of the North-West European Bronze Age. *Oxford Journal of Archaeology* 38, 164–88.

Foulds, E.M. 2017. *Glass Beads from Iron Age Britain: a social approach*. Oxford: Archaeopress.

Fowler, C. 2001. Personhood and social relations in the British Neolithic with a study from the Isle of Man. *Journal of Material Culture* 6, 137–63.

Fowler, C. 2004. Identity politics: personhood, kinship, gender and power in Neolithic and early Bronze Age Britain. In E. Casella and C. Fowler (eds), *The Archaeology of Plural and Changing Identities: beyond identification*. New York: Kluwer Academic/Plenum Press, 109–34.

Fowler, C. 2013. *The Emergent Past: a relational realist archaeology of Early Bronze Age mortuary practices*. Oxford: Oxford University Press.

Fowler, C. 2017. Relational typologies, assemblage theory and Early Bronze Age burials. *Cambridge Archaeological Journal* 27, 95–109.

Fox, C. 1932. *The Personality of Britain*. Cardiff: National Museum of Wales and Press Board of the University of Wales.

Fox, C. 1958. *Pattern and Purpose: a survey of early Celtic Art in Britain*. Cardiff: National Museum of Wales.

Frankenstein, S. and Rowlands, M. 1978. The internal structure and regional context of Early Iron Age society in south-western Germany. *Bulletin of the Institute of Archaeology* 15, 73-112.

Fraser, J. 1913. Note of the discovery of a steatite urn in Harray, Orkney. *Proceedings of the Society of Antiquaries of Scotland* 47, 420–2.

Frere, S., Bennett, P., Rady, J. and Stow, S. 1987. *Canterbury Excavations: intra- and extra-mural sites, 1949-55 and 1980-1984*. Canterbury: Kent Archaeological Society.

Frieman, C. 2012. Going to pieces at the funeral: Completeness and complexity in Early Bronze Age jet 'necklace' assemblages. *Journal of Social Archaeology*, 12(3), 334–55.

Garrow, D. 2012. Odd deposits and average practice. A critical history of the concept of structured deposition. *Archaeological Dialogues* 18, 85–115.

Garrow, D. and Gosden, C. 2012. *Technologies of Enchantment? Exploring Celtic Art 400 BC to AD 100*. Oxford: Oxford University Press.

Garwood, P. 2007. Vital resources, ideal images and virtual lives. Children in Early Bronze Age funerary ritual. In S. Crawford and G. Shepherd (eds), *Children and Social Identity in the Ancient World*. Oxford: Oxbow Books, 63–82.

Gerloff, S. 1975. *The Early Bronze Age Daggers in Great Britain*. Munich: Prähistorische Bronzefunde, 6(2).

Gibson, A. 1978. *Bronze Age Pottery in the North-East of England*. Oxford: British Archaeological Report 56.

Gibson, A. 2002. *Prehistoric Pottery in Britain and Ireland*. Stroud: Tempus.

Gibson, A. and Bayliss, A. 2010. Recent work on the Neolithic round barrows of the Upper Great Wold Valley, Yorkshire. In J. Leary, T. Darvill and D. Field (eds), *Round Mounds and Monumentality in the British Neolithic and Beyond*. Oxford: Neolithic Studies Group Seminar Papers 10, 72–107.

Gibson, A. and Stern, B. 2006. Report on the University of Bradford pilot project into the absorbed residue analysis of Bronze Age pigmy cups from Scotland, England and Wales. In A. Gibson (ed.), *Prehistoric Pottery: some recent research*. Oxford: British Archaeological Report S1509, 69–78.

Gibson, A. and Woods, A. 1997. *Prehistoric Pottery for the Archaeologist*. Leicester: Leicester University Press.

Gibson, A., MacPherson Grant, N. and Stewart, I. 1997. A Cornish vessel from farthest Kent. *Antiquity* 71, 438–41.

Gibson, A., Bayliss, A., Heard, H., Mainland, I., Ogden, A., Bronk Ramsey, C., Cook, G., Plicht, J. van der and Marshall, P. 2009. Recent research at Duggleby Howe, North Yorkshire. *Archaeological Journal* 166, 39–78.

Gibson, C. and Knight, S. 2007. A Middle Iron Age settlement at Weston Down Cottages, West Colley, Hampshire. *Proceedings of the Hampshire Field Club and Archaeological Society* 62, 1–34.

Gilchrist, R. 2008. Magic for the dead? The archaeology of magic in later medieval burials. *Medieval Archaeology* 52(1), 119–59.

Gilchrist, R. 2019. *Sacred Heritage: monastic archaeology, identities, beliefs.* Cambridge: Cambridge University Press. https://doi.org/10.1017/9781108678087.

Gilchrist, R. and Sloane, B. 2005. *Requiem: The medieval monastic cemetery in Britain.* London: Museum of London Archaeology.

Giles, M. 2000. 'Open-weave, close-knit': archaeologies of identity in the later prehistoric landscape of East Yorkshire. Unpublished PhD Thesis, University of Sheffield.

Giles, M. 2006. Collecting the past, constructing identity: the antiquarian John Mortimer and the Driffield Museum of Antiquities and Geological Specimens. *Antiquaries Journal* 86, 279–316.

Giles, M. 2008. Seeing red: the aesthetics of martial objects in the British and Irish Iron Age. In D. Garrow, C. Gosden and J.D. Hill (eds), *Rethinking Celtic Art.* Oxford: Oxbow Books, 59–77.

Giles, M. 2012. *A Forged Glamour: landscape, identity and material culture in the Iron Age.* Oxford: Windgather Press.

Giles, M. 2013. The Danes Graves wheel-headed pin. In M. Endt-Jones (ed.), *Coral. Something Rich and Strange.* Liverpool: Liverpool University Press, 47–8.

Giles, M. 2016. Reconstructing death: the chariot burials of Iron Age East Yorkshire. In H. Williams and M. Giles (eds), *Archaeologists and the Dead: mortuary archaeology in contemporary society.* Oxford, Oxford University Press, 409–32.

Giles, M., Green, V. and Peixoto, P. 2019. Wide connections: women, mobility and power in Iron Age East Yorkshire. In P. Halkon (ed.), *The Arras Culture of Eastern Yorkshire.* Oxford: Oxbow Books, 47–66.

Gosden, C., Green, C., Cooper, A., Creswell, M., Donnelly, V., Franconi, T., Glyde, G., Kamash, Z., Mallet, S., Morley, L., Stansbie, D. and ten Harkel, L. 2021. *English Landscapes and Identities: investigating landscape change from 1500 BC to AD 1086.* Oxford: Oxford University Press.

Gough, R. 1780. *British Topography. Or, An Historical Account of what has been done for Illustrating the Topographical Antiquities of Britain and Ireland.* London: J. Nichols and T. Payne.

Grajetzki, W. 2014. *Tomb Treasures of the Late Middle Kingdom. The Archaeology of Female Burials.* Philadelphia PA: University of Pennsylvania Press.

Grant, W. 1933. A chambered mound at Westness, Rousay, Orkney. *Proceedings of the Society of Antiquaries of Scotland* 68, 71–3.

Grant, W. 1937. Excavation of Bronze Age burial mounds at Quandale, Rousay, Orkney. *Proceedings of the Society of Antiquaries of Scotland* 71, 72–84.

Green, C. 2011. *Winding Dali's Clock: the construction of a fuzzy temporal-GIS for archaeology.* Oxford: British Archaeological Reports S2234.

Greenfield, E. 1959. The excavation of three round barrows at Puncknowle. *Proceedings of the Dorset Natural History and Archaeological Society* 106, 63–76.

Greenwell, W. 1865. Notices of the examination of ancient grave-hills in the North Riding of Yorkshire. *Archaeological Journal* 22(1), 241–63.

Greenwell, W. 1877. *British Barrows. A Record of Sepulchral Mounds in Various Parts of England.* Oxford: Clarendon Press.

Greenwell, W. 1890. Recent researches in barrows in Yorkshire, Wiltshire, Berkshire etc. *Archaeologia* 52, 1–72.

Greenwell, W. 1906. Early Iron Age burials in Yorkshire. *Archaeologia* 60, 251–324.

Griffiths, S. 2016. Beside the ocean of time: A chronology of Neolithic burial monuments and houses in Orkney. In C. Richards and R. Jones (eds), *The Development of Neolithic House Societies in Orkney.* Oxford: Windgather Press, 254–302.

Grinsell, L. 1953. *The Ancient Burial Mounds of England* (2nd edn). London: Methuen.

Grinsell, L. 1959. *Dorset Barrows.* Dorchester: Dorset Natural History and Archaeological Society.

Grinsell, L. 1961. The breaking of objects as a funerary rite. *Folklore* 72(3), 475–91.

Guido, M. 1978. *The Glass Beads of the Prehistoric and Roman Periods in Britain and Ireland.* London: Society of Antiquaries of London.

Hahn, H. and Weiss, H. (eds) 2013. *Mobility, Meaning and the Transformation of Things.* Oxford: Oxbow Books.

Halkon, P. 2013. *The Parisi: Britons and Romans in Eastern Yorkshire.* Stroud: History Press.

Hallam, D. 2015. The Bronze Age Funerary Cups of Northern England. Unpublished MPhil Dissertation, University of Bradford.

Hallam, E. and Hockey, J. 2001. *Death, Memory and Material Culture.* Oxford: Berg.

Hallam, E., Hockey, J. and Howarth G. 1999. *Beyond the Body: death and social identity.* London: Routledge.

Hambleton, E. 1999. *Animal Husbandry Regimes in Iron Age Britain: a comparative study of faunal assemblages from British Iron Age sites.* Oxford: British Archaeological Report 282.

Hambleton, E. 2008. *Review of Middle Bronze Age-Late Iron Age Faunal Assemblages from Southern Britain.* Portsmouth: English Heritage.

Hamilakis, Y. and Jones, A. 2017. Archaeology and assemblage. *Cambridge Archaeological Journal* 27(1), 77–84.

Hamilton, M. and Whittle, A. 1999. Grooved Ware of the Avebury area: styles, contexts and meanings. In Cleal and MacSween (eds) 1999, 36–47.

Hamilton, S. 2007. Cultural choices in the 'British Eastern Channel Area' in the late pre-Roman Iron Age. In C. Haselgrove and T. Moore (eds), *The Later Iron Age in Britain and Beyond.* Oxford: Oxbow Books, 81–106.

Hanley, R. and Sheridan, J.A. 1994. A Beaker cist from Balblair, near Beauly, Inverness District. *Proceedings of the Society of Antiquaries of Scotland* 124, 129–39.

Haraway, D. J. 2003. *The Companion Species Manifesto: dogs, people, and significant otherness.* Chicago IL: Prickly Paradigm Press.

Harding, A. 1984. *The Mycenaeans and Europe.* London: Academic.

Harding, D. 2016. *Death and Burial in Iron Age Britain.* Oxford: Oxford University Press.

Harper, S. 2012. 'I'm glad she has her glasses on. That really makes the difference'. Grave goods in English and American funeral rituals. *Journal of Material Culture* 17(1), 43–59.

Harris, O.J.T. 2013. Relational communities in Neolithic Britain. In C. Watts (ed.), *Relational Archaeologies: humans, animals, things.* London: Routledge, 173–89.

Harris, O.J.T. 2018. Both permeable and partible: exploring the body world of Early Neolithic Britain. In P. Bickle and E. Sibbesson (eds), *Neolithic Bodies.* Oxford: Neolithic Studies Group Seminar Papers 15, 7–24.

Harris, O.J.T. and Cipolla, C.N. 2017. *Archaeological Theory in the New Millennium: introducing current perspectives.* London: Routledge.

Harrison, S. 2011. *John Robert Mortimer. The Life of a Nineteenth Century East Yorkshire Archaeologist.* Pickering: Blackthorn Press.

Hart, P. 2005. 'Beauforts', North Foreland Avenue, Broadstairs, Kent: Archaeological Report. Birchington-on-sea: Trust for Thanet Archaeology, unpublished client report.

Haselgrove, C. 1984. Romanisation before the Conquest: Gaulish precedents and British consequences. In T.F.C. Blagg and A.C. King (eds), *Military and Civilian in Roman Britain: cultural relationships in a frontier province.* Oxford: British Archaeological Report 136, 5–63.

Haselgrove, C. 2001. Iron Age Britain and its European setting. In J. Collis (ed.), *Society and Settlement in Iron Age Europe.* Sheffield: J.R. Collis, 37–72.

Hawkes, C.F.C. 1959. The ABC of the British Iron Age. *Antiquity* 33(131), 170–82.

Hawley, W. 1910. Notes on barrows in South Wiltshire. *Wiltshire Archaeological Magazine* 36, 625–6.

Hayden, C. with Stafford, E. 2006. *The Prehistoric Landscape at White Horse Stone, Aylesford, Kent.* Oxford: Oxford Wessex Archaeology Joint Venture unpublished report. Available at: https://doi.org/10.5284/1008829 (accessed 19 September 2021).

Healy, F. 1995. Pots, pits and peat: ceramics and settlement in East Anglia. In I. Kinnes and G. Varndell (eds), *'Unbaked Urns of Rudely Shape': essays on British and Irish pottery for Ian Longworth.* Oxford: Oxbow Monograph 55, 173–84.

Hedges, J. 1983. *Isbister: a chambered tomb in Orkney*. Oxford: British Archaeological Report 115.

Helms, M. 1988. *Ulysses Sail: an ethnographic odyssey of power, knowledge, and geographical distance*. Princeton NJ: Princeton University Press.

Henshall. A. 1963. *The Chambered Tombs of Scotland*. Vol. 1. Edinburgh: Edinburgh University Press.

Henshall. A. 1972. *The Chambered Tombs of Scotland*. Vol. 2. Edinburgh: Edinburgh University Press.

Hertz, R. 2009 [1960]. *Death and the Right Hand*. London: Routledge.

Higham, T., Chapman, J. Slavchev, V., Gaydarska, B., Honch, N., Yordanov, Y. and Dimitrova, B. 2007. New perspectives on the Varna cemetery – AMS dates and social implications. *Antiquity* 81(313), 640–54.

Hill, J.D. 1995. *Ritual and Rubbish in the Iron Age of Wessex: a study on the formation of specific archaeological record*. Oxford: British Archaeological Report 242.

Hill, J.D. 1997. The end of one kind of body and the beginning of another kind of body? Toilet instruments and 'Romanization' in southern England during the first century A.D. In A. Gwilt and C. Haselgrove (eds), *Reconstructing Iron Age Societies. New Approaches to the British Iron Age*. Oxford: Oxbow Monograph 71, 96–107.

Hill, J.D. 2002. Wetwang chariot burial. *Current Archaeology* 15, 410–12.

Hill, J.D., Evans, C. and Alexander, M. 1999. The Hinxton Rings – a Late Iron Age cemetery at Hinxton, Cambridgeshire, with a reconsideration of northern Aylesford-Swarling rites. *Proceedings of the Prehistoric Society* 65, 243–73.

Hockey, J., Komaromy, C. and Woodthorpe, K. (eds) 2010. *The Matter of Death. Space, Place and Materiality*. London: Palgrave Macmillan.

Hodder, I. 2012. *Entangled. An Archaeology of the Relationships Between People and Things*. Hoboken NJ: Wiley-Blackwell.

Holden, E. 1972. A Bronze Age Cemetery-barrow on Itford Hill, Beddington, Sussex. *Sussex Archaeological Collections* 110, 70–117.

Hosek, L. and Robb, J. 2019. Osteobiography: a platform for bioarchaeological research. *Bioarchaeology International* 3(1), 1–15.

Hoskins, J. 1998. *Biographical Objects. How Things Tell the Stories of People's Lives*. Abingdon: Routledge.

Hudson, W.H. 1910. *A Shepherd's Life. Impressions of the South Wiltshire Downs*. New York: E.P. Dutton.

Hughes, H.H. 1939. A Beaker burial at Llithfaen, Caernarvonshire. *Archaeologia Cambrensis* 94(1), 91–110.

Hunter, F. 2019. A northern view of Arras: or, we have chariots too. In P. Halkon (ed.), *The Arras Culture of Eastern Yorkshire*. Oxford: Oxbow Books, 133–62.

Hurcombe, L. 2014. *Perishable Material Culture in Prehistory. Investigating the Missing Majority*. London: Routledge.

Hurd, H. 1911. *Some Notes on Recent Archaeological Discoveries at Broadstairs*. Broadstairs: Broadstairs Printing and Publishing Company.

Hutchins, J. 1774. *The History and Antiquities of the County of Dorset*. London: W. Bowyer and J. Nichols.

Ingold, T. 1994. Introduction to culture. In T. Ingold (ed.), *Companion Encyclopaedia of Anthropology: humanity, culture and social life*. London and New York: Routledge, 329–49.

Ingold, T. 2007. *Lines. A Brief History*. London: Routledge.

Ingold, T. 2011. *Being Alive: essays on movement, knowledge and description*. London, Routledge.

Innes, L. 2016. The cist on the foreshore at Lopness, Sanday, Orkney (AR019). Glasgow: GUARD Archaeology unpublished report. Available at: https://archaeologyreportsonline.com/reports/2016/ARO19.html (accessed 19 September 2021).

Jackson, C. 2016. Blue Beads from Gardom's Edge. *Journal of Glass Studies* vol. 58, 11–19.

Jay, M. and Richards, M.P. 2006. Diet in the Iron Age cemetery population at Wetwang Slack, East Yorkshire, UK: carbon and nitrogen stable isotope evidence. *Journal of Archaeological Science* 3, 653–62.

Jay, M. and Richards, M.P. 2007. British Iron Age diet: stable isotopes and other evidence. *Proceedings of the Prehistoric Society* 73, 169–90.

Jenkins, R. 1996. *Social Identity*. London: Routledge.

Jewitt, L.F.W. 1870. *Grave Mounds and their Contents*. London: Groombridge and Sons.

Johns, C. 2006. An Iron Age sword and mirror cist burial from Bryher, Isles of Scilly. *Cornish Archaeology*, 41–2 (2002–3), 1–79.

Johnston, R. 2020. *Bronze Age Worlds: a social prehistory of Britain and Ireland*. Abingdon: Routledge.

Jones, A. 1998. Where eagles dare: animals, landscape and the Neolithic of Orkney. *Journal of Material Culture* 3, 301–24.

Jones, A. 2001. Drawn from memory: the archaeology of aesthetics and the aesthetics of archaeology in earlier Bronze Age Britain and the present. *World Archaeology* 33(2), 334–56.

Jones, A. 2002. A biography of colour: colour, material histories and personhood in the Early Bronze Age of Britain and Ireland. In A. Jones and G. MacGregor (eds), *Colouring the Past: the significance of colour in archaeological research*. Oxford: Berg, 159–74.

Jones, A. 2005. Lives in fragments? Personhood and the British Neolithic. *Journal of Social Archaeology* 5, 193–224.

Jones, A. 2010. Layers of meaning: concealment, memory and secrecy in the British Early Bronze Age. In D. Borić (ed.), *Archaeology and Memory*. Oxford: Oxbow Books, 105–20.

Jones, A. 2012. *Prehistoric Materialities: becoming material in prehistoric Britain and Ireland*. Oxford: Oxford University Press.

Jones, A.M. 2005. *Cornish Bronze Age Ceremonial Landscapes c. 2500-1500 BC*. Oxford: British Archaeological Report 394.

Jones, A.M. 2010. Excavation of a barrow on Constantine Island, St Merryn, Cornwall. *Cornish Archaeology* 48–9, 67–97.

Jones, A.M. 2016. *Preserved in the Peat: an extraordinary Bronze Age burial on Whitehorse Hill, Dartmoor, and its wider context*. Oxford: Oxbow Books.

Jones, A.M. and Goskar, T. 2017. Hendraburnick 'Quoit': recording and dating rock art in the west of Britain. *Time and Mind* 10, 277–92.

Jones, A.M. and Mikulski, R. 2015. After the storm: an Early Bronze Age cist burial at Harlyn Bay, Cornwall, 2014. *Cornish Archaeology* 54, 139–56.

Jones, A.M. and Quinnell, H. 2006. Cornish Beakers: new discoveries and perspectives. *Cornish Archaeology* 45, 31–69.

Jones, A.M. and Quinnell, H. 2011. The Neolithic and Bronze Age in Cornwall, *c.* 4000 cal BC to *c.* 1000 cal BC: an overview of recent developments. *Cornish Archaeology* 50, 197–229.

Jones, A.M. and Quinnell, H. 2014. *Lines of Archaeological Investigation Along the North Cornish Coast*. Oxford: British Archaeological Report 594.

Jones, A.M., Marley, J., Quinell, H. and Hartgroves, H. 2011. On the beach: new discoveries at Harlyn Bay, Cornwall. *Proceedings of the Prehistoric Society* 77, 89–109.

Jones, S. 1997. *The Archaeology of Ethnicity. Constructing Identities in the Past and Present*. London: Routledge.

Jope, M. 2000. *Early Celtic Art in the British Isles*. Oxford: Oxford University Press.

Jordan, A. 2016. Her mirror, his sword: unbinding binary gender and sex assumptions in Iron Age British mortuary tradition. *Journal of Archaeological Method and Theory* 23(3), 870–99.

Joy, J. 2009. Reinvigorating object biography: reproducing the drama of object lives. *World Archaeology* 41(4), 540–56.

Joy, J. 2010. *Iron Age Mirrors. A Biographical Approach*. Oxford: British Archaeological Report 518.

Joy, J. 2015. Connections and separation? Narratives of Iron Age art in Britain and its relationship with the Continent. In H. Anderson-Whymark, D. Garrow and F. Sturt (eds), *Continental Connections exploring cross-channel relationships from the Mesolithic to the Iron Age*. Oxford: Oxbow Books, 145–65.

Joy, J. 2016. Hoards as collections: re-examining the Snettisham Iron Age hoards from the perspective of collecting practice. *World Archaeology* 48(2), 239–53.

Joyce, R.A. and Gillespie, S.D. (eds) 2015. *Things in Motion. Object Itineraries in Anthropological Practice*. Santa Fe, NM: SAR Press.

Jupp, P. 2006. *From Dust to Ashes. Cremation and the British Way of Death*. London: Palgrave Macmillan.

Kaliff, A. 2005. The grave as concept and phenomenon. In T. Artelius and F. Svanberg (eds), *Dealing with the Dead: archaeological perspectives on prehistoric Scandinavian burial ritual*. Stockholm: Riksantikvarieambetets forlag, 125–42.

Kelly, D. 1971. Quarry Wood Camp: a Belgic oppidum. *Archaeologia Cantiana* 86, 55–84.

Kinnes, I. 1979. *Round barrows and Ring-ditches in the British Neolithic*. London: British Museum Press.

Kinnes, I. and Longworth, I.H. 1985. *Catalogue of the Excavated Prehistoric and Romano-British Material in the Greenwell Collection*. London: British Museum Press.

Klass, D. 1996. *Continuing Bonds: new understandings of grief*. London: Routledge.

Knight, M., Ormrod, T. and Pearce, S. 2015. *The Bronze Age Metalwork of South Western Britain: a corpus of material found between 1983 and 2014*. Oxford: British Archaeological Report 610.

Knight, M., Ballantyne, R., Zeki, I. R. and Gibson, D. 2019. The Must Farm pile-dwelling settlement. *Antiquity* 93(369), 645–63.

Kopytoff, I. 1986. The cultural biography of things: commoditization as process. In A. Appadurai (ed.), *The Social Life of Things: commodities in cultural perspective*. Cambridge: Cambridge University Press, 64–92.

Krmpotich, C., Fontein, J. and Harries, J. 2010. The substance of bones: the emotive materiality and affective presence of human remains. *Journal of Material Culture* 15(4), 371–84.

Ladle, L. and Woodward, A. 2009. *Excavations at Bestwall Quarry, Wareham 1992–2005*. Dorchester: Dorset Natural History and Archaeological Society.

Lakoff, G. 1987. *Women, Fire and Dangerous Things: what categories reveal about the mind*. Chicago IL: University of Chicago Press.

Lamb, R. 1981. Investigation of a Short Cist with Cremation Burial at Blomuir, Holm, Orkney. Unpublished manuscript. Accessed in Orkney HER, September 2018.

Latour, B. 1993. *We Have Never Been Modern* (trans. C. Porter). Cambridge MA: Harvard University Press.

Latour, B. 2005. *Reassembling the Social: an introduction to actor-network-theory*. Oxford and New York: Oxford University Press.

Laver, P.G. 1927. The excavation of a Tumulus at Lexden, Colchester. *Archaeologia* 76, 241–54.

Law, R. 2008. The Development and Perpetuation of a Ceramic Tradition: The Significance of Collared Urns in Early Bronze Age Social Life. Unpublished PhD thesis, University of Cambridge.

Leigh, C. 1700. *Natural History of the County of Cheshire, Lancashire and the Peak in Derbyshire with an Account of the British, Phoenician, Armenian, Gr. and Rom. Antiquities in those Parts*. Oxford: privately printed.

LiPuma, E. 1998. Modernity and forms of personhood in Melanesia. In M. Lambek and A. Strathern (eds), *Bodies and Persons: comparative views from Africa and Melanesia*. Cambridge: Cambridge University Press, 53–79.

Longworth, I. 1984. *Collared Urns of the Bronze Age in Britain and Ireland*. Cambridge: Cambridge University Press.

Lubbock, C. 1865. *Pre-historic Times, as Illustrated by Ancient Remains, and the Manners and Customs of Modern Savages*. London: Williams and Norgate.

Lucas, G. 2012. *Understanding the Archaeological Record*. Cambridge: Cambridge University Press.

Lynch, F. 1970. *Prehistoric Anglesey*. Llangefni: Anglesey Antiquarian Society.

Lynch, F. 1972. Report on the re-excavation of two Bronze Age cairns in Anglesey: Bedd Branwen and Treiorwerth. *Archaeologia Cambrensis* 120, 11–83.

Lynch, F. 1984. Moel Goedog Circle I Complex Ring Cairn, Harlech. *Archaeologia Cambrensis* 133, 8–50.

Lynch, F. 1991. *Prehistoric Anglesey* (2nd edn). Llangefni: Anglesey Antiquarian Society.

Lynch, F. 1993. *Excavations in the Brenig Valley: A Mesolithic and Bronze Age Landscape in North Wales.* Bangor: Cambrian Archaeological Association.

Mack, J. 2008. *The Art of Small Things.* London: British Museum Press.

Madgwick, R. 2010. Bone modification and the conceptual relationship between humans and animals in Iron Age Wessex. In J. Morris and M. Maltby (eds), *Integrating Social and Environmental Archaeologies: reconsidering deposition.* Oxford: British Archaeological Report S2077, 66–82.

Malafouris, L. 2015. How did the Myceneans remember? Death, matter and memory in the early Mycenean World. In C. Renfrew, M. Boyd and I. Morley (eds), *Deaths, Rituals, Social Order and the Archaeology of Immortality in the Ancient World: 'death shall have no dominion'.* Cambridge: Cambridge University Press, 303–314.

Macgregor, A. and Impey, O. 1997. *The Origins of Museums. The Cabinet of Curiosity in Sixteenth and Seventeenth Century Europe.* Oxford: Ashmolean Museum.

Maltby, M. 2002. Animal bone from graves. In S. Davies, P. Bellamy, M. Heaton and P. Woodward (eds), *Excavations at Alington Avenue, Fordington, Dorchester, Dorset, 1984-87.* Dorchester: Dorset Natural History and Archaeological Society Monograph 15, 168–70.

Manby, T. 1980. Bronze Age settlement in eastern Yorkshire. In J. Barrett and R. Bradley (eds), *Settlement and Society in the British Later Bronze Age.* Oxford: British Archaeological Report 83(ii), 307–70.

Manby, T. 1986. The Bronze Age in western Yorkshire. In T.G. Manby and P. Turnbull (eds), *Archaeology in the Pennines. Studies in Honour of Arthur Raistrick*, Oxford: British Archaeological Report 158, 55–125

Manby, T. 1988. The Neolithic period in eastern Yorkshire. In T. Manby (ed.) *Archaeology in Eastern Yorkshire.* Sheffield: University of Sheffield, 35–88.

Manby, T. 1994. Appendix: Type 1 Food Vessels. In D. Coombs, The excavation of two Bronze Age round barrows on Irton Moor, Yorks, 1973. *Yorkshire Archaeological Journal* 66, 36–40, 48–50.

Manby, T. 1995. Skeuomorphism: some reflections of leather, wood and basketry in Early Bronze Age pottery. In I. Kinnes, and G. Varndell (eds), *Unbaked Urnes of crudely shape': essays on British and Irish pottery for Ian Longworth.* Oxford: Oxbow Books, 81–8.

Manby, T. 1999. Grooved Ware in Yorkshire and northern England: 1974–1994. In Cleal and MacSween (eds) 1999, 57–75.

Manby, T. 2004. Food Vessels with handles. In A.M. Gibson and J.A. Sheridan (eds), *From Sickles to Circles: Britain and Ireland at the time of Stonehenge.* London: Tempus, 215–42.

Margetts, A. 2012. Post-Excavation Assessment and Updated Project Design Report: Land at Leysdown Road Warden Bay in Leysdown, Isle of Sheppey. London: Archaeology South East unpublished report series [https://doi.org/10.5284/1054951] (accessed 19 September 2021).

Margetts, A. 2018. *WEALDBAERA: Excavations at Wickhurst Green, Broadbridge Heath and the landscape of the West Central Weald.* Portslade: Spoilheap Press.

Marsden, B.M. 1974. *The Early Barrow Diggers.* Aylesbury: Shire.

Matthews, S. 2008. Other than bronze: substances and incorporation in Danish Bronze Age hoards. In C. Hamon and B. Quilliec (eds), *Hoards from the Neolithic to the Metal Ages. Technical and Codified Practices.* Oxford: British Archaeological Report S1758, 103–20.

Matthews, S. 2017. At world's end: the Channel Bronze Age and the emergence and limits of the Atlantic complex. In A. Lehoërff and M. Talon (eds), *Movement, Exchange and Identity in Europe in the 2nd and 1st Millennia BC: beyond frontiers.* Oxford: Oxbow Books, 49–62.

Maynard, D.J. 1978. Dorset archaeology in 1977. Wimborne St Giles, Oakley Down. *Proceedings of the Dorset Natural History and Archaeological Society* 99, 125–6.

McGrath, K., Rowsell, K., Gates St-Pierre, C. *et al.* 2019. Identifying archaeological bone via non-destructive ZooMS and the materiality of symbolic expression: examples from Iroquoian bone points. *Scientific Reports* 9, 11027 [https://doi.org/10.1038/s41598-019-47299-x]

McKinley, J. 1993. Bone fragment size and weights of bone from modern British cremations and its implications for the interpretation of archaeological cremations. *International Journal of Osteoarchaeology* 3, 283–7.

McKinley, J. 1994. A pyre and grave goods in British cremation burials; have we missed something? *Antiquity* 68, 132–4.

McKinley, J. 1997. Bronze Age 'barrows' and funerary rites and rituals of cremation. *Proceedings of the Prehistoric Society* 63, 129–45.

McKinley, J. 2006. Cremation ... the cheap option? In R. Gowland and C. Knüsel (eds), *The Social Archaeology of Funerary Remains*. Oxford: Studies in Funerary Archaeology 1, 81–8.

McKinley, J., Leivers, M., Schuster, J., Marshall, P., Barclay, A. and Stoodley, N. 2015. *Cliffs End Farm, Isle of Thanet, Kent: a mortuary and ritual site of the Bronze Age, Iron Age and Anglo-Saxon period with evidence for long-distance maritime mobility*. Salisbury: Wessex Archaeology.

McNee, B. 2012. The Potters' Legacy: production, use and deposition of pottery in Kent, from the Middle Bronze Age to the Early Iron Age. Unpublished PhD thesis, University of Southampton.

Megaw, R. and Megaw, V. 1989. *Celtic Art: from its beginnings to the Book of Kells*. London: Thames & Hudson.

Melton, N., Montgomery, J., Knüsel, C. J., Batt, C., Needham, S., Pearson, M. P., Sheridan, A., Heron, C., Horsley, T., Schmidt, A., Evans, A., Carter, E., Edwards, H., Hargreaves, M., Janaway, R., Lynnerup, N., Northover, P., O'Connor, S., Ogden, A., Taylor, T., Wastling, V. and Wilson, A. 2010. Gristhorpe Man: an Early Bronze Age log-coffin burial scientifically defined. *Antiquity* 84, 796–815.

Melton, N., Knüsel, C.J. and Montgomery, J. (eds) 2013. *Gristhorpe Man. A Life and Death in the Bronze Age*. Oxford: Oxbow Books.

Mepham, L. 1997. Pottery. In Fitzpatrick 1997a, 114–38.

Mercer, R. and Healy, F. 2008. *Hambledon Hill, Dorset, England. Excavation and Survey of a Neolithic Monument Complex and its Surrounding Landscape*. Swindon: English Heritage.

Metcalf, P. and Huntington, R. 1991. *Celebrations of Death* (2nd edn). Cambridge: Cambridge University Press.

Miles, H. 1975. Barrows on the St Austell Granite, Cornwall (Watch Hill, Caerloggas, Trenance, Cocksbarrow). *Cornish Archaeology*, 14, 5–83.

Miles, W. 1826. *A Description of the Deverel Barrow, Opened A.D. 1825*. London: Nichols & Son.

Moore, H. and Wilson, G. 1995. Two Orcadian cist burials: excavations at Midskaill, Egilsay and Linga Field, Sandwick. *Proceedings of the Society of Antiquaries of Scotland* 125, 237–51.

Morgan, L.H. 1877. *Ancient Society: or researches in the lines of human progress, from savagery, through barbarism to civilization*. New York: Holt.

Mortimer, J.R. 1900. Notes on the history of the Driffield Museum of Antiquities and Geological Specimens. *Proceedings of the Yorkshire Geological and Polytechnic Society* 14, 88–96.

Morse, M. 2005. *How the Celts Came to Britain*. Stroud: Tempus.

Mortimer, J. 1905. *Forty Years' Researches. British and Saxon Burial Mounds of East Yorkshire*. Hull: Brown & Sons.

Must Farm. 2019. Post-ex dairy 10: specialist analyses part three: glass and non-glass beads. Available at: http://www.mustfarm.com/post-dig/post-ex-diary-10-specialist-analyses-part-three/ (accessed 14 July 2021).

National Museums Scotland n.d. *Neolithic dog skull*. Available at: https://www.nms.ac.uk/explore-our-collections/stories/scottish-history-and-archaeology/neolithic-dog-skull/ (accessed 7 June 2021).

Needham, S. 1983. The Early Bronze Age Axeheads of Central and Southern England. Unpublished PhD thesis, University College Cardiff.

Needham, S. 1987. The Bronze Age. In D.G. Bird and J. Bird (eds), *The Archaeology of Surrey to 1540*. Guildford: Surrey Archaeological Society, 97–137.

Needham, S. 1988. Selective deposition in the British Early Bronze Age. *World Archaeology* 20, 229–48.

Needham, S. 1996. Chronology and periodisation in the British Bronze Age. *Acta Archaeologica* 67, 121–40.

Needham, S. 2000. Power pulses across a cultural divide: cosmologically driven acquisition between Armorica and Wessex. *Proceedings of the Prehistoric Society* 66, 151–207.

Needham, S. 2001. When expediency broaches ritual intention: the flow of metal between systemic and buried domains. *Journal of the Royal Anthropological Institute* NS 7, 275–98.

Needham, S. 2005. Transforming Beaker culture in North-West Europe; processes of fusion and fission. *Proceedings of the Prehistoric Society* 71, 171–17.

Needham, S. 2006. Precious cups of the Early Bronze Age. In S. Needham, K. Parfitt and G. Varndell (eds), *The Ringlemere Cup: precious cups and the beginning of the Channel Bronze Age*. London: British Museum Press, 53–68.

Needham, S. 2008. Exchange, object biographies and the shaping of identities, 10,000–1000 BC. In J. Pollard (ed.), *Prehistoric Britain*. London: Blackwell, 310–29.

Needham, S. 2009. Encompassing the sea: 'maritories' and Bronze Age maritime interactions. In P. Clarke (ed.), *Bronze Age Connections: cultural contact in prehistoric Europe*. Oxford: Oxbow Books, 12–37.

Needham, S. 2015. A revised classification and chronology for daggers and knives. In Woodward and Hunter (eds) 2015, appendix I, 1–19.

Needham, S. 2017. Transmanche in the Penard/Rosnoën stage. Wearing the same sleeve or keeping at arm's length? In A. Lehoërff and M. Talon (eds), *Movement, Exchange and Identity in Europe in the 2nd and 1st Millennia BC: Beyond Frontiers*. Oxford: Oxbow Books, 31–48.

Needham, S. and Anelay, G. in press. *Barrows at the Core of Bronze Age Communities: Petersfield Heath excavations, 2014-18, in their regional context*. Leiden: Sidestone.

Needham, S., Lawson, A. and Woodward, A. 2010. 'A noble group of barrows': Bush Barrow and the Normanton Down Early Bronze Age cemetery two centuries on. *Antiquaries Journal* 90, 1–39.

Needham, S., Parham, D. and Frieman, C. 2013. *Claimed by the Sea: Salcombe, Langdon Bay and other marine finds of the Bronze Age*. York: Council for British Archaeology Research Report 173.

Needham, S., Kenny, J., Cole, G., Montgomery, J., Jay, M., Davis, M., and Marshall, P. 2017. Death by combat at the dawn of the Bronze Age? Profiling the dagger-accompanied burial from Racton, West Sussex. *Antiquaries Journal* 97, 65–117.

Newman, T. 1976. The jet necklace from Kyloe. *Archaeologia Aeliana* 5 ser 4, 177–82.

Niblett, R. 1999. *The Excavation of a Ceremonial Site at Folly Lane, Verulamium*. London: Society for the Promotion of Roman Studies.

Nisbet, R.A. 1969. *Social Change and History: aspects of the western theory of development*. Oxford: Oxford University Press.

Nowakowski, J., 1991. Trethellan Farm, Newquay. The excavation of a lowland Bronze Age settlement and Iron Age cemetery. *Cornish Archaeology* 30, 5–242.

Nowakowski, J. 1995. The excavation of a complex barrow at Trelowthas Manor Farm, Probus 1995. *Cornish Archaeology* 34, 206–11.

Nowakowski, J.A. 2007. *Excavations of a Bronze Age landscape and a post-Roman industrial settlement 1953-1961, Gwithian, Cornwall. Assessment of key datasets (2005-2006), Volume I*. Truro: Cornwall County Council. https://doi.org/10.5284/1000200 (accessed 21 June 2021).

Nowakowski, J., Quinnell, H., Sturgess, J., Thomas, C. and Thorpe, C. 2007. Return to Gwithian: shifting the sands of time. *Cornish Archaeology* 46, 13–76.

O'Brien, W. 2012. The Chalcolithic in Ireland: a chronological and cultural framework. In M. Allen, J. Gardiner and A. Sheridan (eds), *Is there a British Chalcolithic? People, Place and Polity in the Later 3rd Millennium BC*. Oxford: Prehistoric Society Research Papers 5, 211–25.

O'Brien, W. 2004. *Ross Island: mining, metal and society in early Ireland.* Galway: National University of Ireland.

O'Brien, W. 2014. *Prehistoric Copper Mining in Europe: 5000-500 BC.* Oxford: Oxford University Press.

O'Connor, B. 1980. *Cross-Channel Relations in the Later Bronze Age.* Oxford: British Archaeological Report S91.

O'Connor, B. 1991. Bronze Age metalwork from Cranborne Chase: a catalogue. In J. Barrett, R. Bradley, and M. Hall (eds), *Papers on the Prehistoric Archaeology of Cranborne Chase.* Oxford: Oxbow Monograph 11, 231–41.

Olalde, I., Brace, S., Allentoft, M. *et al.* 2018. The Beaker phenomenon and the genomic transformation of northwest Europe. *Nature* 555, 190–6.

Olivier, L. 1999. The Hochdorf 'princely' grave and the question of the nature of archaeological funerary assemblages. In T. Murray (ed.), *Time and Archaeology.* London: Routledge, 109–38.

Olivier L. 2001. Duration, memory and the nature of the archaeological record. In H. Karlsson (ed.), *It's About Time: the concept of time in archaeology.* Gothenburg: Bricoleur Press, 61–70.

Olsen, 2012. After interpretation: remembering archaeology. *Current Swedish Archaeology* 20, 11–34.

Owoc, M. 2001. The times, they are a changin': experiencing continuity and development in the Early Bronze Age funerary rituals of south-western Britain. In Brück (ed.) 2001a, 193–206.

Owoc, M. 2002. Munselling the mound: the use of soil colour as metaphor in British Bronze Age funerary ritual. In A. Jones and G. MacGregor (eds), *Colouring the Past: the significance of colour in archaeological research.* Oxford: Berg, 127–40.

Pader, E.J. 1982. *Symbolism, Social Relations and the Interpretation of Mortuary Remains.* Oxford: British Archaeological Report S130.

Parfitt, K. 1995. *Iron Age Burials at Mill Hill, Deal.* London: British Museum Press.

Parfitt, K. 1998. A late Iron Age burial from Chilham Castle, near Canterbury, Kent. *Proceedings of the Prehistoric Society* 64, 343–51.

Parke, A.L. 1951. Barrows on Oakley Down, Wimborne St Giles. *Proceedings of the Dorset Natural History and Antiquarian Field Club* 72, 91–2.

Parker Pearson, M. 1982. Mortuary practices, society and ideology: an ethnoarchaeological study. In I. Hodder (ed.), *Symbolic and Structural Archaeology.* Cambridge: Cambridge University Press, 99–113.

Parker Pearson, M. 1995. Southwestern Bronze Age pottery. In I. Kinnes and G. Varndell (eds), '*Unbaked Urns of Rudely Shape: essays on British and Irish pottery for Ian Longworth.* Oxford: Oxbow Monograph 55, 89–100.

Parker Pearson, M. 1999a. Food, sex and death: cosmologies in the British Iron Age with particular relevance to East Yorkshire. *Cambridge Archaeological Journal* 9, 43–69.

Parker Pearson, M. 1999b. *The Archaeology of Death and Burial.* Stroud: Sutton.

Parker Pearson, M., Sheridan, A. and Needham, S. 2013. Bronze Age tree-trunk coffin graves in Britain. In Melton *et al.* (eds) 2013, 29–66.

Parker Pearson, M., Sheridan, A. Jay, M. Chamberlain, A. Richards, M. and Evans, J. (eds) 2019. *The Beaker People: isotopes, mobility and diet in prehistoric Britain.* Oxford: Prehistoric Society Research Papers 7.

Patchett, F. 1944. Cornish Bronze Age pottery, part I. *Archaeological Journal* 101, 17–49.

Patchett, F. 1950. Cornish Bronze Age pottery, part II. *Archaeological Journal* 107, 44–65.

Pauketat, T.R. 2013. *An Archaeology of the Cosmos. Rethinking Agency and Religion in Ancient America.* Abingdon: Routledge.

Pauketat, T.R. and Alt, S.M. 2018. Water and shells in bodies and pots: Mississippian rhizome, Cahokian poiesis. In E. Harrison-Buck and J.A. Hendon (eds), *Relational Identities and Other-than-Human Agency in Archaeology.* Boulder CO: University Press of Colorado, 72–99.

Payne, G. 1911. Researches and discoveries in Kent 1908–1910. *Archaeologia Cantiana* 29, lxxvi–lxxxvi.

Pearce, J. 2015. A civilised death? The Interpretation of Roman Provincial Grave Good Assemblages. In J.R. Brandt, M. Prusac and H. Roland (eds), *Death and Changing Rituals. Function and Meaning in Ancient Funerary Practices.* Oxford: Studies in Funerary Archaeology 7, 223–48.

Pearce. S. 1983. *The Bronze Age Metalwork of South Western Britain.* Oxford: British Archeological Report 120.

Pearce, S. 2007. *Visions of Antiquity. The Society of the Antiquaries of London 1707-2007.* London: Society of Antiquaries of London.

Perkins, D. 2000. A Gateway Island: an exploration of evidence for the existence of a cultural focus in the form of a 'gateway community' in the Isle of Thanet during the Bronze Age and Early and Middle Iron Ages. Unpublished PhD thesis, University College London.

Perkins, D. and Gibson, A. 1991. A Beaker burial from Manston, near Ramsgate. *Archaeologia Cantiana* 108, 11–27.

Pétrequin, P., Cassen, S., Errera, M., Klassen, L., Sheridan, A. and Pétrequin, A.-M. (eds) 2012. *Jade. Grandes haches alpines du Néolithique européen. Ve et IVe millénaires av. J.-C.* Besançon: Presses Universitaires de Franche-Comté and Centre de Recherche archéologique de la Vallée de l'Ain.

Petrie, G. 1859. Description of antiquities in Orkney recently examined, with illustrative drawings. *Proceedings of the Society of Antiquaries of Scotland* 2 (1854–7), 60–1.

Petrie, G. 1871. Notice of excavations, and discovery of cists containing large stone urns in Stronsay, Orkney. *Proceedings of the Society of Antiquaries of Scotland* 8, 347–51.

Philp, B. 2014. *Discoveries and Excavations Across Kent: digging up the past!* Dover: Kent Archaeological Rescue Unit.

Pierpoint, S. 1980. *Social Patterns in Yorkshire Prehistory, 3500-750 BC.* Oxford: British Archaeological Report 74.

Piggott, C. 1938. A Middle Bronze Age barrow and Deverel-Rimbury urnfield at Latch Farm, Christchurch, Hampshire. *Proceedings of the Prehistoric Society* 4(1), 169–87.

Piggott, S. 1938. The Early Bronze Age in Wessex. *Proceedings of the Prehistoric Society* 4, 52–106.

Piggott, S. 1946. The chambered cairn of 'the Grey Mare and Colts'. *Proceedings of the Dorset Natural History and Archaeological Society* 67, 30–3.

Piggott, S. 1954. *Neolithic Cultures of the British Isles.* Cambridge: Cambridge University Press.

Piggott, S. 1962. *The West Kennet Long Barrow: Excavations 1955-56.* London: HMSO.

Pitt-Rivers, A. 1888. *Excavations in Cranborne Chase Vol II. Excavations in Barrows near Rushmore. Excavations in the Romano-British Village Rotherly.* Rushmore: privately printed.

Pouncett, J. 2019. Neolithic Occupation and Stone Working on the Yorkshire Wolds. Unpublished PhD thesis, University of Oxford.

Prag, J. (ed.) 2016. *The Story of Alderley: living with the Edge.* Manchester: Manchester University Press.

Prideaux, C. and Payne, E. 1944. Bincombe Barrow, Ridgeway Hill, Dorset. *Proceedings of the Dorset Natural History and Antiquarian Field Club* 65, 38–52.

Rady, J. and Holman, J. 2019. *Beneath The Seamark: 6,000 years of an Island's History. Archaeological Investigations at 'Thanet Earth', Kent 2007-2012.* Canterbury: Canterbury Archaeological Trust.

Rahtz, P. and Apsimon, A. 1962. Excavations at Shearplace Hill, Sydling St Nicholas, Dorset, England. *Proceedings of the Prehistoric Society* 28, 289–328.

Rajkovača, V. forthcoming. Faunal remains – large vertebrates. In M. Knight, R. Ballantyne, A. Cooper, D. Gibson, and I. Robinson Zeki (eds), *Must Farm Pile-dwelling Settlement. Volume 2. Specialist reports.* Cambridge: Cambridge Archaeological Unit.

Randsborg, K. 1973. Wealth and social structure as reflected in Bronze Age burials – a quantitative approach. In C. Renfrew (ed.), *The Explanation of Culture Change: models in prehistory.* London: Duckworth, 565–70.

Rapport, N. and Overing, J. 2000. *Social and Cultural Anthropology: the key concepts.* London: Routledge.

RCAHMS. 1946. *The Royal Commission on the Ancient and Historical Monuments of Scotland. Twelfth Report with an Inventory of the Ancient Monuments of Orkney and Shetland.* Edinburgh: HMSO.

RCAHMS. 1984. *The Royal Commission on the Ancient and Historical Monuments of Scotland. The Archaeological Sites and Monuments of Eday and Stronsay, Orkney Islands Area.* Edinburgh: Archaeological Sites and Monuments of Scotland 23

RCAHMW. 1964. *Caernarfonshire Vol III. A Survey and Inventory by the Royal Commission on Ancient and Historical Monuments in Wales and Monmouthshire.* Cardiff: HMSO.

Reilly, S. 2003. Processing the dead in Neolithic Orkney. *Oxford Journal of Archaeology* 22, 133–54.

Renfrew, C. 1973. Wessex as a social question. *Antiquity* 47, 221–5.

Renfrew, C. 1974. Space, time and polity. In M.J. Rowlands and J. Friedman (eds), *The Evolution of Social Systems.* London: Duckworth, 89–114.

Renfrew, C. 1979. *Investigations in Orkney.* London: Report of the Research Committee of the Society of Antiquaries of London 38.

Richards, C. 1988. Altered images: a re-examination of Neolithic mortuary practices in Orkney. In J.C. Barrett and I. Kinnes (eds), *The Archaeology of Context in the Neolithic and Bronze Age: recent trends.* Sheffield: Sheffield University Press, 42–56.

Richardson, B. 2016. An Emblem of the Immortal Spirit? Salt plates from St James's and Park Street Burial Grounds. London: MOLA Headland Infrastructure. Available at: https://molaheadland. com/salt-plates-from-st-james-and-park-street-burial-grounds/ (accessed 15 July 2021).

Richmond, A., Coates, G. and Hallybone, C. 2010. Bar Pasture Farm, Pode Hole Quarry, Peterborough, Phase 1. Archaeological interim report. Phoenix Archaeology Report PC259a. York: Archaeology Data Service [distributor] https://doi.org/10.5284/1006428 (accessed 19 September 2021).

Ritchie, A. 2009. *On the Fringe of Neolithic Europe: excavation of a chambered cairn on the Holm of Papa Westray, Orkney.* Edinburgh: RCAHMS.

Ritchie, J. and Ritchie, A. 1974. Excavation of a barrow at Queenafjold, Twatt, Orkney. *Proceedings of the Society of Antiquaries of Scotland* 105, 33–40.

Robb, J. 2002. Time and biography. In Y. Hamilakis, M. Pluciennik and S. Tarlow (eds), *Thinking Through the Body: archaeologies of corporeality.* London: Kluwer/Academic, 145–63.

Roberts, B. 2007. Adorning the living but not the dead: a reassessment of Middle Bronze Age ornaments in Britain. *Proceedings of the Prehistoric Society* 73, 135–67.

Roberts, B., Boughton, D., Dinwiddy, M., Doshi, N., Fitzpatrick, A., Hook, D., Meeks, N., Woodward, A. and Woodward, P. 2015. Collapsing commodities or lavish offerings? Understanding massive metalwork deposition at Langton Matravers, Dorset during the Bronze Age-Iron Age transition. *Oxford Journal of Archaeology* 34, 365–95.

Rohl, B. and Needham, S. 1998. *The Circulation of Metal in the British Bronze Age: the application of lead isotope analysis.* London: British Museum Press.

Rowlands, M. 1993. The role of memory in the transmission of culture. *World Archaeology* 25(2), 141–51.

Rugg, J.J. 2017. Materiality, identity and mutability: irresolvable tensions within burial reform. In J. Bradbury and C. Scarre (eds), *Engaging with the Dead: exploring changing human beliefs about death, mortality and the human body.* Oxford: Studies in Funerary Archaeology 13, 210–16.

Russell, M., Smith. M., Cheetham, P., Evans, D. and Manlet, H. 2019. The girl with the chariot medallion: a well-furnished, Late Iron Age Durotrigian burial from Langton Herring, Dorset. *Archaeological Journal* 176(2), 196–230.

Russell, V. and Patchett, F.M. 1954. A Beaker from Trevedra farm, St Just-in-Penwith. *Proceedings of the West Cornwall Field Club* 1(2), 41–2.

Russell, V. and Pool, P.A.S. 1964. Excavation of a menhir at Try, Gulval. *Cornish Archaeology* 3, 15–26.

Saul, F.P. 1972. The human skeletal remains of Altar de Sacrificios: An osteobiographic analysis. *Papers of the Peabody Museum* 63(2), 3–123.

Saville, A. 1990 *Hazleton North, Gloucestershire, 1979-82: The Excavation of a Neolithic Long Cairn of the Cotswold-Severn Group*. London: English Heritage.

Savory, H.N. 1955. A Corpus of Welsh Bronze Age Pottery: Beakers. *Bulletin of the Board of Celtic Studies*, 16(3), 215–41.

Saxe, A. 1970. Social Dimensions of Mortuary Practice. Unpublished PhD thesis, University of Michigan.

Scarre, C. 2015. Parallel lives? Neolithic funerary monuments and the Channel divide. In H. Anderson-Whymark, D. Garrow and F. Sturt (eds), *Continental Connections: exploring cross-Channel relationships from the Mesolithic to the Iron Age*. Oxford: Oxbow Books, 78–98.

Schulting, R. and Bradley, R. 2013. Of human remains and weapons in the neighbourhood of London: new AMS 14C dates on Thames 'river skulls' and their European context. *Archaeological Journal* 170(1), 30–77.

Schulting, R., Sheridan, A., Crozier, A. and Murphy, E. 2010. Revisiting Quanterness: new AMS dates and stable isotope data from an Orcadian chamber tomb. *Proceedings of the Society of Antiquaries of Scotland* 140, 1–150.

Scott, L. 1935. The chambered cairn of Clettraval, North Uist. *Proceedings of the Society of Antiquaries of Scotland* 69, 480–536.

Scott, L. 1948. The chamber tomb of Unival, North Uist. *Proceedings of the Society of Antiquaries of Scotland* 82, 1–49.

Sebald, W. 1998. *The Rings of Saturn*. London: New Directions Publishing.

Service, E.R. 1962. *Primitive Social Organisation: an evolutionary perspective*. New York: Random House.

Shanks, M. and Tilley, C. 1982 Ideology, symbolic power and ritual communication: a reinterpretation of Neolithic mortuary practices. In I. Hodder (ed.), *Symbolic and Structural Archaeology*. Cambridge: Cambridge University Press, 129–54.

Sharman, P. 2007. *Excavation of a Bronze Age Site at Loth Road, Sanday, Orkney*. Scottish Archaeology Internet Reports 25 [https://doi.org/10.5284/1017938].

Sharman, P. 2009. Steatite funerary urns in the Early Prehistoric Northern Isles. In A. Forster and V. Turner (eds), *Kleber: Shetland's oldest industry. Shetland Soapstone Since Prehistory*. Lerwick: Shetland Amenity Trust, 39–47.

Sharples, N. 1985. Excavations at Pierowall Quarry, Westray, Orkney. *Proceedings of the Society of Antiquaries of Scotland*, 75–125.

Sharples, N. 2010. *Social Relations in Later Prehistory: Wessex in the first millennium BC*. Oxford: Oxford University Press.

Shennan, S. 1975. The social organisation at Branč. *Antiquity* 49, 279–87.

Shennan, S. 1982. Ideology, change and the European Early Bronze Age. In I. Hodder (ed.), *Symbolic and Structural Archaeology*. Cambridge: Cambridge University Press, 155–61.

Shennan, S. 1986. Central Europe in the third millennium BC: an evolutionary trajectory for the beginning of the European Bronze Age. *Journal of Anthropological Archaeology* 5(2), 115–46.

Shepherd, A. 2012. Stepping out together: men, women, and their Beakers in time and space. In M.J. Allen, J. Gardiner and A. Sheridan. (eds), *Is there a British Chalcolithic? People, Place and Polity in the Late 3rd Millennium*. Oxford: Prehistoric Society Research Papers 5, 257–80.

Shepherd, I.A.G. 1986. *Powerful Pots: Beakers in north-east prehistory*. Aberdeen: Anthropological Museum, University of Aberdeen.

Sheppard, T. 1900. *A Descriptive Catalogue of the Specimens in the Mortimer Museum*. London: A. Brown and Sons.

Sheppard, T. 1949. Miniature Bronze Age cinerary urns. *Transactions of the East Riding Antiquarian Society* 29, 1–4.

Sheridan, J.A. 2004. Scottish Food Vessel chronology revisited. In A.M. Gibson and J.A. Sheridan (eds), *From Sickles to Circles: Britain and Ireland at the time of Stonehenge.* Stroud: Tempus, 243–69.

Sheridan, J.A. 2007. Scottish Beaker dates: the good, the bad and the ugly. In M. Larsson and M. Parker Pearson (eds), *From Stonehenge to the Baltic: living with cultural diversity in the third millennium BC.* Oxford: British Archaeological Report S1692, 91–123.

Sheridan, J.A. 2010. The neolithization of Britain and Ireland: the big picture. In B. Finlayson and G. Warren (eds), *Landscapes in Transition: understanding hunter-gatherer and farming landscapes in the early Holocene of Europe and the Levant.* Oxford: Council for British Research in the Levant Supplementary Series 8, 89–105.

Sheridan, J.A. and Davis, M. 2002. Investigating jet and jet-like artefacts from prehistoric Scotland: the National Museums of Scotland project. *Antiquity* 76, 812–25.

Sheridan, J.A. and Shortland, A. 2003. Supernatural power dressing. *British Archaeology* 70, 18–23.

Sheridan, J.A. and Shortland, A. 2004. '... beads which have given rise to so much dogmatism, controversy and rash speculation': faience in Early Bronze Age Britain and Ireland. In I. Shepherd and G. Barclay (eds), *Scotland in Ancient Europe.* Edinburgh: Society of Antiquaries of Scotland, 263–79.

Simpson, D. 1968. Food Vessels: associations and chronology. In J.M. Coles and D.D.A Simpson (eds), *Studies in Ancient Europe: essays presented to Stuart Piggott.* Leicester: Leicester University Press, 197–211.

Simpson, D., Gregory, R.A. and Murphy, E.M. 2003. Excavations at Manish Strand, Ensay, Western Isles. *Proceedings of the Society of Antiquaries of Scotland* 133, 173–89.

Skeates, R. 1993. Mediterranean coral: its use and exchange in and around the Alpine region during the Later Neolithic and Copper Age. *Oxford Journal of Archaeology* 12, 281–92.

Smiles, S. 2008. Thomas Guest and Paul Nash in Wiltshire: two episodes in the artistic approach to British antiquity. In S. Smiles and S. Moser (eds), *Envisioning the Past: archaeology and the image.* Abingdon: Blackwells, 133–57.

Smith, R.A. 1911. On late Celtic antiquities discovered at Welwyn, Herts. *Archaeologia* 63, 1–30.

Smith, M. and Brickley, M. 2009. *People of the Long Barrows: life, death and burial in the earlier Neolithic.* Stroud: History Press.

Smith, R. J. C., Healy, F., Allen, M., Barnes, I. and Woodward, P. J. 1997. *Excavations along the Route of the Dorchester By-pass, Dorset, 1986-8.* Salisbury: Wessex Archaeology Report 11.

Sørensen, M.L.S. 1997. Reading dress: the construction of social categories and identities in Bronze Age Europe. *Journal of European Archaeology* 5(1), 93–114.

Sofaer, J.R. 2006. *The Body as Material Culture: a theoretical osteoarchaeology.* Cambridge: Cambridge University Press.

Sparey-Green, C. 1987. *Excavations at Poundbury, Dorchester, Dorset, 1966-1982. Volume I: the settlements.* Dorchester: Dorset Natural History and Archaeological Society Monograph 7.

St George Gray, H. and Prideaux, C. 1905. Barrow-digging on Martinsdown. *Proceedings of the Dorset Natural History and Antiquarian Field Club* 26, 7–22.

Standish, C., Dhuime, B., Hawkesworth, C. and Pike, A. 2015. A non-local source of Irish Chalcolithic and Early Bronze Age gold. *Proceedings of the Prehistoric Society* 81, 149–77.

Stanley, W. and Way, A. 1868. Ancient interments and sepulchural urns found in Anglesey and North Wales, with some account of examples in other localities. *Archaeologia Cambrensis* Ser 3 56, 217–93.

Stansbie, D. 2016. The Circulation of Flesh: regional food producing/consuming systems in southern England 1500 BC–AD 1086. Unpublished PhD thesis, University of Oxford.

Stead, I.M. 1965. *The La Tène Cultures of East Yorkshire.* York: Yorkshire Philosophical Society.

Stead, I.M. 1967. A La Tène III Burial at Welwyn Garden City. *Archaeologia* 101, 1–62.

Stead, I.M. 1976. The earliest burials of the Aylesford Culture. In G. Sieveking, I. Longworth, K. Wilson and G. Clark (eds), *Problems in Economic and Social Archaeology.* London: Duckworth, 401–16.

Stead, I.M. 1979. *The Arras Culture.* York: Yorkshire Philosophical Society.

Stead, I.M. 1986. A group of Iron Age barrows at Cowlam, North Humberside. *Yorkshire Archaeological Journal* 58, 5–16.

Stead, I.M. 1988. Chalk figurines of the Parisi. *Antiquaries Journal* 68, 9–29.

Stead, I.M. 1991. *Iron Age Cemeteries in East Yorkshire. Excavations at Burton Fleming, Rudston, Garton-on-the-Wolds, and Kirkburn.* London: English Heritage/British Museum Press.

Stead, I.M. and V. Rigby 1986. *Baldock: the Excavation of a Roman and Pre-Roman Settlement 1968-75.* London: Britannia Monograph 7.

Stebbing, W.P.D. 1951. Researches and discoveries in Kent. Neolithic burials found in 1949, Nethercourt, Ramsgate. *Archaeologia Cantiana* 64, 150–1.

Stephens, M. forthcoming. *Chariots, Swords and Spears: Iron Age burials at the foot of the East Yorkshire Wolds.* Oxford: Oxbow Books.

Stephens, M. and Ware, P. 2019. The Iron Age cemeteries at Pocklington and other excavations by MAP. In P. Halkon (ed.), *The Arras Culture of Eastern Yorkshire.* Oxford: Oxbow Books, 17–32.

Stevens, S. 2003. Archaeological Investigations at Hawkinge Aerodrome, Hawkinge, Kent. London: Archaeology South East unpublished client report 677.

Stevenson, J. 2013. *Living by the Sword: the archaeology of Brisley Farm, Ashford, Kent.* Brighton: Spoilheap Monograph 6.

Stillingfleet, E. W. 1846. Account of the opening of some barrows on the Wolds of Yorkshire, *Proceedings of the Archaeological Institute Meeting, York 1846,* 26–32.

Strathern, M. 1988. *The Gender of the Gift.* Berkeley CA: University of California Press.

Stukeley, W. 1740. *Stonehenge, a Temple Restored to the British Druids.* London: Innes and Manby.

Sumbler, M. 1999. The Stratigraphy of the Chalk Group in Yorkshire and Lincolnshire. Keyworth: British Geological Society Technical Report WA/99/02. Unpublished report, available at http://nora.nerc.ac.uk/id/eprint/509937/ (accessed 22 September 2021).

Sweet, 2001. Antiquaries and antiquarianism in eighteenth century England. *Eighteenth-Century Studies* 34(2), 181–206.

Sykes, N. 2014. *Beastly Questions: animal answers to archaeological issues.* London: Bloomsbury.

Sykes, N., Beirne, P., Horowitz, A., Jones, I., Kalof, L., Karlsson, E., King, T., Litwak, H., McDonald, R.A., Murphy, L.J., Pemberton, N., Promislow, D., Rowan, A., Stahl, P.W., Tehrani, J., Tourigny, E., Wynne, C.D.L., Strauss, E. and Larson, G. 2020. Humanity's best friend: a dog-centric approach to addressing global challenges. *Animals* 10 (3), 502 [https://doi.org/10.3390/ani10030502].

Tarlow, S. 1992. Each slow dusk a drawing down of blinds. *Archaeological Review from Cambridge* 11, 125–40.

Tarlow, S. 2012. The archaeology of emotion and affect. *Annual Review of Anthropology* 41, 169–85.

Taylor, B., Conneller, C., Milner, N., Elliott, B., Little, A., Knight, B. and Bamforth, M. 2018. Human lifeways. In N. Milner, C. Conneller and B. Taylor (eds), *Star Carr Volume 1: a persistent place in a changing world.* York: White Rose University Press, 245–72 [https://doi.org/10.22599/book1]

Teather, A. and Chamberlain, A. 2016. Dying embers: fire-lighting technology and mortuary practice in Early Bronze Age Britain. *Archaeological Journal* 173 (2), 188–205.

Thomas, J. 1991. *Rethinking the Neolithic.* Cambridge: Cambridge University Press.

Thomas, J. 1999. *Understanding the Neolithic.* London: Routledge.

Thomas, J. 2000. Death, identity and the body in Neolithic Britain. *Journal of the Royal Anthropological Institute* 6, 653–68.

Thomas, J. 2002. Archaeology's humanism and the materiality of the body. In Y. Hamilakis, M. Pluciennik and S. Tarlow (eds.), *Thinking Through the Body.* London: Kluwer Academic, 29–45.

Thomas, N. and Hartgroves, S. 1990. A Beaker cist grave at Harrowbarrow. *Cornish Archaeology* 29, 52–9.

Thomas, R. and McFadyen, L. 2010. Animals and Cotswold-Severn long barrows: a re-examination. *Proceedings of the Prehistoric Society* 76, 95–114.

Thorpe, I. and Richards, C. 1984. The decline of ritual authority and the introduction of Beakers into Britain. In R. Bradley and J. Gardiner (eds), *Neolithic Studies: a review of some current research*. Oxford: British Archaeological Report 133, 67–84

Thurnam, J. 1869. On ancient British barrows especially those of Wiltshire and adjoining counties (part I: long barrows). *Archaeologia* 42, 161–244.

Thurnam, J. 1872. On ancient British barrows, especially those of Wiltshire and the adjoining counties (part II: round barrows). *Archaeologia* 43(2), 285–552.

Tilley, C. 1995. Rock as resources: landscapes and power. *Cornish Archaeology* 34, 5–57.

Timberlake, S. 2009. Copper mining and metal production at the beginning of the British Bronze Age. In P. Clark (ed.), *Bronze Age Connections: cultural contact in prehistoric Europe*. Oxford: Oxbow Books, 94–121

Trigger, B. 2006. *A History of Archaeological Thought* (2nd edn). Cambridge: Cambridge University Press.

Trudgian, P. and Apsimon, A. 1976. A Trevisker Series Bronze Age Urn from Largin Wood, Broadoak. *Cornish Archaeology* 13, 112–14.

Tylor, E.B. 1871. *Primitive Culture: researches into the development of mythology, philosophy, religion, art, and custom*. London: John Murray.

Ucko, P. 1969. Ethnography and the archaeological interpretation of funerary remains. *World Archaeology* 1, 262–90.

Van der Noort, R. 2006. Argonauts of the North Sea – a social maritime archaeology for the 2nd millennium BC. *Proceedings of the Prehistoric Society* 72, 267–87.

van Gennep, A. 1960. *Rites of Passage*. Chicago: University of Chicago Press.

Vandkilde, H. 2016. Bronzization: the Bronze Age as pre-modern globalization. *Prähistorische Zeitschrift* 91, 103–223.

Vander Linden, M. 2013. A little bit of history repeating itself: theories of the Bell Beaker phenomenon. In A. Harding and H. Fokkens (eds), *The Oxford Handbook of the European Bronze Age*. Oxford: Oxford University Press, 68–81.

Wacher, J. 1959. Litton Cheney excavations. *Proceedings of the Dorset Natural History and Archaeological Society* 80, 160–77.

Waddell, J. 1995. The Cordoned Urn tradition. In I. Kinnes and G. Varndell (eds), '*Unbaked Urns of Rudely Shape': essays on British and Irish pottery for Ian Longworth*. Oxford: Oxbow Monograph 55, 113–22.

Waddington, K. and Sharples, N. 2007. Pins, pixies and thin dark earth. *British Archaeology* 94, 28–33.

Wainwright, G. 1967. Excavation of a round barrow on Worgret Hill, Arne, Dorset. *Proceedings of the Dorset Natural History and Archaeological Society* 87, 119–25.

Walter, T. 1996. A new model of grief: bereavement and biography. *Mortality* 1(1), 17–25.

Warne, C. 1866. *The Celtic Tumuli of Dorset. An Account of Personal and Other Researches in the Sepulchral Mounds of the Durotriges*. London: John Russell Smith.

Warren, G. and Neighbour, T. 2004. Quality quartz: working stone at a bronze age kerbed cairn at Olcote, near Calanais, Isle of Lewis. *Norwegian Archaeological Review* 37, 83–94.

Watkins, C. 2013. *The Undiscovered Country: journeys among the dead*. London: Vintage.

Webley, L. 2015. Rethinking Iron Age connections across the Channel and North Sea. In H. Anderson-Whymark, D. Garrow and F. Sturt (eds), *Continental Connections: exploring cross-Channel relationships from the Mesolithic to the Iron Age*. Oxford: Oxbow Books, 122–44.

Webley, L. Adams, S. and Brück, J. 2020. *The Social Context of Technology: non-ferrous metalworking in later prehistoric Britain and Ireland*. Oxford: Prehistoric Society Research Papers 11.

Wessex Archaeology. n.d. The Amesbury Archer. Available at: https://www.wessexarch.co.uk/our-work/amesbury-archer (accessed 15 July 2021)

Wessex Archaeology 2008a. Allasdale Dunes, Barra, Western Isles, Scotland. Archaeological Evaluation and Assessment of Results. Salisbury: Wessex Archaeology unpublished client report 65305.01.

Wessex Archaeology 2008b. Area A, Waterbrook Park, Ashford, Kent: post-excavation assessment. Salisbury: Wessex Archaeology unpublished client report 65742.02

Wessex Archaeology. 2010. *Margetts Pit, Margetts Lane, Burham, Kent: post-excavation assessment report.* Salisbury: Wessex Archaeology unpublished client report.

Wheeler, M. 1943. *Maiden Castle, Dorset.* London: Report of the Research Committee of the Society of Antiquaries of London 12.

Whimster, R. 1981. *Burial Practices in Iron Age Britain.* Oxford: British Archaeological Report 90.

White, D. 1982. *The Bronze Age Cremation Cemeteries at Simon's Ground, Dorset.* Dorchester: Dorset Natural History and Archaeological Society Monograph 3.

Whittle, A. 2003. *The Archaeology of People. Dimensions of Neolithic Life.* Abingdon: Routledge.

Whittle, A., Bayliss, A. and Healy, F. 2011. *Gathering Time: dating the early Neolithic enclosures of southern Britain and Ireland.* Oxford: Oxbow Books.

Wilkin, N. 2011. Animal remains from Late Neolithic and Early Bronze Age funerary contexts in Wiltshire, Dorset and Oxfordshire. *Archaeological Journal* 168, 64–95.

Wilkin, N. 2013. Food Vessel Pottery Early Bronze Age Funerary Contexts in Northern England: A Typological and Contextual Study. Unpublished PhD Thesis, University of Birmingham.

Wilkin, N. 2017. Combination, composition and context. Readdressing British Middle Bronze Age ornament hoards (*c.* 1400–1100 cal. BC). In T.F. Martin and R. Weetch (eds), *Dress and Society: contributions from archaeology.* Oxford: Oxbow Books, 14–47.

Wilkin, N. and Vander Linden, M. 2015. What was and what would never be: changing patterns of interaction and archaeological visibility across north-west Europe from 2500 to 1500 cal BC. In H. Anderson-Whymark, D. Garrow and F. Sturt (eds), *Continental Connections: exploring cross-Channel relationships from the Mesolithic to the Iron Age.* Oxford: Oxbow, 99–121.

Wilkinson, R. 2019. Iron Age Metalwork Object Hoards of Britain, 800 BC–AD 100. Unpublished PhD Thesis, University of Leicester.

Williams, A. and Le Carlier de Veslud, C. 2019. Boom and bust in Bronze Age Britain: major copper production from the Great Orme mine and European trade, *c.* 1600–1400 BC. *Antiquity* 93, 1178–96.

Williams, H. 2003. Material culture as memory: combs and cremation in early medieval Britain. *Early Medieval Europe* 12(2), 89–128.

Williams, H. 2006. *Death and Memory in Early Medieval Britain.* Cambridge: Cambridge University Press.

Williams, H. 2015. Toward an archaeology of cremation. In C.W. Schmidt and S. Symes (eds), *The Analysis of Burned Human Remains* (2nd edn). London: Academic Press, 259–93.

Williamson, W.C. 1834. *Description of the tumulus, lately opened at Gristhorpe, near Scarborough.* Scarborough: C.R. Todd.

Willis, C. 2019. Stonehenge and Middle to Late Neolithic cremation rites in mainland Britain (*c.* 3500–2500 BC). Unpublished PhD thesis, University College London Institute of Archaeology.

Wilson, D. 1851. *The Archaeology and Prehistoric Annals of Scotland.* Edinburgh: Sutherland and Knox.

Wiseman, R., Allen, M. and Gibson, C. 2021. The inverted dead of Britain's Bronze Age barrows: a perspective from Conceptual Metaphor Theory. *Antiquity* 95, 720–34.

Witmore, C. 2014. Archaeology and the New Materialisms. *Journal of Contemporary Archaeology* 1, 203–46.

Woodward, A. 1995. Vessel size and social identity in the Bronze Age of southern Britain. In I. Kinnes and G. Varndell (eds), *'Unbaked Urns of Rudely Shape': essays on British and Irish pottery for Ian Longworth.* Oxford: Oxbow Monograph 55, 195–202.

Woodward, A. 2000. *British Barrows. A Matter of Life and Death.* Stroud: History Press.

Woodward, A. 2009. The pottery. In Ladle and Woodward (eds) 2009, 200–71.

Woodward, A. and Hunter, J. 2011. *An Examination of Prehistoric Stone Bracers from Britain*. Oxford: Oxbow Books.

Woodward, A. and Hunter, J. 2015. *Ritual in Early Bronze Age Grave Goods*. Oxford: Oxbow Books.

Woodward, A., Hunter, J., Ixer, R., Maltby, M., Potts, P.J., Webb, P.C., Watson, J.S. and Jones, M.C. 2005. Ritual in some Early Bronze Age grave goods. *Archaeological Journal* 162(1), 31–64.

Woodward, P. 1983. The excavation of two barrows and the associated field system on Cowleaze Pasture, Winterbourne Steepleton, Dorset. *Proceedings of the Dorset Natural History and Archaeological Society* 104, 1735.

Woodward, P. 1991. *South Dorset Ridgeway. Field Survey and Excavations 1977-84*. Dorchester: Dorset Natural History and Archaeological Society Monograph 8.

Worsaae, J.J.A. 1849. *The Primeval Antiquities of Denmark* (trans and enlarged by W.J. Thoms). London: John Henry Parker.

Wright, T. 1852. *The Celt, the Roman, and the Saxon: a history of the early inhabitants of Britain, down to the conversion of the Anglo-Saxons to Christianity*. London: Arthur Hall, Virtue & Co.

Wright, T. 1859. On the remains of a primitive people in the south-east corner of Yorkshire; with some remarks on the early ethnology of Britain. *Proceedings of the Geological and Polytechnic Society of the West Riding, Yorkshire* 3, 465–91.

Young. D.J. 2015. Distinctive Deposits at Neolithic Tombs of Yorkshire and Orkney. Unpublished MA thesis, University of Reading.

Zusak, M. 2007. *The Book Thief*. London: Doubleday.

Index

Entries in bold refer to the Illustrations and Tables.